Tourism on the Verge

Series editors
Pauline J. Sheldon
University of Hawaii, Honolulu, Hawaii, USA

Daniel R. Fesenmaier
University of Florida, Gainesville, Florida, USA

More information about this series at http://www.springer.com/series/13605

Dianne Dredge • Szilvia Gyimóthy
Editors

Collaborative Economy and Tourism

Perspectives, Politics, Policies and Prospects

Springer

Editors
Dianne Dredge
Department of Culture & Global Studies
Aalborg University
Copenhagen SV, Denmark

Szilvia Gyimóthy
Department of Culture & Global Studies
Aalborg University
Copenhagen SV, Denmark

ISSN 2366-2611 ISSN 2366-262X (electronic)
Tourism on the Verge
ISBN 978-3-319-51797-1 ISBN 978-3-319-51799-5 (eBook)
DOI 10.1007/978-3-319-51799-5

Library of Congress Control Number: 2017942749

Printed on acid-free paper

This Springer imprint is published by Springer Nature
The registered company is Springer International Publishing AG
The registered company address is: Gewerbestrasse 11, 6330 Cham, Switzerland

Preface

The collaborative economy is, quite possibly, one of the most significant driving forces shaping the future of tourism. Described as a disruptive innovation that is contributing to the de/restructuring of economic and social systems, its ramifications extend in all directions, and its impacts on and consequences for tourism are enormous. As a consequence, explorations of the collaborative economy and its intersections with tourism require a multidisciplinary and multi-focal approach, and it requires us to move fluidly across different disciplinary lenses, frameworks and concepts. We need to weave together the global and local, to appreciate public and private spheres, to be critical of the politics and be attuned to highly contextualised landscapes of power. No wonder that tourism scholars have generally watched developments in the collaborative economy from the sidelines, not knowing where to start, how to approach it or what to prioritise in the myriad of questions emerging about its impacts. Coming from this perspective, our approach to this book has been underpinned by our interest in excavating the theoretical and practical territory of the collaborative economy and tourism. It is by no means a definitive exploration but one we see as particularly important if we are to be future-oriented scholars and teachers.

To date, there has been limited investigation into the character, depth and breadth of these disruptions and the creative opportunities for tourism that are emerging from these shifts. This book provides this platform and addresses both theoretical and practical insights into the future of tourism in a world that is, paradoxically, both increasingly collaborative and individualised.

This book belongs in the Springer Series *Tourism on the Verge*. The series is edgy, it pushes the conceptual envelope, it is future oriented and it addresses deeply complex and challenging issues. *Collaborative Economy and Tourism: Perspectives, Politics, Policies and Prospects* takes an interdisciplinary, cross-sectoral lens to explore the collaborative dynamics that are disrupting, re-creating and transforming processes of tourism production and consumption. It also explores the way that governments, industry and the new public sphere—global civil society, networks and governance—are dealing with these transcendental changes to create and re-create capacities to innovate, control and manage the collaborative economy.

Copenhagen, Denmark
August 2016

Dianne Dredge
Szilvia Gyimóthy

Acknowledgements

In developing this edited volume, the authors would like to acknowledge the wonderful support, good humour and inspiration provided by our close working colleagues in TRU, the support of Aalborg University and the very positive feedback we have received from our colleagues in the European Commission's D-GROWTH (Directorate-General for International Market, Industry, Entrepreneurship and SMEs).

Dianne would especially like to thank Pauline Sheldon, Roberto Daniele, Johan Edelheim, Caryl Bosman, Tazim Jamal, Szilvia Gyimóthy, Carina Ren, Martin Trandberg Jensen, Adriana Budeanu, Anders Sørensen, Renuka Mahadevan, Gillian Warry and Bobbie Kay for their generous inspiration and unending patience, humour and light. I am truly grateful for their generous inspiration, love and laughter.

Szilvia is truly grateful for the ceaseless encouragement of Dianne and the original perspectives you have brought into our discussions. Special thanks go to Martin Trandberg Jensen and Carina Ren for their inspiration and collegial support, as well as to Jane Widtfeldt Meged, Mia Larson, Can Seng Ooi, Johannes Vangsen, Britta Timm Knudsen and Anders Sørensen for their friendship and wit. Finally, we would like to recognise the importance of creative writing and thinking spaces, most notably Klitgaarden, Torvehallerne, Ristinge and Professor Kan's Collaboratorium.

Contents

List of Contributors

Rita Cannas is Assistant Professor in Management and Business Communication, University of Cagliari, Sardinia, Italy. She holds a PhD in Economics (University of Bologna), a Master of Research Methodology in Business degree (University of Strathclyde) and a Marie Curie Fellowship (University of Malta). She coordinated a Master of Management for sustainable and responsible tourism at the Study Centre for Youth Tourist (CTS) in Rome (Italy). Her research interests include sustainable tourism management, particularly in Mediterranean coastal destinations; tourism seasonality; cultural and heritage tourism; and social entrepreneurship.

Jaeyeon Choe is a Senior Lecturer in Events and Leisure, Faculty of Management at Bournemouth University. She is a fellow of the Royal Geographical Society and visiting scholar at the Centre for Asian Tourism Research, Chiang Mai University. Since she completed her PhD in Tourism Management (Minor in Cultural Anthropology) at the Pennsylvania State University, she has contributed to the field publishing her work in peer-reviewed academic journals, conference proceedings and book chapters, including high impact journals such as *Current Issues in Tourism* and *Leisure Studies Journal*. She primarily researches religious/spiritual tourism, cross-cultural study, Chinese consumer behaviour, migration and well-being.

Mathilde Dissing Christensen has a Masters degree in Geography and Communication from Roskilde University. As a research assistant, she has explored the material cultures of biking and cross-cultural encounters in public space. Currently, Mathilde is a PhD student at Roskilde University (DK) and Drexel University (USA), where her dissertation focuses on Airbnb and the ongoing negotiation of private and public spheres amongst users of the platform.

Helene Balslev Clausen holds a PhD and is a researcher at Aalborg University (Denmark). Her expertise lies in Latin American politics and culture, tourism, mobilities and social entrepreneurship. Her main areas of research interest include transnational mobilities and tourism, social enterprise, community participation and

Latin American studies. In addition, she is coordinator for several research projects financed by the Mexican Research Council (CONACYT—SECTUR) including *El fomento y la promoción turística* in collaboration with Mario A. Velázquez (2016).

Jonathon Day is an Associate Professor in Purdue University's School of Hospitality and Tourism Management, and has over 20 years' experience in destination management. An award-winning marketer, Dr Day has worked with destination marketing organisations in Australia, New Zealand and the USA. Dr Day is committed to ensuring tourism is a force for good in the world. Dr Day's research interests focus on sustainable tourism, responsible travel and strategic destination governance within the tourism system. He is interested in the role of business in solving grand challenges through corporate social responsibility programmes and social entrepreneurship.

Dianne Dredge is Professor of Tourism and Destination Development in the Department of Culture and Global Studies, Aalborg University, Denmark. Originally trained as an environmental and urban planner, her research interests are in collaborative economy, tourism policy ecologies and the role of education in social innovation and community capacity building. In her research and consulting activities, she adopts embedded community case study methodologies, community participation and human-centred design approaches. She is co-editor of Stories of Practice: Tourism Planning and Policy (Ashgate, 2011).

Daniel Guttentag is an Assistant Professor in Hospitality and Tourism Management at the College of Charleston, located in Charleston, South Carolina. He holds a Ph.D. in Recreation and Leisure Studies and a Master's degree in Tourism Policy and Planning, both from the University of Waterloo in Ontario, Canada. He is interested in tourism innovations, particularly peer-to-peer short-term rental services like Airbnb. Daniel has previously published on a range of topics, including Airbnb, virtual reality, volunteer tourism and casino gambling behaviour.

Szilvia Gyimóthy is an Associate Professor in Market Communications in Tourism and Head of Research at the Tourism Research Unit, Department of Culture and Global Studies, Aalborg University, Denmark. Her research focuses on strategic placemaking and competitive differentiation of regions in the experience economy. She has studied the narrative repositioning of European destinations along culinary inventions, outdoor adventures and popular culture. In the past years, she has been investigating the novel value-creation mechanisms of digital collaborative endeavours and the potentials of the sharing economy for urban and coastal destinations alike. She is co-editor of Tourism Social Media: Transformations in Identity, Community and Culture (Emerald, 2013).

Anne Hardy is a Senior Lecturer at the University of Tasmania and the Director of the Tourism Research and Education Network (TRENd). She is a specialist in tribal marketing, the drive tourism and recreational vehicle market and issues related to sustainability. Her research has been conducted both in Australia and overseas, including in Canada, the UK and New Zealand. Anne is particularly interested in collaborative research that forms two-way linkages between the university and the broader tourism industry.

Maria del Pilar Leal Londoño holds an international PhD and an MSc in Geography, Territorial Planning and Environmental Management (University of Barcelona). She has collaborated in international consultant companies in Germany and Colombia. She has also been a guest lecturer in tourism in Colombia and Spain and has been a guest researcher at the Scottish Rural College in Scotland and the University of Heidelberg in Germany. She has published several articles in different languages about food, tourism and territorial development. Currently, she is the academic director of the Bachelor and Master Degrees at Ostelea International School of Tourism & Hospitality, Barcelona.

Katrín Anna Lund is an anthropologist and Associate Professor in the Department of Geography and Tourism at the University of Iceland. Her research is on landscape, place, narratives and modes of travelling in southern Spain, Scotland and Iceland. She is a co-editor of the volume Conversations with Landscape, published with Ashgate 2010.

F. Xavier Medina holds a PhD in social anthropology (University of Barcelona). He is the Director of the Department of Food Systems, Culture and Society of the Universitat Oberta de Catalunya (UOC), Barcelona. He is also Director of the UNESCO Chair on "Food, Culture and Development" at the same university. He is currently the Chair of the European section of the International Commission on the Anthropology of Food and Nutrition (ICAF). He is the Director of the International Interdisciplinary Research Group on Tourism (GRIT-EAE). He is also the author or editor of a dozen of books and more than 150 papers in scientific journals.

Gunnar Thór Jóhannesson is Associate Professor at the Department of Geography and Tourism, University of Iceland. His research interests are in the areas of entrepreneurship in tourism, tourism policy and destination development as well as research methodologies. He is a co-editor of Tourism Encounters and Controversies: Ontological Politics of Tourism Development, published with Ashgate in 2015.

D. Michael O'Regan is a Senior Lecturer in Events and Leisure at Bournemouth University, UK. He worked alongside the National Tourism Development Authority of Ireland before joining Gulliver and later Wicklow County Tourism as Marketing Executive. He has a PhD from the School of Sport and Service Management (University of Brighton). His research interests are slow, alternative, historic, future and cultural mobilities. He has recently published articles in relation to hitchhiking, a backpacker habitus and the sharing economy.

Juho Pesonen is the head of eTourism research at the Centre for Tourism Studies in the University of Eastern Finland. In his research, Juho focuses on how information and communication technologies are changing tourism with the emphasis on consumer behaviour. In particular, he studies market heterogeneity and the possibilities it creates for different tourism stakeholders. He has published in numerous academic journals including Journal of Travel Research and Journal of Travel & Tourism Marketing.

Greg Richards is Professor of Placemaking and Events at NHTV Breda University of Applied Sciences and Professor of Leisure Studies at the University of Tilburg in the Netherlands. He has worked on projects for numerous national governments, national tourism organisations and municipalities, and he has extensive experience in tourism research and education.

Iis P. Tussyadiah is Reader in Hospitality and Digital Experience with the School of Hospitality and Tourism Management at the University of Surrey (UK). She investigates the roles of information technology in shaping traveller behaviour and experiences and transforming the travel and tourism industry. In particular, she focuses on the use of information technology for behavioural design in various tourism contexts. She has published her work in Annals of Tourism Research, Journal of Travel Research and other tourism and hospitality journals. She has received several best paper awards in international conferences such as ENTER, ADM and I-CHRIE.

Mario Alberto Velázquez García is Associate Professor at Colegio del Estado de Hidalgo (Mexico). He holds a PhD in Sociology from el Colegio de México, Mexico, and is member of the *National System of Research* (SNI). His main research interests include social movements, tourism and the collaborative economy. Mario has coordinated several major research projects about tourism financed by Mexican Research Council (CONACYT—SECTUR).

Jane Widtfeldt Meged is Associate Professor, PhD and academic coordinator at the Tourist Guide Diploma Program at Roskilde University. Her research interests are in the micro-sociology of co-produced tourism experiences, the working life of front personnel in the experience economy, the collaborative tourism economy and networked IT-driven innovation in guided tours.

Collaborative Economy and Tourism

Dianne Dredge and Szilvia Gyimóthy

Abstract The digital collaborative economy is one of the most fascinating developments to have claimed our attention in the last decade. Not only does it defy clear definition, but its historical links back to non-monetised sharing and gift economies and its contemporary foundations in monetising idle assets and spare capacity make it difficult to theorise. In this chapter, we lay the foundation for a social science approach to the exploration of the collaborative economy and its relationship with tourism. We argue that "collaborative" and "economy" should be conceptualised in a broad and inclusive manner in order to avoid narrow theorisations and blinkered accounts that focus only on digitally-mediated, monetised transactions. A balance between individual and collective dimensions of the collaborative economy is also necessary if we are to understand its societal implications.

Keywords Collaborative economy • Collaborative consumption • Tourism • Critical studies • Sharing • Globalisation

1 Introduction

On February 2, 2014 Amsterdam launched its *Amsterdam Sharing City* campaign and officially became Europe's first named sharing city. Since that time the City has embraced a diversity of sharing activities and has actively sought to facilitate both digital and non-digital forms of sharing economy. Amsterdam promotes the benefits of the sharing economy as a means of achieving the dual goals of economic innovation and sustainability. Following Amsterdam's lead, other world cities including Paris, London and Singapore have also opened their doors to policy reforms that could facilitate the sharing economy. But it has been a complicated and politically volatile journey for many other cities.

Berlin, Barcelona, San Francisco and New York are just some of the cities that have sought to find policy solutions to a range of impacts emerging in different

D. Dredge (✉) • S. Gyimóthy
Department of Culture and Global Studies, Aalborg University, A.C. Meyers Vænge 15, Copenhagen 2450, Denmark
e-mail: dredge@cgs.aau.dk; gyimothy@cgs.aau.dk

D. Dredge, S. Gyimóthy (eds.), *Collaborative Economy and Tourism*,
Tourism on the Verge, DOI 10.1007/978-3-319-51799-5_1

sectors, most notably the ride sharing and collaborative economy accommodation sectors. Debate has been highly political and marred in controversy. Most of the concerns being raised relate to the perceived impacts of extractive, profit-driven models of the collaborative economy such as Airbnb and Uber. However, whether responsibility can be directly attributed to these extractive collaborative economy models, or whether they have simply exacerbated pre-existing and historically-situated problems is a matter of debate (Dredge, Gyimóthy, Birkbak, Jensen, & Madsen, 2016).

For us, as the editors and authors of this volume, the collaborative economy is one of the most fascinating developments to have gained attention over the last decade. What is the collaborative economy? What are its impacts on and consequences for tourism? What does it mean for society at large? Is it desirable? How should we manage it? What can governments do? What can incumbent industry actors do to address the unfolding change? These questions have been raised numerous times in different fora and almost everyone has an opinion. Who then should we believe? And whose advice should we take? We cannot pretend to offer definitive advice given the highly contextualised nature of current debates and issues. However, in taking a social science approach, we seek to deepen understandings, provide alternative conceptualisations and ways of framing the problems and opportunities, and in the process uncover new and creative ways of addressing the issues at hand.

We start our explorations acknowledging that the collaborative economy is not a new phenomenon, but is linked to very old forms of economic exchange including the sharing and gift economies (Belk, 2010). However, in its contemporary digital form, wide reaching social, economic, environmental and political consequences cross sectoral boundaries and create contradictions and tensions that require considerable skill, patience and knowledge to unravel. Technology has sped up the rolling out of this digital collaborative economy, it has enabled everyone with a mobile device and an Internet connection to become a micro-entrepreneur, and it has facilitated global market access to a range of previously untapped products, services and experiences. In the process, in just 10 years, small start-ups with a virtual platform as their main asset have grown into global corporations dwarfing traditional competitors such as hotel chains, taxi and car rental companies. Such has been the scale and speed of the collaborative economy's development that governments, incumbent industry actors and communities are now grappling to unravel and understand the emerging consequences and to identify appropriate and acceptable actions (Dredge & Gyimóthy, 2015).

For researchers unafraid of the challenge and willing to transcend disciplinary divides, the collaborative economy represents a veritable playground. Rittel and Weber (1973) first coined the term "wicked problem" to describe policy problems that defy neat description, where there is no clear identifiable solution, and where addressing the problem requires actions on multiple fronts where no single actor has complete authority and control. Fast forward 40 years and Rittel and Weber could have written their seminal paper about the collaborative economy today. The collaborative economy epitomises the disruptive rescaling of economic structures and practices of a postmodern, post-structural world (Beck, Giddens, & Lash, 1994; Giddens, 1990; Harvey, 1989). It demonstrates individualisation in mass markets; the speed of global digital transactions exemplify time-space compression; and the global nature of digital platforms demonstrates a liquid organisation reminiscent of Bauman's liquid modernity (Bauman, 2000).

At the same time, Botsman and Rogers (2011) and Gansky (2010) argue that the collaborative economy responds to the need for alternative economies that address over-consumption and the unsustainable trajectories of modern capitalism (Harvey, 1996; Healy, 2009). While this argument is often cited, in the absence of evidence it has been increasingly questioned, and a very important distinction has been made between the extractive and generative collaborative economy models (Bauwens, 2005; Scholz, 2016). While this distinction is discussed below, these contributions flag a much greater level of critical engagement and more robust attempts to build a knowledge base about the collaborative economy. This book contributes to this larger project.

The aim of this book is to explore and theorise the nature, character and operation of the collaborative economy and its relationship with tourism. We seek to expand the narrow focus often taken on the collaborative economy that conceptualises it as a set of digitally mediated peer-to-peer transactions. Instead, we take a wider more holistic view of what collaborative economy might look in social and economic life in tourism settings. Our focus is deliberately broad in order to capture perspectives, ideas and intersections between "collaboration" and "economy" and "tourism". For the editors and authors, the collaborative economy is a theoretical, conceptual and practical playground where we "play" with different ways of seeing, understanding and engaging with the collaborative economy and tourism. In the process we also encourage readers to play with the ideas and understandings that unfold, reflecting back to their own disciplinary framings, theoretical preferences and practical experiences. As a caveat, we do not claim that the following chapters provide a comprehensive analysis. Rather, their role is to prompt us to think critically and creatively about the collaborative economy so that we can crystallise these insights with our own experiences and understandings to develop a deeper appreciation of its problems and potentials.

2 What Is the Collaborative Economy?

Defining the collaborative economy is a much more slippery and elusive task than readers first imagine. The most commonly cited definition is that of Botsman (2013) who defines it as:

> . . .an economy built on distributed networks of connected individuals and communities versus centralized institutions, transforming how we can produce, consume, finance, and learn.

But as discussed in a critical evaluation of definitions and key concepts in Gyimóthy and Dredge (2017), definitions of the collaborative economy have come under increasing scrutiny. Scholars and practitioners, anchored in different disciplinary perspectives and interests, have offered different definitions and terminologies and have attempted to categorise it in various ways and for their own purposes. Not surprisingly, there is a mounting number of definitions that emphasise various aspects of the collaborative economy including innovation and market growth; disruption to business chains; the ethical characteristics of the sharing transaction; or its contribution to economic transformation.

We see the challenge of defining the collaborative economy as something of a moving target. On one hand, the characteristics of the collaborative economy are on the move as new innovations emerge, as disciplinary contributions highlight various attributes of exchange, and as the consequences and implications become more apparent. On the other hand, for governments to understand and develop their positions, to undertake analysis, and to respond with considered policies, definitions are important. To this end, the European Commission (2016) has developed a definition that offers characteristics and dimensions that may be operationalised in research and policy:

> . . .the term "collaborative economy" refers to business models where activities are facilitated by collaborative platforms that create an open marketplace for the temporary usage of goods or services often provided by private individuals. The collaborative economy involves three categories of actors: (i) service providers who share assets, resources, time and/or skills—these can be private individuals offering services on an occasional basis ('peers') or service providers acting in their professional capacity ("professional services providers"); (ii) users of these; and (iii) intermediaries that connect—via an online platform—providers with users and that facilitate transactions between them ('collaborative platforms'). Collaborative economy transactions generally do not involve a change of ownership and can be carried out for profit or not-for-profit.

While we see value in various attempts to define the collaborative economy for specific purposes, we are cautious that any attempt to offer a decisive definition will create boundaries around how authors engage with the two key words: "collaborative" and "economy". We conceptualise the collaborative economy as a much wider phenomenon, it has a much longer history, and it includes a variety of collaborative transactions that extend well beyond the current focus on digital platforms, monetised transactions and the disruption currently caused by particular models. In our excavations of the collaborative economy and tourism, we see the collaborative economy as including, but not limited to, the digital collaborative economy. We include a range of different types of collaborative transactions (e.g. social transactions, monetised and non-monetised transactions, ethical transactions based on moral responsibility, etc.), and we embrace different models ranging from extractive for-profit models to commons or generative models (Kostakis & Bauwens, 2014; Scholz, 2014).

Our commitment to adopting this wider interpretation is based on our belief that a narrow definition could limit a fuller understanding of what the collaborative economy in tourism might be and how it impacts economic, social and political life.

So, for our own purposes in the development of this book, we have deliberately sought not to define the collaborative economy in a clear-cut manner in these early stages, but to inductively return to this challenge in the concluding chapter.

3 Approach and Scope

The approach taken in each of the following chapters varies, however there are some common threads. In this volume, we have sought to encourage multi/trans/postdisciplinary approaches to explorations of the collaborative economy in tourism. While the disciplinary backgrounds and preferences of chapter authors have influenced their engagement with the subject matter, the hard and dirty work of translating, synthesising and making sense of the world of collaborative economy also comes with the challenge of recognising how one's own perspective and voice gets interwoven into the text (Anderson-Gough & Hoskins, 2005). To this end, authors have drawn upon and woven together different disciplinary influences and have used different methods of data collection and analysis.

In keeping with this approach, we have also asked the authors to adopt a critical stance. This criticality takes different forms. Some authors have been inspired by radical and Marxist interpretations and have been critical to the power relations, silenced voices and injustices that characterise aspects of the collaborative economy; they have sought to highlight the impacts of collaborative economy on class/labour relations; and they have excavated the manner in which collaborative economy capitalism has contributed (or not) to the redistribution of assets and wealth from the commons to private interests. Others have taken on a different approach to criticality, placing emphasis on the process of translating their data into stories and to the articulation of their perspectives and to those of others. In doing so, they have tuned in to the logocentricism of their own writing and positionality and have tried to balance this with respect for the voices of others (Fuller & Kitchin, 2004).

We have encouraged the investigation and interpretation of values, and how those values are transformed into decisions and actions in the collaborative economy. This direction has inspired a variety of quantitative and qualitative research approaches and methodologies, including surveys, descriptive statistical analysis, interviews and dialogic approaches, participant observation, reflective accounts and story-telling that have sought to question what is really going on. In addressing this challenge, we seek to examine the way that governments, industry and the public sphere can and are responding to the challenges presented by the collaborative economy and we discuss what these changes mean for the future of tourism as a set of social, economic, cultural, environmental and political practices. The collected volume thus becomes a varied account of collaborative economy and tourism and an ideal foundation for future research.

In setting out the broad aim, approach and scope in this way, our hope is that readers will start to appreciate the complexities of the collaborative economy and refrain from simply aligning it with Airbnb or Uber as the dominant market models. The collaborative economy is consistent with and symptomatic of broader meta-sociological trends including late modernism, post-structuralism, (post)globalisation and (post)neoliberalism. Understanding this broader context, and sharpening our theoretical as well as practical understandings of the collaborative economy, in its macro-micro interrelations, is essential for more informed and appropriate responses to the future challenges it presents.

4 Why Study the Collaborative Economy?

There are many reasons why greater focus should be given to researching the intersections of collaborative economy and tourism but three main reasons underpin the development of the approach and scope to this book. First, the collaborative economy has fuelled a range of disruptive innovations and understanding the nature and implications of this change is essential when contemplating the future of tourism. These disruptive innovations include *product innovations* that have, for example, increased the range and diversity of products and on-demand services available (e.g. guiding and personal services, health, recreation and leisure equipment sharing, etc.) that facilitate the delivery of customised services to mass markets (Owyang, Samuel, & Grenville, 2014; Rifkin, 2014). *Process innovations* have been unlocked by the matching of micro-producers and consumers via sharing mobile apps thereby cutting out intermediaries and improving cost efficiencies. *Management innovations* are demonstrated in, for example, online on-demand reservation and payment options that reduce friction in transactions and the need for and cost of labour (Stokes, Clarence, & Rinne, 2014). *Market innovations* can be found in the development of reputational mechanisms such as user feedback and ratings systems, which have been effectively used to build markets and customer loyalty (Belk, 2014). These innovations have wide-ranging effects, the consequences of which have not been fully explored, but are likely to have significant ramifications for the future of tourism.

Second, the collaborative economy has attracted significant media attention. It has been hotly debated and self-proclaimed experts are multiplying at an astonishing rate. Dredge and Gyimóthy (2015) have argued that this new and highly volatile space has become characterised by a large number of experts who have diagnosed the problem and applied their own lens to identify potential solutions. Asymmetries of information have emerged depending on the (self)interests of these experts. The scholarly voice has largely been missing from these debates. As editors, we believe that it is important to add scholarly analyses into these debates, to introduce alternative ways of problematising and analysing the issues and to deepen understandings.

Third, and related to the above, Dredge and Gyimóthy (2015) have identified a number of myths that have emerged and that require deeper and more balanced assessment including:

- That collaborative economy social technologies unlock hidden wealth.
- That the collaborative economy embraces openness, inclusivity and the commons; it reallocates wealth across the value chain, and it carries the seeds of a more fair, just and equal society.
- That the collaborative economy focuses on community lifestyle and living local movements, it is an antidote to the failures of capitalism, and it contributes to a moral turn in consumer decision-making.
- That the collaborative economy represents a free unfettered and more efficient market place where producers and consumers exchange goods and services and without the heavy-handed regulation.
- That the collaborative economy possesses the capacity to self-regulate and address market failures.

These myths are variously addressed by chapter authors and will be reflected upon in the conclusions.

5 Collaborative Economy Actors

The collaborative economy is characterised by a number of stakeholder groups that can be broadly divided into the following interdependent and overlapping groups described below (see Dredge et al., 2016). These groupings are not exclusive: actors may belong to more than one group and move between groups over time. Their interests may also converge or conflict depending on the social, economic, political and environmental factors at play. While these groupings are indicative, they are nevertheless useful in conceptualising the relational setting[1] of the collaborative economy.

Consumers Consumers are those that purchase and consume the goods and services offered in collaborative economy.

Providers Providers are a large and diverse group of stakeholders, motivated by a variety of reasons, who offer the use of their assets, resources, expertise, knowledge and labour to a collaborative network for their consumption. The resource, asset or service that providers offer may not necessarily be idle or spare, but may be a specific investment made for the purposes of offering it on a collaborative platform as an alternative business model.

[1]To our knowledge there is no research examining the network characteristics of collaborative economy tourism accommodation stakeholders to date. The conceptualisation in this chapter will therefore be useful in future studies of this nature.

New Service Entrepreneurs New service entrepreneurs are often small and micro-business operators who provide goods and services that support the collaborative economy sector and in the process contribute to new ecologies of entrepreneurship and business opportunity. These may include, for example, meet and greet hospitality services, destination concierge services, cleaning services and key exchange services.

Local Residents and Community Local residents may be directly or indirectly impacted by the collaborative economy. These are, for example, the residents in neighbouring houses and apartments that must deal with local impacts (e.g. noise and nuisance caused by tourist behaviour, loss of community cohesion, impacts of community facilities, impacts on rental and property prices, etc.) of collaborative economy accommodation. This group of stakeholders may also take other roles from time to time, including Consumers and/or Providers.

Incumbent Operators Incumbent actors or industry operators are those traditional providers (e.g. hotels, taxi companies) that, as a result of the growth in the collaborative economy, face pressures such as increased competition, inequitable regulatory burdens, and traditional business models and supply chains are being challenged. These stakeholders include individual businesses, destination management organisations and other interest-based organisations (e.g. rental agencies, B&B associations, etc.).

Collaborative Economy Platforms or Networks Collaborative economy platforms take a variety of organisational forms. They may include both digital platforms and non-digital peer-to-peer networks, and may be extractive or commons-based.[2] Regardless of organisational form, collaborative economy platforms/networks add value by providing the context and forum for the transaction. This value adding may be in terms of administrative services, customer verification procedures, advertising and peer rating mechanisms.

Governments Supra-national agencies, national, regional and local governments have a role in protecting public interests, in facilitating innovation and societal

[2]The extractive collaborative economy is a model where approximately 15% of the value created is diverted to the platform company and its investors and 85% is earned by the provider. Extractive platforms do not invest back into the provider's asset, product or labour, earning criticism that they are merely extracting and redistributing wealth from the commons rather than generating sufficient new value for a host or community to thrive, be socially fair and sustainable. The commons collaborative economy is based on three broad social movements: (i) sustainable citizenship; (ii) fairness based around the creation and distribution of value that is shared; and (iii) the commons movement which embeds a commitment to open source and sharing for a vibrant society. The commons collaborative economy is more often a ground up initiative and any profit is invested back into the commons (Bauwens, 2005).

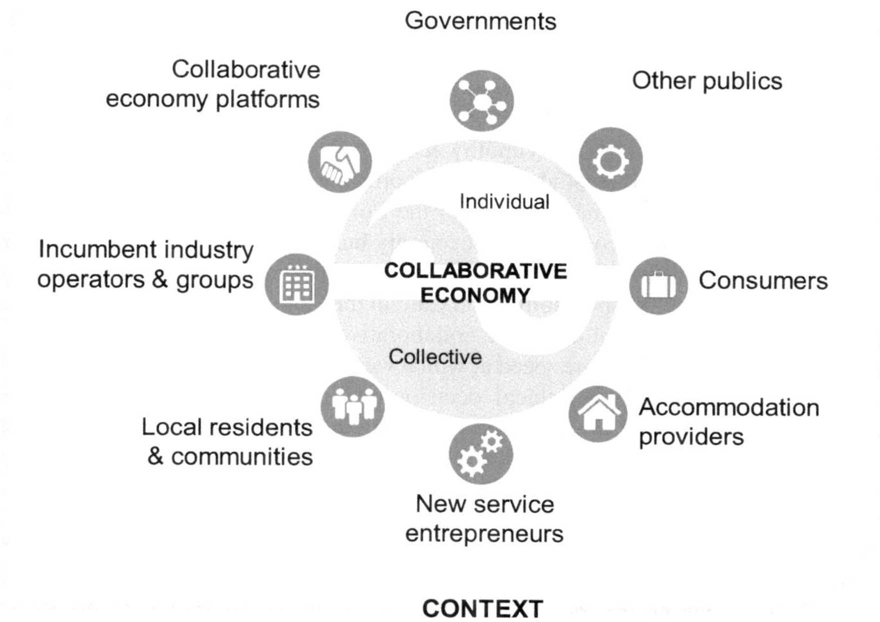

Fig. 1 Relational approach to studying the collaborative economy

interest. Roles and responsibilities vary, and government approaches are also influenced by institutional cultures and historical policy decisions.

Other Publics There are a range of other (future) stakeholders and interests that may not yet be apparent, whose voices may not yet have emerged, and these may vary from location to location. These interests may be important in the future, and for this reason, these stakeholders are acknowledged here in order to prompt policy makers and regulators to think beyond the immediate discussions taking place about regulating the collaborative economy.

Figure 1 shows a visual representation of this relational setting, raising attention to the context in which these relations play out. It also seeks to acknowledge both the individual dimensions (such as individual motivations, peer-to-peer transactions between individuals) and the collective dimensions (such as the formation of networks, tribes, platforms and the impacts on other publics) in the collaborative economy. The chapters that follow highlight the diverse relational characteristics of the collaborative economy at theoretical, pragmatic and contextualised levels.

6 Structure of this Book

Based on the above outline, our explorations of the collaborative economy and tourism can be loosely grouped into three major themes. Following this introduction, the first set of chapters engages in theoretical explorations of the collaborative economy and tourism. In the chapter "Definitions and Mapping the Landscape in the Collaborative Economy" (Gyimóthy & Dredge), the foundation is laid for the broad interpretation of the collaborative economy and tourism that we adopt in this book. In the chapter "Business Models of the Collaborative Economy", Gyimóthy explores the diversity of collaborative economy business models helping to build a deeper appreciation for the various motivations underpinning collaborative transactions. Dredge (see "Responsibility and Care in the Collaborative Economy") then examines moral responsibility in the collaborative economy and tourism arguing that we need to slow down the speed at which we move from problem identification to response and to nurture ethical decision-making that cares for the various interests at play. In the chapter "Sociology of the We-conomy: Understanding Networked Cultures", Gyimóthy takes as her starting point, the networked relations of the collaborative economy by examining the sociology of the "we-conomy". The final chapter in this section, "Politics, Policy and Regulatory Perspectives in the Collaborative Economy" (Dredge), examines the political landscape, the path dependencies created by previous industrial policy approaches, and the influence of neoliberal ideologies on policy and regulation in the collaborative economy.

In Part II, the second set of chapters explores the disruptions, innovations and transformations of the collaborative economy from a kaleidoscope of perspectives. In the chapter "Regulating Innovation in the Collaborative Economy: An Examination of Airbnb's Early Legal Issues", Guttentag captures the complexity of regulatory issues characterising the world's largest accommodation sharing platform and lays out the challenges for both the company, regulators and incumbent industry actors. Shifting the focus to free walking tours, (see "Free Walking Tour Enterprises in Europe: An Evolutionary Economic Approach"), Leal Londoño and Medina explore free walking tours as a manifestation of collaborative economy in tourism, and they pay particular attention to way in which these companies are embedded in traditional capitalist models of tourism production and consumption. In the chapter "Airbnb: Turning the Collaborative Economy into a Collaborative Society", O'Regan and Choe ask why critical questions are not being raised about the collaborative economy, and they explore what the authors consider to be an unbalanced, short-term and ahistorical rhetoric fostered by collaborative economy evangelists. Richards opens up a discussion of the collaborative economy and tourism from a geographical perspective in the chapter "Sharing the New Localities of Tourism". In this chapter, the way that the collaborative economy is contributing to the co-creation of tourism spaces and contributing to the restructuring of tourist cities is examined. In the chapter "Working Life in the Collaborative Tourism Economy", Meged and Christensen explore how workers in the collaborative tourism economy craft meaning and identity in work and discuss transformations in the established labor market induced by the collaborative economy. Day then draws our attention to the impact of the collaborative economy on destination management organisations (see "Collaborative Economy and Destination Marketing Organisations: A Systems Approach") identifying key challenges for the future.

Part III examines the encounters and communities in collaborative economy and tourism. In the chapter "Embedding Social Values in Tourism Management: Community Currencies as Laboratories of Social Entrepreneurship?", Cannas takes us to Sardinia. She explores the Sardex mutual credit system and its role and value in tourism. From Sardinia we travel to Iceland where Jóhannesson and Lund (see "Improvising Economy: Everyday Encounters and Tourism Consumption") explore an improvised collaborative encounter in the Icelandic Museum of Sorcery and Witchcraft. In the process they open up the notion of collaboration and how collaborative encounters affect the growth of tourism economies. Hardy (see "Community and Connection: Exploring the Outcomes of the Collaborative Economy Through Recreational Vehicle Use") continues along these lines by exploring the tribal characteristics of collaborative encounters of RVers drawing attention to the importance of non-monetised transactions in the collaborative economy. In "Collaborative Consumption in Tourism in Latin America: The Case of Brazil, Mexico, Argentina, Columbia and Chile", Clausen and Velázquez challenge our understanding of the collaborative economy in the Global North. They frame the collaborative economy as an extension of historical economic models in Latin America and argue that understandings of collaborative phenomena are currently limited by its framing in post-industrial societies. In the last chapter in this Part, Pesonen and Tussyadiah (see "Peer-to-Peer Accommodation: Drivers and User Profiles") return to the digital collaborative economy, offering insights into the users and non-users of P2P accommodation services and how they differ from each other in terms of the personal and behavioural factors.

The insights and understandings of these chapters contribute to an unravelling of a collaborative economy landscape that extends well beyond the current and relatively narrow discussion of the digital collaborative economy and the dominant extractive models that we are familiar with. In the final chapter, (see "New Frontiers"), Dredge and Gyimóthy identify and confront these challenges offering insights into the myths previously identified and a research agenda for the future.

References

Anderson-Gough, F., & Hoskins, K. (2005). What is it to be post-disciplinary? The dirty business of translation. In *Critical policy studies—Enacting critical management: Integration of the critical and the technical*. University of Cambridge. Accessed June 8, 2016, from http://doi.org/10.1017/CBO9781107415324.004

Bauman, Z. (2000). *Liquid modernity*. Cambridge: Polity.

Bauwens, M. (2005). 1000 days of theory—The political economy of peer production. *cTheory, 12/1/2005*. Accessed June 8, 2016, from www.ctheory.net/articles.aspx?id=499

Beck, U., Giddens, A., & Lash, S. (1994). *Reflexive modernization: Politics, tradition and aesthetics in the modern social order*. Cambridge: Polity Press.

Belk, R. (2010). Sharing. *Journal of Consumer Research, 36*(5), 715–734.

Belk, R. (2014). You are what you can access: Sharing and collaborative consumption online. *Journal of Business Research, 67*(8), 1595–1600.

Botsman, R. (2013). *The sharing economy lacks a shared definition*. Accessed May 21, 2016, from https://www.fastcoexist.com/3022028/the-sharing-economy-lacks-a-shared-definition#4

Botsman, R., & Rogers, R. (2011). *What's mine is yours: How collaborative consumption is changing the way we live*. New York: Collins.

Dredge, D., & Gyimóthy, S. (2015). The collaborative economy and tourism: Critical perspectives, questionable claims and silenced voices. *Tourism Recreation Research, 40*(3), 286–302. doi:10.1080/02508281.2015.1086076.

Dredge, D., Gyimóthy, S., Birkbak, A., Jensen, T. E., & Madsen, A. K. (2016). *The impact of regulatory approaches targeting collaborative economy in the tourism accommodation sector: Barcelona, Berlin, Amsterdam and Paris*. Impulse Paper No.9. Brussels: European Commission.

European Commission. (2016). *A European agenda for the collaborative economy*. Brussels: European Commission.

Fuller, D., & Kitchin, R. (2004). *Radical theory/critical praxis: Making a difference beyond the academy?* Vernon, BC: Praxis (e)Press.

Gansky, L. (2010). *The mesh: Why the future of business is sharing*. New York: Penguin Books.

Giddens, A. (1990). *The consequences of modernity*. Cambridge: Polity Press.

Gyimóthy, S., & Dredge, D. (2017). Definitions and mapping the landscape in the collaborative economy. In D. Dredge & S. Gyimóthy (Eds.), *Collaborative economy and tourism: Perspectives, politics, policies and prospects*. Cham: Springer.

Harvey, D. (1989). *The condition of postmodernity*. Oxford: Blackwell.

Harvey, D. (1996). On planning the ideology of planning. In S. Campbell & S. Fainstein (Eds.), *Readings in planning theory* (pp. 176–197). Cambridge: Blackwell.

Healy, S. (2009). Alternative economies. In R. Kitchin & N. Thrift (Eds.), *International encyclopedia of human geography*. (online) (pp. 338–344).

Kostakis, V., & Bauwens, M. (2014). *Network society and future scenarios for a collaborative economy*. New York: Palgrave MacMillan.

Owyang, J., Samuel, A., & Grenville, A. (2014). *Sharing is the new buying: How to win in the collaborative economy*. Accessed November 28, 2015, from http://tms.visioncritical.com/sites/default/files/pdf/sharing-new-buying-collaborative-economy-report.pdf

Rifkin, J. (2014). *The zero marginal cost society: The internet of things, the collaborative commons, and the eclipse of capitalism*. New York: Palgrave MacMillan.

Rittel, W., & Weber, M. (1973). Dilemmas in a general theory of planning. *Policy Sciences, 4*(2), 155–169.

Scholz, T. (2014). *The politics of the sharing economy*. Accessed November 27, 2015, from http://ourworld.unu.edu/en/the-politics-of-the-sharing-economy

Scholz, T. (2016). *Platform cooperativism: Challenging the corporate sharing economy*. New York: Rosa Luxemburg Stiftung.

Stokes, K., Clarence, E., & Rinne, A. (2014). *Making sense of the UK collaborative economy*. London: Nesta. Accessed May 5, 2015, from http://www.nesta.org.uk/publications/making-sense-uk-collaborative-economy

Part I
Theoretical Explorations

Definitions and Mapping the Landscape in the Collaborative Economy

Szilvia Gyimóthy and Dianne Dredge

Abstract This chapter examines definitions of the collaborative economy and maps out the landscape of collaborative economy in tourism. We cast a wide and inclusive net, acknowledging that the collaborative economy is found in the intersection of two words: "collaborative" and "economy". Any attempt to narrow its definition to digitally-mediated, monetised transactions limits the potential understandings that we may develop about this phenomenon. We argue that the collaborative economy involves collaboration through which there is an exchange of resources, assets or services. By corollary, researchers should pay attention to the properties of that exchange, the relational qualities of the actors directly and indirectly involved, and the social, economic, political and environmental factors that influence that exchange.

Keywords Collaborative Economy • Collaborative Consumption • Tourism • Critical Studies • Sharing • Key Terms

1 What's in a Term?

Sharing economy. Gift economy. Gig economy. Access economy. On-demand economy. We-conomy. The collaborative economy is known by many names, all of which are attempts to capture or accentuate different features (Belk, 2014a, 2014b; Dredge & Gyimóthy, 2015). In this chapter, we call it the collaborative economy, but in doing so we are keen not to limit the full array of understandings that might inductively emerge from the following chapters. Moreover, it is important to understand this phenomenon in context, since the digital collaborative economy has burst upon our consciousness in the last decade as a new, disruptive and innovative development and, in the process, obscured the very important on-going work of, for example, the commons or community economy. It has demanded our attention in social media, in urban politics, in our consumer choices,

S. Gyimóthy (✉) • D. Dredge
Department of Culture and Global Studies, Aalborg University, A.C. Meyers Vænge 15, Copenhagen 2450, Denmark
e-mail: gyimothy@cgs.aau.dk; dredge@cgs.aau.dk

D. Dredge, S. Gyimóthy (eds.), *Collaborative Economy and Tourism*,
Tourism on the Verge, DOI 10.1007/978-3-319-51799-5_2

and now, in our research. But what is in a name? And why might it be important to consider its meaning in a deeper way? These are the central questions of this chapter, which help us to lay the foundation for the remainder of this book. In answering these questions, it is important to acknowledge that it is not, as some believe, a new development, and so it is here we begin.

Sharing, gift and barter economies have always existed in closely-knit communities. Anthropologists, ethnologists and sociologists have studied these collaborative transactions for centuries, drawing attention to the multiple motivations, interests and agendas that underpin these transactions (Belk, 2010; Mauss, 1922/1990; Rehn, 2014). In these explorations, excavating what "collaboration" means has been key, and has been linked to aspects such as community capital building, social cohesion and informal social welfare systems. In the last 10 years, the digital collaborative economy has usurped our attention. Social and economic conditions have fed the growth of mobile technologies and access to the Internet has allowed access to products and services at unparalleled scales. The digital collaborative economy, epitomised by platform capitalists such as Airbnb and Uber, have drawn our attention, and in the process, a "new" economic activity known as the collaborative economy has emerged (Botsman & Rogers, 2011; Gansky, 2010). The rise of this new collaborative economy has prompted *Time* magazine to claim it as one of the top ten ideas to change the world (Walsh, 2011).

Taking into account these historical threads, this chapter examines definitions and key terms. In doing so we seek to cast a wide net, to be inclusive, and to acknowledge that the collaborative economy is in fact, the intersection of two words: "collaborative" and "economy" and that attempts to narrow its definition to digitally-mediated, monetised transactions limits the potential understandings we may develop about this phenomenon. Our approach is to acknowledge that the collaborative economy involves collaboration through which there is an exchange of resources, assets or services. Transactions may be monetised or non-monetised and may take place for a variety of motivations ranging from very utilitarian "You have what I want or need" commercial transactions to communitarian "I give, swap or share because I want to help my community for a better world" exchanges. There are both individual and collective dimensions to these transactions. The characteristics of exchange, the relational qualities of actors, and any contextual influences are relevant grounds for the explorations contained in this book.

2 Key Terms and Definitions

2.1 Historical Roots

In anthropological studies, sharing can be traced back to historical concepts such as gift, exchange or barter economies. Sharing and gift-giving within family, close kin and friends are often characterised by non-monetary exchanges between people who know each other. Barter systems have existed and shaped society since prehistoric times, and cultural anthropologists have studied the cultural norms and conventions governing them for over a century (Derrida, 1992; Humphrey, 1985; Mauss, 1922/1990). Belk (2007) and other social anthropologists have theorised the social and cultural features of sharing, defining it succinctly as "nonreciprocal, pro-social behaviour" (Frey & Meier in Benkler, 2004, p. 275). The altruistic act of sharing serves a social purpose: to forge and reinforce social bonds between individual members of a group or community. Sharing encapsulates the collective use or consumption of commodities without compensation or permanent transfer of ownership. In contrast, gift giving, swapping and bartering rely on reciprocity and permanent transfer ownership where no monetary transaction is involved. In these exchanges, relationships between giver and receiver are generally founded on mutual trust, intimacy, empathy, care or other relations of proximity.

Contemporary sharing economy phenomena differ significantly from the types of exchange defined above. They increasingly, but not always, involve interactions among strangers and transcend a geographically defined community. Exchange is most often monetised, systematised in a business model, and facilitated by technology. In recent conceptualisations, the exchange of services has also been added to the array of goods being shared. The first generation of *faux sharing* commercial ventures (a term coined by Belk, 2014a) emerged in the 1980s. For instance, Michael Linton developed the Local Exchange Trading System (LETS) to facilitate the exchange of in-kind services within members of a small community in British Columbia (Linton, 1984). With the advent of the Internet and the social technologies of Web 2.0, the opportunities to liaise on a global scale have multiplied. Lisa Gansky labelled digital interconnectedness '*the mesh*' (Gansky, 2010), emphasising the variety of new, peer-to-peer (P2P) distribution platforms to access goods and services. In tourism these include couchsurfing, house-swapping, dinner sharing, ridesharing and others.

Twentieth-century consumer cultures have developed along the credo 'you are what you own' (Belk, 1988). Hence, consumable possessions have been considered significant accessories of identity construction, an observation also made within tourism studies (Holstein & Gubrium, 2000; Wearing & Wearing, 1996; Welk, 2004). However, contemporary consumer narratives are less frequently framed around the ownership of consumables and enduring goods. Jeremy Rifkin (2000) claims in his influential book, *The Age of Access*, that temporary access to possessions is becoming increasingly more important than ownership. As technological platforms enable zero-threshold, real time access to a range of experience economy commodities (e.g. music, films, books), the worth of identity-forming possessions becomes obsolete. Such *access-based economy* business models are becoming attractive innovation opportunities within tourism and the hospitality industry, exemplified by timeshare and office-on-demand concepts in urban hotels. Intangible tourist experiences, such as local guided tours or dining experiences with locals, are also examples. Common to these collaborative concepts is that they are facilitated by *matchmaker intermediaries* (e.g. Airbnb, Wimdu, VRBO, etc) and can be thus characterised as *market-mediated access* (Bardhi & Eckhardt, 2012) rather than *auto-mediated* peer-to-peer exchanges orchestrated by individuals between other individuals. However, given the rapid rise and worldwide dispersal of market-mediated digital platforms, there is no widespread agreement on a single terminology.

On a slightly different note, the strategic management and marketing literature has also addressed the shift from production to service societies, reconceptualising the market as an interaction platform (Normann & Ramirez, 1993; Prahalad & Ramaswamy, 2004). This conceptualisation acknowledges the rise of dialogic and collaborative value co-creation between firms and customers. Service marketers even go so far as to claim a paradigm shift away from utilitarian logic of transaction exchange towards a new, service-dominant logic (Lusch & Vargo, 2006; Vargo & Lusch, 2004). This perspective upgrades (depicted earlier as passive) customers to a more active role, highlighting their significance as repositories of intangible resources such as knowledge, skills and competences. Although these thoughts bring important conceptual advances in regards to highlighting interactive value constellations in collaborative economy, the kernel of value creation is still theorised as a market relationship (i.e. the provider-customer dyad), which neglects other collaborative formats.

2.2 Reincarnations and Innovations in Terms

The term "collaborative consumption" was first coined by Felson and Spaeth (1978) who were interested in studies of joint and social consumption activities such as collaboratively buying a pitcher of beer as a more effective option than purchasing individual glasses. Published 20 years before the Internet, understandably there was no explicit focus on intermediation or technological platforms in their work. Botsman and Rogers (2011) appropriated and re-interpreted the term to include both auto-mediated and market-mediated monetised 'sharing, bartering, lending, trading, gifting and swapping activities'. For Botsman, collaborative consumption represents a superior and enlightened economy: "a system activating the untapped resources of assets through models and marketplaces that enable greater efficiency and access" (*ibid*, p. 24). Belk (2014b, p. 1597) finds this to be a "mis-specified" use of the term because "it is too broad and mixes marketplace exchange, gift-giving, and sharing". Indeed, some forms of collaborative consumption such as couchsurfing do not involve monetised transactions and explicitly forbid it. Instead, Belk offers an inclusive definition: "people coordinating the acquisition and distribution of a resource for a fee or other compensation" (Belk, 2014b, p. 1597). Such a definition, he argues, is superior because it incorporates both monetised exchange and sharing. So, even in its short life, these definitional debates illustrate that the term is already embedded with multiple meanings, and has been distanced from Felson and Spaeth's original conceptualisation. More recently, a new term *collaborative economy* (subsequently used in this book) has gained momentum in an effort to recognise that these collaborative constellations also extend beyond consumption "to make better use of skills, goods and other useful things" (Stokes et al., 2014, p. 10).

2.3 A Genealogy of Definitions

Our explorations reveal much about the purposes for which definitions are developed, and, by corollary, their strengths and limitations. Genealogic investigations reveal not less than 18 terms related to the sharing economy. These terms often frame the sharing economy as a hybrid, digitally facilitated, alternative economic model embedded in (or rediscovering) deep-rooted cultural, moral and ecological rationales. Different conceptualisations take their point of departure in human ecology, computer science and neoclassic microeconomics, anthropology, postmodern sociology, philosophy, politics and cultural theory. As such, collaborative economy metaphors are formulated along and unite previously incompatible ideas. For example:

1. Models of economic systems combine social concepts using terms such as circuit, regime, networks, ties, transactions and relationships.
2. Economic transactions have been combined with cultural and moral perspectives to derive terms such as lifestyle micro-entrepreneurship, connected consumption and moral economy.
3. Ideas of efficiency and enhanced value creation are combined in terms such as zero marginal costs, full interconnectedness, direct exchange, optimised capacity use and the recirculation of idling resources.

Table 1 lists these terms and identifies the various streams of authorship and disciplinary inspirations that have contributed to their development. It is noteworthy to mention that most recent conceptualisations are postdisciplinary in nature—bridging, crossing and moving beyond classic scientific disciplinary boundaries.

These discussions reveal that definitions struggle to capture aspects such as technology-facilitated transactions, the nature of relationships beyond the immediate exchange, the temporary sharing or pooling of resources, and so on. Conceptualisations are primarily directed at connecting historical lines of thought, or to reflect business logics including digital intermediation and interconnectedness, temporary access and exchange of possessions, and the effective mobilisation of idle resources. Underlying the discourse is also an unquestioned neoclassic notion of "perfect markets", where full and complete information is available to both providers and consumers are well informed, monopolies do not exist and prices are not manipulated. This perfect market, we know, does not exist (Koopman, Mitchell, & Thierer, 2014; Mason, 2015). Instead, complex, contested and asymmetry-ridden relationships among actors (i.e. producers, consumers,

Table 1 A chronological illustration of the genealogy of the concept of the sharing economy

Term	Author	Definition	Metaphor
Human ecology	Hawley (1950) *Human Ecology: A Theory of Community Structure*	Human populations organise themselves in communities (symbiotic and commensalistic relationships) to adapt to their environment. Joint and **coordinated performance** to gain sustenance	Ecosystem (biology)
Collaborative consumption	Felson and Spaeth (1978) Adapting the ideas of Hawley to consumer behaviour	"Actors of collaborative consumption [are] **events** in which one or more persons consume economic goods or services in the process of engaging in **joint activities** with one or more others" (Felson & Spaeth, 1978, p. 614)	Community (sociology, human ecology, consumer behaviour)
Access economy	Rifkin (2000) *The Age of Access: A New Culture of Hypercapitalism*	**Property regimes** have changed to **access regimes** characterised by short-term limited use of assets controlled by networks of suppliers	Transaction exchange (neoclassical microeconomics)
Moral economy	Bauman (2003) *Liquid Love and Human Bonds*	"A community, neighbourhood, circle of friends, partners in life and partners for life [. . .] fellows in the on-going, never-ending **joint effort** of shared life building and making shared life liveable" (Bauman, 2003, p. 70)	Culturally embedded human/ist coexistence (postmodern sociology)
Social sharing	Benkler (2004) *Sharing Nicely: On Shareable Goods and the Emergence of Sharing as a Modality of Economic Production*	Sharing is nonreciprocal **prosocial behaviour**. [. . .] Social sharing and exchange is becoming a common **modality** of producing valuable desiderata at the very core of the most advanced economies—in information, culture, education, computation, and communications sectors (Benkler, 2004, p. 278)	Transactional exchange (neoclassical microeconomics)
Alternative post-capitalist economies	Gibson-Graham (2006) *A post-capitalist politics* and *Take back the economy* Gibson-Graham, Cameron, and Healy (2013)	Envisions, politicises and enacts economic transformation by empowering **placed-based community** approaches to unlocking diverse economies	Post-capitalist social movement (marxist inspired alternative economies)

(continued)

Table 1 (continued)

Term	Author	Definition	Metaphor
Collaborative consumption v. 2.0	Botsman and Rogers (2011) *What's Mine Is Yours: How Collaborative Consumption is Changing the Way We Live*	A **system** activating the untapped value of assets through models and marketplaces that enable greater efficiency and access (Botsman, 2014b, p. 24)	Circular system (neoclassical microeconomics, systems theory)
Collaborative lifestyles	Botsman and Rogers (ibid.) Adapting the ideas of Felson and Spaeth (1978) and Rifkin (2000)	Collaborative **Lifestyles**: "people with similar interests are **banding** together to share and exchange less tangible assets such as time, space, skills, and money" (Botsman & Rogers, 2011, p. 73)	Lifestyle (cultural theory)
The Mesh (aka the sharing society)	Gansky (2010) *Why the Future of Business is Sharing?*	Digital technologies of Web 2.0 provide full **interconnectedness** among people to access and distribute goods and services at the exact moment they need them, without the burden and expense of owning them	Mesh = highly interconnected network of computers (computing science)
Circuits of commerce	Zelizer (2010)	Circuits are **social transactions** and [...] consist of dynamic, meaningful, incessantly negotiated interactions among individuals, households, organisations, or other social entities, [based on] distinctive media (for example, legal tender or localised tokens) and an array of organised, differentiated transfers (for example, gifts or compensation)	Transactional circuits (neoclassical microeconomics)
Access-based consumption	Bardhi and Eckhardt (2012) Adapting the ideas of Jeremy Rifkin to P2P transport/carsharing	**Transactions** that may be market mediated in which no transfer of ownership takes place (Bardhi & Eckhardt, 2012, p. 881)	Market-mediated transactions (neoclassical microeconomics)
Peer-to-peer economy	Bauwens et al. (2012)	P2P **business models** allow direct exchanges among peers and entail a variety of platforms on which citizens rent, sell and share things without the involvement of shops, banks, agencies and other intermediaries	Exchange system (neoclassical microeconomics)

(continued)

Table 1 (continued)

Term	Author	Definition	Metaphor
Moral economy (of alternative tourism)	Germann Molz (2013) Adapting the ideas of Bauman (2003) to P2P tourism phenomena e.g. Couchsurfing	Based not on the exchange of money but on **cooperation and generosity**, shared goods and services, mutual help and support a moral economy involves a far **different kind of exchange** from the market economy (Molz, 2013)	Exchange system (cultural economics)
Sharing vs. Pseudo-sharing	Belk (2007, 2010, 2014a) Synthesises ideas from anthropology (gift giving and sharing] with the proponents of collaborative consumption	Collaborative consumption is an **economic model** based on sharing, swapping, trading, or renting products and services enabling access over ownership. [. . .] **Coordinated acquisition and distribution of a resource** for a fee or other compensation (Belk, 2014b, p. 1597)	Economic model based on more-than-economic, coordinated transactions (cultural economy)
Connected consumption	Schor and Fitzmaurice (2015) *Collaborating and Connecting: The emergence of the sharing economy*	Connected Consumption is based on a **culture of access, use, and re-circulation** of used goods as alternatives to traditional private ownership. (Schor & Fitzmaurice, 2015)	Culturally conditioned collaborative behaviour (cultural economy)
Collaborative commerce	Sigala (2015) Adapting Huang and Benyucef's (2013) ideas on social e-commerce	Collaborative commerce creates an **exchange economy** whereby customers become producers/suppliers and sellers of their own travel goods by negotiating and bartering exchanges for trading these goods even without having the use of money. Such C2C transactions provide alternative travel goods that can also enhance tourism sustainability by generating various forms of social value (Sigala, 2015, p. 3)	Collaborative value co-creation (neoclassic microeconomics, service marketing)
Sharing economy	Lessig (2008) *Remix: Making art and Commerce Thrive in the Hybrid Economy*, among others	**The Sharing Economy is a socio-economic ecosystem** [. . .] which embeds sharing and collaboration at its heart [. . .]. **It includes the shared creation, production, distribution, trade and consumption of goods and services by different people and organisations.** (Matovska, 2015)	**Socio-economic system** (human ecology, microeconomics, cultural theory)

(continued)

Table 1 (continued)

Term	Author	Definition	Metaphor
Hybrid economy	Rifkin (2015) *The Zero Marginal Cost Society: The Internet of Things, the Collaborative Commons, and the Eclipse of Capitalism*	"The plummeting of marginal costs is spawning a hybrid economy—part capitalist market and part **Collaborative Commons**—with far reaching implications for society. [...] In this new world, social capital is as important as financial capital, access trumps ownership, sustainability supersedes consumerism, cooperation ousts competition, and "exchange value" in the capitalist marketplace is increasingly replaced by "**sharable value**" on the "Collaborative Commons" (Rifkin, 2015, p. 2)	Digitally facilitated socio-economic system (human ecology, microeconomics, cultural theory and computing science)

intermediaries, governments and civil society) are present but not acknowledged, and there is no acknowledgement of fundamentally different rationales underpinning collaboration.

2.4 Key Features

So what are we left with if we acknowledge all of these weaknesses and limitations in current definitions? Our own view is that the these attempts at defining what we are calling "the collaborative economy" are very useful in laying the groundwork for research, particularly if we are critical to their strengths, weaknesses and limitations. We acknowledge that, for some researchers, definitions are useful in delimiting the scope of the phenomenon under investigation, but they can also limit more complex postdisciplinary and poststructural understandings of practices that can be deeply woven into economic and social life. To this end, we seek not to define the collaborative economy in any schema that might limit our investigations at the outset, but we are keen to raise attention to the following features that provide a useful focus for research:

- The nature of the transaction itself such as the characteristics of the connections, motivations for the transactions, the resources, assets, services exchanged, tools/techniques of mediation and so on.

- The relational characteristics of the actors involved in the exchange including, for instance, the influence of ethics, emotions (trust, empathy, reciprocity, mutuality, responsibility, solidarity, etc.); social factors (ties, bonds, reputation, etc.); issues of power, equality and justice.
- The contextual factors that influence the exchange (social, economic, environmental, political conditions).
- The impacts and consequences of the collaborative economy over time and space on the self and other.

3 Mapping the Landscape of Collaborative Economy and Tourism

3.1 Extent of Collaborative Economy in Tourism

Tourism has traditionally been framed as an industry, and governments have commonly responded with a range of neoliberal industry policy measures aimed at boosting investment, increasing competitiveness, marketing and promotion to increase consumer awareness, and reducing barriers to growth (Dredge & Jenkins, 2007; Halkier, 2010). However, growing concerns over environmental impacts, resource depletion, climate change, poverty, and regular and persistent financial crises have prompted calls for alternative socio-political models of tourism that can more effectively address sustainable development (Burns & Bibbings, 2009; Mosedale, 2012). It is within this ideological space that the collaborative economy has gained momentum in tourism. Figure 1 shows the potential extent of collaborative opportunities in tourism from the consumer's perspective, and identifies examples in food, travel services, health and wellness, currency exchange, travel companions and support, accommodation and work space, transport and education.

3.2 Enabling Conditions

There are a number of broad societal conditions that have fed the rise of the collaborative economy. This growth has predominantly been in commercial, for-profit, extractive models of the collaborative economy in tourism and has emerged as a response to several problems characterising late modern capitalism in general, and the traditional tourism industrial system in particular. First, and partially as a result of our consumption-oriented culture in Western societies, redundancy is present in the form of dead capital, idling assets and latent expertise. For example, empty apartments, rooms and couches, idle cars, bicycles and boats can all now be accessed by visitors in a destination using the technology-mediated

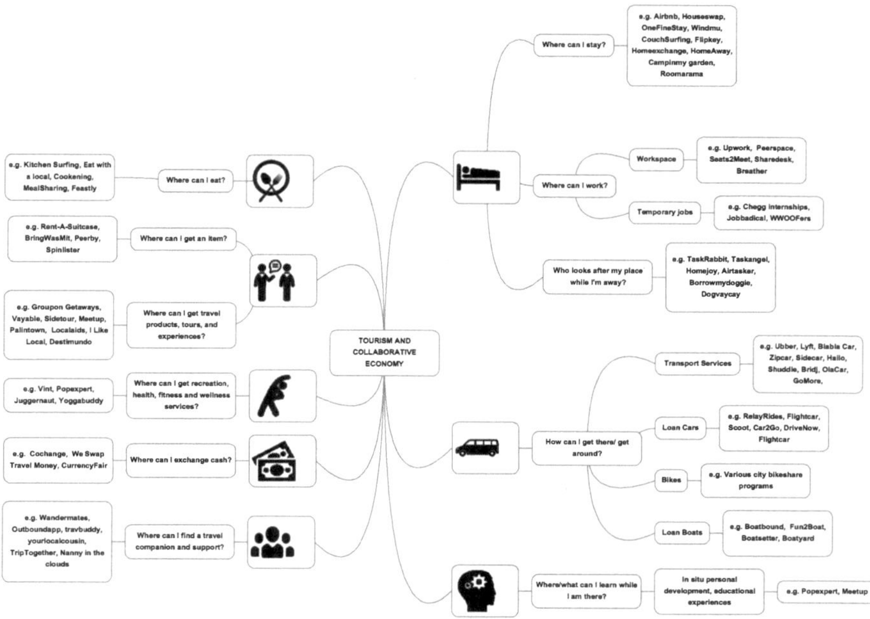

Fig. 1 The collaborative economy and tourism

platforms indicated in Fig. 1. Local expertise and knowledge idling in underemployed workers can be monetised by offering guided tours, concierge services or dining experiences with local hosts. According to protagonists, not only do these idle assets add product diversity, but they can also provide local actors, once previously excluded from the tourism economy, with the opportunity to generate economic and/or other benefits. Such opportunities can fuel entrepreneurialism and expand the scope of trade (Botsman, 2014a; Koopman et al., 2014).[1]

Second, in the existing tourism system, high transaction costs and distorted information between market actors can reduce consumer trust and visitor satisfaction, push up costs and inhibit repeat visitation. However, protagonists of the

[1]This argument is much cited in the literature and rests on altruistic ideas about the motivations of actors to address consumerism and "do good". However, we feel compelled to offer a counter view to this argument. Frictionless transactions at minimal or no cost in the collaborative economy have created incentives for those with capital to invest. Investment properties and other goods are purchased for the purpose of offering them in the collaborative economy on a commercial basis. Not only does this allow the provider to bypass normal regulatory processes (e.g. land use planning, consumer protections, etc.) but lower transaction costs make the product or service highly competitive especially in price-sensitive markets. Thus, incentives exist for commercial motives to be foregrounded and collaborative/sharing motives become less important in the market-mediated digital collaborative economy.

collaborative economy in tourism posit that tools, such as peer-to-peer feedback where both suppliers and consumers are rated, can build trust and facilitate authentic host-visitor relations not achievable within traditional tourism systems. It allows customers and providers to transact directly enabling idling resources to be used, and it also minimises transaction costs. The ITB (2014, p. 27) explains: "...they [intermediaries] are attractive because they offer lower prices, better accessibility, ease of use and 'a user-focused mission' including transparency and interactive communication". This digital transparency and comparability of offers/prices benefits consumers, and increases the availability of niche products and specialised alternatives, including the return of 'genuine' cross-cultural encounters (Yannopoulou, 2013).

Third, asymmetries of regulation have impeded innovation, allowed some producers to capture and take advantage of regulations, and have restricted the entry of new entrepreneurs and ideas into the marketplace (Koopman et al., 2014). For instance, costs of insurance, accreditation, industry memberships, licenses and so on are passed onto consumers and built into pricing structures. In the accommodation sector, products can be overregulated by bureaucratic quality control systems and costly consumer and eco labelling. The result is an inhospitable hospitality industry (Ritzer & Jurgenson, 2010). Mitchell (2014) explains further: "Uber is successful because it *isn't* a cartelized taxi company" and therefore it does not need to pass on the costs of heavy and cumbersome regulation. Regulations have a way of locking in the status quo and rendering innovation more difficult, whereas collaboration based around digital platforms offers greater flexibility and access to the marketplace.

Fourth, as discussed above, the preferences of the postmodern tourist extend beyond the streamlined and impersonal experiences, services and products often associated with the traditional tourism system. Consuming travel is intimately bound to identity construction and narratives of authentic encounters with local cultures. Driven by the ambition of deviating from the beaten track, new generations of travellers are converging on digital platforms to retrieve recommendations and information from fellow travellers and local residents, i.e. sources other than traditional market intermediaries (ITB Berlin, 2014; World Travel Market, 2014), and to explore alternative experiences. Airbnb and other accommodation platforms offer opportunities for guests to stay in treehouses, refurbished jumbo jets, concrete drain pipes, vintage caravans and ski jumps, thereby meeting postmodern demands.

Fifth, destination competition and innovation in the traditional tourism system can be thwarted by difficulties in attracting capital investment or by what bankers might consider "safe" investments. As Botsman (2014b) explains: "Airbnb's model is 'asset light'; it does not need to build or own inventory, but instead facilities access to existing assets, such as spare rooms, holiday houses, entire islands or treehouses". In this way, the collaborative economy offers a way of overcoming barriers to innovation, investment and product diversity.

3.3 *Extractive Versus Generative Collaborative Models*

The market-mediated digital collaborative economy has taken hold relatively quickly as a result of these enabling conditions and, as will be discussed later, a wide range of models has emerged (see Gyimóthy's chapter "Business Models of the Collaborative Economy"). However, it is important to note in our broader mapping of the collaborative economy in tourism that these enabling conditions have predominantly empowered extractive models of collaborative economy over commons-based, communitarian or generative models.

In extractive models, for-profit platform capitalists extract on average 15% of the value created by providers and distribute it back to themselves and their investors. Bauwens (2005) has argued that this redistribution of wealth makes the rich richer and makes market-mediated matchmaker collaborative economy platforms nothing more than traditional capitalism. He argues for a generative commons model of the collaborative economy where the collective of hosts and service providers benefit from reinvestment and there is no redistribution of wealth away from the collective. In tourism, such models have not yet emerged that we are aware of, but may provide an opportunity in the future (Dredge, Gyimóthy, Birkbak, Jensen, & Madsen, 2016).

In the absence of alternative collaborative economy models, the extractive model epitomised by Airbnb, Wimdu, VRBO and others continues to hurtle forward with some estimating that the collaborative economy now accounts for approximately 40% of the overall world outbound accommodation market (ITB Berlin, 2014). However, we know little about its wider impacts on local, regional and national economies and whether (or how) it might lead to the restructuring of tourism systems. We know even less about how it will it affect citizens and communities in different geographical settings, or how it will transform guest-host relationships. These questions provide the stimulus for the research in subsequent chapters.

4 Conclusions

There is no doubt that the collaborative economy is full of contradictions. The collaborative economy is linked to the past but is innovative and disruptive in the present and future. It is deeply individualistic and personalised, yet global in its reach and local in its consequences. To date, research efforts examining the collaborative economy have predominantly focused on its effects and uptake in the marketplace, its influences and consequences for certain stakeholders, the range and potential impacts of policy responses, and on various sectors and market segments. Some impacts, such as those associated with Uber and Airbnb, have dominated much of the discussion and certain agendas and interests have tended to frame research (Dredge & Gyimóthy, 2015). Indeed, the collaborative economy is also much wider, more complex and involves a greater diversity of models than those models discussed above.

In tourism, investigations into the characteristics, impacts and consequences of the collaborative economy have only just started to emerge. These investigations need to take into account the broad range of definitions and interpretations available instead of jumping to conclusions that it is only a market-mediated digital platform phenomenon. To date, there has been a tendency to focus on a few collaborative economy platforms and business models, and research has only scratched the surface of the very complex and interconnected socio-political and economic characteristics of collaborative economy. Our interest is to explore the collaborative economy as it unfolds in different contexts, at different global to local scales, and to apply a range of theoretical and contextual lenses to better understand this phenomenon. We seek to challenge the notion that the extractive models of platform capitalism are the only possible models of collaborative economy. Our position instead is that the collaborative economy involves a range of transactions, is underpinned by different motivations, that various forms of collaboration are present, and not all are monetised. We also call attention to the need for more research examining the deep structural changes in the economy that are associated with collaborative economy, and the need to examine the range of new organisational and business models and practices that are uprooting traditional modes of operation.

Acknowledgement Some sections of this chapter have been inspired by Dredge, D. and Gyimóthy, S. (2015). The collaborative economy and tourism: Critical perspectives, questionable claims and silenced voices, *Tourism Recreation Research, 40*(3), 286–302.

References

Bardhi, F., & Eckhardt, G. M. (2012). Access-based consumption: The case of car sharing. *Journal of Consumer Research, 39*(December), 881–898.

Bauman, Z. (2003). *Liquid love: On the frailty of human bonds*. Cambridge: Polity.

Bauwens, M. (2005). 1000 days of theory—The political economy of peer production. *cTheory, 12/1/2005*. Accessed May 21, 2016, from www.ctheory.net/articles.aspx?id=499

Bauwens, M., Mendoza, N., & Iacomella A. (2012). *Synthetic overview of the collaborative economy*. Report by Orange Labs and P2P Foundation. Retrieved from http://p2p.coop/files/reports/collaborative-economy-2012.pdf

Belk, R. (1988). Possessions and the extended self. *Journal of Consumer Studies, 15*, 139–168.

Belk, R. (2007). Why not share rather than own? *The ANNALS of the American Academy of Political and Social Science, 611*(1), 126–140.

Belk, R. (2010). Sharing. *Journal of Consumer Research, 36*(5), 715–734.

Belk, R. (2014a). Sharing versus pseudo-sharing in web 2.0. *Anthropologist, 18*(1), 7–23.

Belk, R. (2014b). You are what you can access: Sharing and collaborative consumption online. *Journal of Business Research, 67*(8), 1595–1600.

Benkler, Y. (2004). Sharing nicely: On shareable goods and the emergence of sharing as a modality of economic production. *The Yale Law Journal, 114*, 237–358.

Botsman, R. (2014a). *Collaborative economy services: Changing the way we travel*. Accessed May 9, 2015, from http://www.collaborativeconsumption.com/2014/06/25/collaborative-economy-services-changing-the-way-we-travel/
Botsman, R. (2014b). Sharing is not just for startups. *Harvard Business Review, 92*(3), 23–26.
Botsman, R., & Rogers, R. (2011). *What's mine is yours: How collaborative consumption is changing the way we live*. New York: Collins.
Burns, P. M., & Bibbings, L. J. (2009). The end of tourism? Climate change and societal changes. *Journal of the Academy of Social Sciences, 4*(1), 31–51.
Derrida, J. (1992). *Given time I. Counterfeit money*. Chicago: University of Chicago Press.
Dredge, D., & Gyimóthy, S. (2015). The collaborative economy and tourism: Critical perspectives, questionable claims and silenced voices. *Tourism Recreation Research, 40*(3), 286–302.
Dredge, D., & Jenkins, J. (2007). *Tourism policy and planning*. Brisbane: Wiley.
Dredge, D., Gyimóthy, S., Birkbak, A., Jensen, T. E., & Madsen, A. K. (2016). *The impact of regulatory approaches targeting collaborative economy in the tourism accommodation sector: Barcelona, Berlin, Amsterdam and Paris*. Impulse Paper No. 9. Brussels: European Commission.
Felson, M., & Spaeth, J. L. (1978). Community structure and collaborative consumption: A routine activity approach. *American Behavioral Scientist, 21*(4), 614–624.
Gansky, L. (2010). *The mesh: Why the future of business is sharing*. New York: Penguin Books.
Germann Molz, J. (2013). Social networking technologies and the moral economy of alternative tourism: The case of couchsurfing.org. *Annals of Tourism Research, 43*, 210–230.
Gibson-Graham, J. K. (2006). *A postcapitalist politics*. Minneapolis: University of Minnesota Press.
Gibson-Graham, J. K., Cameron, J., & Healy, S. (2013). *Taking back the economy: An ethical guide for transforming communities*. Minneapolis: University of Minnesota Press.
Halkier, H. (2010). EU and tourism development: Bark or bite? *Scandinavian Journal of Hospitality and Tourism, 10*(2), 92–106.
Hawley, A. (1950). *Human ecology: A theory of community structure*. New York: Ronald Press.
Holstein, J. A., & Gubrium, J. F. (2000). *The self we live by: Narrative identity in a postmodern world*. New York: Oxford University Press.
Huang, Z., & Benyoucef, M. (2013). From e-commerce to social commerce: A close look at design features. *Electronic Commerce Research and Applications, 12*(4), 246–259.
Humphrey, C. (1985). Barter and economic disintegration. *Man, 20*, 48–72.
ITB Berlin. (2014). *ITB world travel trends report 2014/2015*. Berlin: Messe Berlin GmbH.
Koopman, C., Mitchell, M., & Thierer, A. (2014). *The sharing economy and consumer protection regulation: The case for policy change*. Arlington: George Mason University.
Lessig, L. (2008). *Remix: Making art and commerce thrive in the hybrid economy*. NewYork: Penguin.
Linton, M. (1984). The LETsystem: A local currency that works. *In Context, 7*. Accessed May 21, 2016, from http://www.context.org/iclib/ic07/linton/
Lusch, R. F., & Vargo, S. L. (2006). *The service-dominant logic of marketing: Dialog, debate, and directions*. Armonk: M. E. Sharpe.
Mason, P. (2015). *Airbnb and Uber's sharing economy is one route to dotcommunism*. Accessed May 21, 2016, from http://www.theguardian.com/commentisfree/2015/jun/21/airbnb-uber-sharing-economy-dotcommunism-economy
Mauss, M. (1922/1990). *The gift: Forms and functions of exchange in archaic societies*. London: Routledge.
Matovska, B. (2015). *What is the sharing economy*. Retrieved from http://www.thepeoplewhoshare.com/blog/what-is-the-sharing-economy/
Mitchell, M. (2014). *The sharing economy*. Accessed May 5, 2015, from http://neighborhoodeffects.mercatus.org/2014/09/30/the-sharing-economy/

Mosedale, J. (2012). Diverse economies and alternative economic practices in tourism. In I. Ateljevic, N. Morgan, & A. Pritchard (Eds.), *The critical turn in tourism studies: Creating an academy of hope* (pp. 194–207). London: Routledge.
Normann, R., & Ramirez, R. (1993). Designing interactive strategy. *Harvard Business Review, 71* (4), 65–77.
Prahalad, C. K., & Ramaswamy, V. (2004). Co-creation experiences: The next practice in value creation. *Journal of Interactive Marketing, 18*(3), 5–14.
Rehn, A. (2014). Gifts, gifting and gift economies: On challenging capitalism with blood, plunder and necklaces. In M. Parker, G. Cheney, V. Fournier, & C. Land (Eds.), *The routledge companion to alternative organization* (pp. 195–209). London: Routledge.
Rifkin, J. (2000). *The age of access: The new culture of hypercapitalism, where all of life is a paidfor experience*. New York: Putman.
Rifkin, J. (2015). *The zero marginal cost society: The Internet of things, the collaborative commons, and the eclipse of capitalism*. New York: Palgrave Macmillan.
Ritzer, G., & Jurgenson, N. (2010). Production, consumption, prosumption: The nature of capitalism in the age of the digital "prosumer". *Journal of Consumer Culture, 10*(1), 13–36.
Schor, J. B., & Fitzmaurice, C. J. (2015). Collaborating and connecting: The emergence of the sharing economy. In L. Reisch & J. Thogersen (Eds.), *Handbook on research on sustainable consumption* (pp. 410–425). Cheltenham, UK: Edward Elgar.
Sigala, M. (2015). Collaborative commerce in tourism: Implications for research and industry. *Current Issues in Tourism, 20*(4), 346–355. doi:10.1080/13683500.2014.982522.
Stokes, K., Clarence, E., & Rinne, A. (2014). *Making sense of the UK collaborative economy*. London: Nesta. Retrieved from http://www.nesta.org.uk/
Vargo, S. L., & Lusch, R. F. (2004). Evolving to a new dominant logic for marketing. *Journal of Marketing, 68*, 1–17.
Walsh, B. (2011). 10 ideas that will change the world. *Time Magazine*. Accessed March 14, 2015, from http://content.time.com/time/specials/packages/article/0,28804,2059521_2059717_2059710,00.html
Wearing, B., & Wearing, S. (1996). Refocussing the tourist experience: The flaneur and the choraster. *Leisure Studies, 15*(4), 229–243.
Welk, P. (2004). The beaten track: Anti tourism as an element of backpacker identity construction. In G. Richards & J. Wilson (Eds.), *The global nomad. Backpacker travel in theory and practice* (pp. 77–91). Clevedon: Channel View Publications.
World Travel Market. (2014). *World travel market global trends report 2014*. Berlin: ITB.
Yannopoulou, N. (2013). User-generated brands and social media: Couchsurfing and Airbnb. *Contemporary Management Research, 9*(1), 85–90.
Zelizer, V. A. (2010). *Economic lives: How culture shapes the economy*. Princeton, NJ: Princeton University Press.

Business Models of the Collaborative Economy

Szilvia Gyimóthy

Abstract Collaborative business models are often equated with disruptive commercial endeavors, epitomised by a handful large global sharing platforms. They represent a certain archetype of business model, extracting profit from market-mediated peer exchanges. A narrow focus on for-profit models obstructs coming to terms with the full scope of the collaborative economy phenomena, driven by purposes and actors beyond commercial market domains. This chapter attempts to broaden this perspective by reviewing alternative value creation mechanisms and presents emerging business model archetypes.

Keywords Collaborative economy • Business models • Value creation • Value platforms • Communitarian business model • Profit extractive business model • Collaborative lifestyles • Place based cooperatives

1 Introduction

Airbnb. Vayable. Getmyboat. OffWeFly. EatWith. Gearshare. Travelbuddy. Collaborative business models are becoming attractive within tourism, encompassing a wide range of digitalised platforms where people can share or swap tangible resources, services, expertise and experiences. A wide range of assets are made accessible to meet the needs and demands of potential tourists, opening up collaboration on multiple levels and networks. Collaborative platforms tap into the capacities of peer travellers and local community members simultaneously. They are empowered (or involuntarily made) to play new roles and take responsibilities previously carried out by commercial and public actors. Consumers become part-time marketers, intermediaries and quality supervisors. Citizens undertake the role of part-time destination ambassadors and suppliers of a range of tourism products and services. Take the example of free guided tours in metropolitan cities, which are often run by self-employed expats, bypassing not only industrial operators, but

S. Gyimóthy (✉)
Department of Culture and Global Studies, Aalborg University, A.C. Meyers Vænge 15, Copenhagen 2450, Denmark
e-mail: gyimothy@cgs.aau.dk

D. Dredge, S. Gyimóthy (eds.), *Collaborative Economy and Tourism*,
Tourism on the Verge, DOI 10.1007/978-3-319-51799-5_3

also local regulative and control systems (addressed by Meged & Dissing, 2017; Leal Londoño & Medina, 2017). Nevertheless, the business model of free guided tours is fundamentally different from that of rideshare and peer accommodation rental, not only in terms of purpose, alternative recruitment and distribution systems, but also in terms of the benefits and impact they generate.

It is important to acknowledge the diversity of value creating objectives, mechanisms and the disruptive scope of various collaborative phenomena. In order to provide a clear understanding of the different types business models that co-exist in the collaborative economy, this chapter contributes threefold. First, it condenses the main tenets of the business model literature; second, it reviews early attempts to categorise collaborative and sharing business models and; third, based on these, it identifies generic criteria along which we can distinguish collaborative business endeavours in tourism.

2 Business Models and Value Creating Mechanisms

Since the turn of the millennium, the business model as a conceptual tool has received increased attention in a range of subfields in management (strategy, sustainable production, e-commerce, technology and innovation) and among practitioners. The network school of strategic management enables us to rethink competitive advantage and value perceptions along more porous firm boundaries and dynamic capabilities. It has been acknowledged that value is not created autonomously by a firm, but rather in collaboration with other firms and market players (Beattie & Smith, 2013; Zott, Amit, & Massa, 2011). Although definitions differ, there is broad agreement that the business model is a new unit of analysis, distinct from the product, firm, network or sector. By focusing on collaborative ties and value co-creating activities between firms and their stakeholders, business model analysis takes a holistic approach to explaining "how firms do business" (Zott & Amit, 2010).

Business models capture the essence of a firm's competitive strategy by defining three key components; its value proposition (benefits offered to target segments), its value creation mechanisms (resources, supplier and distribution channels and partners) and value capture (cost structures and revenue models) (Osterwalder & Pigneur, 2010). This framework enables us to take firm-level and system-level perspectives simultaneously, and address firm performance both in terms of corporate strategic goals as well as its impacts on stakeholders, environment and society. As such, a structured analysis of business purposes, value creation processes and revenue streams may help to categorise novel concepts on the market into distinct types of business models. For instance, by reviewing a multitude of cases on sustainable innovation, Bocken, Short, Rana, and Evans (2014) developed eight sustainable *business model archetypes*, entailing three technological, three social and two organisational innovations. Archetypes capture the essence of the value proposition, e.g. "maximize material and energy efficiency", "create value from waste" or "deliver functionality rather than ownership" (ibid.). Some of these archetypes are not operated by firms in the traditional sense, but rather through new socio-economic arrangements, public-private partnerships and entrepreneurial initiatives.

3 Early Categorisations of Collaborative Business Models

Developments in digital technologies and interactive communication platforms in the past decade opened up fundamentally new ways to create and deliver value. This has led to rapid expansion of new transaction architectures and unconventional exchange mechanisms, for instance along the fusion of e-commerce and social networking sites (Amit & Zott, 2001; Sigala, 2015). The novelty of collaborative business platforms lies in their hybrid networking functionalities, which may simultaneously serve commercial and social purposes. Some of the new platforms are built around genuine sharing and pooling of resources while others facilitate monetised exchanges among strangers. For instance, Schor and Fitzmaurice (2015) differentiate between four types of sharing: recirculation of goods, swapping services, optimizing the use of durable assets, and building social connections. This hybridity confuses the conceptualisation of new business phenomena, as long as we try to approach them along a classic value chain framework or conceptual dichotomies, such as buyer-seller, user-provider, host-guest or citizen-foreigner. Acknowledging that there are fundamental differences between facilitating sharing among strangers to members of a neighbourhood or an interest community, we must scrutinise various mediation (brokerage) solutions. Platform mediators play a significant role in building and commodifying trust and maintaining social control through the reliance on digital technologies.

Established definitions keep on adopting one particular business model archetype, conceptualising the collaborative economy as a peer-to-peer *marketplace*. For instance, the European Commission defines the collaborative economy as "a complex ecosystem of on-demand services and temporary use of assets based on exchanges via online platforms" (European Commission, 2015, p. 3). Overt focus is given to digital platforms that match people who want to buy, rent or share products and services in the most cost effective way. Operators do not own the property or assets that are traded on their platforms, but they provide immediate, virtual access to assets on a large scale. Such collaborative business models thrive on density and volume, and their success will depend on the enduring availability of a broad supply of goods and/or services (Bardhi & Eckhart, 2012; Gansky, 2010). Capturing a critical volume in the market is determined by two central factors: a broad and far-reaching scaling and a dense and collaborative community (Smolka & Hienerth, 2014. Accordingly, the most significant growth of collaborative business phenomena takes place in cities and urban areas, with a high concentration of resources (capital, property, skills) and year-round demand with high purchase power.

Peer accommodation rental operators (Wimdu, Airbnb, Flipkey and HomeAway) are up-scaled global models of a particular business setup, where profit is extracted for the benefit of the private firm. On these digital platforms, value is generated by members of the public who are neither employees (hence, lacking labor protection), nor have shares in the private firm. This has come to be referred to as platform capitalism or the extractive collaborative economy. However, the collaborative economy also counts other constellations that are mobilised by social capital and generate value in other ways. Carpooling and ridesharing platforms, voluntary welcome services (e.g. Global Greeters) and peer traveller information sites (backpackr.org) facilitate peer collaboration and communication where transactions are not necessarily monetised and captured by single businesses. These models are broadly known as communitarian models of collaborative economy or platform cooperativism. In the broader mapping of collaborative business models we must therefore acknowledge the existence of both platform capitalism and platform cooperativism respectively (Scholz, 2016). In line with this, two generic collaborative business model archetypes are reviewed.

3.1 Corporatised Extractive Models

Koopman, Mitchell, and Thierer (2014) identify five ways in which collaborative businesses create and capture value. First, they mobilise "dead" capital by utilising idle assets (empty apartments, inactive labour, excess knowledge). Second, peer market exchanges are made instantaneous and effective by bringing together multiple buyers and sellers through a simple, standardised mediation process. This lowers transaction and bartering costs, yielding more competitive prices, thereby making collaborative offerings available to previously marginalised customers (Rifkin, 2015). Third, trust between buyers and sellers is enhanced through the transparent peer rating system, which aggregates the evaluation of past consumers. Fourth, reputational feedback mechanisms represent a more direct and instantaneous quality assurance system, that replaces traditional third-party quality control mechanisms such as star classifications. Fifth, the demand-driven setup enhances new innovations and may optimise service and delivery processes. As demonstrated below, competitive advantage is created across all elements of the business model; the value proposition, value creation mechanisms and value capture processes.

Corporatised extractive models are designed along market mediated transactions embedded in strict social control mechanisms. The commercial intermediary secures a powerful position to capture value along the entire process. In order to avoid bypassing the intermediary, full contact addresses are only delivered after payment. In most cases the price is charged at the time of booking, but first transferred to respective hosts 24 hours after departure. Platform operators typically charge 15% to cover transaction and administrative costs, including verification procedures, quality assurance and instructions of the hosts. Furthermore, when taking a closer look at these companies' disclaimers, responsibilities are devolved as far as possible to the parties involved. There is no explicit insurance policy protecting either hosts or guests. The illustrious guarantees (amounting to one million dollars on some platforms) only apply in extreme cases of misconduct, should the company "decide in its sole discretion". Apart from this, the corporate sharing platforms disclaim all warranties regarding the correctness of information provided by the hosts, including the availability, reliability or quality of rented assets or compliance with local laws and regulations. Such disclaimers elegantly bypass the lack of control over health and hygiene, and personal and labour security, which points to multiple problems in the operating and regulating of footloose commercial enterprises across the blurred boundaries of private and commercial hospitality.

These blurred boundaries become controversial as we focus closely on the mass-customised, but allegedly "intimate and authentic" host-guest encounters among strangers. The modular design of market-mediated platforms evokes the design of contemporary digital dating apps, ensuring near or perfect matches between hosts and their guests beforehand. In the business models of peer accommodation rental and social dining, hospitality itself is conditioned and reduced to a number of transparent parameters, elegantly organised along a searchable and bookable menu. As such, the menu operates as a mediator and a buffer between the individual autonomy of customers and structures of power (Korczynski & Ott, 2006). The enticing website listings of hosts appeal to guests' sense of freedom to choose the optimal accommodation or meal experience and the disguised payment through a third party platform enhances the illusion of private hospitality.

The ritualised, selected and standardised presentation of welcoming, service-minded hosts upholds the enchanting myth of guests' sovereignty. Guests are simultaneously reminded and exempted from culturally established hospitality practices; for instance, they are encouraged, but not obliged to bring small gifts for their hosts. On the other hand, they are automatically prompted to use peer rating systems, designed along other online market valuation platforms, like Tripadvisor. Affiliated hosts are evaluated by their patrons subsequent to their visit along a few parameters (e.g. overall experience, welcome or cleanliness). Over time, the peer rating system results in social control and a virtual social hierarchy, where hosts with the highest scores are elevated to a differentiated status (e.g. Airbnb's "superhosts").

This crude meritocratic system is a double-edged sword that mostly benefits the customer. It may simplify the selection process of accommodation providers in the same location, but negative reviews may also expose hosts and their reputation in the long term. The extractive platforms do not protect hosts against biased criticism, let alone invest back into the providers' assets, product or labor. It has been claimed that collaborative economy businesses offer benefits for society on all levels: consumers, citizens, unemployed, entrepreneurs. While sustainable business models have adopted triple bottom line approaches to demonstrate their wider impact, the annual reports of global sharing platforms do not provide a systematic, detailed documentation of their societal, environmental and economic footprint. As such it has been argued that they are merely extracting wealth rather than generating sufficient new value for a community to thrive, be socially fair and sustainable (Slee, 2015).

3.2 Communitarian or Commons Models

At the other end of the spectrum, an alternative to the extractive model is a commons model of the collaborative economy where peer-to-peer mediated sharing is powered by solidarity, mutuality and co-ownership, and where benefits are returned back into building the capacity of users or to the commons (Scholz, 2016). If a surplus is generated, it is invested back to the people who contribute or in the maintenance of the platform itself. Communitarian business platforms models are often a result of bottom-up initiatives and are typically locally-owned (e.g. a municipality, housing cooperative, or potentially even a destination marketing organisation). For instance, neighbourhood help, gear swapping sites or voluntary visitor greeter services are cooperative marketplaces that offer sharing options similar to global platforms but profits would be invested into city projects and community facilities, or distributed amongst participating residents.

The value creation processes of communitarian collaborative business models are fundamentally different from extractive ones. Strong communal ties and mutual consent with the core values of the group implies that trust mechanisms differ from those in extractive models. Trust is paid forward and assessed through commitment, rather reputational capital alone. For instance, to get access to the collective pool of resources, members of communitarian platforms must contribute with in-kind assets (e.g. a room, couch or apartment), reciprocating the contribution of other members. The Couchsurfing community requires all members to be prepared to let their couches out for fellow couchsurfers, hence trust is embedded in a boundary-defining membership (Molz, 2013). The medium of exchange is nonmonetary; couchsurfer hosts offer their time, private property and local knowledge in return for virtual reputation and member endorsements. Another distinct feature of the communitarian model is its auto-mediated organisational setup. Instead of a commercial intermediary, cooperative platforms are either owned and managed by the group itself, or mediated by a public or nonprofit body. For instance, a Danish museum has recently enhanced a regional pilgrimage trail by hosting a digital platform on which hikers may directly connect with local citizens and book experiences ranging from private dinners to birdwatching and berry-picking. The platform, Camønoen.org neither charges for intermediation, nor is responsible for vetting procedures. As the market overtakes quality control mechanisms, the trustworthiness (and ultimately, the survival) of the platform will depend on the volume and support of contributing members.

Communitarian models may also be built around a certain cause or interest such as subcultures, or consumer tribes (backpackers, film fans or foodies). For instance, the Social Dining Network in Cornwall is connecting gastronomy enthusiasts, where the platform not only enables dinner dating but also the exchange of recipes and cooking experiences. The communitarian model thrives on the commitment of its members and reciprocal relationships among them. Collaborative communities create network and information spillover effects and economies of scale, and can best be described as ecosystems with high social impact (Smolka & Hienerth, 2014). As Hardy (2017) points out, collaborations among RVers are built around sharing intangible or immaterial assets (e.g. skills, experiences), where value is not necessarily monetised or bound to discrete one-to-one exchanges. This implies that some communitarian, auto-mediated models are not purely functional transaction sites but also sites of convergence. The value proposition of "promoting a collaborative lifestyle" is enabled on virtual meeting platforms offering diverse interaction opportunities other than market exchanges.

4 Collaborative Business Model Archetypes in Tourism

Based on the generic categories of extractive and communitarian business models it is possible to identify some common features along which collaborative economy business endeavors in tourism can be described and distinguished (Table 1). These are: (1) global peer-to-peer marketplaces to enable temporary access of idle assets; (2) place-based cooperatives enabling small local providers to provide tourism

Table 1 Comparing and contrasting collaborative business models along key characteristics

	Global peer marketplace	Place-based cooperative	Virtual community meeting place
Main purpose	Commercial redistribution system for market exchanges among peers	Trading ecosystem among local community members	Site of convergence for interest communities (tribes)
Value proposition	Optimal use and access to idle durable assets and skills	Recirculate goods and swap services	Promoting a collaborative lifestyle building social connections
Value capture	Extractive: surplus extracted by commercial mediator	Communitarian: surplus recirculated into neighbourhood	Communitarian: recirculated among community members
Scope of collaborative community	Strangers—anyone can participate	Neighborhood or local community (membership criteria apply)	Interest community (membership criteria apply)
Strength of communal ties	Loose	Semi-loose	Strong
Mediating mechanisms	Market-mediated	Publicly mediated	Automediated
Examples	Airbnb Boatflex Free walking tours	Global Greeters Camøno Yays	Couchsurfing Gearshare

services and experiences and finally, (3) virtual community platforms where interest communities converge. Each archetype differs in terms of purpose, value proposition, value capture, scope of the sharing community and the strength of communal ties among members as well as mediation/brokerage mechanisms.

5 Conclusion

Collaborative business models are new structures that cross-appropriate old forms of sharing (e.g. building social connections, recirculating tangible goods, swapping services and intangible assets) with effective digital intermediation to extract value from idle capacity and assets. Business models in the collaborative economy can vary significantly. However, tourism scholars and practitioners have so far mainly been concerned with profit-extractive models even though communitarian models of collaborative economy are well-established in various contexts (see chapters by Cannas, 2017; Clausen & Velázquez, 2017; Hardy, 2017). The extractive model, manifested in a small number of strong global platforms, has tended to dominate the marketplace, facilitated by media coverage and scholars keen to identify and claim lead status in the next "big research theme". This chapter has offered a broader mapping of collaborative models, and has contributed much needed insight by sketching three archetypes with distinct features, scope and value creation mechanisms. A more nuanced typology may shed light by highlighting the existence of alternative, communitarian or commons-based businesses in tourism. These can potentially mobilise resources and communities not only in urban, but also in rural and coastal destinations, usually under-prioritised by industrial investments and development opportunities.

References

Amit, R., & Zott, C. (2001). Value creation in e-business. *Strategic Management Journal, 22*, 493–520.

Bardhi, F., & Eckhardt, G. M. (2012). Access-based consumption: The case of car sharing. *Journal of Consumer Research, 39*, 881–898.

Beattie, V., & Smith, S. J. (2013). Value creation and business models: Refocusing the intellectual capital debate. *The British Accounting Review, 45*(4), 243–254.

Bocken, N. M. P. B., Short, S. W., Rana, P., & Evans, S. (2014). A literature and practice review to develop sustainable business model archetypes. *Journal of Cleaner Production, 65*(1), 42–56.

Cannas, R. (2017). Embedding social values in tourism management: Community currencies as laboratories of social entrepreneurship? In D. Dredge & S. Gyimóthy (Eds.), *Collaborative economy: Perspectives, politics, policies and prospects*. Cham: Springer.

Clausen, H. B., & Velázquez, M. G. (2017). Collaborative economy in tourism in Latin America: The case of Argentina, Colombia, Chile and Mexico. In D. Dredge & S. Gyimóthy (Eds.), *Collaborative economy and tourism: Perspectives, politics, policies and prospects*. Cham: Springer.

European Commission. (2015). *Upgrading the single market: More opportunities for people and business*. https://ec.europa.eu/transparency/regdoc/rep/1/2015/EN/1-2015-550-EN-F1-1.PDF

Gansky, L. (2010). *The mesh: Why the future of business is sharing*. New York: Penguin Books.

Germann Molz, J. (2013). Social networking technologies and the moral economy of alternative tourism: The case of couchsurfing.org, *Annals of Tourism Research*, 43, 210–230.

Hardy, A. (2017). Community and connection: Exploring non-monetary aspects of the collaborative economy through recreation vehicle use. In D. Dredge & S. Gyimóthy (Eds.), *Collaborative economy and tourism: Perspectives, politics, policies and prospects*. Cham: Springer.

Koopman, C., Mitchell, M., & Thierer, A. (2014). *The sharing economy and consumer protection regulation: The case for policy change*. Arlington, VA: Mercatus Center, George Mason University.

Korczynski, M., & Ott, U. (2006). The menu in society: Mediating structures of power and enchanting myths of individual sovereignty. *Sociology, 40*(5), 911–928.

Leal Londoño, M. P., & Medina, F. X. (2017). Free walking tour enterprises in Europe: An evolutionary economic approach. In D. Dredge & S. Gyimóthy (Eds.), *Collaborative economy and tourism: Perspectives, politics, policies and prospects*. Cham: Springer.

Meged, J. W., & Christensen, M. D. (2017). Working within the collaborative tourist economy: The complex crafting of work and meaning. In D. Dredge & S. Gyimóthy (Eds.), *Collaborative economy and tourism: Perspectives, politics, policies and prospects*. Cham: Springer.

Osterwalder, A., & Pigneur, Y. (2010). *Business model generation: A handbook for visionaries, game changers, and challengers*. Hoboken, NJ: Wiley.

Rifkin, J. (2015). *The zero marginal cost society: The internet of things, the collaborative commons, and the eclipse of capitalism*. New York: Palgrave MacMillan.

Scholz, T. (2016). *Platform cooperativism: Challenging the corporate sharing economy*. Accessed June 12, 2016, from http://www.rosalux-nyc.org/wp-content/files_mf/scholz_platformcooperativism_2016.pdf

Schor, J. B., & Fitzmaurice, C. J. (2015). Collaborating and connecting: The emergence of the sharing economy. In L. Reisch & J. Thogersen (Eds.), *Handbook on research on sustainable consumption*. Cheltenham: Edward Elgar.

Sigala, M. (2015). Collaborative commerce in tourism: Implications for research and industry. *Current Issues in Tourism, 20*(4), 346–355. doi:10.1080/13683500.2014.982522.

Slee, T. (2015). *What's yours is mine: Against the sharing economy*. New York: OR Books.

Smolka, C., & Hienerth, C. (2014). *The best of two worlds: Conceptualizing trade-offs between openness and closedness for sharing economy models*. Paper presented at the 12th International Open and User Innovation Workshop, Harvard Business School, Harvard University, Boston, MA, USA.

Zott, C., & Amit, R. (2010). Business model design: An activity system perspective. *Long Range Planning, 43*(2/3), 216–226.

Zott, C., Amit, R., & Massa, L. (2011). The business model: Recent developments and future research. *Journal of Management, 37*(4), 1019–1042.

Responsibility and Care in the Collaborative Economy

Dianne Dredge

Abstract This paper explores moral responsibility in the collaborative economy using examples from the collaborative economy accommodation sector as the context to excavate key issues and challenges. The paper traverses difficult philosophical terrain in order to better understand the relationship between concepts such as ethics, responsibility and moral action in the collaborative economy. The traditional approach is for governments to adopt universal rules to determine who is responsible for what consequences and to prescribe remedies so that actors can 'earn' the claim of being responsible. However, the global and liquid nature of the collaborative economy operating across jurisdictions and the difficulty and lack of interest in implementing strict regulatory frameworks that contradict neoliberal free market ideology suggest that utilitarian and rule bound approaches to defining and apportioning responsibilities are unlikely. A care ethics approach to responsibility, that relies on articulating values, establishing emotional connections to place and people/communities, and that encourages public-private collaborative action towards a caring end is argued to be a potential way forward.

Keywords Responsibility • Care ethics • Collaborative economy • Tourism • Accommodation sharing • Planning • Policy

1 Introduction

If you believe some reports, in May 2016 Berlin's government banned Airbnb (Berlin has banned Airbnb, 2016; Oltermann, 2016; Payton, 2016). The legislation, which evoked considerable controversy in the media and ignited concern across the world, was introduced in response to brewing tensions some of which were explained by Hollersen and Mingels (2012) some four years earlier:

> In this odd environment, two types of people are coming into conflict: On the one hand, there are the foreigners, or new Berliners, who are looking for something to buy. On the

---

D. Dredge (✉)
Department of Culture and Global Studies, Aalborg University, A.C. Meyers Vænge 15, Copenhagen 2450, Denmark
e-mail: dredge@cgs.aau.dk

D. Dredge, S. Gyimóthy (eds.), *Collaborative Economy and Tourism*,
Tourism on the Verge, DOI 10.1007/978-3-319-51799-5_4

> other, there are the locals, the old Berliners, who wonder how much longer they'll be able to stay. Those in the first group tend to look up as they walk the streets, checking out buildings and looking for good investments. Those in the second are just trying to get home.
>
> Despite these differences, they are all anxious. The foreigners are anxious about their modest assets, which they hope to convert into valuable real estate before the euro goes bust. Meanwhile, native Berliners are worried about the city they call home. And this anxiety, which affects all of Germany and many other European countries, is being transformed into a euphoria of sorts in the Berlin real estate market.

Hollersen and Mingels identified just two perspectives: local residents and mobile investors/new residents. Local residents within apartment complexes were living with the daily impacts of visitors coming and going and the City was growing at a rapid rate with the tenants association claiming that 45,000 new Berliners were searching for accommodation each year (Berliner Mieter Gemeinschaft, 2016). The Senate was interested in protecting the interests of Berliners, both present and future, so housing availability and affordability were key concerns. The legislation required that approval for commercial accommodation be sought (i.e. where property owners were not resident), and owners had been given 2 years to secure these permissions. The intention of the legislation was to stop residential housing—and particularly social housing—being illegally converted into short-term commercial accommodation. Further, in recent personal communications with this author, a government official further clarified that "the Senate Department for Urban Development and the Environment does not undertake any regulatory activity with regard to the tourism sector, the sharing economy, the collaborative economy or the hotel and guesthouse sector" and that "the new law does not contain any regulatory elements that are specifically targeted at the tourism sector, the sharing economy or the collaborative economy" (Dredge, Gyimóthy, Birkbak, Jensen, & Madsen, 2016). Put simply, the legislative response was simply designed to protect housing availability and affordability and not ban any particular platform. So, while collaborative economy accommodation platforms and some second homeowners and property investors might have been adversely affected by the new legislation, the claim that Airbnb had been banned was an exaggeration. Lawmakers, taking into account their duties and responsibilities as elected representatives to their constituencies, were simply making ethical decisions about what were appropriate actions to protect public interests.

Not only does this episode illustrate inaccurate reporting of the developments in Berlin (and why we need to remain critical to the claims in media in particular), but it also illustrates the complexity of ethical decision-making faced by policymakers. Policymakers have to decide what issues are more or less important, what values they will uphold, what values can be traded-off, what stakeholders they answer to, and, ultimately, what are responsible actions from a government's perspective bearing in mind their legal and moral responsibilities to citizens, communities and the private sector. These decisions are based on ethical considerations and inevitably result in winners and loosers. In the above case, sharing platform companies were perceived to be the loosers, and Berliners in search of affordable housing, were the winners.

Smith and Duffy (2003), Fennell (2006) and Jamal and Menzel (2009) argue for strengthening philosophical engagement with the ethical dimensions of tourism development. This is the challenge to which this chapter responds. At a global level, supporters of the collaborative economy reiterate that it is a sustainable alternative to current consumption-oriented modes of economic activity (Owyang, Samuel, & Grenville, 2014). Botsman (2010) explains:

> ...I believe we're actually in a period where we're waking up from this humongous hangover of emptiness and waste, and we're taking a leap to create a more sustainable system built to serve our innate needs for community and individual identity. I believe it will be referred to as a revolution, so to speak—when society, faced with great challenges, made a seismic shift from individual getting and spending towards a rediscovery of collective good.

But is the collaborative economy really a more responsible economy? Do these claims of responsibility translate into more responsible behaviours by the range of actors involved in the collaborative economy? The starting point for this chapter is that moral responsibility in the collaborative economy is a reflection of our identities (i.e. who we are and what we want to be). Notions of responsibility are socially constructed and politically framed, so it is important to be critical of what we claim as responsible. To this end, this chapter seeks to encourage greater theoretical reflection on the ethics of what ought to be done or not be done, what is right and wrong, good and bad, and how this gets played out in collaborative economy practices (Lawton, Van der Wal, & Huberts, 2016).

2 Why Are Ethics Important?

There are four key reasons why a deeper exploration of ethics in the collaborative economy is urgently needed. First, *the disruptive nature of the collaborative economy demands immediate action which should be proactive not reactive*. In the collaborative economy responsibility for addressing impacts and consequences are complex and distributed (Anderson & Um, 2015; Leigh, 2016; Slee, 2016). The speed of change means that politics is driving public responses. Reflection and theorising, if done at all, is post-hoc. Not only is greater understanding of the ethical decisions and trade-offs in collaborative economy practices needed, but we also need tools and frameworks to help us deliberate.

Second, *moral responsibility is relational*. The collaborative economy is a distributed system comprising a range of actors including service providers, property owners, investors, consumers and platform capitalists. It also relies on public assets and common pool resources, such as publicly funded tourism marketing activities, and intangible community assets and attractions that are not acknowledged within peer-to-peer transactions. As a result, the effects of the collaborative economy can impact upon a range of actors and public interests beyond those involved in direct transactions (Dredge & Gyimóthy, 2015). For example, residential communities, future residents and property investors may not necessarily be directly involved in peer-to-peer transactions but may experience the consequences of collaborative economy practices. Moral responsibility in the collaborative economy therefore involves multi-lateral relations.

Third, *responsibility in the collaborative economy requires public-private action*. The governance literature reminds us that neither public nor private sectors have exclusive control and negative externalities[1] are a shared responsibility (Haufler, 2013; Vigoda, 2002). Collaborative economy platform actors have displayed quite varied willingness to act and their behaviour and attitudes towards the impacts of the collaborative economy have at times raised controversy (Sundararajan, 2014). The very different organisational cultures and values of the platforms mean that reaching an understanding of ethical responsibility requires dialogue and shared understanding.

Fourth, *the liquid organisation of the collaborative economy makes assigning responsibilities difficult*. Liquid organisation denotes a fluid organisational form that does not have rigid boundaries or membership and it is characterised by autonomous actors operating to pursue their own loosely aligned values (Clegg & Baumeler, 2010). Globalisation has facilitated the operation of liquid organisations where responsibilities can be shifted elsewhere or even avoided. The collaborative economy comprises a myriad of such liquid organisational platforms and practices, which governments have found difficult to deal with (Monbiot, 2014, 2015; US Federal Trade Commission, 2015).

Together, these reasons highlight that the collaborative economy is dynamic, liquid and resistant to the rule bound ways that governments assign responsibilities and make laws (i.e. a justice ethics approach). Instead, impacts and issues vary and expectations and values (i.e. what might be good or bad, right or wrong) differ so that universal principles and rules are difficult, if not impossible, to identify. Furthermore, relationships between actors spread out in all directions so that good actions towards one set of stakeholders might not yield desirable results in another set of stakeholders (e.g. resident communities in destinations). Herein lies the difficulty of thinking about moral responsibility in the collaborative economy.

This chapter does not, therefore, seek to determine or make any universal claims about who should take responsibility for what issues and impacts. My intention instead is to promote critical thinking about ethics and to move beyond superficial claims that the collaborative economy is more responsible than current models of economic production and consumption, a claim that Dredge and Gyimóthy (2015) see as hollow and lacking in evidence. Drawing from care ethics, the chapter argues that it is possible to excavate some core values that can help move us towards a normative theory of responsibility in the collaborative economy. However, before exploring the nature of caring and responsibility in the tourism accommodation

[1]A negative externality is a cost or impact suffered by a third party (e.g. a community group or resident) as a result of an economic transaction between two parties. In a simple example, residents in an apartment building may be subject to the disruptive behaviours of sharing accommodation guests even through they are external to the transaction between the provider (host), the guests and the collaborative economy platform.

collaborative economy it is first important to briefly explore key terms and concepts.

3 Key Terms and Concepts

Ethics is a branch of philosophy that explores what is right and wrong, good and bad, and helps us to make decisions about what we ought to do or not to do. Different theoretical strands within the philosophy of ethics help us to theorise, systemise and determine what ought to be done. Determining responsibility inevitably involves moral questions about what is the right course of action (deontological ethics); what action will lead to the best and most acceptable consequence (consequentialist ethics); and what is the most virtuous thing to do in order that society lives well and flourishes (virtue ethics). Traditional discussions of moral responsibility—whether we deserve praise or blame for our actions—are quite complex philosophical questions and often require consideration of what sort of person we are and want to be; what we can do within the capacities and limitations that we possess; how we understand and interpret all the possible actions that are open to us; and how much control we have to undertake action. While deeper discussion is not possible here, it is important to note that when governments make decisions and enact laws that determine who is responsible for what, they rely on universal principles and rules that can be applied equally, are accountable (to whom is another question!) and justifiable. The case of Berlin above illustrates that these universal rules and principles are underpinned by emotional and political responses to the problem and the value systems that permeate the debate.

Moral responsibility is the consideration of whether a response or action deserves praise or blame, and is often associated with a sense of duty, fairness or obligation. Being responsible implies praise for a given action, while being irresponsible implies blame for the negative consequences of an action. A philosophical view on moral responsibility invokes a much deeper discussion than I currently have space for in this chapter. Instead, my intention is to retain a pragmatic focus on exploring responsibility as moral agency in the collaborative economy.

Four key observations are raised with respect to moral responsibility. First, the concept of responsibility cannot be simply cast as individual action undertaken within private life; it also encompasses the actions of groups or collectives of individuals operating jointly and/or on behalf of others (Boston, Bradstock, & Eng, 2010). This perspective opens up the opportunity for us to consider the ethical dimensions of how groups of actors such as politicians, policy makers and private sector representatives work collectively to take morally responsible decisions and actions for the public interest as in the above example in Berlin. Second, consideration of what moral responsibility is in the collaborative economy invokes a range of reactive emotions including empathy, care, goodwill, thoughtfulness, and so on (Shafer-Landau, 2013). In the Berlin case, policymakers were empathetic to the poor who were experiencing a housing affordability crisis. Third, the process wherein an individual or collective assigns praise or blame involves rule-bound and value-based judgements. This socialisation of responsibility means that certain actions are expected to be more or less responsible. The controversy arose in Berlin because two sets of values about what is responsible—protecting housing for the poor and support for the collaborative economy as a market innovation—came into conflict. On this point, Ims and Jakobsen in Bina and Guedes Vaz (2011, p. 176) warn that we need to pay greater attention to what kind of people and values our current economic systems foster, because this affects the character and collective moral agency of society to be responsible for our actions.

In line with this thinking, a *care ethics* approach to responsibility is adopted. *Care ethics* draws attention to the interdependent relationship between self and other, where caring for the other is not a rational, rule-bound exercise but one in which deliberation takes into account contextual, relational and emotional considerations (e.g. Gilligan, 1982; Noddings, 1984; Robinson, 2010). Care ethics highlights the mutually independent, connected and potentially vulnerable and asymmetric relations between states, institutions and individuals (Collins, 2015). It recognises that moral responsibility involves reciprocity, mutuality and dependency in the face of unequal power and resources (Pettersen, 2011). This relational ontology of care, and its reciprocal mode of caring for others, offers a framing of responsibility that is not as well developed in conventional ethical theories and is suited to the collaborative economy.

Emerging out of feminist writings in the 1980s and 1990s, care ethics raises attention to the way that men and women construct moral problems differently (e.g. see Gilligan, 1982; Noddings, 1984; Tronto, 1993). Gilligan's work explored questions of responsibility, the role of the self and others, and she focused attention on the distinction between the ethics of care and ethics of justice. She noted that women tend toward an ethics of care, framing responsibility as a relational and deeply personal response to care for the self and others. In the ethics of justice, responsibility is constructed around legal rules and concepts such as fairness, rights, sanctions or consequences, and tends to be masculine in orientation (McKeon, 1957; Ricoeur, 2000). Gilligan (1982) argued that the mature human practises both ethics of care and ethics of justice: girls had a more developed ethics of care as a result of the closer relationships developed with their primary caregiver (generally the mother) and that boys' disconnection with women at an earlier age was a driving factor in perpetuating patriarchal societies (p. xxiii).

Building upon this early work, and broadening its application beyond gendered practices of caring and responsibility, Tronto (1993) built a normative ethics of care and argued that care ethics was broadly applicable to moral dilemmas in society. Tronto (1993) defined "care" as "everything we do to maintain, continue, and repair our world so that we can live in it as well as possible" (p. 103). Thinking of responsibility as caring invites us to think of the moral landscape in terms of the way we conceptualise an issue, how we see and interpret injustice and inequity, and also how we might respond given our interdependence to others in the issue (Engster & Hamington, 2013). In this way, the ethics of care rebalances the dominance of universalising and rule-bound ideas about ethics as justice towards ethics as a relational and contextualised response motivated by a desire to sustain, nurture and protect (Held, 2005; Stensöta, 2016).

Public policy has been characterised as "what governments choose to do or not to do" (Dye, 1978). The object of public policy ultimately determines who wins and looses and how the benefits and costs of those actions are distributed among present and future actors. Returning to Berlin, as described in the introduction to this chapter, what government chooses to do about the conversion of residential apartments into collaborative economy accommodation is an ethical issue. What interests should government care for and prioritise in their policy response? European labour and capital mobility benefits the middle classes who are able to invest and profit in second homes that they can advertise on platforms such as Airbnb. Increased tourism associated with the sharing economy accommodation sector contributes to economic growth producing economic indicators that might also make elected representatives look good. The poor will bear the costs in terms of rising housing costs and decreased supply. Elected officials might act in their own self-interest or they might seek to address a broader collective set of public interests. In doing so, they are required to understand, evaluate and make trade-offs about what is more or less important, and who will shoulder the benefits and costs of those decisions. Public policy addressing the collaborative economy accommodation sector therefore involves quite complex ethical decisions ranging from how the problem is framed; what are potential actions and their consequences; what values and actions are prioritised or cared for; and how these consequences are valued and by whom.

Influenced by rationalism, modern policymaking has commonly adopted universal rules and abstract reasoning to determine a moral position on what should be done. Issues were framed and decisions made based on, for example, cost-benefit analysis and other techniques that removed emotions such as empathy, compassion, caring and so on (Held, 2014). Ironically, these deliberations are usually underpinned by a set of values that are not always explicit, and can be deeply embedded and ideological but these were obscured under the guise of rationalism. For example, Bramwell (2011) and Dredge and Jenkins (2007, 2012) discuss the shifting ideological landscape shaping the role of government including the desirability for the operation of free markets and declining support for interventionist policy. Furthermore, as Porritt (2007) argues, these neoliberal values associated with the global economy have become so embedded that there is no longer any discursive space available to consider ethical questions about what governments ought to do or where their responsibility lies. Instead, responsibility has become a matter of what actions will support global economic development within the parameters of a neoliberal agenda. This point is taken up further in the next section, where in trying to isolate some core values in the ethics of care in the collaborative economy, we also need to confront the unquestioned values embedded in neoliberalism that dictate definitions of responsibility that tend to prioritise markets and growth over other societal issues.

4 Core Values of Care and Responsibility

Proponents of the collaborative economy argue that collaborative economy innovation unlocks idling assets. Monetising these assets contributes to goals such as economic growth and job creation, and it opens up ecologies of economic innovation leading to increased competition (Botsman, 2010). These advantages are aligned with neoliberal values, and the unquestioned acceptance of these values provides some policymakers with clear direction on what ought to be done with respect to the collaborative economy—i.e. what we need to do to embrace its growth potential and avoid regulatory measures that might stymie its development. However, drawing from Porritt's (2007) earlier point, these values are so embedded that the notion of responsibility in the collaborative economy is unquestioned, and our consideration of responsible actions are narrowed to only those that feed the rolling out and consolidation of neoliberalism. The rationale underpinning neoliberalism is built on abstract rules and universal laws that require us to remove feelings and emotions and to make objective, "considered judgements" about what ought to be done (Held, 2014). Ironically, these "considered judgements" are based on deeply embedded values and subjectivities that assume responsible actions are those that lead to greater competition, free markets and growth. To date, reflection and the questioning of these neoliberal values in the collaborative economy have occurred on the margins of mainstream discussion (e.g. see Bauwens, 2005; Scholz & Schneider, 2016; Slee, 2016). They have also had to compete with the well-resourced research and media campaigns of collaborative economy platforms.

Critics seeking to broaden the notion of responsibility beyond neoliberal values have also argued that the extractive model exploits precariat[2] workers where their labour is subsumed into the product (Slee, 2016); it extracts wealth from common pool resources, redistributes and privatises it (Slee, 2016); and it is disruptive to communities and residents who bear the costs of overcrowding, rent increases, housing shortages and declining community cohesion without receiving benefits (Bauwens, 2005; Scholz & Schneider, 2016). For these critics, responsibility in the extractive collaborative economy entails being responsive to the impacts and negative externalities of the collaborative economy, the burden of which is currently being shouldered by the precariat (e.g. informal workers, silenced communities, the urban poor) (Slee, 2016). Here, a care ethics approach appears a useful alternative to help flesh out a broader understanding of responsibility in the collaborative economy.

Care ethicist, Virginia Held (2014, p. 109) argues "morality is less a matter of rational recognition and more a matter of taking responsibility for particular other

---

[2]The term "economic precariat" refers to the increasing number of people living precariously in late modern capitalism. They generally lack the security of a living wage and the predictability of regular income. The precariat often have to undertake extensive unpaid labour in order to remain in the labour force, and the phenomenon is often associated with underemployment.

persons in need". She argues against a rational approach and calls for greater attention to contextual, relational and emotional factors in determining responsibility. She argues that the relational approach triggers a different kind of action that fosters caring for human values. Building upon the work of Gilligan (2013), the ethics of care offers resistance to injustice, to the silencing of alternative voices and to the distancing of democracy, conditions that characterise current neoliberal modes of governance.

But while the ethics of care is appealing as a way of re-orienting our deliberations on what ought to be done, a caring ontology is difficult to capture in normative guidance (Held, 2014; Pettersen, 2011). Normative theories attempt to provide us with general guidance on how we should act or behave. A normative theory of care is difficult to articulate because care, as discussed above, rests on relational qualities that are contextual, emotional and cannot be easily coded into general principles (Collins, 2015). Despite these reservations, some care ethicists remain undeterred arguing that we cannot afford to give up and that it is possible to identify "the normative heart of care" to guide us (Pettersen, 2011; Stensöta, 2016).

Pettersen (2011, p. 54) argues a twofold normative approach to care being "the universal condemnation of exploit and hurt, and the universal commitment to human flourishing". The relationship between the two values is further explained:

> Care as a normative value is indeed related to the ideal of not inflicting harm, but it must also include a reasonably limited commitment to actively working for the prevention of harm. Furthermore, the normative value of care is related to the ideal of contributing to the promotion of good, but it must be narrowed down in order to not entail self-sacrifice or the sacrificing of the well-being of a third part. Care, the normative core of the ethics of care, can be portrayed as a merging of the principle of non-maleficence when it is expanded to allow for certain types of interventions, and the principle of beneficence when it is restricted to the prevention of systematic self-sacrifice and the surrendering of the concrete others' interests (Pettersen, 2011, p. 54).

Public policy researchers have also tried to capture a normative basis for care ethics. Stensöta (2016), for example, argues for a public ethics of care (PEC) as a general approach to facilitate policy formation and implementation that builds, nurtures, sustains and protects relationships that promote societal well-being. Drawing from the literature (e.g. see Barnett & Land, 2007; Held, 2005; Stensöta, 2016; Tronto, 1993), the following core features can be identified:

1. *Context matters*. A caring response necessarily requires an appreciation of the experiences, capacities, histories and relationships with others.
2. *Relationships matter*. A caring response recognises relational entanglements, interdependence and dependence, and the flow of impacts and consequences in different directions.
3. *Values and emotions matter*. Emotions, such as empathy, injustice and inequity, and values such as respect, reciprocity and mutuality inform and motivate moral commitment and can trigger deeper and more personal actions.
4. *Individual and collective action matter*. Care ethics involves an action orientation that is both an individual and a collective responsibility to care.

In taking into consideration these above dimensions, care ethics opens up a political thought project that triggers deeper philosophical thinking about how we can frame responsibility as our capacity to care and be morally responsible for others; it allows us to examine the relational consequences of actions; and it prompts us to think about aspects such as generosity and obligation to whom and for what purpose (Hooft, 2016; Massey, 2004). However, this normative heart of care ethics is not complete or exhaustive, and care ethicists argue that a mature approach to responsibility will also take into account a justice perspective (Pettersen, 2011).

In developing this normative core of care ethics, theorists draw attention to the role of the moral agent, their situatedness within their personal sphere, and their role in society, as a citizen, as a professional, as an economic, social and political actor. As a practice, care ethics requires continuous negotiation of caring—for one's own interests, for others' interests, and for the collective interests of society. On one hand an overemphasis on altruistic care and concern for others is debilitating, undermining autonomy, integrity and personal growth. On the other hand, a self-centred approach to care can be equally isolating, leading to narcissism, violence and intolerance. To avoid overdeveloped altruism or self-centredness, an understanding of the core values of care discussed above and the capacity to reflect upon care in context are essential. Thus, moving care ethics from a philosophical position to pragmatic normative guidance requires that we "analyze and articulate value systems, draw attention to problems and possibilities, and supply well-founded justification when necessary" (Pettersen, 2011, p. 61). In the following section, the challenges of caring within the collaborative economy are discussed.

5 Responsibility and Caring in the Collaborative Economy Accommodation Sector

In the literature, discussions of responsibility in the collaborative economy have generally circulated around two broad overlapping themes: (1) a justice inspired view of ethical responsibility based on rules about who ought to take responsibility for various impacts and consequences (Cannon & Chung, 2015; Koopman, Mitchell, & Thierer, 2014); and (2) discussions about where *moral responsibility* lies in the collaborative economy (Bauwens, 2005; P2P Foundation, 2015). However, and as previously discussed, caring is an individual and a collective activity and caring relationships, motivations and values go in all directions. The discussion below illustrates just two types of caring that have been expressed in the collaborative economy accommodation sector[3]: hosts caring for guests, and a platform caring for

[3]These expressions of caring have been chosen only to illustrate the challenges, however there are mutiple expressions of caring and fuller investigation of all these expressions is a potential line of future inquiry.

the broader community. These are used for illustrative purposes and are not intended to represent a comprehensive discussion of caring in the collaborative economy.

In the first, collaborative economy platforms are keen to project hosts' commitment to caring for guests:

> If you can, make someone feel special. That cannot be explained. Nothing gives you joy like making someone happy. That is, I think, the reason that motivates me to be a host. Being a host, it's not a very, very, casual decision. Being a host is a responsibility. India's a dynamic country. My objective is, if someone comes here they should be connected to the place in the right way. Me, as a host, I think is kind of connecting these different dots together, a kind of narrator. … We have an old (Indian) scripture: "Your mother is a god. Your father is a god. And your guest is a god". The presence of the guest here is that you treat them as your family. They trust me, and I trust them. And that's the reason it works. So hospitality, if you ask me, is about taking care, It's about welcoming with an open heart…' (Transcript from host, Airbnb, 2016).

Readers might make a cynical quip about whether this passage expresses genuine caring or is an attempt by Airbnb to highlight a competitive advantage that differentiates the homestay product[4] offered by its hosts from the commercial hospitality sector. Cynicism aside, the above passage draws attention to the potential for genuine caring between accommodation providers and guests to be present in the collaborative economy accommodation sector. Caring in this case demonstrates all the above core values—context-dependent, relational, emotional and values-based and it is action-oriented at individual and collective levels. However, the use of this quote on Airbnb's website suggests that caring may also be a staged or managed claim and that caring about the business is heavily intertwined in the motivation to care for guests.

Second, caring is also manifested at a collective level as evidenced in the Airbnb Community Compact released at the Airbnb Open in Paris in late 2015:

> Based on our core principles to help make cities stronger, Airbnb is committed to working with cities where our community has a significant presence and where there is support for the right of people to share their homes, both when they are present and when they are out of town (Airbnb, 2015).

Airbnb further indicates a willingness to work with cities around the world to "treat every city personally and help ensure our community pays its fair share of hotel and tourist taxes"… (i.e. caring is context dependent) "to build an open and transparent community"… (i.e. caring as a value) and to "promote responsible home sharing to make cities stronger" (i.e. caring for communities through action) (Airbnb, 2015). The impacts of short-term rental accommodation are threatening the very presence of Airbnb in some cities (Ikkala & Airi, 2015; Kassam, 2015; New York State Department of the Attorney General, 2014). In response, Airbnb has launched an

[4]The Airbnb product comprises the rental of whole apartments, rooms and beds. In most destinations, homestay experiences (taken to mean the renting of a room or a bed where the host is onsite and personal service is provided) makes up a relatively smaller proportion of the product offer than whole apartments where the host is absent.

action platform (www.airbnbaction.com) that outlines its commitment to addressing various impacts, including addressing the concerns of hosts, communities and governments. The platform is clearly intended to engage directly in this debate by acknowledging concerns and by helping to maintain a positive constructive debate. The Community Compact (Airbnb 2015) further states:

> Based on our core principles to help make cities stronger, Airbnb is committed to working with cities where our community has a significant presence and where there is support for the right of people to share their homes, both when they are present and when they are out of town.

In this quote, Airbnb is not taking responsibility for the impacts emerging at a community level, but is expressing a willingness to work collaboratively to address emerging issues. In this sense, the Community Compact might be regarded as an expression of Airbnb's corporate social responsibility intentions. The extent to which Airbnb is responsible for a range of issues currently being linked to the platform's growth (e.g. housing supply and affordability issues, resident-visitor impacts) is a contested point. Many of these issues are derived from historical policies and pre-existing conditions in housing, tourism marketing, property investment and labour mobility (see Dredge et al., 2016). The linking of housing supply and affordability issues with Airbnb, whose operations *may* have exacerbated problems in some cities, has resulted in calls for the platform to take responsibility for wicked policy issues well beyond its capacity and responsibility despite its immense power as a corporate citizen. The global nature of the organisation further exacerbates the difficulty of deciding where responsibility starts and ends. Moreover, accommodation providers are not employees but independent operators, so Airbnb's obligations are ill-defined in relation to the broader commitments that the company is undertaking in its Community Compact.

The platform and their providers have *some* responsibility for contributing to the wicked problems associated with the collaborative economy housing accommodation sector, but the extent and nature of this responsibility is very unclear. The platform must work collectively with its accommodation providers; providers must work collaboratively with their market (guests); and platforms, providers and the market must work collaboratively with governments to address the issues. This discussion demonstrates that responsibility is both an individual and a collective issue, and is a public-private concern. Responsibility is also an expression of the caring relationship between the individual/collective. The Community Compact also illustrates Airbnb's relational and contextualised city-by-city approach.

However, the global and liquid nature of collaborative economy platforms operating across jurisdictions, and governments' difficulty in implementing regulatory approaches (which would go against neoliberal ideology that promotes economic innovation), suggest that utilitarian and rule bound approaches to defining and apportioning responsibilities are problematic. A care ethics approach to responsibility, that relies on articulating values, establishing emotional connection to place and people/communities, and that encourages public-private collaborative action towards a caring end may offer a way forward in addressing community impacts. The object of caring is a central consideration here, since individuals and collectives can simultaneously care for very different ends. Caring about markets, growth, corporate image and reputation are traded off against caring for communities and people. The critical point here is that who is cared for, and what is cared about are complex issues that do not receive the attention they deserve.

6 Discussion

This chapter has argued that care ethics offers an alternative approach to defining moral responsibility in the collaborative economy and has briefly explored two expressions of caring in the collaborative economy accommodation sector: hosts caring for guests, and a collaborative economy platform (extractive model) taking moral responsibility for impacts on communities. In undertaking this exploration of how care ethics might be used to guide moral responsibility in the collaborative economy, the deep political entanglements between global and local, between public and private, between individual and collective, and between self and other have been (albeit briefly) excavated. These entanglements should be understood as dynamic tensions, simultaneously pushing and pulling stakeholders' attention, resources and action to care for some interests and impacts more or less. Care ethics, as a philosophical approach to moral responsibility, sees action as both a personal and collective response to relationships, emotions, values and context. In conceptualising moral responsibility in this way, it is possible to balance rule-bound and universal approaches to ethics with an ethics of care.

The challenge lies in moving the care ethics approach from a philosophical pledge to normative directions and actions. The opportunity to introduce care ethics relies on unlocking the opportunities that exist in the space between the fast moving, liquid, global and highly politicised world in which issue identification takes place and where action happens. Focusing on the opportunities to care that exist within this space, to increase our capacity to care and take moral responsibility requires that we resist quick judgement and expedient policy solutions. It requires deliberation, reflection, mutual recognition and co-created understanding of the impacts and consequences of the collaborative economy.

In the above discussion of care ethics in the collaborative economy we identified four core values: context matters; understanding relations matters; values and emotions matter; and individual and collective action matters. But when and where in the policy and decision making process can these aspects be fully considered? In the rapid, often contested and highly pressured arena of public policy and media-led debate, it is often difficult to find the opportunity to consider who should we care for and what should we care about. We need to slow down and expand the "space" of deliberation. We need to expand the space of opportunity that lies between two steps in policymaking—between issue identification and decision making—so that we may discuss and deliberate more fully on the notion of care.

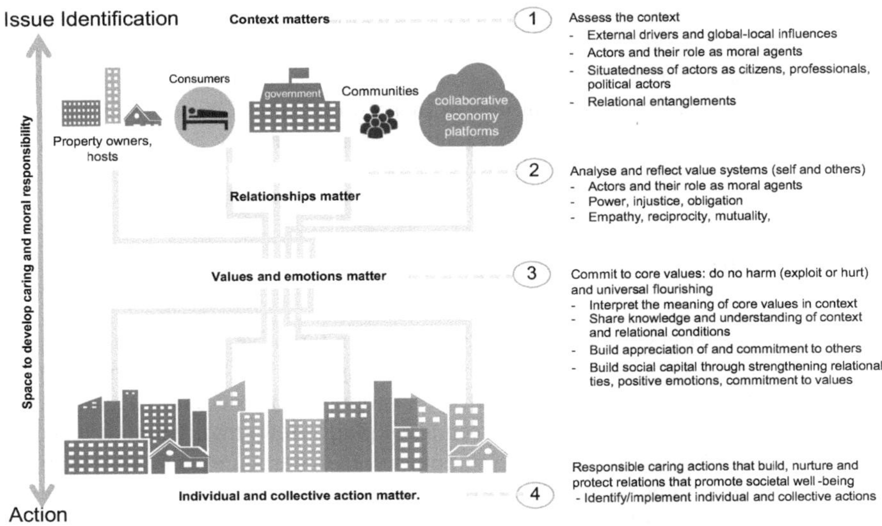

Fig. 1 Space of caring and moral responsibility in the collaborative economy

Figure 1 conceptualises and expands this space between issue identification, decision making and action drawing upon the earlier discussed directions from care ethics. In this figure, we start by acknowledging that context matters and that analysis of the context is also important. Relationships also matter, so we need to identify the range actors and understand their relational entanglements. Values and emotions also matter, so emotional connections and commitments between actors need to be understood expanded and deliberated upon. Considered actions at both individual and collective levels can then emerge.

Figure 1 is a conceptual framework that identifies opportunities for expanding the space between issue identification and action, a space for creative exploration, deliberation, and for the development of caring and moral responsibility. The Figure acknowledges that interest structures are complex and that relations extend in all directions. There will be shared values as well as individual values and these common interests will co-exist with mutually exclusive interests.

7 Conclusions

The focus of this chapter has been on exploring moral responsibility in the collaborative economy using a care ethics approach, and the extractive collaborative economy accommodation is used as the context for exploration. The chapter has traversed difficult philosophical terrain in order to investigate relationships between concepts such as ethics, responsibility and policy action. The traditional approach is for governments to adopt universal rules (justice ethics) to determine who is responsible for what consequences and to prescribe remedies or consequences. However, attempts to develop universal rules that prescribe roles and responsibilities have proven to be highly political, difficult to implement, and significant questions remain over the effectiveness of such approaches. Moreover, the diversity of sharing economy models means that determining universal rules is a difficult task. Factors that have contributed to this impasse include: the liquid, mobile and global character of the collaborative economy; high levels of individualisation and self-interest of heterogeneous stakeholders (platforms, hosts, consumers, residents, governments, etc.); the highly contextualised and location specific nature of impacts; and the power differentials that exist between powerful and well-resourced platforms and governments and communities.

These factors mean that not only is it difficult to establish rules and responsibilities, but the limitations of state sovereignty mean that implementing these rules and demanding platforms and other actors take on responsibility defined by external actors is fraught with difficulty. Under these circumstances it becomes clear that responsible actions need to be generated from the emotional and interdependent relationships and connections that actors have to the problem and to the consequences of their actions on others. In order to do this, greater attention of the space between issue identification and action is required.

Acknowledgement The author wishes to thank Associate Professor Tazim Jamal and Professor Johan Edelheim for their invaluable comments and robust discussion on earlier drafts of this chapter. The usual caveats apply—any omissions, errors and shortcomings are entirely my own.

References

Airbnb. (2015). *The Airbnb community compact*. Accessed May 21, 2016, from https://www.airbnbaction.com/compactdetaileden/

Airbnb. (2016). *Hosting standards*. Accessed April 20, 2016, from https://www.airbnb.com/hospitality

Anderson, L., & Um, S. (2015). *Behind the bargains: How the sharing economy impacts health*. Toronto: Wellsley Institute.

Barnett, C., & Land, D. (2007). Geographies of generosity: Beyond the "moral turn". *Geoforum, 38*(6), 1065–1075. doi:10.1016/j.geoforum.2007.02.006.

Bauwens, M. (2005, December 1). 1000 days of theory—The political economy of peer production. *cTheory*. Accessed May 22, 2016, from www.ctheory.net/articles.aspx?id=499

Berlin has banned Airbnb. (2016). Accessed May 21, 2016, from http://www.huhmagazine.co.uk/11457/berlin-has-banned-airbnb

Berliner Mieter Gemeinschaft. (2016). *Tenant report*. Accessed May 30, 2016, from http://www.bmgev.de/mieterecho/mieterecho-online/ihk-bericht.html

Bina, O., & Vaz, S. G. (2011). Humans, environment and economies: From vicious relationships to virtuous responsibility. *Ecological Economics, 72*, 170–178. doi:10.1016/j.ecolecon.2011.09.029.

Boston, J., Bradstock, A., & Eng, D. (2010). Ethics and public policy. In *Public policy why ethics matters* (pp. 1–20). Canberra: ANU Press.

Botsman, R. (2010). The case for collaborative consumption. *TED Talk*. Accessed May 21, 2016, from https://www.ted.com/talks/rachel_botsman_the_case_for_collaborative_consumption/transcript?language=en

Bramwell, B. (2011). Governance, the state and sustainable tourism: A political economy approach. *Journal of Sustainable Tourism, 19*(4/5), 459–477.

Cannon, B., & Chung, H. (2015). A framework for designing co-regulation models well-adapted to technology-facilitated sharing economies. *Santa Clara Computer and High—Technology Law Journal, 31*(1), 23–96.

Clegg, S., & Baumeler, C. (2010). Essai: From iron cages to liquid modernity in organization analysis. *Organization Studies, 31*(12), 1713–1733. doi:10.1177/0170840610387240.

Collins, S. (2015). *The core of care ethics*. London: Palgrave MacMillan.

Dredge, D., & Gyimóthy, S. (2015). The collaborative economy and tourism: Critical perspectives, questionable claims and silenced voices. *Tourism Recreation Research, 40*(3), 286–302. doi:10.1080/02508281.2015.1086076.

Dredge, D., Gyimóthy, S., Birkbak, A., Jensen, T. E., & Madsen, A. K. (2016). *The impact of regulatory approaches targeting collaborative economy in the tourism accommodation sector: Barcelona, Berlin, Amsterdam and Paris* (Impulse Paper No. 9). Brussels: European Commission.

Dredge, D., & Jenkins, J. (2007). *Tourism policy and planning*. Brisbane: Wiley.

Dredge, D., & Jenkins, J. (2012). Australian national tourism policy: Influences of reflexive and political modernisation. *Tourism Planning and Development, 9*(3), 231–251. doi:10.1080/21568316.2012.678379.

Dye, T. R. (1978). *Understanding public policy* (3rd ed.). Englewood Cliffs: Prentice Hall.

Engster, D., & Hamington, M. (2013). Introduction. In *Care ethics and political theory* (Vol. 15, pp. 583–605). Oxford: Oxford University Press.

Fennell, D. (2006). *Tourism ethics*. Clevedon: Channel View Publications.

Gilligan, C. (1982). *In a different voice*. Cambridge, MA: Harvard University Press.

Gilligan, C. (2013). *Joining the resistance*. Cambridge: Polity Press.

Haufler, V. (2013). *A public role for the private sector: Industry self-regulation in a global economy*. New York: Carganie Institute.

Held, V. (2005). *The ethics of care: Personal, political, and global*. Oxford: Oxford University Press.

Held, V. (2014). The ethics of care as normative guidance: Comment on Gilligan. *Journal of Social Philosophy, 45*(1), 107–115. doi:10.1111/josp.12051.

Hollersen, W., & Mingels, G. (2012). *Real estate boom threatens to end dream of affordable life in Berlin*. Accessed May 29, 2016, from http://www.spiegel.de/international/germany/real-estate-boom-threatens-to-end-dream-of-affordable-life-in-berlin-a-859420.html

Hooft, S. V. (2016). Ricoeur on responsibility. *Borderlands, 3*(1), 1–6.

Ikkala, T., & Airi, L. (2015, March 14–18). *Monetizing network hospitality: Hospitality and sociability in the context of Airbnb*. Cscw Conference. Vancouver, BC: Canada.

Jamal, T., & Menzel, C. (2009). Good actions in tourism. In J. Tribe (Ed.), *Philosophical issues in tourism* (pp. 227–243). Bristol: Channel View Publications.

Kassam, A. (2015). Airbnb fined €30,000 for illegal tourist lets in Barcelona. *The Guardian*. Accessed July 7, 2016, from https://www.theguardian.com/technology/2014/jul/07/airbnb-fined-illegal-tourist-lets-barcelona-catalonia

Koopman, C., Mitchell, M., & Thierer, A. (2014). *The sharing economy and consumer protection regulation: The case for policy change*. Arlington: Mercatus Center.

Lawton, A., Van der Wal, Z., & Huberts, L. (2016). The scope and scale of ethics in public policy and management. In *Ethics in public policy and management: A global research companion*. Abingdon: Routledge.

Leigh, A. (2016). *Sharing the benefits of the sharing economy*. Accessed March 9, 2016, from http://www.policyforum.net/sharing-benefits-sharing-economy/

Massey, D. (2004). Geographies of responsibility. *Geografiska Annaler, 86B*, 5–18.

McKeon, R. (1957). The Development and the significance of the concept of responsibility. *Revue Internationale de Philosophie, 13*(1), 3–32.
Monbiot, G. (2014). Taming corporate power: The key political issue of our age. *The Guardian.* Accessed May 21, 2016, from https://www.theguardian.com/commentisfree/2014/dec/08/taming-corporate-power-key-political-issue-alternative
Monbiot, G. (2015). Uber and the lawlessness of 'sharing economy' corporates. *The Guadian.* Accessed May 21, 2016, from https://www.theguardian.com/technology/2015/jul/28/uber-lawlessness-sharing-economy-corporates-airbnb-google
New York State Department of the Attorney General. (2014). *Airbnb in the city.* New York. http://www.ag.ny.gov/pdfs/AIRBNB REPORT.pdf
Noddings, N. (1984). *Caring: A feminine approach to ethics and moral education.* Berkley: University of California Press.
Oltermann, P. (2016). *Berlin ban on Airbnb short-term rentals upheld by city court.* Accessed May 21, 2016, from https://www.theguardian.com/technology/2016/jun/08/berlin-ban-airbnb-short-term-rentals-upheld-city-court
Owyang, J., Samuel, A., & Grenville, A. (2014). *Sharing is the new buying: How to win in the collaborative economy.* Accessed November 28, 2015, from http://tms.visioncritical.com/sites/default/files/pdf/sharing-new-buying-collaborative-economy-report.pdf
P2P Foundation. (2015). Commons transition: Policy proposals for an open knowledge commons society. Amsterdam: P2P Foundation. http://commonstransition.org/wp-content/uploads/2014/11/Commons-Transition_-Policy-Proposals-for-a-P2P-Foundation.pdf
Payton, M. (2016). *Berlin stops Airbnb renting apartments to tourists to protect affordable housing.* Accessed May 21, 2016, from http://www.independent.co.uk/news/world/europe/airbnb-rentals-berlin-germany-tourist-ban-fines-restricting-to-protect-affordable-housing-a7008891.html
Pettersen, T. (2011). The ethics of care: Normative structures and empirical implications. *Health Care Anals, 9*(1), 51–64.
Porritt, J. (2007). *Capitalism as if the world matters.* London: Earthscan.
Ricoeur, P. (2000). *The concept of responsibility: An essay in semantic analysis.* Chicago: Chicago University Press.
Robinson, F. (2010). After liberalism in world politics? Towards an international political theory of care. *Ethics and Social Welfare, 4*(2), 130–144. doi:10.1080/17496535.2010.484257.
Scholz, T., & Schneider, N. (2016). *The rise of platform cooperativism. A new vision for the future of work and a fairer internet.* New York: OR Books.
Shafer-Landau, R. (2013). *Ethical theory: An anthology* (2nd ed.). Malden: Wiley Blackwell.
Slee, T. (2016). *What's yours in mine: Against the sharing economy.* New York: OR Books.
Smith, M., & Duffy, R. (2003). *The ethics of tourism development.* London: Routledge.
Stensöta, O. (2016). A public ethics of care: Bringing ethics of care into public ethics research. In A. Lawnton, Z. Van der Wal, & L. Huberts (Eds.), *Ethics in public policy and management: A global research companion.* Abingdon: Routledge.
Sundararajan, A. (2014). *What Airbnb gets about culture that Uber doesn't.* Accessed May 22, 2016, from https://hbr.org/2014/11/what-airbnb-gets-about-culture-that-uber-doesnt
Tronto, J. (1993). *Moral boundaries: A political argument for an ethic of care.* New York: Routledge.
US Federal Trade Commission. (2015). *The "sharing" economy: Issues facing platforms, participants, and regulators.* New York: US Federal Trade Commission.
Vigoda, E. (2002). From responsiveness to collaboration: Governance, citizens, and the next generation of public administration. *Public Administration Review, 62*(5), 527–540.

Networked Cultures in the Collaborative Economy

Szilvia Gyimóthy

Abstract This chapter charts diverse approaches to conceptualising the cultures of connection characterising the collaborative economy. To decode the "we-conomy", we revisit classic notions of coexistence, collaboration and bonding in communities. Informed by a multidisciplinary review (touching upon human ecology, sociology, anthropology and cultural theory), the chapter identifies distinct theoretical frameworks to describe the constitution of communities and discusses their relevance to the collaborative economy. These frameworks explain the drivers of communitarian behaviour and resource circulation, and together open up for multidimensional interpretations of social exchange in the collaborative economy. The chapter concludes with a critical reflection on the challenges of understanding the collaborative economy in tourism, particularly when discourses are dominated by a communitarian logic that overshadows the presence of other, and more pervasive, capitalist logics.

Keywords Communities • Networked cultures • Peer-to-peer networks • Collaborative economy • Tourism • Hybrid forms of exchange

1 Introduction

> Before the Industrial Revolution, people tended to cluster in small towns and farming communities, where citizens built tight-knit relationships over the course of many years. In an economic system like that, where everybody knows everybody else, there's a natural incentive to treat people well [...] On a broader level, the members of these small, homogeneous communities knew that their neighbours probably saw the world in the same way they did, holding the same morals and belief systems, which made it easier to conduct business with them. The sharing economy [...] suggests a return to pre-industrial society, when our relationships and identities—social capital, to use the lingo—mattered just as much as the financial capital we had to spend (Tanz, 2014).

S. Gyimóthy (✉)
Department of Culture and Global Studies, Aalborg University, A.C. Meyers Vænge 15, Copenhagen 2450, Denmark
e-mail: gyimothy@cgs.aau.dk

D. Dredge, S. Gyimóthy (eds.), *Collaborative Economy and Tourism*,
Tourism on the Verge, DOI 10.1007/978-3-319-51799-5_5

The quote above illustrates a prevailing and optimistic suggestion about the radical societal transformative power of the collaborative economy. It conveys the vision of a closely-knit (g)local society, emerging as an alternative to the alienated market economy, driven by greed, egocentrism and calculative rationalism. The village community is resurrected and upscaled, thanks to mediating infrastructures and algorithms with warranties of transparency and equality. Contemporary social networking platforms enable exchanges and interconnectedness among complete strangers by institutionalising trust using sophisticated digital technologies. The proponents of the collaborative economy frequently refer to the widespread success of global tourism entrepreneurial phenomena (Airbnb, EatWith, Lyft, HomeAway) to prove their point of the advent of a new era of digitally enabled intimacy between fellow human beings.

Indeed, the most compelling narrative about the sharing economy is the utopian *return* to the times in human history where people lived in egalitarian communities—a utopia that has actually never existed (Sparks, 2015). Peer-to-peer networks on the social web appropriate the metaphors of face-to-face communitarian constellations by stretching and infusing new meaning into terms such as sharing, collaboration and symbiotic relationships. We must therefore address the implications of adopting an unsubstantiated, ahistoric and essentialist notion of the community as the central analytical concept to understand collaborative phenomena. This chapter challenges this naïve framing by adding critical insights into the momentum of the collaborative economy. Using a sociology of markets perspective, it addresses the question: How has the collaborative economy achieved such broad appeal so rapidly, expanding along the discourse of a disruptive force that will change the world?

To make sense of the collaborative economy (often called the "we-conomy"), the chapter disentangles analytical endeavors focusing on how communities are constituted via their transactions. In order to decode new cultures of connection characterizing the collaborative economy, it charts diverse disciplinary approaches to communities and networked societies and related conceptions of human coexistence, collaboration and bonding. Four distinct theoretical frameworks are identified to explain exchanges in the collaborative economy. To qualify and contrast these frameworks, two themes are addressed in depth: the drivers of communitarian behavior (i.e. what is the "glue" that binds networked cultures together?) and the characteristics of resource circulation (i.e. how do people trade commodities?). The chapter concludes with a critical reflection on the challenges of understanding the collaborative economy in tourism, particularly when discourses are dominated by a communitarian logic that overshadows the presence of other capitalist logics.

2 The Constitutive Logic of Communities

Since the eighteenth century, social scientists have attempted to theorise the character of human co-existence, addressing the question: why and how do people organise themselves into communities? Why do we engage in joint efforts, build collectives and share resources? How have communities evolved over time and across societies? How are digital technologies shaping and shaped by collective human activities? Human ecologists, economic sociologists, social anthropologists and cultural theorists put forward fundamentally different views on the constitutive logic of communities, each framed by an evolutionary take on their representative empirical contexts: human evolution as a part of complex adaptive systems, the maturation and diversification of market exchanges, the rise and decline of capitalist societies and the progress of consumer cultures.

As a consequence, there exists an ontological disparity within social sciences; communities are being depicted along entirely different tenets and structural metaphors. In Table 1, and as described below, four frameworks or perspectives

Table 1 Conceptual approaches to communities in the collaborative economy

	Ecological-substantivist logic	Utilitarian logic	Symbolic interactionist logic	Communitarian logic
Ethos	Functionalist: coordinated performance to sustain populations	Opportunist: optimising the benefits for the individual	Positional: semiotic negotiation of societal status	Altruistic: care and giving out of moral responsibility
Type of social connectedness and resource circulation	Socio-economic teamwork for the optimal use of scarce resources or idle assets	One-to-one barter transactions to maximise value in exchange, diversified brokers	Complex socio-cultural ties to trade and co-construct symbolic capital	Shared sociality (mutuality) and inclusive relations
Value of connectedness	Joint survival	Individual prosperity through alliances	Bonding for distinction, belonging to a community positions identity	Collaborative care Reciprocity to level out social inequalities
Value-making logic	Subsistence: to survive through more efficient collaboration	Extractive: to maximise profit per transaction	Meritocratic: status positioning among peers	Distributive: collaborative commons
Metaphors to describe structural characteristics	Flat/mesh (similar to ecosystems and computer networks)	Circuits of commerce (similar to value chains with diversified actors)	Communities of consumption (similar to tribal hierarchies)	Inclusive communities

are identified (the ecological-substantivist, the utilitarian, the communitarian and the symbolic-interactionist) to illustrate this diversity. Each provides concurrent explanations regarding the constitutive logic and the forms of human co-existence. Taken together, these perspectives offer notions that may strengthen a more nuanced theorisation of collaborative economy, including its communitarian ethos, models of social connectedness and diverse forms of value creation underlying the joint use of resources. Attempts to theorise the collaborative economy may therefore start with exploring how seemingly incompatible ideas about community dynamics can be intersected and converged to better understand hybrid forms of exchange and collaboration (Dredge & Gyimóthy, 2015).

2.1 The Substantivist Perspective: Community as Self-organising Ecosystem

Amos Henry Hawley's seminal work on *Human Ecology: A Theory of Community Structure* (1950) provides an ecological framework to analyse aggregating patterns in human populations. His argument is that people would band together in symbiotic relationships to adapt to their environment and optimise the use of scarce resources. Hunter-gatherer societies were organised along smaller units (a clan of related families), each playing functional roles in sustaining the community. Inequalities within the boundaries of the clan would be leveled out, where those who had more capacity than needed shared with those who had not. This interdependence has led to joint activities, such as the pooling and hierarchical redistribution of resources and knowledge, and subsequently laid the foundations of complex social institutions orchestrating and coordinating livelihoods. As communities expanded in size, exchange structures become more complex, leading to the stratification of society. Market capitalism brought about an asymmetric accumulation of individual wealth, culminating in unsustainable growth trajectories on a global level. Hence, resource effectiveness and the pooling of spare capacity among individuals became yet again a fundamental priority of sustainable societies and in the discourse of collaborative economy (Botsman & Rogers, 2011). Ridesharing, for instance, is a case of collaboration for sustaining a society through more efficient use of resources that has implications on both individual and collective levels. Commuters sharing a ride instead of driving separate vehicles are not only saving money and time each, but also reduce their environmental footprint by releasing less carbon-dioxide into the atmosphere.

The ecological-substantivist perspective defines the formation of human communities as coordinated performance to survive difficult conditions. It is perhaps more actual than ever, when contemporary societies are coping with economic and environmental pressures, and the depletion of Earth's resources necessitates effective teamwork for the subsistence of its over seven billion inhabitants. The functionalist ethos of optimal resource use and effective systems was revitalised in early conceptualisations of the sharing economy. Benkler's (2004) notion of *commons-based peer production* and Botsman and Rogers' (2011) reclaiming of Felson and Spaeth's (1978) term *collaborative consumption* depicts communities as sociotechnical ecosystems. Resource scarcity and technological advances are identified as key drivers of emergent socio-economic systems enabling sharing on a broad geographical scale (Botsman, 2014; Lessig, 2008; Rifkin, 2000). Property regimes are being replaced by access regimes, where consumers are connected to suppliers through networks bypassing traditional intermediaries (Rifkin, 2000). In the past few years, digital network technologies have given life to vastly diverse CBPP-phenomena, ranging from crowdsourced software innovations to the swapping of homes and private accommodation. The rapid rise and scale of new peer production and exchange platforms provided Benkler with a plausible argument to conclude "social sharing and exchange is becoming a common modality of economic production" (Benkler, 2004, p. 278). In a similar vein, Lisa Gansky (2010) used a computer network analogy ("the mesh") to characterise the Sharing Society as a flat and fully interconnected digital global marketplace, enabling direct, on-demand interactions among individuals to optimise resource circulation.

There is a certain romanticisation about unmediated encounters within online communities that are collaborating for the greater good. As Sparks argues, discourses in the sharing economy reinstate the village and its neighbourly interactions, yet these invoked times never actually existed (Sparks, 2015, p. 30). Void of historical justification and context, the universal community is a hyperreal simulacrum (Baudrillard, 1994), that is, a plausible projection of the past without any factual grounding in reality. Pre-industrial, feudal societies were not particularly egalitarian and peer-to-peer connectivity on a global scale was simply not possible before the rise of the social web and Internet technologies.

The sociotechnical ecosystem metaphors introduced above are built on a naïve understanding of interconnectedness without addressing the social dynamics as well as constraints of self-organizing systems among people. Equating human collaboration with production systems or with an interlocked mesh of computer networks distorts the notion of how people interact in groups. While computers are absolutely capable of negotiating ever-increasing quantities of digital data to find optimal and effective choices, the human mind has limited capacity to cope with complexity.

In 1992, Dunbar suggested that the size of the brain's neocortex imposes a limit to the number of stable interpersonal relationships people can handle. He conducted a series of experiments among human communities to establish the typical size of a social network, estimating a stable group size between 100 and 200 individuals (i.e. the Dunbar number). Dunbar's Number has been tested and validated in studies of online communities (Gonçalves, Perra, & Vespignani, 2011), confirming that our social and cognitive capabilities of maintaining social relations online do not increase with new technological affordances. Despite the possibility of being continuously connected with unlimited other individuals, online collaborative platforms do not automatically reproduce communities characterised by deep, egalitarian and symbiotic social ties. The coordinated acquisition and distribution of goods and services among 50 peers or above necessitates a set of digital tools enabling sharing or exchanges on a larger scale. Socio-economic transactions are organised along intermediating algorithms, including modular search, connection, rating and review systems. Market mediated collaborative platforms list their best performing providers to facilitate consumer decisions, thereby obstructing the transparency of available offers. For instance, Airbnb search results always suggest available superhosts as first options. Rather than being flat and egalitarian, these constellations are organised along particular social hierarchies, coordinated by the commercial platform owner (the broker of online peer exchanges). This leads us to the second explanatory framework of networked communities, namely that of market exchanges and the problematisation of commercial brokerage.

2.2 The Utilitarian Perspective: Community as Market Exchange Platform

As argued above, communities in the sharing economy are complex constellations, which are being produced, regulated and connected within socio-economic systems termed "circuits of commerce" (Zelizer, 2010). The utilitarian perspective presents an alternative constitutive logic for communities, in which the "glue" binding human societies is framed through trade and transactions. The analogy of the pre-modern village prevails (Sparks, 2015), but this time collaboration between people becomes a means of economic progress and growth, rather than joint survival. The foundational myth of the sharing economy is thus also inspired by a neoclassic microeconomic ethos that has been around for over two centuries. Back then, the economist Adam Smith naturalised bartering (the most primitive version of market exchange) as a human trait: "There is certain propensity in human nature ... the propensity to truck, barter, and exchange one thing for another" (Smith, 1776, p. 25). Market exchange denotes a transaction between two parts, when one part transfers the ownership of a commodity (or an intangible resource) to another part. The transfer of ownership is reciprocated by monetary or non-monetary compensation and hence conceptualised as a calculated and rational exchange, free of moral obligations transcending the transaction itself. The value of traded resources becomes marketised (as value-in-exchange), depending on their worth in a given transaction context framed by demand-supply configurations. Most collaborative platforms facilitating monetised exchanges follow the valuation practices of the market economy. For example, Airbnb's or Uber's prices are calculated based on the attractiveness and availability of a given ride or room at a specific time and location.

The utilitarian perspective adopts a marketplace analogy to understand human interactions, and implicitly suggests that there can be put a price tag on all aspects of human life. Derived from the tenets of social exchange theory (social psychology), it is claimed that individuals are opportunistic in all social and economic transactions, attempting to optimise the benefits for themselves. The concepts of "rational man" and "reasoned action" have been the privileged departure point in consumer studies and economic analysis, also inspiring the egocentric notion of the extended self (Belk, 1988, 2013). This instrumental trading logic is also perceptible in Botsman and Rogers' (2011, p. 73) analysis of emergent peer-to-peer sharing phenomena. Self-interest is identified as the main *raison d'être* for re/circulation of resources in the collaborative economy:

> I lived in New York for 10 years, and I am a big fan of "Sex and the City." Now I'd love to watch the first movie again as sort of a warm-up to the sequel coming out next week. So how easily could I swap our unwanted copy of "24" for a wanted copy of "Sex and the City?" Now you may have noticed there's a new sector emerging called swap-trading. Now the easiest analogy for swap-trading is like an online dating service for all your unwanted media. What it does is use the Internet to create an infinite marketplace to match person A's "haves" with person C's "wants," whatever they may be (Botsman, 2010).

Critics of the utilitarian perspective (Arnould & Rose, 2015; M.A.U.S.S., 1996) warn against making sense of human and social phenomena solely along a self-interested market discourse. Accordingly, this logic naturalises and prioritises egocentric motives and expectations of return in the analysis of peer-to-peer exchanges. As Arnould and Rose (2015) point out, utilitarianism not only reduces human life to economism and the rationality of markets, but also reproduces modernist dichotomies, which isolates market exchanges from gift giving, opportunism from altruism and generosity from self-interest. However, contemporary collaborative economy phenomena defy such clear-cut distinctions. For instance, the video testimonials of EatWith chefs (a dinnersharing platform) emphasise the gratifying experience of bringing people together and share the enjoyment of culinary delights:

> [...] To get to see their faces and see their eyes light up when they take the first bite.... That's just priceless.... that long mmmm-sound, that's what I love. That's what I cook for! (EatWith, 2014).

The gratification gained from guests' compliments resonates well with Telfer's (2000) notion of hospitableness, identifying it as a benevolent, compassionate action, driven by the desire for being with, pleasing and entertaining others. At the same time, EatWith hosts do get decent compensation for their efforts; hence, they represent both ulterior and altruistic motives. Collaborative phenomena, like dinnersharing, are partly governed by capitalist market logic and partly by social capital and collaborative values (Rifkin, 2015). In order to fully understand collaborative lifestyles and consumption, we must take note of cultural analytical approaches which consider utilitarian and altruistic perspectives simultaneously.

2.3 The Symbolic-Interactionist Logic: Community as Ideological Kinship

Arguably, the collaborative economy is not just a technological and economic phenomenon, but also an ideological manifest and movement characterising the cultural economy of the new millennium. As such, it can be understood using cultural approaches to societal analysis, being sensitive to the sociocultural context of consumption phenomena. Consumer culture theory (CCT) conceptualises the integration of consumers into communities and takes inspiration in tribal metaphors to describe their social hierarchy and organising principles (Arnould & Thompson, 2005; Maffesoli, 1996). Inspired by the principles of distinction and social stratification put forward by Pierre Bourdieu, consumer culture theorists would argue that consumption is a self-defining act in which individuals position themselves by exploiting the symbolic meanings associated with commodities. In this view, goods, services, tourism destinations, and even private homes, are accessories used to fabricate a compelling story of the self and enhance status among peers. Staying at a private Airbnb accommodation instead of a hotel room signifies a reflexive and daring traveller identity in opposition to that of the mass tourist (searching for authentic encounters away from the "beaten track"). The symbolic-interactionist perspective suggests that the worth of commodities is defined through the value added during the act of consumption (value-in-use), and hence, dependent on the semiotic fabric of a given cultural context. Status-enhancing symbols and meanings follow the trends of fashion and thus incessantly negotiated in social interactions among individuals, subcultures, commercial actors and other social entities. In contemporary tourism, "going local" (i.e. tapping into the everyday life of a place visited) is one of the most enduring narratives, through which individuals construct their traveller identities.

Consumption and consumer goods are not only a tool to construct a distinct identity that sticks out from the mass, but also a way to signal belonging and identification with like-minded others. Seen from this lens, the constitutive logic of consumer communities is an ideological kinship of people sharing a passion for a commodity, brand, leisure activity or lifestyle. For instance, urban hipsters made fairtrade products, vintage clothing and organic food fashionable, establishing a new regime of conscious consumption through their everyday market choices. Consumer communities are constructed around the identities, relationships, signs, rituals and everyday practices of members (Cova, Kozinets, & Shankar, 2007) who may converge on physical events or virtual platforms to nurture and intensify social bonds. Contrasted to a conceptualisation of the community bound to a certain locality (as in the ecological and utilitarian logic), this perspective sees communities as virtual, footloose and networked across geographical space.

It is quite straightforward to deconstruct the ethos of "new" collaborative lifestyles promoted by Botsman and Rogers (2011) with the help of symbolic-interactionism. The "global sharing community" exhibits remarkable similarities with the so-called Californian ideology (Barbrook and Cameron, in Sparks, 2015), driven by visions of an egalitarian ecotopia, well illustrated in Airbnb's community compact:

> Airbnb is a people-to-people platform—of the people, by the people and for the people—that was created during the Great Recession to help people around the world use what is typically their greatest expense, their home, to generate supplemental income. Airbnb creates economic opportunity [...] at a time when economic inequality is a major challenge. Airbnb democratizes travel so anyone can belong anywhere. [...] Airbnb is home to good travelers and good neighbors who contribute to their communities (Airbnb, 2015).

The Californian ideology is a cultural hybrid of San Francisco's hipster bohemianism, passion and colourful individual expressions and the maverick spirit of Silicon Valley's new high-tech startups. When in 2014 Airbnb relaunched its brand manifesto with the polymorphous logo "Belo", it subtly appropriated the values and ideals of the Californian ideology as well as those of backpacker subcultures to demarcate the company's brand community. In a similar vein, The Compact in Paris (2015) and the 2016 Airbnb Open Hosting Festival in Los Angeles was an internal branding performance (or corporate domestication) to strengthen hosts' sense of attachment and commitment to the company: "*At Airbnb Open, we celebrate the spirit of belonging through which we care for our guests and embrace them as part of our family.*" It has been suggested that part of Airbnb's success lies in carefully crafted narrative strategies to recruit and maintain their hosts. Douglas Atkin, the Global Head of Community and Mobilization at Airbnb is the author of the book titled 'The Culting of Brands: Turn Your Customers Into True Believers' (Atkin, 2004), which analyses and relates the social dynamics of cult brand communities (Apple, Harley-Davidson) to those of real cults (Unification Church and the Hare Krishna movement). He pointed out that cult brands address and engage with their devotees by invoking community identification and loyalty. "It's easy to see the same kind of cult-like enthusiasm for Airbnb among its users, a kind of evangelism, a sense that they are taking an enlightened path and even helping to change the world" (Strong, n.d.).

The limits of the symbolic-interactionist perspective are related to the framing of collaborative phenomena as a *consumer* culture trend, opportunistically harnessed by venture capitalists. It equates the collaborative economy with a certain cluster of global platforms, connecting, driven and benefited by people with high cultural, digital and networking capital. It is capable of identifying contemporary narrative representations of the self or of analysing the situated value of symbolic transactions among members of consumer tribes, but it fails to provide a more holistic, socially grounded and generalised explanation of communitarian movements. This may be attributed to the fact that the symbolic-interactionist logic (similar to the utilitarian view) takes its point of departure in individual behaviour to explain larger social phenomena. We will now turn our attention to the communitarian logic, pinpointing the norm of generosity and inclusion as a driver of human coexistence.

2.4 The Communitarian Logic: Community as a Solidaristic Cohesion

The advent of free market economies and consolidating capitalist systems by the twentieth century has led to functionalist and meritocratic logic infusing all aspects of personal and social life. The consequences of individual interests, economic rationality and the spreading of utilitarianism greatly concerned modern sociologists. In particular, Emile Durkheim and his nephew, Marcel Mauss attempted to reinvoke social commitment (charity, solidarity and community care) to maintain social cohesion and long-term peaceful coexistence. In his seminal work *The Gift*, Mauss (1990 [1925]) conceptualised gift-exchanges as the social glue in society (Sleeboom-Faulkner, 2014), hence, defining the constitutive logic of communities along the pursuit of solidarity, reciprocity and congeniality.

The gift as a special form of moral exchange has been extensively discussed within anthropology and sociology (Mauss, 1990; Otnes & Beltramini, 1996; Sahlins, 1972). As already noted above, Marcel Mauss maintained that gift is central to maintain long-term social relationships "marked by the balance between generosity and obligation, self-interest and solidarity" (Sleeboom-Faulkner, 2014, p. 324), and as such, brings benefits to a larger group rather than between two individuals. Opposed to market exchanges, gift-giving is not a simple dyadic affair, with an ulterior motive of maximising benefits for the individual. Theories on gift-giving describe reciprocal relationships between giver and receiver, which are conditioned by mutual trust, intimacy or other types of proximities (e.g. kinship).

Mauss' work is echoed in both early and recent analyses of moral economies as an emergent alternative to contemporary Western societal structures. For instance, Scott (1976) described the communitarian interests underlying peasant communities in Southeast Asia and contrasted them to capitalist societies thriving on self-interest. Later, proponents of post-capitalist social movements (Gibson-Graham, 2006), the moral economy (Bauman, 2003; Germann Molz, 2013; Gold, 2004) and the hybrid economy (Rifkin, 2015) envisioned new societal dynamics based on cooperation and generosity, involving a new type of generalised exchange, also referred as "mutuality" by Arnould and Rose (2015). The constitutive logic of communities in the communitarian perspective is pro-social, altruistic behaviour, where giving and caring is a moral imperative to maintain and reproduce a shared social vision (e.g. sustainability, social security and support). Market exchange and dyadic transactions are replaced by the distributive logic of collaborative commons, characterised by joint ownership, cooperative appropriation of resources and access-based consumption. Within collaborative commons, the sustainable limits to resource extraction are agreed upon by the community and surplus is reinvested or re-circulated among members.

The communitarian perspective suggests that patterns of social cohesion and kinship in small groups are also valid on a larger scale, and transferable to urban neighbourhoods or global virtual communities. However, a larger geographic scope will affect how members are related to each other, modifying the density, intensity and proximity of personal relationships. It has been argued that social distance will have an influence on how we return a favour, so that people in closer relationships are more likely to act unselfishly than in remote ones (Sahlins, 1972). Consequently, the concept of reciprocity should be nuanced on three distinct levels. Generalised reciprocity or mutuality, understood as an altruistic act without expectations of direct return is typically observable among closely related individuals (ibid.). In contrast, relationships between strangers and distant individuals tend to be more opportunistic, where individuals benefit at the expense of others. Finally, balanced reciprocity denotes a direct exchange between equivalents. It can be argued that commercial collaborative economy models in tourism are designed to facilitate balanced reciprocity rather than generalised reciprocity. Platforms explicitly define the terms of transaction and exchange between the host and the guest, but there are no procedures for re-circulating the gains of individual transactions within the broader host community.

3 Towards a Hybrid Understanding of Networked Cultures

Networked cultures and communities are often highlighted as the backbone of the collaborative economy, engaging in new social practices transcending the boundaries of public and private spheres. In order to address this complexity, four perspectives were introduced above, each providing a distinct conceptualisation of communitarian ethos, dynamics and resource circulation. As single analytical approaches, their polarised interpretations may be partially inadequate to fully understand the collaborative economy, where social dynamics are equally characterised by substantivist, utilitarian, symbolic and communitarian logics. Economic sociologists (Granovetter, 1985; Polányi, 1968) were early to point out that all economic activities, including exchange are embedded in a non-economic context, such as cultural values, social relationships and moral concerns. This complicates the theorisation of resource circulation, which conceptually distinguishes between gift-giving, market exchange and sharing. The hybrid character of collaborative economy blurs such distinctions; the emerging forms of "sharing" and "pseudo-sharing" (Belk, 2014) cannot be understood independently of gift-giving and market exchanges.

In order to address the social embeddedness of collaborative economic phenomena, we must develop frameworks that are sensitive to capture overlapping motives behind resource pooling mechanisms (Fig. 1). These may entail pragmatic reasons (convenience and resource scarcity) suggested by the substantive-ecological perspective; symbolic statements related to identity construction (distinction and belonging) as well as communitarian imperatives (altruism and reciprocity), where giving is an act of shared sociality. Networked cultures in the collaborative economy governed simultaneously by these six motives, solicit analytical

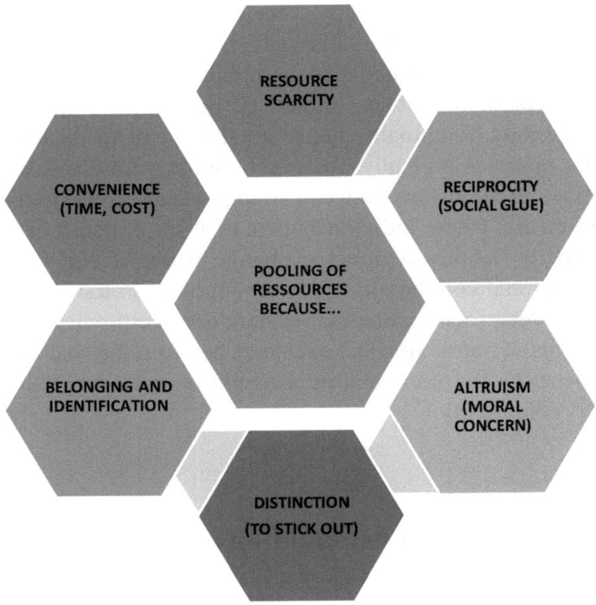

Fig. 1 Hybrid motives of joint use of resources

frameworks from previously incompatible domains. These are: (1) models of economic systems (circuit, regime, networks and ties, transactions, relationships); (2) cultural and moral perspectives on human coexistence (negotiation, lifestyle, stewardship, pro-social behaviour, collaborative symbiosis) and; (3) ideas of efficiency and enhanced value creation (zero marginal costs, full interconnectedness, direct exchange, optimised capacity use, recirculation of idle resources). To qualify emergent social and communitarian practices in the collaborative economy, future studies must look into the intersections of these domains. Such an approach can problematise how utilitarian, eco-ethical and solidaristic ideals are balanced in market-community relationships on different geographical levels, and how are they negotiated and institutionalised in emergent disruptive business models.

4 Conclusion: The Red Herring of Sharing

The collaborative economy has been labeled as a disruptive force that will change the world (Walsh, 2011). The four perspectives introduced in this chapter offer an explanation for the rapid global diffusion and appeal of tourism and travel related collaborative businesses. Airbnb and other platforms harness the communitarian ideals of sustainable, eco-ethical and solidaristic co-existence, and emphasise personal bonding and social cohesion instead monetised market exchanges. In this fuzzy context, the term "sharing" is a red herring (a misnomer) that has been misappropriated to occupy a market position by tapping into consumers' need for caring, connection and communitarian values. Epitomised by neologisms such as "sharing economy", "sharing platforms", "sharewares" and so on, the term of sharing has been re-imagined and reinvigorated across different domains, denoting widely different social practices, some of which having actually very little to do with sharing.

Let us therefore revisit the notion of sharing and review its conceptualisation in the study of communities and networked cultures. Social anthropologists have long acknowledged the structuring role of sharing in social relationships and in societies at large. Since the rise of the social web, it has gained renewed interest by sociologists (Belk, 2007, 2014), linguists (John, 2013) and social anthropologists (Arnould & Rose, 2015). They all agree that the contemporary use of the term is fraught with ambiguity and complexity. In a recent etymological essay, John (2013) differentiates between no less than five contemporary meanings of sharing, including, among others; acts of distribution (e.g. sharing a box of chocolate), acts of communication (sharing experiences) and acts of participation. Jenny Kennedy (2015) explores the conceptual boundaries of sharing in relation to other social theories of exchange. Based on a synthesis of various streams of literature she suggests that there exist three distinct ontological perspectives on sharing (economic, distributive and social) when describing the practices of networked communities practice. Accordingly, sharing is simultaneously used to denote an economy driven by social capital (i.e. the sharing economy/collaborative economy), a mode of online resource distribution (i.e. sharing platforms) and a site of social intensification (symbolic exchanges and bonding among community members).

The return of authentic relationships with private hosts has a particular allure in contemporary tourism (Russo & Richards, 2016), where local cultures are commoditised, packaged and distributed by multinational tour operators. The disruptive impact of new tourism collaborative platforms can also be attributed to a skillful manipulation of the communitarian discourse, promoting sharing and belonging, while disguising the capitalist fundament of their business model (Slee, 2015). They position themselves in opposition to the incumbent industry (travel intermediaries and corporate hospitality chains), who are framed as uncaring opportunistic players that contribute to, rather than alleviate, socio-economic inequality across the world (Millard, 2016). As Strong (n.d.) notes: "The sharing economy has cleverly made established brands dangerously out of touch. If they do attempt to criticise the business model then they can appear like dinosaurs out of step with the hip new economy".

Sharing is positioned as a "morally correct act", transporting its rhetoric and positive associations to companies facilitating peer transactions against a fee. In the book, "What is yours is mine" Slee (2015) demonstrates how the ideals of community, generosity and participation are hijacked and twisted to scaffold extractive business models, for instance, that of Airbnb. Hosts are recruited through the company's founding myth of some poor guys renting out their air beds to supplement their income, while prospective guests are seduced by the illusion that their peer purchase will benefit locals. With slogans such as *Belong anywhere* or *Live like a local*; tourists are invited to take on the role of reflexive citizens and contribute to build strong communities and good neighbourhoods. In reality, Airbnb is a hyper capitalist venture, which does not redistribute the benefits from idle property rental among community members. Despite allegations of contributing to housing pressures and gentrification, the company is reluctant to take civic responsibility to deal with local problems arising from illegal rental and tax evasion in European cities hit by a tourism boom (Dredge, Gyimóthy, Birkbak, Jensen, & Madsen, 2016).

The collaborative economy in tourism is more than a circular marketplace allowing peers to trade physical commodities and private hospitality. It also reconfigures conventional actor constellations and respective roles previously assigned to local hosts, local governments, transient visitors and footloose global enterprises. Armed with professional lobbyists advocating for the cult of sharing, innovation and peer-to-peer trust, the new commercial platforms have been successful in persuading local decision makers to legalise them on favourable terms (Slee, 2015; 2016). They claim that their algorithmically enhanced business models are more effective to regulate their service providers, and the free market will ensure quality control more effectively than public administrations would do. As a result, analytical portrayals of the sharing economy tend to equal it with hyper-capitalist, extractive business models, and disregard communitarian models. Nonetheless, there is a vast number of small-scale initiatives (tool libraries, dinnersharing, toy and garment swaps) that are conceived around genuine sharing, serving the needs of a community rather than maximising revenue.

This chapter has explored the roots and dominance of the communitarian discourse in the collaborative economy, pointing out that present sharing phenomena are driven by multiple competing logics. In order to move beyond oversimplified and romanticised notions of collaboration, solidarity, sustainability and social responsibility, we need to break apart the sharing economy discourse and be more critical to the claims of its cult brands. Strong (n.d.) offers a pragmatic approach to distinguish between extractive and communitarian endeavors. This includes exploring the propagated cult philosophy and identifying potential inconsistencies between strategic communication and actual deeds. Special attention is required to monitor the organisations' ethical practices regarding worker's rights, health and safety, payment of taxes and recirculation of benefits.

References

Airbnb. (2015). *Community compact*. Retrieved from https://www.airbnbaction.com/wp-content/uploads/2015/11/Airbnb-Community-Compact.pdf

Arnould, E. J., & Rose, A. S. (2015). Mutuality: Critique and substitute for Belk's "sharing". *Marketing Theory*, 1–25.

Arnould, E. J., & Thompson, C. J. (2005). Consumer Culture Theory (CCT): Twenty years of research. *Journal of Consumer Research, 31*(4), 868–882.

Atkin, D. (2004). *The culting of brands: Turn your customers into true believers*. New York: Portfolio (Penguin Group).

Baudrillard, J. (1994). *Simulacra and simulation*. Michigan: University of Michigan Press.

Bauman, Z. (2003). *Liquid love: On the frailty of human bonds*. Cambridge: Polity Press.

Belk, R. (1988). Possessions and the extended self. *Journal of Consumer Studies, 15*, 139–168.

Belk, R. (2007). Why not share rather than own? *The Annals of the American Academy of Political and Social Science, 611*(1), 126–140.

Belk, R. W. (2013). Extended self in a digital world. *Journal of Consumer Research, 40*, 477–500.

Belk, R. (2014). You are what you can access: Sharing and collaborative consumption online. *Journal of Business Research, 67*(8), 1595–1600.

Benkler, Y. (2004). Sharing nicely: On shareable goods and the emergence of sharing as a modality of economic production. *The Yale Law Journal, 114*, 237–358.

Botsman, R. (2010). *The case for collaborative consumption*. TED-talk, transcript. Retrieved from https://www.ted.com/talks/rachel_botsman_the_case_for_collaborative_consumption/transcript

Botsman, R. (2014). Sharing is not just for startups. *Harvard Business Review, 92*(3), 23–26.

Botsman, R., & Rogers, R. (2011). *What's mine is yours: How collaborative consumption is changing the way we live*. London: Collins.

Cova, B., Kozinets, R. V., & Shankar, A. (2007). Tribes, Inc.: The new world of tribalism. In B. Cova, R. V. Kozinets, & A. Shankar (Eds.), *Consumer tribes*. Oxford, UK: Butterworth-Heinemann.

Dredge, D., & Gyimóthy, S. (2015). Collaborative economy and tourism: Critical perspectives, questionable claims and silenced voices. *Tourism Recreation Research, 40*(3), 286–302. doi:10.1080/02508281.2015.1086076.

Dredge, D., Gyimóthy, S., Birkbak, A., Jensen, T. E., & Madsen, A. K. (2016). *The impact of regulatory approaches targeting collaborative economy in the tourism accommodation sector: Barcelona, Berlin, Amsterdam and Paris* (Impulse Paper No. 9). Brussels: European Commission.

Dunbar, R. I. M. (1992). Neocortex size as a constraint on group size in primates. *Journal of Human Evolution, 22*, 469–482.

Eatwith. (2014). *EatWith Coreen in San Francisco*. Retrieved from https://www.youtube.com/watch?v=KaAcYjWUZPk

Felson, M., & Spaeth, J. L. (1978). Community structure and collaborative consumption: A routine activity approach. *American Behavioral Scientist, 21*(4), 614–624. doi:10.1177/000276427802100411.

Gansky, L. (2010). *The mesh: Why the future of business is sharing*. New York: Penguin Books.

Germann Molz, J. (2013). Social networking technologies and the moral economy of alternative tourism: The case of couchsurfing.org. *Annals of Tourism Research, 43*, 210–230.

Gibson-Graham, J. K. (2006). *A postcapitalist politics*. Minneapolis: University of Minnesota Press.

Gold, L. (2004). *The sharing economy: Solidarity networks transforming globalization*. Burlington, VT: Ashgate.

Gonçalves, B., Perra, N., & Vespignani, A. (2011). Modeling users' activity on twitter networks: Validation of Dunbar's number. *PLoS ONE, 6*(8), e22656. doi:10.1371/journal.pone.0022656.

Granovetter, M. (1985). Economic action and social structure: The problem of embeddedness. *The American Journal of Sociology, 91*(3), 487.

Hawley, A. (1950). *Human ecology: A theory of community structure*. New York: Ronald Press.

John, N. A. (2013). The social logics of sharing. *The Communication Review, 16*(3), 113–131.

Kennedy, J. (2015). Conceptual boundaries of sharing. *Information Communication and Society, 19*(4), 461–474.

Lessig, L. (2008). *Remix: Making art and commerce thrive in the hybrid economy*. New York: Penguin.

M.A.U.S.S. (1996). *L'Obligation de Donner: la De'couverte Sociologique Capitale de Marcel Mauss*. Paris: La Découverte/M.A.U.S.S.
Maffesoli, M. (1996). *The time of the tribes*. London: Sage.
Mauss, M. (1990). *The gift: Forms and functions of exchange in archaic societies*. London: Routledge.
Millard, D. (2016). *The sharing economy is not your friend*. Retrieved from http://www.vice.com/read/the-case-against-airbnb-and-uber
Otnes, C., & Beltramini, R. F. (1996). *Gift giving: A research anthology*. Bowling Green: Popular Press.
Polányi, K. (1968). The economy as instituted process. In E. LeClair & H. Schneider (Eds.), *Economic anthropology* (pp. 126–145). New York: Holt, Rinehart and Winston.
Rifkin, J. (2000). *The age of access: The new culture of hypercapitalism, where all of life is a paid-for experience*. New York: Putman.
Rifkin, J. (2015). *The zero marginal cost society: The internet of things, the collaborative commons, and the eclipse of capitalism*. New York: Palgrave MacMillan.
Russo, A. P., & Richards, G. (2016). *Reinventing the local in tourism producing, consuming and negotiating place*. Bristol: Channel View Publications.
Sahlins, M. (1972). *Stone age economics*. Chicago: Aldine Publishing.
Scott, J. C. (1976). *The moral economy of the peasant*. New Heaven: Yale University Press.
Slee, T. (2015). *What's yours is mine: Against the sharing economy*. New York: OR Book.
Slee, T. (2016). *What is yours is mine: The greed behind the new sharing economy*. Retrieved from http://www.afr.com/leadership/entrepreneur/whats-yours-is-mine-the-greed-behind-the-new-sharing-economy-20160525-gp3yfo#ixzz4K30OflpR
Sleeboom-Faulkner, M. (2014). The twenty-first-century gift and the cocirculation of things. *Anthropological Forum: A Journal of Social Anthropology and Comparative Sociology, 24* (4), 323–337.
Smith, A. (1904/1776). *An inquiry into the nature and causes of the wealth of nations* (5th ed.). London: Methuen. Retrieved from http://www.econlib.org/library/Smith/smWN13.html#B.IV. Ch. 2.
Sparks, K. (2015). *The sharing economy: The production, consumption, and regulation of community in the digital economy*. Thesis, Swarthmore College.
Strong, C. (n.d.). *Airbnb and Hotels: What to do about the sharing economy?* Retrieved from https://www.wired.com/insights/2014/11/hotels-sharing-economy/
Tanz, J. (2014). *How Airbnb and lyft finally got Americans to trust each other*. Retrieved from https://www.wired.com/2014/04/trust-in-the-share-economy/
Telfer, E. (2000). The philosophy of hospitableness. In C. Lashley & A. Morrison (Eds.), *In search of hospitality: Theoretical debates and perspectives*. Oxford: Butterworth-Heinemann.
Walsh, B. (2011). 10 ideas that will change the world. *Time*. Retrieved from http://content.time.com/time/specials/packages/article/0,28804,2059521_2059717_2059710,00.html
Zelizer, V. A. (2010). *Economic lives: How culture shapes the economy*. Princeton, NJ: Princeton University Press.

Policy and Regulatory Challenges in the Tourism Collaborative Economy

Dianne Dredge

Abstract The choice of policy approach and regulatory framework in dealing with the collaborative economy rests on two fundamental factors—that government decisions should be based on good sound knowledge and that this knowledge should be above politics. In the newly emerging and rapidly growing collaborative economy, these conditions are difficult to meet. The dynamic restructuring of power relations, new stakeholders and information asymmetries can obscure what is really going on. Some authors offer valuable meso-level explorations of policy and regulatory issues in different sub-sectors of the collaborative economy. However, these solutions are often based on assumptions about government sovereignty and power relations that do not necessarily apply in the slippery global world of platform capitalism. This chapter seeks to undertake a critical exploration of the factors and values that permeate and circulate in policy discussions about the collaborative economy at a macro-level. The rendering of the socio-political landscape as complex, dynamic and value-laden dictates that policy approaches and regulatory solutions are subjective and influenced by prevailing ideology, available knowledge and the path dependencies created from historical events and approaches. These influences have a crucial role to play in the identification of alternative regulatory solutions, the evaluation of these alternatives, and the adoption of preferred approaches.

Keywords Collaborative economy • Sharing economy • Regulation • Policy • Governance

1 Introduction

In addressing policy and regulation in the collaborative economy, it is first important to distinguish between two very broad interpretations of the collaborative economy that may attract very different policy and regulatory responses from

D. Dredge (✉)
Department of Culture and Global Studies, Aalborg University, A.C. Meyers Vænge 15, Copenhagen 2450, Denmark
e-mail: dredge@cgs.aau.dk

D. Dredge, S. Gyimóthy (eds.), *Collaborative Economy and Tourism*,
Tourism on the Verge, DOI 10.1007/978-3-319-51799-5_6

governments. Both draw upon the rhetoric of collaboration, sharing, community, sustainability and trust, but they are quite distinct in terms of their underpinning values and the nature of government responses that may be appropriate. The first interpretation reflects traditional notions of sharing; this collaborative economy has been around for millennia and is deeply embedded in, for example, indigenous cultural practices such as potlash, and in the gift and favour economies (Mauss, 1925; Rehn, 2014). In contemporary western societies, this sharing has been associated with visions of communitarianism and cooperativism that seek to restore small-scale personal exchange as a means of taking back communities from the individualism and consumerism that characterises twentieth century capitalism (Gibson-Graham, Cameron, & Healy, 2013; Slee, 2016). Translated into the digital world, Scholz (2016) argues for platform cooperativism a movement made up of co-owned digital platforms where democracy, mutuality and communitarian ideals invigorate genuine sharing and solidarity.

The second interpretation has also appropriated the terms 'sharing economy' and 'collaborative economy' but shares little in common with communitarian values. It is a disruptive, digitally-mediated version of the collaborative economy known as platform capitalism. This second version of the collaborative economy, also known as the peer-to-peer, sharing, gig or platform economy, also calls upon a rhetoric of sustainability, trust and openness, and is becoming a major change agent in many sectors of the economy including tourism (Botsman & Rogers, 2011; Stokes, Clarence, & Rinne, 2014). PWC (2015) estimated that the five main sharing sectors—peer to peer lending, online staffing, peer-to-peer accommodation, car sharing and music and video streaming—generate $15 billion in global revenues but could be generating up to $335 billion worldwide by 2025. But this version of the collaborative economy, which is underpinned by venture capital and characterised by profit motivations, and has produced in a few short years a large number of billionaires, is not based on the above traditional notions of sharing, gifting or mutuality (Slee, 2016). For governments, the massive growth of this digitally-mediated collaborative economy has presented a range of policy and regulatory problems.

This chapter focuses on the policy and regulatory challenges associated with this second interpretation of the collaborative economy. The digitally mediated collaborative economy is multiplying at lightening speed where almost anything can be shared or accessed via mobile technologies. As producers and consumers connect virtually in this liquid mobile world, the geographies of markets and regulation and the sovereignty of nation states to manage their domestic economies and to raise taxes have almost become redundant (OECD, 2013). As a result of this digital collaborative economy, it has become possible to customise the mass production of accommodation, food experiences, transport and personal services by accessing both the idling resources and the labour of an increasing band of micro-entrepreneurs. In the process, existing tourism business models and traditional supply chains are coming under increasing pressure to adapt and transform. Traditional domestic taxation regimes, labour laws, health and safety regulations are just some of the existing regulatory protections that can be evaded by this fluid digital collaborative economy and that create an uneven, and often onerous, playing field for incumbent industry actors (Scholz, 2016).

The landscape of power and regulation with respect to policy-making has also changed. The global expansion and capital value of platforms such as Airbnb, Wimdu, Flipkey, Lyft and Uber for example, have given rise to new, mobile and very powerful platform capitalists with extraordinary power to manage, manipulate or even disregard policy and regulatory discourses (Monbiot, 2015). In addition to these platforms, a range of new policy actors is also emerging that defy traditional stakeholder classifications. Peers (www.peers.org) is one such organization, which is a membership organization representing an extensive coalition of collaborative economy platforms, and it was also behind a political movement to galvanise Airbnb hosts to vote against attempts to tighten regulation of short-term accommodation rental in San Francisco (Fast Company, 2013; Slee, 2016). Freelancers (www.freelancersunion.org) is another type of organization that acts as a kind of union for independent workers many of whom work in the collaborative economy. To the uninitiated, it is difficult to distinguish between the two organisations, yet their motives and the interests they prioritise are vastly different.

The aim of this chapter is to explore the challenges faced by governments in dealing with policy and regulation in this digitally mediated tourism collaborative economy. Some authors have offered valuable meso-level explorations of policy and regulatory issues dealing with collaborative economy accommodation (e.g. Guttentag, 2013; Miller, 2015) and transport (e.g. Ha, 2013; Meelen & Frenken, 2015). The contribution of this chapter is to add to this rich emergent landscape of knowledge, by providing a meta-discussion and conceptual foundation that assists in understanding the particular tensions, contradictions and values underpinning the challenges faced by governments.

2 In Whose Interests? The Policy Dilemma

Policy and regulation are important tasks undertaken by government: they create the conditions for societies to function in an orderly manner; they protect rights, attribute legal responsibility and, importantly, they directly and indirectly shape the social limits, expectations and desires that influence how individuals operate in society. The development of appropriate policy and regulation rests on two fundamental precepts—that government decisions should be based on good sound knowledge and that this knowledge should 'rise above politics' (Fischer, Torgerson, Durnová, & Orsini, 2015, p. 1). During the latter part of the twentieth century however, modern rational scientific approaches to policy-making have crumbled, and its become increasingly apparent that technical policy knowledge in not neutral. Critical policy analysts call for increased attention to the way in which knowledge is framed, policy discourses are socially engineered, and the values underpinning decision-making influence outcomes that benefit certain groups and individuals (Considine, 1994; Fischer, 2003). This critical perspective provides the lens to understand what is going on in the tourism collaborative economy and the policy and regulatory challenges that are emerging.

The collaborative economy is mooted as a disruptive innovation that embodies a more efficient and sustainable use of existing resources and assets and a move away from an industrial growth paradigm. Proponents of this digital collaborative economy invoke a moral mission to make the world more sustainable, more accessible and more connected by accessing idling resources (e.g. rooms, beds, goods, space) and the expertise of a growing body of freelance workers (Botsman, 2014; Stokes et al., 2014):

> It's about empowering people to make meaningful connections, connections that are enabling us to rediscover a humanness that we've lost somewhere along the way, by engaging in marketplaces like Airbnb, like Kickstarter, like Etsy, that are built in personal relationships versus empty transaction (Botsman cited in Slee, 2016, p. 20).

But in spite of this language of altruism and caring, the digital collaborative economy is largely made up of for-profit commercial entities and the funding of the sector is mostly derived from profit-seeking venture capital (Slee, 2016). The role of this venture capital is to advance economic innovation by supporting a robust network of activities aimed at financing, selecting, collectively learning, embedding and signalling innovations (Ferrary & Granovetter, 2009). Together these activities systematically 'select the most promising projects of the region, signal the best start-ups to the business community, accumulate and spread entrepreneurial knowledge in the cluster and embed the interdependent agents of the network' (Ferrary & Granovetter, 2009, p. 354). The power of these networks to promote and empower certain economic development discourses and social movements, and to apply pressure on policymakers and elected officials, has resulted in the accumulation of asymetric knowledge, the emergence of monopoly power and a diffusion of political power away from the state (Stiglitz, 1999; Strange, 1996). As a result, it is important to critically evaluate the policy discourses around the collaborative economy, and to excavate the origin and values of the knowledge that is being reproduced and for what purpose. In other words, the dilemma lies in understanding the difference between what we are told is a good or appropriate policy direction and whose interests and agendas are embedded in this framing of the issues.

The moral value of the digital collaborative economy is corroborated and reproduced in a dense network of Silicon Valley entities that co-produce knowledge to support and embed these interpretations in policy discourses and practices. For instance, Airbnb has commissioned research using another Silicon Valley start-up, CleanTech, to support the notion that its users are more environmentally aware and their practices more sustainable than the traditional hotel sector (Airbnb, 2014). In another example, Fast Company[1] (2013) draws attention to how Airbnb's

[1]Fast Company itself is owned by Mansueto Ventures. According to its own website the company focuses on innovation in technology, etho-nomics (ethical economics), leadership, and design.

political interests are advanced in invisible ways by, for example, calling upon a network of for-profit and not-for profit companies or creating its own entities. Douglas Atkin, Airbnb's Global Head of Community, co-founded the abovementioned membership based organization Peers, which is aimed at 'making the sharing economy work for the people who power it' (see Fig. 1). The website offers links to independent workers' insurance; it suggests places to find work by linking to platforms such as Airbnb, VRBO, Homestay, Instacart, Lyft and so on (see Fig. 2); and it offers advice on tax, personal safety nets and writing letters to policy makers in support of the 'modern (collaborative economy) workforce' (Peers, 2016). However, Fast Company draws attention to the fact that that the majority of members listed on Peers webpage are for-profit platform companies (Fast Company, 2013; Peers, 2016). One of Peer's tasks was to galvanise hosts into a voting block to resist Proposition F, an attempt by the municipality to tighten

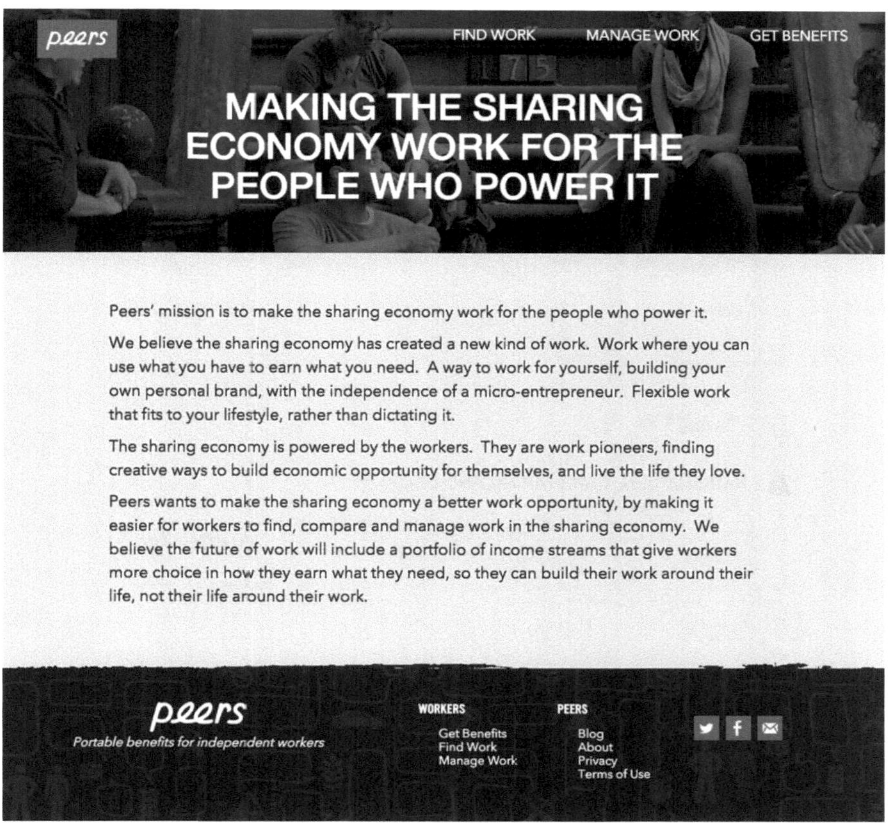

Fig. 1 Screenshot of Peers (http://www.peers.org/about/)

Fig. 2 Screenshot of Peers (http://www.peers.org/find-work/)

short term accommodation regulations in San Francisco (Fast Company, 2013; O'Donnovan, 2015; Slee, 2016). Using Peers, Airbnb reportedly spent US$8 million on this campaign and organised more than 400 volunteers in a door knock event (Somerville, 2015).

Arguments that the collaborative economy assists in the formation of stronger, more authentic social connections feed into a carefully crafted policy position that the collaborative economy is a positive and much-needed innovation and therefore deserving of a 'light-touch regulatory approach'. Airbnb's own carefully crafted Community Compact manifesto (Airbnb, 2015) positions itself as wanting to work in partnership with city administrations and will co-operate by providing information (i.e., basic highly standardised reports) and may even collect local taxes where appropriate, in return for this light regulatory touch.

These examples illustrate a complex multi-pronged approach that collaborative economy platforms use to engage in policy discourses in order to pursue their interests. The emergence of these new stakeholder coalitions such as Peers, illustrates that traditional categories of stakeholders do not apply and that coalitions further obscure traditional interest structures. When asked about whose interests were being represented, a social movements consultant working to progress Airbnb's interests in New York replied:

> We no longer live in a binary space of business versus the grassroots. Businesses can be part of social change, just like nonprofits. This space between social benefit and economic benefit is where the sharing economy is growing fast (Foster cited in Fast Company, 2013).

Fast Company (2013) further clarifies:

> Foster says that the agenda of Peers is wide open and will be defined by its membership. If the actions taken so far benefit companies like Airbnb, they also benefit its hosts, who earn an average of $5,000 a year. That's the nature of the sharing economy. "Erica and Brian in Grand Rapids don't see themselves as defending corporate Airbnb," she says. "It's their room in their house and their income that they're fighting for."

The above discussion illustrates the complex multi-value, multi-interest policy setting that governments are required to negotiate in responding to the collaborative economy. But there are some key tensions residing within this policy landscape: On one hand governments have a commitment to economic growth, innovation and competitiveness and this appears to go hand-in-hand with claims that the collaborative economy can secure more sustainable and less resource consumptive ways of living. On the other hand, there are a range of consequences and impacts emerging from the tourism collaborative economy, the full extent of which are not yet known. Not only is governments' information poor, but the slippery global nature of the digital collaborative economy means that governments have less and less power to address these impacts through policy and regulation. Collaborative economy platforms exploit this paradox by generating information and engineering the policy discourse towards its own ends. Governments' ideological commitment to neoliberalism and to the framing of tourism within an industry policy approach has also created path dependent logics that constrain creative policy solutions that can interfere with the march of hard line neoliberalism. These path dependent logics—tourism industrial policy and neoliberalism—are explored in the following sections.

3 Cracks in the System? Tourism and Industrial Policy

The modern capitalist system has become an increasingly complex system of production and consumption shaped by the dogma of industrial policy that seeks to enhance competitiveness, facilitate efficient production by lowering costs and reduce barriers to growth (Stiglitz, 1999; Walton, 1987; Warwick, 2013). Historically, drawing upon readings of liberalism and Adam Smith's notion of the invisible hand, there has been a presumption that markets would correct their own failures. In this view, the private sector operating out of self-interest would protect the circumstances influencing its own production, and would therefore take steps to avoid any negative consequences that would affect growth. Elected representatives, believing in this ability of the free market to regulate itself, systematically removed barriers to economic growth. It also became fashionable to attribute economic success to liberalisation, privatisation and the free hand of deregulation rather than pursue structural reform (Stiglitz, Lin, & Monga, 2013; Wade, 2012). As a result, and particularly since the 1970s, governments in many countries have actively sought to reduce regulation, arguing that interventionist policies were undesirable and impeded perfect market function. However, markets have been conclusively shown to be imperfect, market failures persist, information for markets to operate has been asymmetric, and governments have not treated industry sectors equally (Stiglitz et al., 2013; The Guardian, 2002). The result has been the creation of a very uneven playing field where (often hidden) public subsidies and administrative measures have created distortions and public policies have favoured some industries over others.

In tourism, and despite growing evidence of market imperfections including tourism's contribution to climate change, natural resource and community impacts, there has been a persistent belief in neoliberal non-interventionist approaches to tourism policy. In most countries, tourism has been treated as an export industry,[2] as a regional development tool, and as a strategy for economic diversification and employment generation (Bramwell & Lane, 2010). Developing economies have also been subject to this ideology as a result of coercive pressures from international funding agencies. As a result, tourism has been cast as an industry, an employment generator, a source of foreign exchange earnings and has been dominated by market stimulation policies. Efforts to address market failures, structural inequities and asymmetric information have been de-emphasised. Moreover, tourism has generally been afforded less policy emphasis compared to other industry sectors such as car manufacturing (which has received significant subsidies in many countries), and mining and natural resources. With a high proportion of SMEs and the fragmentation of the sector, targeting policy initiatives is also

---

[2]We note that tourism is characterised by partial industrialisation and, while it does not follow traditional models of industrial production and consumption, governments have often adopted industrial policy approaches to manage it.

complicated and may have contributed to lacklustre policy development in tourism (Dredge & Jenkins, 2012; Halkier, 2010).

This preference for an industry policy approach affects government-stakeholder relations. The industry policy approach entails close consultation with private sector interests and policies and actions that support and facilitate key industry interests: economic growth and competitiveness. This process facilitates flows of information between government and business; it produces a shared understanding between government and industry of the (growth) values to be pursued, and in the process public resources are directed towards assisting industry ends. Large multinational corporations often enjoy considerable power in this process as a result of their market presence and the jobs they create, which in turn affords greater access to policy makers and support for their interests (Dredge & Jenkins, 2012).

Not surprisingly, government policies have tended to fall into three broad categories designed to address the concerns of predominantly corporate stakeholders. Policies address such things as initiatives to increase tourism demand (e.g. remove barriers to growth, open up idling assets such as waterfronts and national parks); initiatives to improve productivity (e.g. maintain minimum wages and labour protections); initiatives to attract investment (e.g. reduce environmental regulation and red tape); and policies to address certain market failures (e.g. to support governance arrangements that enhance industry co-ordination). This industrial policy approach has given rise to a kind of mutual intensification of interests between governments and incumbent industry interests, and it highlights the inadequacy of democratic systems of government to engage the broader interests of civil society (Dean, 2014).

Here, the issue of regulatory capture is particularly pertinent. Regulatory capture occurs when government regulators come to advance the interests of the industry entities being regulated (e.g. hotels and taxis). For example, regulations can become so complex that regulators need the help of the industry, who have the relevant market knowledge, to regulate. The dense relational ties that develop between incumbent industry actors and regulators can result in a build up of power and knowledge in cartels that keep others from entering the market (Koopman, Mitchell, & Thierer, 2014). The collaborative economy challenges these established relations because peer-to-peer transactions can bypass regulatory requirements and have significant detrimental effects on incumbent business models as shown in the taxi industry (Koopman et al., 2014; Monbiot, 2015; Parliament of NSW, 2015).

The rise of the collaborative economy has disrupted this traditional alignment of stakeholder interests and flows of power. Traditionally large tourism operators have enjoyed access to policy makers and elected representatives, and small and medium sized enterprises, which make up the majority of the tourism industry, have had less access and have been less able to advocate their interests in policy-making processes. The entrance of platform companies are disrupting the marketplace, challenging the sustainability of traditional business models and supply chains, and the landscape of power relations. As discussed above, hosts earning $5000 per year are aligning with platform companies worth billions; incumbent stakeholders are subject to onerous policy and regulation that, while was once thought to protect them, are now impeding innovation and adaptation; and governments are faced with mounting pressure to do something about the consequences of a digital economy that is global and mobile enough to avoid domestic regulation. On one hand, governments would like to encourage this disruption-unlocking innovation. On the other hand, incumbent industry interests (who have kept governments in power) are demanding action to regulate the collaborative economy. Here, we now turn to examine the policy and regulatory challenges of the collaborative economy.

4 Regulatory Challenges

The literature identifies a large, overlapping and complex set of policy and regulatory challenges related to the tourism collaborative economy. Table 1 summarises these issues. This table is not a comprehensive list of all challenges, but rather it captures the breadth of issues that have been raised across various jurisdictions and policy contexts. Delving into the details of different sectors within the collaborative economy (e.g. accommodation, transport, personal services and so on) will likely reveal further and specific challenges but is outside the current task. The literature drawn upon in the development of Table 1 is global in nature, suggesting that many of the challenges that are emerging are shared across international contexts and jurisdictions.

In the opening section of this chapter it was noted that the choice of policy and regulation rests on two fundamental factors—that government decisions should be based on good sound knowledge and that this knowledge should 'rise above politics' (Fischer et al., 2015, p. 1). We also noted that knowledge about the tourism collaborative economy is not value neutral but is underpinned by established values, beliefs and expectations about the role of government and acceptable levels of intervention. In the second section of this chapter, the political nature of tourism collaborative economy policy-making was discussed and it emerged that there are power and knowledge asymmetries at play and there are stakeholder relations that defy traditional classifications and management approaches. This rendering of the socio-political landscape as complex, dynamic and value-laden dictates that policy approaches and regulatory solutions are subjective and influenced by prevailing ideology, available knowledge and the path dependencies created from historical choices (Henning, Stam, & Wenting, 2013). These influences have a crucial role to play on the identification of alternative regulatory solutions, the evaluation of these alternatives, and the adoption of preferred approaches. We now turn to explore approaches to regulating the tourism collaborative economy.

Table 1 Some policy challenges in the tourism collaborative economy

Type of policy challenge	References
Ideological and practical concerns	
Free riding on collective resources. Sharing and exchange through collaborative platforms can encourage free-riding of resources and services provided by public authorities (e.g. tourism marketing and promotion, recreation and leisure services).	Koopman et al. (2014)
Flexibility vs. *Certainty.* Evolutionary, require balancing flexibility to innovate against creating the certainty needed for generating business confidence, investment attraction, etc.	Johal and Zon (2015)
Rights vs. *freedoms.* Government responses must balance what is good for society versus what is merely profit-driven and good for the individual's or company's private interest.	Monbiot (2015) and Goudin (2016)
Distribution of benefits (who wins and looses). Governments need to understand who are the winners and losers, and what can be done to minimise the negative effects on marginalised groups/ actors.	Juul (2015) and Goudin (2016)
Policy mobilities. There is a propensity to adopt and adapt policy measures in one jurisdiction to another. However, innovation is context dependent. What is innovative and brings net positive benefits in one setting may not be the same in another setting.	Juul (2015) and Dredge and Gyimóthy (2015)
Information. There is no transparency of data or information to inform evidence-based policy approaches. It is unknown whether the collaborative economy brings new economic value and what type.	Scholz (2016) and Cannon and Chung (2015)
Responsibility. There is little consensus on who is responsible for the negative externalities emerging from the collaborative economy. Global companies operate outside domestic laws making it difficult to attribute any responsibility to them.	Cannon and Chung (2015)
Power and governance. Power shifts from public towards private sector are exacerbated in the collaborative economy. Establishing good governance arrangements and collaboration in the collaborative economy represents new challenges.	Hartl, Hofmann, and Kirchler (2015) and OECD (2016)
Economic implications	
Relationship between regulation and innovation. Regulatory responses may impede or promote innovation. Understanding the effects of potential regulatory approaches on innovation in the collaborative economy is required.	Ranchordás (2015) and Autoritat Catalana del la Competencia (2014)
Relationship between regulation and competition. Regulatory responses need to take into account the effects of the collaborative economy on competition between actors within the 'new collaborative economy', and between incumbent industry and the new collaborative economy actors. The risk of collaborative economy monopolies is a concern noted in several jurisdictions.	Koopman et al. (2014) and Johal and Zon (2015)
Impact on incumbent industry actors. Established regulatory regimes can give rise to regulatory capture by powerful incumbents. Regulators may come to see the world as the incumbent actors do, and rely on their knowledge, making 'new' thinking difficult.	Koopman et al. (2014) and Johal and Zon (2015)

(continued)

Table 1 (continued)

Type of policy challenge	References
Taxation	
Tax base erosion. Collaborative platforms are usually global companies and their organisation and operation are organised to exploit and optimise tax arrangements. Collaborative economy platforms are contributing to tax base erosion and profit shifting raising issues of fairness.	OECD (2013) and Parliament of NSW (2015)
Tax collection. Digital transactions on global platforms make it difficult for governments to collect taxes. Collaborative tax arrangements where platforms collect tax herald a further shift in control away from government and the privatisation of public functions such as tax collection.	Koopman et al. (2014) and Goudin (2016)
Land use planning	
Licensing. Local land use planning laws generally define owners' rights with respect to renting/sharing their house/apartment/room. Different jurisdictions are making laws and taking very different approaches to addressing impacts creating and create uneven playing fields.	Starr (2015) and Kassam (2015)
Nuisance. Local authorities have a responsibility to address nuisance effects (e.g. noise, overcrowding and illegal activities (e.g. pop-up brothels and drug labs).	Koopman et al. (2014) and Starr (2015)
Community impacts. Unregulated sharing activities at mass scale can impact on local communities.	Starr (2015)
Labour	
Minimum wage. Labour has been subsumed into production. Collaborative economy workers don't often make minimum wage, income security or have basic worker protections. A decline in labour conditions could result.	Scholz (2016), Cannon and Chung (2015) and BIBA (2015)
Workplace health and safety. Traditional workplace health and safety regulation and enforcement is not practical in the collaborative economy. Lack of knowledge, awareness of temporary workforces exacerbate the problem of maintain hard-won protections by the labour movement.	BIBA (2014)
Legal aspects—rights, risks and liabilities	
Impact of regulation on individual rights. Many sharing practices have not traditionally required regulation and its been considered a personal right, choice and practice to 'share' a room or couch or home. Regulations may need to challenge existing rights and freedoms.	BIBA (2014) and Monbiot (2015)
Business models and entities. Business models and practices adopted by small and micro-entrepreneurs can be blurred with personal finances and practices making it difficult to identify producers and enforce compliance with policies and regulations.	US Federal Trade Commission (2015)
Consumer protections. Given the global context of platform companies and the emergence of new peer-to-peer providers that lack knowledge of consumer laws, consumers need to be protected more than ever.	Koopman et al. (2014), Parliament of NSW (2015) and BIBA (2014)

5 Approaches to Regulation

Regulatory approaches are concrete forms of intervention that are implemented either by public authorities alone or in partnership with other stakeholders (e.g. private sector interests, NGOs). Howlett and Ramesh (1995) point out that there are as many regulatory approaches as there are policy issues, a situation that has emerged because regulatory solutions mutate in response to local political discourses and geo-institutional contexts. Other researchers have attempted to build taxonomies of regulatory approaches based on attributes such as the level of government involvement; levels of public resourcing; and levels of government control (Bemelmans-Videc, Rist, & Vedung, 2010; Dredge & Jenkins, 2007). While these taxonomies are useful in understanding the broad landscape of regulatory responses that might be available by mixing levels of intervention, resources and control, they still do not account for the dynamic 'moving map' of ideas and values that underpins regulation (Brenner, Peck and Theodore, 2010).

In an attempt to better understand the widespread regulatory transformations taking place since the 1980s, Brenner et al. (2010) take a macro evolutionary approach. They draw attention to the fact that approaches to regulation have been underpinned by neoliberalism and that it is essential to understand its evolution in order to better appreciate how regulatory structures and practices have been produced and reproduced (Dean, 2014; Peck & Theodore, 2010). In their view, neoliberalism is a broad, dynamic and inconsistent thought project based on various value-driven ideologies (e.g. globalisation, marketisation, commoditisation, growth, limited government intervention, etc.). The interpretation of this neoliberal thought project takes place within geo-institutional contexts. As a result, approaches to regulation are often experimental, variegated forms of policy transfer drawn from other jurisdictions and locally contextualised.

So what does this mean for the regulation of the collaborative economy? The collaborative economy itself has been framed as a response to neoliberal imperatives where the marketisation and commodification of peoples' lives and their assets are extensions of a market-based economy (Slee, 2016). Transnational policy transfer has attempted to create a homogenised policy space in which global platform capitalist can play, but the influences of local politics and path dependencies have created a variegated regulatory space. The success of the collaborative economy relies on digital connectedness that allows producers and consumers to trade effectively and efficiently while bypassing cumbersome regulations. Collaborative economy platforms might acknowledge that some regulation might be necessary to address negative externalities, however heavy intervention undermines the very conditions on which the collaborative economy depends.

But there are contradictions in this position. Earlier sections of this chapter demonstrate that market failures are already emerging, and the intensity and impact of these may indeed undermine the socio-political conditions needed for the collaborative economy's success. These in-built contradictions suggest that regulatory approaches to the tourism collaborative economy require careful consideration. The aims of regulation need to be considered in context and unthinking adoption of regulatory frameworks drawn from elsewhere should be avoided. Inter-jurisdictional policy transfer can homogenise the regulatory space, but such solutions are embedded with the neoliberal values of other politico-institutional contexts and may 'lead to unpredictable, unintended, and intensely variegated outcomes' (Peck cited in Brenner et al., 2010, p. 335).

In exploring the political landscape, the path dependencies created by previous industrial policy approaches and the influence of neoliberal ideologies, the above discussion has explored the policy and regulatory challenges associated with the tourism collaborative economy. So where does this interrogation of regulatory challenges leave us in dealing with the tourism collaborative economy? What insights can we draw from the above discussion and what opportunities do we have to shape policy and regulation?

6 Discussion

Earlier in this paper we highlighted a widely held maxim that government decisions about appropriate policy and regulatory approaches should be based on good sound knowledge and that this knowledge should 'rise above politics' (Fischer et al., 2015, p. 1). In considering the range of possible policy and regulatory approaches, it is important to consider a number of factors. First, it is important to reflect on how knowledge inputs are framed and enter into policy discourses. Second, it is essential to question what values and ideologies may be taken for granted in, for example, industry policy or neoliberal ideologies that are (often unthinkingly) translated from one context to another. Third, it is wise to reflect on the particular socio-political and geo-institutional characteristics that make a local policy discourse unique. Fourth, critically reflecting on how policy discourses are socially engineered by various stakeholders can reveal information and power asymmetries, silent voices and hidden issues. It is in the spirit of remaining open and reflexive to these power and informational influences that we flesh out below a broad policy and regulatory landscape.

In returning to the two types of collaborative economy that were identified in the introduction to this chapter—platform capitalism and platform cooperative—Fig. 3 sets out a continuum of policy and regulatory choices and uses these as anchors at each end. This Figure is not intended to present a normative vision of two opposing approaches, but instead tries to illustrate that there are different value positions and choices ranging from a zombie-like adherence to neoliberal values (e.g. marketisation, commoditisation, growth, etc.) to a socially-oriented communitarian approach. This is the 'moving map' of ideas and values that underpin the choice of policy approaches and regulatory frameworks (Brenner et al., 2010), where shifts may occur over time from one to the other side of the continuum depending on local contextualised discourses. The value of this conceptualisation is to release us from an oppressive all-encompassing market-driven

Market approaches		**Social communitarian approaches**
Platform capitalism	Collaborative economy model	Platform cooperativism
Privatization of value extracted from sharing	What happens to the value produced	Re-invest back to the commons
Labour subsumed into production of the good or service (and most likely undervalued)	Labour	Supports worker solidarity by combating wage theft, exploitation, erosion of established worker benefits, etc.
Returns proportioned between shareholders and asset owners, producers	Stakeholders	Returns to workers, asset owners, producers
Unlocking innovation potential and ecologies of small/micro entrepreneurship	Focus of policy	Social policy focused on regulatory frameworks that support cooperative platforms that promote fairness
No or limited regulation of collaborative economy activities	Focus of regulation	Regulation supports collaborative economy workers, working conditions and rights
Mobility of policy ideas and approaches that facilitate the extension of global platforms (and possibly enhance monopoly power of platforms)	Global-local nexus	Ecosystems of local collaborative business ecosystems that may link on a global scale through shared value systems

Fig. 3 Continuum of policy and regulatory approaches

version of neoliberalism, and to demonstrate that there is a broader set of choices available in how to deal with the tourism collaborative economy. In some socio-political and geo-jurisdictional contexts, a style of policy and regulation for the collaborative economy that is more socially oriented may be more acceptable. In other words, and building on the notion that neoliberalism is not an internally consistent and cohesive theory but exists along a number of dimensions outlined in Fig. 3, then it becomes possible to interfere with these logics to find policy and regulatory solutions that do not simply reinforce "hard" neoliberal approaches.

7 Conclusions

The aim of this chapter was to explore the challenges faced by governments in dealing with policy and regulation in the digitally mediated tourism collaborative economy. While some authors have undertaken meso-level explorations of policy and regulatory issues dealing with collaborative economy accommodation, this chapter has provided a conceptual foundation that assists in understanding the policy choices available. In fleshing out these broader influences, the paper has explored the political landscape, the path dependencies created by previous industrial policy approaches and the influence of neoliberal ideologies on policy and regulation.

In addressing these aspects, we have drawn attention to the inherent contradictions and tensions that governments face in regulating the collaborative economy. On one hand governments have a desire to promote innovation and to unlock new economic ecologies that support economic growth. To do this a "light regulatory approach" is sought by proponents. On the other hand, an unfettered collaborative economy can lead to a range of market failures that can destabilise long established industrial modes of production and consumption; it can contribute to tax base erosion; it can induce poverty by allowing workers to fall below the living wage; and it can erode labour protections, health and safety standards. The pace of growth in the collaborative economy demands that governments address the concerns of and impacts upon incumbent actors, new players, communities, workers, and emergent stakeholder groups.

The chapter has demonstrated that not only is it becoming clear that traditional industry policy approaches are inadequate in dealing with the range of emerging policy and regulatory issues, but the complexity of the tourism collaborative economy policy space and the interdependency and complexity of policy problems calls for new approaches. These new approaches require an ecological ontology—i.e. an awareness of the interrelatedness of different policy issues and a move away from a binary division that pits industrial policy against social policy. They also call for an appreciation of the moving map of values that underpin the neoliberal discourses that influence our choice of policy and regulatory approaches. Only when we become aware of these influences can we start to appreciate the choices available and the opportunities to reflexively engage in tourism policy discourses about the collaborative economy.

References

Airbnb. (2014). *Airbnb claims homesharing more sustainable than going to a green hotel*. Accessed November 28, 2015, from https://www.airbnb.dk/press/news/new-study-reveals-a-greener-way-to-travel-airbnb-community-shows-environmental-benefits-of-home-sharing-eu

Airbnb. (2015). *The Airbnb community compact*. Accessed May 5, 2016, from https://www.airbnbaction.com/wp-content/uploads/2015/11/Airbnb-Community-Compact.pdf

Autoritat Catalana del la Competencia. (2014). *Peer-to-peer transactions and competition*. Barcelona. Accessed May 21, 2016, from http://acco.gencat.cat/web/.content/80_acco/documents/arxius/actuacions/ES_7_2014_TRANSACTIONS_BETWEEN_EQUALS_AND_COMPETITION_ENG.pdf

Bemelmans-Videc, M. L., Rist, R., & Vedung, E. O. (2010). *Carrots, sticks and sermons: Policy instruments and their evaluation*. New Brunswick: Transaction.

BIBA. (2014). *A BIBA guide to the sharing economy*. London. Accessed May 21, 2016, from https://view.publitas.com/biba/a-biba-guide-to-the-sharing-economy/page/1

BIBA. (2015). *A BIBA Brokers' guide to case law legal update*. Accessed May 21, 2016, from https://view.publitas.com/biba/a-biba-brokers-guide-to-case-law-legal-update/page/1

Botsman, R. (2014). *Collaborative economy services: Changing the way we travel*. Accessed May 9, 2015, from http://www.collaborativeconsumption.com/2014/06/25/collaborative-economy-services-changing-the-way-we-travel/

Botsman, R., & Rogers, R. (2011). *What's mine is yours: How collaborative consumption is changing the way we live*. New York: Collins.

Bramwell, B., & Lane, B. (2010). Editorial: Sustainable tourism and the evolving roles of government planning. *Journal of Sustainable Tourism, 18*(1), 1–5.

Brenner, N., Peck, J., & Theodore, N. (2010). After neoliberalization? *Globalizations, 7*(3), 327–345.

Cannon, B., & Chung, H. (2015). A framework for designing co-regulation models well-adapted to technology-facilitated sharing economies. *Santa Clara Computer and High Technology Law Journal, 31*(1), 23–96.

Considine, M. (1994). *Public policy: A critical approach*. Melbourne: Macmillan.

Dean, M. (2014). Rethinking neoliberalism. Journal of Sociology, 50(2), 150–163. http://doi.org/10.1177/1440783312442256

Dredge, D., & Gyimóthy, S. (2015). The collaborative economy and tourism: Critical perspectives, questionable claims and silenced voices. *Tourism Recreation Research, 40*(3), 286–302. doi:10.1080/02508281.2015.1086076.

Dredge, D., & Jenkins, J. (2007). Policy instruments, implementation and evaluation. In *Tourism planning and policy*. Brisbane: Wiley.

Dredge, D., & Jenkins, J. (2012). Australian national tourism policy: Influences of reflexive and political modernization. *Tourism Planning and Development, 9*(3), 231–251.

Fast Company. (2013). *Is peers the sharing economy's future or just a great silicon valley PR stunt?* Accessed April 4, 2016, from http://www.fastcompany.com/3022974/tech-forecast/is-peers-the-sharing-economys-future-or-just-a-great-silicon-valley-pr-stunt

Ferrary, M., & Granovetter, M. (2009). The role of venture capital firms in Silicon Valley's complex innovation network. *Economy and Society, 38*(2), 326–359. doi:10.1080/03085140902786827.

Fischer, F. (2003). *Reframing public policy: Discursive politics and deliberative practices*. Oxford: Oxford University Press.

Fischer, F., Torgerson, D., Durnová, A., & Orsini, M. (2015). Chapter 1: Introduction to critical policy studies. *Handbook of critical policy studies* (pp. 2–24). Cheltenham: Edward Elgar.

Gibson-Graham, J. K., Cameron, J., & Healy, S. (2013). *Take back the economy: An ethical guide for transforming communities*. Minneapolis: University of Minnesota Press.

Goudin, P. (2016). The cost of non-Europe in the sharing economy: Economic, social and legal challenges and opportunities. Brussels: European Parliamentary Research Service. http://www.europarl.europa.eu/RegData/etudes/STUD/2016/558777/EPRS_STU(2016)558777_EN.pdf

Guttentag, D. (2013). Airbnb: Disruptive innovation and the rise of an informal tourism accommodation sector. *Current Issues in Tourism, 18*(12), 1192–1217. doi:10.1080/13683500.2013.827159.

Ha, A. (2013). *California regulator passes first ridesharing rules: A big win for Lyft, SideCar and Uber*. Accessed April 26, 2015, from http://techcrunch.com/2013/09/19/cpuc-ridesharing-regulations/

Halkier, H. (2010). EU and tourism development: Bark or bite? *Scandinavian Journal of Hospitality and Tourism, 10*(2), 92–106. doi:10.1080/15022250903561952.

Hartl, B., Hofmann, E., & Kirchler, E. (2015). Do we need rules for "what's mine is yours"? Governance in collaborative consumption communities. *Journal of Business Research*, 1–8. doi:10.1016/j.jbusres.2015.11.011.

Henning, M., Stam, E., & Wenting, R. (2013). Path dependence research in regional economic development: Cacophony or knowledge accumulation? *Regional Studies, 47*(8), 1348–1362.

Howlett, M., & Ramesh, M. (1995). *Studying public policy: Policy cycles and policy subsystems*. Toronto: Oxford University Press.

Johal, S., & Zon, H. (2015). *Policymaking for the sharing economy: Beyond whack-a-mole*. Toronto: Mowat Center. https://mowatcentre.ca/wp-content/uploads/publications/106_policymaking_for_the_sharing_economy.pdf

Juul, M. (2015). *The sharing economy and tourism: Tourist accommodation*. Brussels. http://www.europarl.europa.eu/RegData/etudes/BRIE/2015/568345/EPRS_BRI(2015)568345_EN.pdf

Kassam, A. (2015). Airbnb fined €30,000 for illegal tourist lets in Barcelona. *The Guardian*. Accessed July 7, 2015, from https://www.theguardian.com/technology/2014/jul/07/airbnb-fined-illegal-tourist-lets-barcelona-catalonia

Koopman, C., Mitchell, M., & Thierer, A. (2014). *The sharing economy and consumer protection regulation: The case for policy change*. Arlington: Mercatus Center.

Mauss, M. (1925). *The gift: Forms and functions of exchange in archaic societies*. London: Cohen and West.

Meelen, T., & Frenken, K. (2015). Stop saying uber is part of the sharing economy. *Fast Company*. Accessed May 17, 2016, from http://www.fastcoexist.com/3040863/stop-saying-uber-is-part-of-the-sharing-economy

Miller, S. R. (2015). First principles for regulating the sharing economy. *SSRN Electronic Journal, 54*. http://doi.org/10.2139/ssrn.2568016

Monbiot, G. (2015). *Uber and the lawlessness of 'sharing economy' corporates*. Accessed May 5, 2016, from https://www.theguardian.com/technology/2015/jul/28/uber-lawlessness-sharing-economy-corporates-airbnb-google

O'Donnovan, C. (2015). Airbnb is building an army. *BuzzFeed News*. Accessed May 5, 2016, from http://www.buzzfeed.com/carolineodonovan/airbnb-is-building-a-political-army#.fdXojrO5E

OECD. (2013). *Action plan on base erosion and profit shifting*. Paris: Organisation for Economic Cooperation and Development.

OECD. (2016). *OECD tourism trends and policies 2016. OECD tourism trends and policies 2016*. Paris: Organisation for Economic Cooperation and Development.

Parliament of NSW. (2015). *Uber and Airbnb: The legal and policy debate in NSW*. Sydney: Parliament of NSW.

Peck, J., & Theodore, N. (2010). Mobilizing policy: Models, methods, and mutations. *Geoforum, 41*(2), 169–174. doi:10.1016/j.geoforum.2010.01.002.

Peers. (2016). *Making the sharing economy work for the people who empower it*. Accessed April 4, 2016, from http://www.peers.org/about/

PWC. (2015). The sharing economy—Sizing the revenue opportunity. Accessed May 5, 2016, from http://www.pwc.co.uk/issues/megatrends/collisions/sharingeconomy/the-sharing-economy-sizing-the-revenue-opportunity.html

Ranchordás, S. (2015). Does sharing mean caring? Regulating innovation in the sharing economy. *Minnesota Journal of Law, Science and Technology, 16*(1), 1–63.

Rehn, A. (2014). Gifts, gifting and gift economies: On challenging capitalism with blood, plunder and necklaces. In M. Parker, G. Cheney, V. Fournier, & C. Land (Eds.), *The Routledge companion to alternative organization* (pp. 195–209). London: Routledge.

Scholz, T. (2016). *Platform cooperativism: Challenging the corporate sharing economy*. New York: Rosaluxemburg Stiftung. Accessed May 21, 2016, from http://www.rosalux-nyc.org/wp-content/files_mf/scholz_platformcoop_5.9.2016.pdf

Slee, T. (2016). *What's yours in mine: Against the sharing economy*. New York: OR Books.

Somerville, H. (2015). Airbnb wages $8 million campaign to defeat San Francisco measure. *Reuters*. Accessed April 5, 2016, from http://www.reuters.com/article/us-airbnb-election-sanfrancisco-idUSKCN0SQ2CJ20151101?feedType=RSS&feedName=businessNews

Starr, A. (2015). *Amendments relating to short-term rentals*. San Fransisco: San Fransisco City Planning Commission. Accessed May 5, 2016, from http://commissions.sfplanning.org/cpcpackets/2014-001033PCA.pdf

Stiglitz, J. (1999). *Public policy for a knowledge economy*. Accessed May 5, 2016, from http://cyberinet04.inet-tr.org.tr/akgul/BT-BE/knowledge-economy.pdf

Stiglitz, J., Lin, J. Y., & Monga, C. (2013). *The rejuvenation of industrial policy*. Accessed April 2, 2016, from https://openknowledge.worldbank.org/bitstream/handle/10986/16845/WPS6628.pdf?sequence=1&isAllowed=y

Stokes, K., Clarence, E., & Rinne, A. (2014). *Making sense of the UK collaborative economy*. Accessed May 5, 2015, from http://www.nesta.org.uk/publications/making-sense-uk-collaborative-economy

Strange, S. (1996). *The retreat of the state: The diffusion of power in the world economy*. Cambridge: Cambridge University Press.

The Guardian. (2002). Joseph Stiglitz: There is no invisible hand. Accessed May 10, 2015, from http://www.theguardian.com/education/2002/dec/20/highereducation.uk1

US Federal Trade Commission. (2015, June 9). *The "sharing" economy: Issues facing platforms, participants, and regulators*. New York: US Federal Trade Commission.

Wade, R. H. (2012). Return of industrial policy? *International Review of Applied Economics, 26* (2), 223–239. doi:10.1080/02692171.2011.640312.

Walton, J. (1987). Theory and research on industrialization. *Annual Review of Sociology, 13*, 89–108.

Warwick, K. (2013). *Beyond industrial policy: Emerging issues and new trends* (OECD Science, Technology and Industry Policy Papers No. 2). OECD Publishing. doi:10.1787/5k4869clw0xp-en

Part II
Disruptions, Innovations and Transformations

Regulating Innovation in the Collaborative Economy: An Examination of Airbnb's Early Legal Issues

Daniel Guttentag

Abstract Airbnb, a service through which ordinary people rent out their spaces to tourists, has become one of the most prominent companies in the collaborative economy. Hundreds of thousands of tourists sleep in Airbnb accommodations every night, yet a large number of these accommodations are actually illegal according to many jurisdictions' regulations on short-term rentals. This situation has made regulatory conflict an omnipresent issue for the company. Such regulatory tensions actually define the early years of many major innovations because the innovations are not perfectly compatible with existing regulatory frameworks. Moreover, Airbnb is a disruptive innovation within the collaborative economy, and operating within a tightly regulated industry, which made regulatory conflicts virtually inevitable for the company. Airbnb's rapid growth has forced policymakers to urgently rethink their applicable regulations by assessing the primary issues and impacts, both positive and negative, surrounding Airbnb—tourism, taxes, consumer protection, and local residents. In response, destinations have taken different approaches to regulating Airbnb, centred on renting restrictions, permits, enforcement, and taxes. As the regulatory landscape continues to evolve, more and more destinations will look to overcome the challenges associated with legalising, regulating, and taxing Airbnb.

Keywords Airbnb • Collaborative economy • Innovation • Regulation • Short-term rentals

1 Introduction

Often considered a poster child of the collaborative economy, Airbnb (www.airbnb.com) is an online service through which ordinary people rent out their spaces as tourist accommodation. Airbnb's popularity has grown exponentially in recent

D. Guttentag (✉)
Hospitality and Tourism Management, College of Charleston, Charleston, SC, USA

Ted Rogers School of Hospitality and Tourism Management, Ryerson University, 350 Victoria Street, Toronto, ON M5B 2K3, Canada
e-mail: dguttentag@yahoo.com

D. Dredge, S. Gyimóthy (eds.), *Collaborative Economy and Tourism*,
Tourism on the Verge, DOI 10.1007/978-3-319-51799-5_7

years, transforming the service from a niche product into a mainstream one. Nevertheless, a large portion of Airbnb accommodations are actually illegal because they contravene local short-term rental laws, and the company has consequently become embroiled in myriad regulatory battles across the globe. This chapter illustrates that such regulatory issues plague many major innovations, both inside and outside of the collaborative economy, because the innovations often do not fit within existing regulatory structures. The chapter subsequently explores the key issues for and against Airbnb that policymakers must consider as they seek an appropriate regulatory response. The chapter next examines the various approaches different jurisdictions are taking towards regulating Airbnb, as related to renting restrictions, permits, enforcement, and taxes. Finally, the chapter explores several challenges that will impact future Airbnb regulatory discussions, and how the regulatory environment surrounding Airbnb will likely evolve.

2 Airbnb and Its Legal Status

Airbnb describes itself as 'a trusted community marketplace for people to list, discover, and book unique accommodations around the world' (Airbnb, 2016a). As is characteristic of the collaborative economy, Airbnb has leveraged new internet and mobile technologies to greatly reduce previous trust and communication barriers, and has thereby modernised and popularised the age-old hospitality practice of ordinary people renting out residences to tourists. Airbnb is not the only company occupying this 'peer-to-peer short-term rental' sector (others include VRBO, Wimdu, and Onefinestay), but Airbnb is indisputably the most prominent. As with many other of these peer-to-peer short-term rental companies, Airbnb is much more than a simple 'matchmaker' platform like craigslist, as Airbnb is involved in numerous aspects of the rental process; for example, Airbnb handles the payments (earning its revenue by charging a commission), promotes security via a host/guest review system and various identity verification measures, offers hosts reimbursement for property damage, and even provides hosts access to free photographers.

Airbnb accommodations range from very modest to luxurious, and usually consist of an entire residence (house or apartment) or a private room in a residence where the host is also present. The level of professionalism ranges considerably, from hosts who periodically list their homes when away on vacation to professionally-managed full-time rental properties. As is typical of the collaborative economy, Airbnb guests are attracted by a combination of cost savings, practical benefits (e.g., household amenities), and an experiential facet based on the opportunity for authentic and unique local experiences and interactions (Guttentag, 2015; Tussyadiah, 2015). Since its inception in 2008, Airbnb's growth has been so swift that any numbers stated here will quickly be outdated, but by the summer of 2015 well over 500,000 guests were using Airbnb every night (Tsotsis, 2015), and by early 2016 the company boasted over two million listings worldwide (Airbnb, 2016a).

Despite this popularity, Airbnb is actually illegal in many jurisdictions due to zoning ordinances and other laws restricting unlicensed short-term rentals. Such issues have followed Airbnb across the globe, from Barcelona (Pellicer, 2014) to Berlin (Vasagar, 2014), from Malta (Cooke, 2013) to Myanmar (Pasick, 2013), from New York (Whitehouse, 2015) to New Orleans (Sayre, 2014), and from Tasmania (Beniuk, 2015) to Tel Aviv (Elis, 2015). Often, unlicensed rentals of under 30 days are prohibited, as is the case in Denver (Nowicki, 2014), Los Angeles (Morris, 2015), New Orleans (where the minimum increases to 60 days in the popular French Quarter) (Sayre, 2014), New York City (which permits such rentals only if the owner is also present) (Whitehouse, 2015), and Vancouver (Gallagher, 2014). Moreover, some jurisdictions have more specific limitations on short-term rentals, such as regarding areas where they can be located, their ratio within the community, the number of times they can be rented annually, or the number of allowable guests (Gottlieb, 2013). In addition to frequently being illegal, Airbnb also generally does not collect and remit the accommodation taxes that traditional forms of accommodation often charge.

Such issues were mostly trivial not long ago, but now that Airbnb and the broader peer-to-peer short-term rental sector have quickly become so immense, government bodies (mostly municipal) around the world are grappling with the question of how to respond. Airbnb's plan clearly was to establish itself as firmly as possible before confronting its regulatory concerns, and simply wait for policymakers to catch up (Yglesias, 2012a). This philosophy and the motives behind it were encapsulated nicely by the co-founder of Lyft, a ride-hailing company in the collaborative economy: 'If we took the approach of, "Hey, let's wait and see what the government does to create a path that is very, very clear for this new industry" ... then we wouldn't be operating anywhere' (Dubner, 2014).

3 Innovation vs. Regulation

Major innovations, by their very nature, often challenge regulatory structures by introducing novel products, services, and business models for which the most pertinent regulations—devised only for what previously existed—do not adequately apply. For example, today there are major regulatory debates surrounding innovations like food trucks, driverless cars, and drones. Airbnb has unsurprisingly argued that the regulations prohibiting its rentals are outdated and have not adapted to reflect modern technologies (e.g., Pedler, 2016), and there is some truth to this claim. As an amusing example, the Ontario Innkeepers Act still devotes significant space to describing when a hotel owner can place a lien on or sell a guest's horse (Johal & Zon, 2015). In addition to often lagging behind innovation, regulations can also unquestionably hinder innovative activities and will more generally limit personal freedoms (Chase, 2015). Nonetheless, regulations are (at least in theory) intended to foster the overall public good (Chase, 2015; Koopman, Mitchell, & Thierer, 2014) and few would question their overall importance. For instance, Airbnb surely would desire regulatory protection against the (hypothetical) emergence of a rival service named Aerobnb. However, finding an ideal level of regulation is challenging, as policymakers must consider a variety goals including ensuring consumer protection, guaranteeing intellectual property, and fostering competition.

Innovations may also prompt regulatory action based on rent-seeking behaviour, as competitors encourage regulation and enforcement to protect their market position and hinder the innovation. Such manoeuvring is perhaps inevitable because innovations can pose an existential threat to incumbent products and businesses. Joseph Schumpeter, an influential Austrian-born economist who is widely recognised as the father of innovation studies, termed this process 'creative destruction,' and describes it as an intrinsic feature of capitalism (Schumpeter, 1942/2008). As he summarises, 'The competition from the new [innovation]... strikes not at the margins of the profits and the outputs of the existing firms but at their foundations and their very lives' (p. 84). Clearly fearing newfound competition from Airbnb, numerous hotel organisations and hotel workers unions, including the American Hotel & Lodging Association (O'Neill, 2014), the British Hospitality Association (Meyer, 2015), the French hotel union UMIH (Jenne, 2015), and the Australian Hotels Association (Ironside, 2015), have publically criticised Airbnb and advocated stricter regulations and enforcement. Such appeals parallel those made by restaurant associations against food trucks (e.g., Carman, 2013) and by taxi commissions against ride-hailing services such as Uber and Lyft (e.g., Greenfield, 2012).

Uber and Lyft, like Airbnb, form part of the collaborative economy, many aspects of which make it ripe for regulatory tensions. Firstly, collaborative economy innovations are based on rapidly advancing internet and mobile technologies, making it difficult for policymakers to keep pace. Secondly, several of the most popular collaborative economy services exist within highly regulated industries, such as Airbnb (short-term accommodation), Uber (transportation), and Prosper (finance). Thirdly, as Airbnb's CEO has highlighted, the collaborative economy has precipitated the emergence of micro-entrepreneurs who are challenging the distinction between businesses and people (Kessler, 2014). This blurring of traditional boundaries raises difficult questions regarding consumer protection (e.g., Should Airbnb accommodations meet the same safety standards as hotels?), where taxation and other liabilities lie (e.g., Is Airbnb liable if a guest is injured in an Airbnb accommodation?), and the employment status of collaborative economy workers (e.g., Should Uber drivers receive employee benefits?).

Moreover, Airbnb represents a specific type of innovation, known as a 'disruptive innovation' (Guttentag, 2015). This term is often overused to describe any novel product that 'disrupts' a market in a more colloquial sense (Yglesias, 2013). However, it really refers to a product whose appeal derives not from improved performance, as one may expect, but it rather underperforms in comparison with prevailing products' key attribute(s) while introducing an alternative package of benefits generally centred on being cheaper, simpler, smaller, or more convenient. In other words, disruptive innovations are inferior 'good enough' products (Christensen, 1997; Christensen & Raynor, 2003). This notion seems to apply directly to Airbnb, which appears to underperform in comparison with traditional accommodations' key performance attributes (e.g., cleanliness, security, and quality assurance), but provides an alternative value proposition centred on its relatively low cost, practical benefits, and experiential authenticity (Guttentag, 2015). Because disruptive innovations are customarily simpler than existing products, they often will not meet existing standards within tightly regulated industries, which has led to regulatory clashes in industries including healthcare (Christensen, Grossman, & Hwang, 2009; Curtis & Schulman, 2006) and legal services (Campbell, 2012). In some cases, strict regulations may even prevent the emergence of disruptive innovations, as these inferior products, though 'good enough' for consumers, are not 'good enough' to meet established regulatory standards (Curtis & Schulman, 2006). Airbnb provides an excellent example of this issue, as Airbnb accommodations often will not meet the safety standards imposed on hotels and other traditional accommodations, and Airbnb emerged by simply ignoring the existing regulatory regime that would have otherwise suffocated it.

4 The Policymaker's Perspective: Airbnb's Issues and Impacts

Being a disruptive innovation within both the collaborative economy and a highly regulated industry, Airbnb's regulatory problems were virtually inevitable. As policymakers are forced to reassess their jurisdictions' relevant regulations in response to Airbnb's rise, they must consider a broad range of issues and impacts, both for and against Airbnb.

4.1 Tourism: Visitors, Traditional Accommodations and DMOs

Airbnb's most direct impacts are on the tourism sector. From a visitor perspective, Airbnb is essentially an unqualified benefit, as it has introduced new accommodations that differ from most existing options by being cheaper and providing a more authentic local experience. Even visitors who stay elsewhere may enjoy lower prices due to the new competition Airbnb offers. Nonetheless, tourism is a business, so from a destination perspective a central question is the potential economic impacts of Airbnb, as economic benefits could help compensate for other drawbacks. Unfortunately, the economic benefits of Airbnb are largely unknown. Airbnb has sponsored economic impact studies in various major cities, touting tens of millions of dollars in economic activity (Airbnb, 2016b), but such studies are inherently biased (Crompton, 2006). Airbnb indisputably is lodging huge numbers of money-spending tourists, but this money may have been spent in a destination anyways, as Airbnb guests may simply use it as a substitute for traditional accommodations. Airbnb therefore may even allow visitors to spend less money overall by spending less on accommodation, although Airbnb contends the majority of its guests spend their accommodation savings elsewhere in a destination (e.g., Airbnb, 2015a, 2015b). Airbnb also touts its economic impacts by boasting that its guests tend to stay longer and spend more money than hotel guests (Airbnb, 2016b). However, it is possible that these behaviours are not actually influenced by Airbnb, and may simply result from Airbnb accommodations being particularly appealing for travellers on relatively long trips.

Nevertheless, regulations should not simply be fashioned to squeeze as much money as possible from tourists, and Airbnb certainly may strengthen the tourism economy in other ways. Airbnb accommodations tend to be spread throughout residential neighbourhoods rather than concentrated in a tourism core, so Airbnb may help to disperse tourist spending (Porges, 2013; Smerd, 2014). Airbnb also may reduce leakage from the local economy, as money is paid to local hosts (minus Airbnb's commission) rather than corporate hotels headquartered elsewhere. Additionally, Airbnb provides 'invisible infrastructure' (Capps, 2014) that can help support major events or seasonal tourist influx without the need for traditional accommodations that may not be sustainable. For example, Airbnb is the official 'alternative accommodation' sponsor of the 2016 Olympic Games in Rio de Janeiro, helping to ease the city's bed shortage (Associated Press, 2015). In addition to such economic benefits, Airbnb stays are purportedly more environmentally-friendly than hotel stays (Snyder, 2014), and the Airbnb host-guest interaction may promote intercultural understanding.

The question of whether Airbnb guests are regularly using Airbnb as a substitute for traditional accommodations has particularly salient implications for the regulatory debate. Airbnb has repeatedly denied that it competes directly with hotels, arguing that it draws a different type of tourist (e.g., Conley, 2014; Titcomb, 2014; Trenholm, 2015). Moreover, hotels in the U.S. have recently enjoyed exceptional performance despite Airbnb's emergence (Griswold, 2015b; Solomon, 2014), and some hoteliers and industry analysts claim Airbnb is too small and distinct from hotels to have a major impact (e.g., Grant, 2013; Karmin, 2015; Marcin, 2014). Nonetheless, while Airbnb's clientele may not perfectly resemble that of hotels, many of the hundreds of thousands of guests using Airbnb every night undeniably would have otherwise stayed in existing accommodations (hotels, hostels, bed-and-breakfasts, etc.). Furthermore, very early on Airbnb did in fact present itself as a hotel alternative (Airbnb, 2016c), and Airbnb is increasingly pushing into the hotel market by targeting business travellers (Newcomer, 2015). In addition, analyses of hotel metrics in Texas (Zervas, Proserpio, & Byers, 2015b), San Francisco (Swig, 2014), and New York City (Vivion, 2015) have concluded Airbnb is hurting hotel occupancy rates and prices, particularly in lower-priced hotels without a strong business clientele.

As was previously noted, the perceived threat of Airbnb has begun to mobilise the traditional accommodation sector, which has called for tighter regulations and stricter enforcement against Airbnb. The common refrain from these incumbents is that they desire a 'level playing field' in which Airbnb pays its taxes and is held to similar regulatory standards (e.g., Carney, 2015; Deese, 2015; Kenney, 2015a). Moreover, if Airbnb is hurting hotels then there could be a negative impact on hotel employment, which some policymakers may wish to protect (Dubner, 2014). This employment issue is partly offset by the money hosts earn and the ecosystem of businesses that have sprung up to serve Airbnb (Shankman, 2014), but collaborative economy jobs have been criticised for being precarious and offering no benefits (e.g., Keen, 2015). Also, Airbnb may have a particularly significant impact on non-hotel accommodations like bed-and-breakfasts (e.g., Kenney, 2015b) and hostels.

Hotels' opposition to Airbnb creates an awkward situation for local destination marketing organisations (DMOs) tasked with destination promotion, as DMOs are largely funded by hotels (via accommodation taxes) and hotels often feature prominently on DMO boards of directors (Sheehan & Ritchie, 2005). Therefore, even if a DMO feels Airbnb benefits a destination (e.g., by facilitating event hosting, fostering a destination's image as hip and trendy, engaging local residents with the local tourism sector, or simply providing a desirable accommodation alternative), the DMO may avoid publicly supporting Airbnb. San Francisco's DMO recently became the first to forge an official partnership with Airbnb (Sciacca, 2015) and Philadelphia followed shortly after (Hilario, 2015), whereas Baltimore's DMO has taken the opposite stance and sought stricter short-term rental restrictions (Munshaw, 2015). However, for the most part DMOs seem to have avoided Airbnb debates and allowed their two main stakeholders—hotels and municipal governments (Sheehan, Ritchie, & Hudson, 2007)—to confront the issue.

4.2 Taxes

In jurisdictions where Airbnb remains illegal and unregulated, it also is generally untaxed. Therefore, policymakers have an economic incentive to legalise, regulate, and tax Airbnb. In major destinations like San Francisco, the tax revenue from Airbnb can reach many millions of dollars (Green, 2015a). Moreover, taxing Airbnb eliminates the 'free rider' problem in which Airbnb and its hosts benefit from destination promotion without contributing to it via an accommodation tax.

Several years ago, Airbnb resisted accommodation taxes, arguing that accommodation tax laws needed to be updated for innovative services like Airbnb (Coté, 2012) and Airbnb hosts should individually be responsible for collecting and remitting the taxes (Levy & Goldman, 2012). However, as Airbnb's regulatory battles heated up, particularly in New York City, Airbnb wisely accepted its tax obligations and began using the promise of tax dollars as a bargaining chip for regulatory acceptance (Hantman, 2014b; Wohlsen, 2013). For example, Airbnb recently sent a letter to all 213 New York State Legislators lamenting the millions of dollars in tax revenue that Airbnb could contribute if the laws were revised (Kerr, 2015). Amusingly, when Airbnb changed its stance on taxes, its hotel industry opponents in New York City, who had previously criticised Airbnb for not paying its taxes, were forced to similarly reverse course and began to oppose Airbnb taxation, worried that tax payments would grant Airbnb more formal legitimacy (Griswold, 2015a; Hantman, 2014c).

4.3 Consumer Protection

Beyond the tax question, when hotels demand a level playing field with Airbnb or when policymakers question its merit, they often reference consumer safety concerns including security, health, and fire safety (e.g., King, 2015; Sreenivasan, 2015; Valencia, 2014). Such concerns are understandable, and in fact one Airbnb guest has died after falling from a broken rope swing (Stone, 2015), another died from carbon monoxide poisoning (with several accompanying guests hospitalised) (Hill, 2015), two separate sexual assaults have reportedly been committed against Airbnb guests (Joshi, 2014; Lieber, 2015b), one guest was bitten by a host's Rottweiler (Lieber, 2015a), and another found a hidden camera in her rental (Brandom, 2015). However, while Airbnb can do more to prevent such tragedies, it must be acknowledged that given the massive number of Airbnb users it is almost unavoidable that some crimes and injuries would occur, and such incidents obviously occur in hotels as well (e.g., Hussain, 2015; Leland, 2015; MacBride & Flores, 2015). Also, the vast majority of Airbnb crimes actually seem to be property crimes perpetrated against hosts rather than guests (e.g., Nerman, 2015; Sernoffsky, 2015), and many Airbnb accommodations are in buildings that already abide by various safety standards.

Airbnb promotes security via identity verification measures and a review system, the latter of which is a defining security feature in many collaborative economy enterprises. Such systems serve the dual purpose of allowing two parties to learn more about one another before agreeing to a transaction, and creating an incentive for both parties to conduct themselves acceptably (Jøsang, Ismail, & Boyd, 2007). Several authors have posited that these self-regulatory reputation-based feedback mechanisms are more effective than traditional government regulatory regimes, and the latter are therefore mostly anachronistic and inefficient (Cohen & Sundararajan, 2015; Grossman, 2015; Koopman et al., 2014; Sundararajan, 2012, 2014). Grossman (2015), for example, envisions a new regulatory paradigm centered on accountability rather than permission, as information accessibility replaces the need for traditional licensing, and companies share data with regulators to help prevent and respond to problems. Koopman et al. (2014) similarly argue that information accessibility has minimised the need for traditional regulations, which should be relaxed for both incumbent businesses and new entrants, and Sundararajan (2014) and Cohen and Sundararajan (2015) advocate almost wholly self-regulatory agencies with limited government oversight.

There is no question that regulatory agencies should exploit the copious real-time data now generated by consumers, which presents some obvious advantages over the information that can be gathered by a licensed inspector. However, one must be careful about overstating the collaborative economy's ability to use reputational feedback mechanisms for self-regulation. Advocating reliance on review mechanisms for consumer protection would seemingly suggest TripAdvisor is sufficient to regulate hotels, which is a notion that Sundararajan (2012) actually presents, but one with which most people would quickly disagree. The problem with relying on user reviews as a regulatory mechanism is that review systems like Airbnb's can exhibit numerous weaknesses. To begin, Airbnb reviews predictably focus on issues like cleanliness, location, and host friendliness, rather than issues like fire safety, the presence of carbon monoxide detectors, or the host's criminal record, which are the sort of issues most likely to be considered by government regulations. Additionally, several aspects of the Airbnb review system may artificially inflate the positivity of reviews: firstly, guests may not wish to post a negative review because it could signal pickiness that would lead future potential hosts to reject reservation requests (Mulshine, 2015); secondly, a guest must complete a stay in order to leave a review, and therefore cannot review a place that was so terrible the guest left early (Paris, 2015); thirdly, guests may be disinclined to criticise an individual person (i.e., the Airbnb host) despite having no issue criticising a faceless hotel property (Ho, 2015); and fourthly, until a recent policy change that postdates many existing reviews, Airbnb published hosts' and guests' reviews immediately, so each were discouraged from criticism out of fear of a retaliatory negative review (Rubin, 2014). Given such issues, it is unsurprising that research has found Airbnb reviews to be extremely positive, as compared with accommodation reviews on other websites (Díaz Armas, Gutiérrez Taño, & García Rodríguez, 2015; Zervas, Proserpio, & Byers, 2015a). In fact, Zervas et al. (2015a) looked at 600,000 Airbnb listings and found 95% enjoyed a 4.5 or 5 star rating, and virtually none had fewer than 3.5 stars. Consequently, rather than providing a substitute for traditional regulations, review systems are better suited to simply complement and bolster traditional regulatory practices, like in New York City where health authorities have used Yelp to help detect outbreaks of foodborne illness (Knox, 2014).

4.3.1 Hosts and Residents

Short-term renting permits Airbnb hosts to leverage what is likely their largest asset to generate additional income, which may help to cover mortgage payments and avert foreclosures (Gottlieb, 2013). In fact, Airbnb often boasts that a large percentage of its hosts use their earnings to help cover mortgage or rent payments and other basic expenses (Airbnb, 2016b). Restricting such economic activity requires a strong justification, and interestingly few have considered whether short-term rental regulations constitute violations of individual property rights, although a recent lawsuit in Tennessee makes this very claim (Garrison, 2015c). Jefferson-Jones (2015) provides the most focused analysis on this question, connecting it to the long history of boarding houses in the U.S. and arguing that short-term rental restrictions do, in fact, represent an unconstitutional 'taking' of private property (i.e., 'inverse condemnation') without just compensation.

Nevertheless, Jefferson-Jones (2015) glosses over some serious concerns with Airbnb accommodations. Whereas Airbnb may provide a net benefit for both the host and guest, it produces a negative externality in terms of its impacts on the host's neighbours, which is notably absent from most other collaborative economy services (e.g., ride-hailing). This concern is a basic reason for zoning laws—much like many people would not want their neighbours hosting weekly garage sales, or opening a mechanic business in their driveway, or running a beauty salon from their living room, it is understandable for people to not want to live across the hall from what is essentially a hotel room. Tourist guests, who may behave more hedonistically when on vacation (Carr, 2002) and have no long-term vested interest in the community, may prove disruptive for nearby residents. For instance, unknown transient guests may raise safety concerns or disturb neighbouring residents by noisily coming and going late at night or partying loudly (e.g., Leland, 2012; Lu, 2015; Shute, 2014). As one Airbnb critic scribbled on an Airbnb subway ad in New York City, 'The dumbest person in your building is passing out a set of keys to your front door!' (Pressler, 2014). Additionally, in neighbourhoods where Airbnb accommodations are abundant—like New York City's East Village (Fermino, 2015) or Paris's Marais (French, Schechner & Verbergt, 2015)—they can more generally harm the fabric of the community by filling purportedly residential areas with throngs of tourists. Consequently, while Airbnb is beloved by many, it has also led to conflicts between neighbours (e.g., CBC News, 2015; Coltrain, 2015) and triggered both informal and organised protests from some community activists (e.g. Curth, 2015; Dzieza, 2015; Langfield, 2014). In effect, Airbnb has produced a sort of 'NIMBYism[1]' in which Airbnb is popular in theory, but many people do not want it near them. In fact, an online poll found that when asked if people should be permitted to rent their rooms to strangers, 26% of respondents answered it should be freely allowed and only 12% answered it should be completely banned, yet when asked if their neighbours should be permitted to rent their rooms to strangers only 17% said it should be freely allowed and 20% stated it should be completely banned (Ali, 2015).

Airbnb also may harm local property markets by reducing housing stock and in turn precipitating an increase in housing prices. Such issues primarily result from residences being used as permanent short-term rentals with absentee hosts, yet there are even reports of landlords evicting tenants in order to convert long-term housing into more lucrative short-term rentals (e.g., Aron, 2015). Nonetheless, it is unclear

[1] 'Not in my backyard'.

to what extent Airbnb truly reduces housing stock. Airbnb claims to make housing more affordable by providing hosts with supplemental income to help cover high rents or mortgages (Hantman, 2014a), and therefore has recently positioned itself as a champion of middle class economic stability (Said, 2015c). The company also portrays its hosts as ordinary people renting spare rooms (Chesky, 2013) and notes that roughly 80–90% of its hosts rent their primary residences (Airbnb, 2016b). However, this number obscures the much larger proportion of Airbnb inventory owned by hosts operating full-time rentals as a more professional enterprise, as has been illustrated in various independent analyses based on data extracted from the Airbnb website. For example, Slee (2014) looked at 14 of the world's largest cities and found an average of 38% of Airbnb accommodations were managed by hosts with multiple listings. Similarly, at the time of writing, data for 32 major worldwide cities extracted from Airbnb and presented on the website insideairbnb.com indicated an average of 64% of the cities' Airbnb listings were for entire homes/ apartments, 37% were managed by hosts with multiple listings, and 83% were available for renting at least 90 days per year. Examining the consequences of such patterns, reports by Airbnb-commissioned consultants, government analysts, and a pro-labor advocacy group have reached contradictory conclusions regarding Airbnb's impact on housing, with some finding Airbnb has minimal impact and others concluding that Airbnb is removing substantial levels of housing stock (Green, 2015b; Kusisto, 2015; Rosen, 2013; Samaan, 2015). It is also nearly impossible to tease out the impact of Airbnb from other important variables like job growth or demographic trends (Rosen, 2013), and Airbnb may be receiving blame better directed at other issues like restrictions on housing development or real estate investing by absentee foreign owners (Badger, 2014; Cutler, K.-M., 2014; Yglesias, 2012b).

5 Existing Regulatory Approaches

Airbnb's regulatory battles have developed into high-stakes and highly contentious affairs, characterised by heated legislative meetings (e.g., Karni, 2015; Mesh, 2014), high-priced lobbying (e.g., O'Brien, 2015; Thomas, 2015), campaign-style advertising (e.g., Mosendz & Smith, 2014), special interest groups (e.g., Hawkins, 2014; Tam, 2013), and citizen protests (e.g., Dzieza, 2015; Swan, 2014). These battles have resulted in destinations taking vastly different approaches to Airbnb. Some destinations have strongly opposed the service, such as New York City, where enforcement against illegal Airbnb accommodations has increased (Fickenscher, 2015), the State Attorney General subpoenaed Airbnb's data and released a critical report on the company's operations (Schneiderman, 2014), a state legislator sponsored a bill that would fine hosts for merely posting an Airbnb listing (Lovett, 2015), and another state legislator secretly recorded her own undercover Airbnb sting operation (Golding, 2015). Likewise, Berlin recently passed a law banning unregistered short-term rentals (Vasagar, 2014); Barcelona recently began experimenting with new punishments for unlicensed short-term rental owners (Quijones, 2015) and fined Airbnb for marketing unlicensed listings (AFP, 2015); and Santa Monica, California recently passed new laws prohibiting short-term rentals in which the host is not present, and established a proactive enforcement department (Lepore, 2015). Nonetheless, during the past few years an increasing number of destinations have made moves towards legalising, regulating, and taxing Airbnb, such as Amsterdam (Weber, 2013b), London (Shankman, 2015), Nashville (Garrison, 2015a), Paris (France 24, 2015), Philadelphia (Lattanzio, 2015), Portland (Law, 2014a), Sacramento (Ortiz, 2015), San Francisco (Musil, 2014), and San Jose, California (Rosenberg, 2014). Developments are occurring so quickly that there is little reason to discuss any particular city in significant detail; rather, it is more useful to examine the key facets of the regulatory regimes that are being contemplated by nearly all destinations and will continue to define the Airbnb regulatory framework well into the future.

5.1 Renting Restrictions: Quotas and More

Much of the new short-term rental legislation focuses on capping the number of nights an entire home can be rented out annually. This focus addresses the concern that a plethora of casual hosts conceal a smaller number of commercial multi-unit operators who receive a large portion of Airbnb's bookings and remove housing stock (Cutler, 2015). For example, Amsterdam now permits renting an entire home for up to 60 days per year (Zabludovsky, 2014); London permits up to 90 days (Shankman, 2015); Paris permits up to four months (Schechner & Verbergt, 2015); Philadelphia permits up to 90 days unlicensed or 180 days with a license (Lattanzio, 2015); Portland requires homeowners to reside on-site at least nine months per year (Law, 2014a); San Francisco permits up to 90 days per year, while also only allowing one rental per host (Brustein, 2014); and San Jose permits up to 180 days per year (Rosenberg, 2014). Taking a much tougher stance on short-term renting, New York City (Whitehouse, 2015), Catalonia (Zillman, 2015), and Santa Monica (Lepore, 2015) allow short-term rentals only if the host is present during the stay, with Catalonia also limiting such rentals to four months annually.

Some destinations are also enacting laws relating to more detailed aspects of short-term renting. For instance, Amsterdam limits rentals to four guests simultaneously (Zabludovsky, 2014); Nashville mandates the number of guests can be no more than twice the number of sleeping rooms (Garrison, 2015a); Portland permits hosts to rent up to two bedrooms (Law, 2014a); and Carlsbad, California restricts rentals to coastal neighbourhoods (Seaside Courier, 2015). Moreover, several cities have taken the stance that the government should not subsidise properties that are used to earn short-term rental profits; for example, Amsterdam prohibits short-term rentals in rent-controlled properties (Dutch News, 2015), a New York City judge evicted a tenant for renting his rent-stabilised apartment on Airbnb (Plautz, 2015a), and Boston ordered the owner of an affordable housing unit to stop renting it on Airbnb (Rocheleau, 2015).

5.2 *Permits and Safety*

In order to promote consumer safety and community wellbeing, many destinations have enacted licensing systems and/or other safety requirements. For instance, Grand Rapids, Michigan requires hosts obtain a $287 rental license (Sidorowicz, 2014), Louisville requires hosts pay a $250 annual licensing fee and comply with health and safety requirements, although the license requirement is waived for hosts who rent out no more than twice per year (Roldan, 2015a); Roanoke, Virginia has created a new 'homestay' permit for short-term renting (Chittum, 2015); Philadelphia requires a rental license for hosts renting out their homes for over 90 days annually (Lattanzio, 2015); Portland requires hosts obtain a $178 permit (that involves a basic safety inspection), acquire a business license, and inform their neighbours and neighbourhood association of their rental intentions (Njus, 2014); and San Francisco requires hosts register in-person at City Hall and pay a $50 fee (Weinberger, 2015). However, initial compliance with licensing regulations has been limited—after roughly one month in Grand Rapids only four of approximately 70 listings were properly licensed (Sidorowicz, 2014); after about six months in Portland only about 10% of its roughly 1600 rentals were properly licensed (Peltier, 2015); and after nearly 1 year in San Francisco only about one-fifth of the city's more than 6000 rentals had applied for a registration (CBS, 2015).

5.3 *Rule Enforcement*

Enforcement may be needed to pressure hosts into complying with licensing requirements and other regulations, but destinations have struggled considerably to institute enforcement measures that are both appropriate and practical. When initially confronted with the rise of short-term rentals, several destinations took an initially tough stance that was later tempered. Some, including Sydney (McKenny, 2014), Perth (Hennessy, 2015), Tasmania (Beniuk, 2015), and the Canary Islands (Perthen, 2012), threatened hosts with excessively large fines of up to hundreds of thousands of dollars, yet it does not appear the violators have ever actually been forced to pay these amounts. Likewise, city officials in both Boulder, Colorado (Kuta, 2015) and Louisville (Lopez, 2015) sent numerous hosts cease-and-desist letters, but in both cases such actions were dropped in favour of re-examining the old short-term rental laws. In fact, reports from numerous destinations—including Amsterdam (Weber, 2013a), Malibu (Stevens & Groves, 2014), and San Diego

(Halverstadt, 2015)—of imminent crackdowns against Airbnb actually preceded more formal regulatory discussions.

Nonetheless, even new regulations have proved extremely difficult to enforce, as illustrated by the non-compliance with licensing requirements. For instance, a Louisville Assistant County Attorney described short-term rental enforcement as 'a nightmare' that has strained staff resources (Roldan, 2015b), the Amsterdam City council claimed its 22 full-time inspectors were not enough to cope with the city's short-term rental complaints (Dutch News, 2014), and San Francisco's short-term rental laws were deemed unenforceable by the department originally tasked with enforcing them (Matier & Ross, 2015b). In response, several locations have significantly expanded their enforcement bodies—San Francisco has created a six-person Office of Short Term Rental Administration (Kokalitcheva, 2015); Santa Monica created a new three-person enforcement department (Lepore, 2015); Quebec has planned to increase its number of inspectors (Presse Canadienne, 2015); and New York City, dealing with a significant rise in complaints (Gartland, 2015), has doubled the budget and more than doubled the staff of its enforcement department (Fickenscher, 2015). Enforcement is challenging because it is often difficult to definitively prove regulatory violations, even though rentals are publicly listed on the Airbnb website. For example, it can take significant time and effort to prove an Airbnb host is not living in a rental property, or that the property is exceeding an annual night quota. Enforcement has traditionally focused on investigating complaints, but numerous places, including New York City (Fickenscher, 2015), Paris (Schechner & Verbergt, 2015), Berlin (Nezik, 2015), and Santa Monica (Lepore, 2015) have transitioned to a more proactive approach in which violators are actively sought out using short-term rental websites.

Some jurisdictions have also considered requiring Airbnb to cooperate with enforcement efforts, either through sharing data or incorporating restrictions into the website. For example, in 2014 Portland's Revenue Division Director proposed requiring Airbnb to provide names and addresses for all local hosts in order to ensure licensing compliance, but the requirement was never established (Law, 2014b). Somewhat similarly, a California law proposed in early 2015 would require Airbnb to provide information on addresses being used for short-term rentals, the nights rented, and the revenue earned (Rosenhall, 2015). Airbnb predictably has resisted such efforts intensely, citing privacy concerns and the burden associated with compliance (e.g., Mason, 2015; Schaal, 2013). Nevertheless, in November 2015 Airbnb somewhat softened its tone by pledging to be 'transparent with our data and information' as part of a broader 'Airbnb Community Compact' (Airbnb, 2015c; Chesky, 2015). The following month Airbnb released anonymous New York City data and promised to make similar releases elsewhere (Isaac, 2015), including San Francisco (Nevius, 2015). Nonetheless, some policymakers criticised the endeavor, arguing that anonymous data was not actionable in terms of aiding enforcement of the existing regulations (Kulwin, 2015). Even without data sharing, there is also the potential for Airbnb to incorporate restrictions directly into its booking engine. For example, San Francisco legislation proposed in early 2015 would have prohibited Airbnb from listing units not in good standing (Cutler, 2015), and the proposed California law mentioned above would require Airbnb to prohibit bookings in jurisdictions where short-term rentals are banned (Mason, 2015). Additionally, Portland demanded Airbnb begin posting host license numbers on the website, threatening a fine of $500 for each host violation, but Airbnb refused to comply and the city did not follow through with the fines (Walters, 2015).

5.4 Taxes

As was previously discussed, Airbnb initially resisted calls to collect and remit taxes, but as its regulatory battles intensified the company changed its attitude and began using taxes to gain acceptance and legitimacy. Indeed, taxation agreements have often closely coincided with moves to legalise Airbnb, such as in Amsterdam (Lomas, 2014); Nashville (Garrison, 2015a); Philadelphia (Lattanzio, 2015); Portland (Law, 2014a); San Jose (Rosenberg, 2014); and San Francisco (Musil, 2014), where Airbnb also agreed to pay back-taxes for several prior years (Matier & Ross, 2015a). It is therefore reasonable to assume that regulatory acceptance will soon come in destinations where Airbnb had recently begun collecting taxes at the time of writing, including Florida (Perry, 2015); Illinois (Ecker, 2015); Malibu (Sawicki, 2015); North Carolina (Knopf, 2015); San Diego (Horn, 2015); Washington, D.C. (Badger, 2015); and Washington state (Plautz, 2015b). These taxation agreements virtually all involve Airbnb collecting and remitting standard accommodation taxes, which means Airbnb and its hosts now contribute towards destination marketing and can no longer be criticized as 'free riders.' Taking taxation a step further, Tucson, Arizona recently raised the property tax rate for short-term rental hosts by reclassifying their properties from residential to commercial (McNamara, 2015), which is a development traditional bed-and-breakfasts have previously fought in some destinations (Stankus, 2012). Also, due to the housing concerns that Airbnb raises, Nashville has earmarked some of its short-term rental tax revenue for an affordable housing fund (Garrison, 2015b), and in early 2016 the mayor of Chicago proposed a 2% surcharge on vacation rentals that would be similarly dedicated towards affordable housing (Spielman, 2016).

6 The Challenging Future of Airbnb Regulation

Because Airbnb has grown so rapidly, policymakers have been forced to tackle this innovation urgently and with little warning. Many cities undoubtedly wish to quickly establish a workable regulatory framework, and presumably Airbnb is similarly eager to be legalised and regulated, as there is widespread speculation that the company will go public in the relatively near future, and major regulatory question marks would complicate an initial public offering (Logan & Alpert Reyes, 2015). The clear trend regarding Airbnb's regulatory landscape is one of increased legalisation, regulation, and taxation. In 2014, the U.S. Conference of Mayors even adopted a resolution in support of 'shareable cities' in which services like Airbnb are legalised with appropriate regulatory controls (Cutler, J., 2014). As Airbnb's current hockey stick growth curve eventually levels off, and the company is further brought into the regulatory fold, Airbnb will be seen less as a maverick service and more of a traditional one. This increased acceptance will likely lead to open competition with hotels, representation on DMO boards, and increased partnerships with other tourism firms (airlines, meeting organizers, etc.). It has become quite apparent that Airbnb has a long-term place in the tourism accommodation market, and it is sensible that policymakers are mostly focusing on using regulation to mitigate negative impacts rather than prohibit the service. To date, however, destinations have struggled to craft suitable regulatory controls that overcome the many challenges posed by Airbnb.

One major complication is that the public holds very mixed opinions toward Airbnb. For example, in November 2015 San Francisco voters rejected a proposed tightening of restrictions on short-term rentals, but the vote was relatively close (55–45%) even though the Airbnb-funded winning 'No' side spent over 15 times as much money campaigning as did the opposition (Said, 2015b). Around the same time, Boulder, Colorado residents voted at a similarly close margin (57.5–42.5%) to accept an ordinance that permitted and taxed short-term rentals (Burness, 2015). Also, a 2015 survey found that the proportion of prospective renters in New York City who were more likely to lease in an Airbnb-friendly building nearly doubled from 10% to 19% within the previous year, yet a slightly larger percentage (20%, down from 25%) still indicated they would be less likely to lease in such a building (Clarke, 2015). Moreover, as was described previously, when asked in an online poll if 'people' should be allowed to rent their rooms to strangers the response was generally positive, but when asked about 'neighbours' more respondents felt the activity should be banned than allowed. Finally, in a 2014 poll in New York City, 56% of respondents agreed that residents should be permitted to rent rooms in their homes to strangers, while 36% felt the practice should be banned (Fischer, 2014; Parry, 2014). In other words, Airbnb is a highly divisive issue and, quite simply, large numbers of people will be displeased with any potential regulatory framework. Nevertheless, the public seems more amenable than not towards allowing and regulating short-term rentals, thus generally paving the way for their continued acceptance, both via legislation and residential policies (e.g., condominium bylaws).

However, shaping a workable short-term rental regulatory framework remains very challenging in large part because Airbnb listings are extremely varied. A spare bedroom that is rented out occasionally and a full property that is rented out year-round are highly distinct, making it very difficult to discuss Airbnb as a whole. As a result, two people can perceive Airbnb on very different terms, with neither being completely right or wrong. Such complications certainly impacted the results from two of the surveys just described, as the question prompts merely asked about renting 'rooms' and avoided mention of entire residences (Fischer, 2014). In fact, some of Airbnb's peer-to-peer short-term rental competitors, like VRBO, only involve renting full residences. Also, as was stated earlier, many Airbnb listings are owned by more professionally-oriented multi-unit operators, and these hosts unsurprisingly account for a disproportionate share of Airbnb revenue. For example, Slee's (2014) analysis of 14 of the world's largest cities found that on average only about 15% of hosts managed multiple listings, but this cohort represented 38% of the total inventory and was estimated to receive about 45% of all bookings. Likewise, a study (sponsored by the American Hotel & Lodging Association) analysing 12 major U.S. markets found hosts operating three or more listings represented just 7% of the hosts but generated 25% of the revenue (O'Neill & Ouyang, 2016), and New York City data released by Airbnb showed that hosts with three or more listings represented just 2% of all hosts but received 24% of all revenue (Popper, 2015). In other words, a large percentage of Airbnb's business derives from permanent operations that often violate local laws, such as annual night quotas, even in places where Airbnb has been legalised (e.g., Brustein, 2014). Though Airbnb would obviously loathe losing this portion of its business, this issue arguably represents many regulators' biggest concern about short-term rentals, and it likely must be sorted out to some degree prior to an Airbnb initial public offering.

Permanent vacation rentals certainly deserve their place in destinations, but it is natural for regulations to distinguish full-time vacation rentals with absentee hosts from other short-term rental properties. Not surprisingly, some destinations, including Nashville (Nashville.gov, 2016); Austin, Texas (AustinTexas.gov, 2016); and Raleigh, North Carolina (Specht, 2015) have enacted or are considering multi-tiered regulatory systems that differentiate between rentals that are and are not owner-occupied principal residences. Even for permanent rentals, Airbnb will likely prompt a general easing of regulations that may ultimately affect other forms of tourism accommodation. Koopman et al. (2014), for example, argue that rather than applying old regulations to new innovations, 'The better alternative is to level the playing field by "deregulating down" to put everyone on equal footing, not by "regulating up" to achieve parity' (p. 19). In particular, bed-and-breakfasts may have their often fairly onerous regulations (Staley, 2007) eased significantly, quite likely to the point that bed-and-breakfasts are not even legislatively distinguished from other peer-to-peer short-term rentals. Hotels will always receive greater regulatory oversight than smaller accommodations, but even they may enjoy an easing of regulations.

Regardless of how their new regulatory frameworks are crafted, as destinations increasingly revise their laws to legalise short-term rentals, they will become less hesitant to prosecute violators, as has occurred in San Francisco (Barmann, 2015). Likewise, destinations will undoubtedly bolster their ability to field and respond to complaints, and more and more destinations will seek out violators proactively. Such actions will further push Airbnb to better comply with local ordinances.

However, the question remains to what degree Airbnb will cooperate directly with local governments, particularly with regards to multi-unit operators. To date, Airbnb has resisted such cooperation, combining open defiance with an appeal for self-regulation. In late 2015 Airbnb's CEO claimed, 'We succeeded not because of [the professional hosts] but in spite of them,' (Said, 2015a), and the company's previously mentioned Community Compact pledged that in cities with long-term housing shortages the company would ensure 'hosts agree to a policy of listing only permanent homes on a short-term basis' (Airbnb, 2015c). Indeed, when comparing New York City Airbnb data subpoenaed by the New York State Attorney General covering the period of January 2010 to June 2014 (Schneiderman, 2014) with data later voluntarily released by Airbnb covering the period of November 2014 to November 2015 (Popper, 2015), the percentage of hosts with at least three unique listings had dropped from 6% to 2% and their share of the total revenue had dropped from 37 to 24%. Also, Airbnb has removed listings from some of its professional operators managing large numbers of properties in New York City (Newcomer, 2016; Walker, 2014), Los Angeles (Logan & Alpert Reyes, 2015), and Amsterdam (Pieters, 2016). Nevertheless, one must appreciate the context of these gestures before perceiving Airbnb as eager to fully cooperate with local regulatory bodies. The New York State Attorney General originally had to subpoena Airbnb to receive its data; full access to the voluntarily released data required an in-person appointment at Airbnb's New York office (Griswold, 2015c); shortly before releasing both the subpoenaed data and the voluntary data Airbnb manipulated its numbers by removing thousands of illegal listings, and the company only acknowledged the second purge after it was discovered by independent analysts (Cox & Slee, 2016; Kerr, 2014; Newcomer, 2016); many of the listings removed in the second purge were soon re-listed by their hosts (Clark, 2016; Cox & Slee, 2016); and bulk removals of professional hosts have only occurred in a few places and only following intense pressure and scrutiny (Kerr, 2014; Kidd, 2015; Logan & Alpert Reyes, 2015).

In other words, it is naive to think Airbnb will readily begin removing illegal accommodations that generate a sizeable portion of its revenue. Nonetheless, it also seems likely that Airbnb will eventually cooperate more closely with local governments by sharing data that can be used to monitor both impacts and regulatory violations, and by taking a more proactive stance in prohibiting listings that egregiously violate local laws. Data sharing is critical to a regulatory system that uses consumer-generated data (Grossman, 2015), and Airbnb undoubtedly understands its need to cooperate more on this front in order to obtain the more modernised regulatory frameworks it has encouraged. Also, while an intervention forcing Airbnb to delist illegal properties would not be unprecedented—U.S. state attorneys general previously pressured craigslist into eliminating its 'adult services' section (Associated Press, 2010)—it is much more probable that greater enforcement against hosts and the threat of stricter regulations will prompt Airbnb to become more proactive in its efforts to limit major violations (e.g., Said, 2016). Indeed, Airbnb's about-face on taxes and the recent softening of its tone on data sharing demonstrate the company is willing to pragmatically shift positions in its quest for greater legitimacy, so although Airbnb will clearly fight hard to defend its turf from regulators, increased future pressure will likely lead to increased compromise. In the end, a world full of outraged policymakers, hosts incurring hefty fines, and public referendums with questionable outcomes is not the ideal environment for Airbnb to thrive, and the company is certainly cognizant of this reality.

7 Conclusion

When considering the regulatory issues surrounding Airbnb, it is also important to remember that Airbnb is a global company operating in diverse destinations with different traditions and needs. Urban destinations with rent-controlled housing are different from beach communities with a long-standing vacation rental tradition; small destinations like Yellowknife, Canada, which is eager for more visitors (Williams, 2015), are different from major destinations like the Canary Islands, which is already so overrun with tourists that it is considering instituting visitor caps (Hutchinson, 2015); and countries with a tradition of significant government intervention are different from countries with a more neoliberal regulatory tradition. Consequently, there is not a one-size-fits-all regulatory framework for all destinations, and policymakers must independently assess the issues surrounding Airbnb in order to formulate the most sensible approach for their communities.

Nonetheless, destinations will often face many of the same questions regarding Airbnb, such as how it impacts tourism, how the service should be taxed, how guests' and hosts' safety can be assured, and how negative externalities can be minimised. These issues have challenged policymakers, but such circumstances often follow major innovations like Airbnb that shake up the status quo. The regulatory challenges created by Airbnb clearly demonstrate how the emerging collaborative economy has produced important and difficult questions about regulation in the digital age. It is a fascinating future, and one which is still being written.

References

AFP. (2015, December 22). Airbnb fined for offering lodgings without permits in Barcelona. *The Local*. Accessed March 14, 2016, from http://www.thelocal.es/20151222/barcelona-city-hall-fines-airbnb

Airbnb. (2015a). Overview of the Airbnb community in Austin, Texas. *Airbnb*. Accessed March 14, 2016, from http://publicpolicy.airbnb.com/wp-content/uploads/2015/10/AustinImpactReport1.pdf

Airbnb. (2015b). Overview of the Airbnb community in New Orleans, Louisiana. *Airbnb*. Accessed March 14, 2016, from http://publicpolicy.airbnb.com/wp-content/uploads/2015/11/NewOrleansImpactReport.pdf

Airbnb. (2015c). The Airbnb community compact. *Airbnb*. Accessed February 23, 2016, from http://publicpolicy.airbnb.com/wp-content/uploads/2015/11/Airbnb-Community-Compact.pdf

Airbnb. (2016a). About us. *Airbnb*. Accessed January 26, 2016, from https://www.airbnb.ca/about/about-us

Airbnb. (2016b). Airbnb economic impact. *Airbnb*. Accessed January 26, 2016, from http://blog.airbnb.com/economic-impact-airbnb/

Airbnb. (2016c). Obama O's: Hope in every bowl. *Airbnb*. Accessed January 26, 2016, from https://www.airbnb.com/obamaos

Ali, R. (2015, February 5). Americans are generally OK with Airbnb unless their neighbors are doing it. *Skift*. Accessed January 26, 2016, from http://skift.com/2015/02/05/americans-are-generally-ok-with-airbnb-unless-their-neighbors-are-doing-it/

Aron, H. (2015, August 19). Why Venice Beach is ground zero for the Airbnb backlash. *LA Weekly*. Accessed January 26, 2016, from http://www.laweekly.com/news/why-venice-beach-is-ground-zero-for-the-airbnb-backlash-5928207

Associated Press. (2010, September 4). Craigslist removes adult services section. *MSNBC*. Accessed January 26, 2016, from http://www.msnbc.msn.com/id/39005873/ns/technology_and_science-tech_and_gadgets/t/craigslist-removes-adult-services-section

Associated Press. (2015, March 28). Airbnb to sponsor 2016 Rio Olympics. *ESPN*. Accessed January 26, 2016, from http://espn.go.com/blog/olympics/post/_/id/4527/airbnb-to-sponsor-2016-rio-olympics

AustinTexas.gov. (2016). Rental types: Three types of short-term rentals. *AustinTexas.gov*. Accessed January 26, 2016, from https://www.austintexas.gov/page/short-term-rental-types

Badger, E. (2014, May 20). Foreign investors are making housing more expensive. Should we tax them for it? *The Washington Post*. Accessed January 26, 2016, from http://www.washingtonpost.com/news/wonkblog/wp/2014/05/20/foreign-home-buyers-are-making-housing-more-expensive-should-cities-tax-them-for-it/

Badger, E. (2015, January 29). Airbnb is about to start collecting hotel taxes in more major cities, including Washington. *The Washington Post*. Accessed January 26, 2016, from http://www.washingtonpost.com/news/wonkblog/wp/2015/01/29/airbnb-is-about-to-start-collecting-hotel-taxes-in-more-major-cities-including-washington/

Barmann, J. (2015, December 14). City cracks down on Airbnb/VRBO law violators, issues $400,000 in penalties. *SFist*. Accessed January 26, 2016, from http://sfist.com/2015/12/14/city_cracks_down_on_airbnbvrbo_law.php

Beniuk, D. (2015, July 26). Kentish Council swoops on Airbnb pensioner. *News.com.au*. Accessed January 26, 2016, from http://www.news.com.au/national/tasmania/kentish-council-swoops-on-airbnb-pensioner/story-fnn32rbc-1227456969278

Brandom, R. (2015, December 16). A woman is suing Airbnb over an alleged hidden camera. *The Verge*. Accessed January 26, 2016, from http://www.theverge.com/2015/12/16/10318300/airbnb-hidden-camera-lawsuit-california

Brustein, J. (2014, October 8). Airbnb gets off easy in San Francisco. Hosts? Not so much. *Bloomberg*. Accessed January 26, 2016, from http://www.bloomberg.com/bw/articles/2014-10-08/airbnb-gets-off-easy-in-san-francisco-dot-its-hosts-not-so-much

Burness, A. (2015, November 3). Boulder voters support tax on Airbnb, reject City Council pay raise. *Daily Camera*. Accessed January 26, 2016, from http://www.dailycamera.com/local-election-news/ci_29067073/early-returns-voters-support-tax-airbnb-vrbo-reject

Campbell, R. W. (2012). Rethinking regulation and innovation in the U.S. legal services market. *New York University Journal of Law & Business, 9*(1), 1–70.

Capps, K. (2014, September 29). The sharing economy could drive down the price of mega-events. *Citylab*. Accessed January 26, 2016, from http://www.citylab.com/tech/2014/09/the-sharing-economy-could-drive-down-the-price-of-mega-events/380908/

Carman, T. (2013, June 5). Its status quo on food trucks after D.C. Council's vote. *The Washington Post*. Accessed January 26, 2016, from http://www.washingtonpost.com/blogs/going-out-guide/wp/2013/06/05/its-status-quo-on-food-trucks-after-d-c-councils-vote/

Carney, T. P. (2015, April 17). Maine innkeepers call for 'level playing field' with Airbnb; governor offers to deregulate everyone. *The Washington Examiner*. Accessed January 26, 2016, from http://www.washingtonexaminer.com/maine-innkeepers-call-for-level-playing-field-with-airbnb-governor-offers-to-deregulate-everyone/article/2563215

Carr, N. (2002). The tourism–leisure behavioural continuum. *Annals of Tourism Research, 29*(4), 972–986.

CBC News. (2015, September 16). Airbnb causing condo conflict in Vancouver. *CBC News*. Accessed January 26, 2016, from http://www.cbc.ca/news/canada/british-columbia/airbnb-condo-vancouver-1.3231426

CBS. (2015, March 4). Most of SF's Airbnb listings technically illegal as homeowners struggle with rigorous new application process. *CBS San Francisco*. Accessed January 26, 2016, from http://sanfrancisco.cbslocal.com/2015/03/04/most-of-sfs-san-francisco-airbnb-listings-technically-illegal-as-homeowners-struggle-with-rigorous-new-application-process/

Chase, R. (2015). *Peers Inc: How people and platforms are inventing the collaborative economy and reinventing capitalism*. New York: Public Affairs.

Chesky, B. (2013, October 3). Who we are, what we stand for. *The Airbnb Blog*. Accessed January 26, 2016, from http://blog.airbnb.com/who-we-are/

Chesky, B. (2015, November 11). Our commitment to communities around the world. *The Airbnb Blog*. Accessed January 26, 2016, from http://blog.airbnb.com/our-commitment-to-communities-around-the-world/

Chittum, M. (2015, July 6). Roanoke eases way for AirBnB rentals. *The Roanoke Times*. Accessed January 26, 2016, from http://www.roanoke.com/news/local/roanoke/roanoke-eases-way-for-airbnb-rentals/article_e8e7209c-b622-5727-b577-0090d8ca98d7.html

Christensen, C. M. (1997). *The innovator's dilemma: When new technologies cause great firms to fail*. Boston: Harvard Business School Press.

Christensen, C. M., & Raynor, M. E. (2003). *The innovator's solution: Creating and sustaining successful growth*. Boston: Harvard Business School Press.

Christensen, C. M., Grossman, J. H., & Hwang, J. (2009). *The innovator's prescription: A disruptive solution for health care*. New York: McGraw-Hill.

Clark, P. (2016, February 25). Airbnb's purged listings are already coming back. *Bloomberg*. Accessed January 26, 2016, from http://www.bloomberg.com/news/articles/2016-02-25/airbnb-s-purged-landlords-are-relisting-their-apartments

Clarke, K. (2015, August 18). An increasing number of NYC renters want to live in Airbnb-friendly buildings: Survey. *New York Daily News*. Accessed January 26, 2016, from http://www.nydailynews.com/life-style/real-estate/nyc-renters-live-airbnb-friendly-buildings-article-1.2329388

Cohen, M., & Sundararajan, A. (2015). Self-regulation and innovation in the peer-to-peer sharing economy. *The University of Chicago Law Review Dialogue, 82*, 116–133.

Coltrain, N. (2015, August 30). Vacation rentals pit neighbor against neighbor. *The Coloradoan*. Accessed January 26, 2016, from http://www.coloradoan.com/story/news/2015/08/30/vacation-rentals/71337842/

Conley, C. (2014, August 29). Airbnb is an old idea with a new tech twist. *Hotel News Now*. Accessed January 26, 2016, from http://www.hotelnewsnow.com/Article/14343/Airbnb-is-an-old-idea-with-a-new-tech-twist

Cooke, P. (2013, October 13). Unlicensed room letting risks penalty of €23,000. *Times of Malta*. Accessed January 26, 2016, from http://www.timesofmalta.com/articles/view/20131013/local/Unlicensed-room-letting-risks-penalty-of-23-000.490062

Coté, J. (2012, April 4). Airbnb, other sites owe city hotel tax, S.F. says. *San Francisco Chronicle*. Accessed January 26, 2016, from http://www.sfgate.com/bayarea/article/Airbnb-other-sites-owe-city-hotel-tax-S-F-says-3457290.php

Cox, M., & Slee, T. (2016, February 10). How Airbnb's data hid the facts in New York City. *Insideairbnb.com*. Accessed January 26, 2016, from http://insideairbnb.com/reports/how-airbnbs-data-hid-the-facts-in-new-york-city.pdf

Crompton, J. L. (2006). Economic impact studies: Instruments for political shenanigans? *Journal of Travel Research, 45*(1), 67–82.

Curth, K. (2015, May 28). Bywater neighbors fed up with airbnb rentals. *Fox 8 WVUE*. Accessed January 26, 2016, from http://www.fox8live.com/story/29185366/bywater-neighbors-fed-up-with-airbnb-rentals

Curtis, L. H., & Schulman, K. A. (2006). Overregulation of health care: Musings on disruptive innovation theory. *Law and Contemporary Problems, 69*(4), 195–206.

Cutler, J. E. (2014, October 21). Cities grappling with challenges of how to tax, regulate short-term rentals. *Bloomberg BNA*. Accessed January 26, 2016, from http://www.bna.com/cities-grappling-challenges-n17179897258/

Cutler, K. M. (2014, November 2). So you want to fix the housing crisis. *TechCrunch*. Accessed January 26, 2016, from http://techcrunch.com/2014/11/02/so-you-want-to-fix-the-housing-crisis/

Cutler, K. M (2015, June 11). Airbnb and the problem of data. *TechCrunch*. Accessed January 26, 2016, from http://techcrunch.com/2015/06/11/airbnb-and-the-problem-of-data/

Deese, H. (2015, January 3). Airbnb, VRBO offer parallels to online music. *The Daily News*. Accessed January 26, 2016, from http://www.memphisdailynews.com/news/2015/jan/3/airbnb-vrbo-offer-parallels-to-online-music/

Díaz Armas, R. J., Gutiérrez Taño, D., & García Rodríguez, F. J. (2015). Airbnb como nuevo modelo de negocio disruptivo en la empresa turística: Un análisis de su potencial competitivo a partir de las opiniones de los usuarios. *Análisis Turístico, 12*. Accessed January 26, 2016, from http://congresoaecit.org/uploads/public/files/modules/congress/18/papers/29.pdf

Dubner, S. (2014, September 4). Regulate this! Full transcript. *Freakonomics*. Accessed January 26, 2016, from http://freakonomics.com/2014/09/04/regulate-this-full-transcript/

Dutch News. (2014, October 12). Amsterdam admits it can't cope with Airbnb inspections. *DutchNews.nl*. Accessed January 26, 2016, from http://www.dutchnews.nl/news/archives/2014/10/amsterdam_admits_it_cant_cope

Dutch News. (2015, February 3). Airbnb starts collecting Dutch tourist tax, but no one knows how much. *DutchNews.nl*. Accessed January 26, 2016, from http://www.dutchnews.nl/news/archives/2015/02/airbnb-starts-collecting-dutch-tourist-tax-but-no-one-knows-how-much/

Dzieza, J. (2015, January 21). Airbnb comes under fire in New York City. *The Verge*. Accessed January 26, 2016, from http://www.theverge.com/2015/1/21/7865959/airbnb-under-fire-new-york-city-city-council

Ecker, D. (2015, December 10). Airbnb to begin collecting full Illinois hotel tax. *Crain's Chicago Business*. Accessed January 26, 2016, from http://www.chicagobusiness.com/article/20151210/NEWS09/151219991/airbnb-to-begin-collecting-full-illinois-hotel-tax

Elis, N. (2015, June 14). Hoteliers demand Tel Aviv taxation on Airbnb room. *The Jerusalem Post*. Accessed January 26, 2016, from http://www.jpost.com/Business-and-Innovation/Hoteliers-demand-Tel-Aviv-taxation-on-Airbnb-room-406018

Fermino, J. (2015, July 29). Airbnb taking up 1 out of 5 vacant apartments in popular New York City zip codes: study. *New York Daily News*. Accessed January 26, 2016, from http://www.nydailynews.com/news/politics/airbnb-takes-1-5-apartments-popular-nyc-zip-codes-article-1.2307521

Fickenscher, L. (2015, July 16). City beefs up unit probing Airbnb abuses. *The New York Post*. Accessed January 26, 2016, from http://nypost.com/2015/07/16/city-beefs-up-unit-probing-airbnb-abuses/

Fischer, B. (2014, September 2). Q-Poll doesn't quite say what Airbnb wants it to say. *New York Business Journal*. Accessed January 26, 2016, from http://www.bizjournals.com/newyork/blog/techflash/2014/09/q-poll-doesnt-quite-say-what-airbnb-wants-it-to.html

France 24. (2015, February 26). Airbnb vows to comply with Paris lodgings tax. *France 24*. Accessed January 26, 2016, from http://www.france24.com/en/20150226-paris-airbnb-cooperate-home-rental-hotels-chesky-france/

French, J., Schechner, S., & Verbergt, M. (2015, June 26). How Airbnb is taking over Paris. *The Wall Street Journal*. Accessed January 26, 2016, from http://graphics.wsj.com/how-airbnb-is-taking-over-paris/

Gallagher, M. (2014, November 19). Airbnb causing condo conflict in Vancouver. *CBC*. Accessed January 26, 2016, from http://www.cbc.ca/news/canada/british-columbia/airbnb-causing-condo-conflict-in-vancouver-1.2839010

Garrison, J. (2015a, February 24). Metro Council approves regulations for Airbnb in Nashville. *The Tennessean*. Accessed January 26, 2016, from http://www.tennessean.com/story/news/politics/2015/02/24/airbnb-nashville-regulations-metro-council/23976931/
Garrison, J. (2015b, April 7). Plan to boost housing fund with Airbnb tax revenue advances. *The Tennessean*. Accessed January 26, 2016, from http://www.tennessean.com/story/news/politics/2015/04/07/plan-boost-housing-fund-airbnb-tax-revenue-advances/25443033/
Garrison, J. (2015c, December 3). Tennessee AG: Airbnb rentals subject to hotel, sales tax. *The Tennessean*. Accessed January 26, 2016, from http://www.tennessean.com/story/news/2015/12/03/tennessee-ag-airbnb-rentals-subject-hotel-sales-tax/76739660/
Gartland, M. (2015, January 21). Neighbors' complaints to 311 over Airbnb are on the rise. *The New York Post*. Accessed January 26, 2016, from http://nypost.com/2015/01/21/neighbors-complaints-to-311-over-airbnb-are-on-the-rise/
Golding, B. (2015, January 12). NYC City Council schedules hearing over Airbnb safety concerns. *The New York Post*. Accessed January 26, 2016, from http://nypost.com/2015/01/12/nyc-city-council-schedules-hearing-over-airbnb-safety-concerns/
Gottlieb, C. (2013). Residential short-term rentals: Should local governments regulate the 'industry'? *Planning & Environmental Law, 65*(2), 4–9.
Grant, M. (2013, March 27). Airbnb.com poses only a small threat to hotel industry. *Euromonitor International*. Accessed January 26, 2016, from http://blog.euromonitor.com/2013/03/airbnbcom-poses-only-a-small-threat-to-hotel-industry.html
Green, E. (2015a, April 10). Airbnb, S.F. trade accusations on tax collection. *The San Francisco Chronicle*. Accessed January 26, 2016, from http://www.sfgate.com/bayarea/article/Airbnb-SF-double-dipping-on-taxes-SF-Airbnb-6190442.php
Green, E. (2015b, May 19). New reports differ on impact of Airbnb on S.F. *The San Francisco Chronicle*. Accessed January 26, 2016, from http://www.sfgate.com/bayarea/article/New-reports-differ-on-impact-of-Airbnb-on-S-F-6271923.php
Greenfield, R. (2012, September 5). Uber runs up against big taxi in New York now. *The Atlantic Wire*. Accessed January 26, 2016, from http://www.theatlanticwire.com/technology/2012/09/uber-runs-against-big-taxi-new-york-now/56529/
Griswold, A. (2015a, February 13). Why Airbnb desperately wants to pay hotel taxes. *Slate*. Accessed January 26, 2016, from http://www.slate.com/articles/business/moneybox/2015/02/airbnb_hotel_taxes_why_does_the_sharing_economy_startup_want_to_pay_them.single.html
Griswold, A. (2015b, July 6). Airbnb is thriving. Hotels are thriving. *Slate*. Accessed January 26, 2016, from http://www.slate.com/articles/business/moneybox/2015/07/airbnb_disrupting_hotels_it_hasn_t_happened_yet_and_both_are_thriving_what.single.html
Griswold, A. (2015c, December 15). Airbnb has a really convoluted process for being "transparent" with New York City. *Quartz*. Accessed January 26, 2016, from http://qz.com/571165/airbnb-is-sharing-more-data-but-in-a-really-convoluted-way/
Grossman, N. (2015). Regulation, the internet way: A data-first model for establishing trust, safety, and security. *Ash Center for Democratic Governance and Innovation*. Retrieved from http://datasmart.ash.harvard.edu/news/article/white-paper-regulation-the-internet-way-660
Guttentag, D. (2015). Airbnb: Disruptive innovation and the rise of an informal tourism accommodation sector. *Current Issues in Tourism, 18*(12), 1192–1217.
Halverstadt, L. (2015, February 9). San Diego's cracking down on Airbnb hosts. *Voice of San Diego*. Accessed January 26, 2016, from http://www.voiceofsandiego.org/topics/news/san-diegos-cracking-down-on-airbnb-hosts/
Hantman, D. (2014a, February 13). Airbnb and housing. *The Airbnb Public Policy Blog*. Accessed January 26, 2016, from http://publicpolicy.airbnb.com/airbnb-housing/
Hantman, D. (2014b, April 14). $21 million more for New York. *The Airbnb Public Policy Blog*. Accessed January 26, 2016, from http://publicpolicy.airbnb.com/21-million-new-york/
Hantman, D. (2014c, April 17). New York hotel lobbyists flip-flop on taxes. *The Airbnb Public Policy Blog*. Accessed January 26, 2016, from http://publicpolicy.airbnb.com/new-york-hotel-lobbyists-flip-flop/

Hawkins, A. J. (2014, December 4). NYC's anti-Airbnb coalition heads west. *Crain's New York Business*. Accessed January 26, 2016, from http://www.crainsnewyork.com/article/20141204/BLOGS04/141209910/nycs-anti-airbnb-coalition-heads-west

Hennessy, A. (2015, March 22). Perth property owners could face $200k fines for nightly rentals. *PerthNow*. Accessed January 26, 2016, from http://www.perthnow.com.au/news/western-australia/perth-property-owners-could-face-200k-fines-for-nightly-rentals/story-fnhocxo3-1227272959129

Hilario, K. (2015, August 31). Visit Philadelphia wants Airbnb hosts to be tourism 'ambassadors'. *Philadelphia Business Journal*. Accessed January 26, 2016, from http://www.bizjournals.com/philadelphia/news/2015/08/31/visit-philadelphia-airbnb-hosts-tourism-hotel.html

Hill, K. (2015, November 9). After a woman was poisoned in an Airbnb, the company started giving out prevention devices. *Fusion*. Accessed January 26, 2016, from http://fusion.net/story/229589/airbnb-death-safety-regulations/

Ho, E. (2015, May 18). Why you should think twice before trusting Airbnb reviews. *Mashable*. Accessed January 26, 2016, from http://mashable.com/2015/05/18/airbnb-reviews/

Horn, J. (2015, July 1). Airbnb to collect San Diego tourist taxes. *The San Diego Tribune*. Accessed January 26, 2016, from http://www.sandiegouniontribune.com/news/2015/jul/01/airbnb-taxes-tot-tourism-rentals-hotels/

Hussain, A. (2015, December 12). Boy's drowning in RWS Hard Rock Hotel pool in June ruled a misadventure. *The Straits Times*. Accessed January 26, 2016, from http://www.straitstimes.com/singapore/boys-drowning-in-rws-hard-rock-hotel-pool-in-june-ruled-a-misadventure

Hutchinson, J. (2015, July 1). 'The Magaluf effect': Canary Islands could impose limits on tourism as increase in visitor numbers is 'killing quality in Spain.' *The Daily Mail*. Accessed January 26, 2016, from http://www.dailymail.co.uk/travel/travel_news/article-3162201/The-Magaluf-effect-Canary-Islands-impose-limits-tourism-increase-visitor-numbers-killing-quality-Spain.html

Ironside, R. (2015, February 6). Rising angst over airbnb operations. *News.com.au*. Accessed January 26, 2016, from http://www.news.com.au/travel/travel-updates/rising-angst-over-airbnb-operations/story-e6frfq80-1227210877547

Isaac, M. (2015, December 1). Airbnb releases trove of New York City home-sharing data. *The New York Times*. Accessed January 26, 2016, from http://www.nytimes.com/2015/12/02/technology/airbnb-releases-trove-of-new-york-city-home-sharing-data.html

Jefferson-Jones, J. (2015). Airbnb and the housing segment of the modern sharing economy: Are short-term rental restrictions an unconstitutional taking? *Hastings Constitutional Law Quarterly, 42*(3), 557–576.

Jenne, A. (2015, August 17). Paris's most prestigious luxury hotels are counting the cost of the Airbnb revolution. *The Independent*. Accessed January 26, 2016, from http://www.independent.co.uk/news/world/europe/pariss-most-prestigious-luxury-hotels-are-counting-the-cost-of-the-airbnb-revolution-10459656.html

Johal, S., & Zon, N. (2015). *Policymaking for the sharing economy: Beyond whack-a-mole*. Toronto, ON: Mowat Centre, University of Toronto. http://mowatcentre.ca/wpcontent/uploads/publications/106_PolicymakingForTheSharingEconomy.pdf

Jøsang, A., Ismail, R., & Boyd, C. (2007). A survey of trust and reputation systems for online service provision. *Decision Support Systems, 43*(2), 618–644.

Joshi, P. (2014, December 20). Spain: Man jailed for raping holidaymakers who rented his flat through AirBnB. *The International Business Times*. Accessed January 26, 2016, from http://www.ibtimes.co.uk/spain-man-jailed-raping-holidaymakers-who-rented-his-flat-through-airbnb-1480434

Karmin, C. (2015, September 29). Airbnb crimps hotels' power on pricing. *The Wall Street Journal*. Accessed January 26, 2016, from http://www.wsj.com/articles/airbnb-crimps-hotels-power-on-pricing-1443519181

Karni, A. (2015, January 20). City Council blasts Airbnb executives in contentious hearing. *The New York Daily News*. Accessed January 26, 2016, from http://www.nydailynews.com/new-york/city-council-blasts-airbnb-executives-contentious-hearing-article-1.2086252

Keen, A. (2015, May 10). Can the sharing economy provide good jobs?—NO: It is a great deal for the owners, but a bad one for workers. *The Wall Street Journal*. Accessed January 26, 2016, from http://www.wsj.com/articles/can-the-sharing-economy-provide-good-jobs-1431288393

Kenney, A. (2015a, February 24). Key questions over Internet rentals, Airbnb emerge at Raleigh meeting. *The News & Observer*. Accessed January 26, 2016, from http://www.newsobserver.com/news/local/counties/wake-county/raleigh-report-blog/article11309984.html

Kenney, A. (2015b, April 19). Raleigh's last bed-and-breakfast to close, blaming Airbnb. *The News & Observer*. Accessed January 26, 2016, from http://www.newsobserver.com/news/local/counties/wake-county/article18917151.html

Kerr, D. (2014, April 21). Airbnb wipes 2,000 NY listings before court hearing. *CNET*. Accessed January 26, 2016, from http://www.cnet.com/news/airbnb-wipes-2000-ny-apartment-listings-before-court-hearing/

Kerr, D. (2015, April 15). Airbnb: Let us pay hotel taxes in New York. *CNET*. Accessed January 26, 2016, from http://www.cnet.com/news/airbnb-let-us-pay-hotel-taxes-in-new-york/

Kessler, A. (2014, January 17). Brian Chesky: The 'sharing economy' and its enemies. *The Wall Street Journal*. Accessed January 26, 2016, from http://www.wsj.com/articles/SB10001424052702304049704579321001856708992

Kidd, G. (2015, October 28). Court upholds €24,000 fine on Amsterdam Airbnb landlord. *NL Times*. Accessed 26 January 2016, from http://www.nltimes.nl/2015/10/28/court-upholds-e24000-fine-on-amsterdam-airbnb-landlord/

King, D. (2015, June 7). Airbnb's impact critiqued at N.Y. hotel conferences. *Travel Weekly*. Accessed January 26, 2016, from http://www.travelweekly.com/Travel-News/Hotel-News/Airbnb-impact-critiqued-at-NY-hotel-conferences

Knopf, T. (2015, May 18). Airbnb to collect and pay taxes in North Carolina. *The News & Observer*. Accessed January 26, 2016, from http://www.newsobserver.com/news/local/counties/wake-county/article21331905.html

Knox, R. (2014, May 22). How Yelp can help disease detectives track food poisoning. *NPR*. Accessed January 26, 2016, from http://www.npr.org/sections/thesalt/2014/05/22/314933875/how-yelp-can-help-disease-detectives-track-food-poisoning

Kokalitcheva, K. (2015, July 2). New San Francisco office will manage and investigate Airbnb landlords. *Fortune*. Accessed January 26, 2016, from http://fortune.com/2015/07/02/san-francisco-airbnb-office-regulations/

Koopman, C., Mitchell, M., & Thierer, A. (2014). *The sharing economy and consumer protection regulation: The case for policy change*. Arlington, VA: Mercatus Center, George Mason University. Accessed January 26, 2016, from http://mercatus.org/sites/default/files/Koopman-Sharing-Economy.pdf

Kulwin, N. (2015, December 21). Airbnb releases anonymized NYC listing data; city councilors call it 'useless'. *Re/code*. Accessed January 26, 2016, from http://recode.net/2015/12/01/airbnb-releases-anonymized-nyc-listing-data-city-councilors-call-it-useless/

Kusisto, L. (2015, March 30). Airbnb pushes up apartment rents slightly, study says. *The Wall Street Journal*. Accessed January 26, 2016, from http://blogs.wsj.com/developments/2015/03/30/airbnb-pushes-up-apartment-rents-slightly-study-says/

Kuta, S. (2015, January 1). Boulder rescinds cease-and-desist orders to homeowners offering Airbnb, VRBO rentals. *The Daily Camera*. Accessed January 26, 2016, from http://www.dailycamera.com/news/boulder/ci_27307446/boulder-rescinds-cease-and-desist-orders-homeowners-offering

Langfield, A. (2014, September 12). Anti-Airbnb coalition aims to counter sharing campaign. *CNBC*. Accessed January 26, 2016, from http://www.cnbc.com/2014/09/12/anti-airbnb-coalition-aims-to-counter-sharing-campaign.html

Lattanzio, V. (2015, June 19). You'll no longer be breaking the law by renting on Airbnb in Philadelphia. *NBC 10*. Accessed January 26, 2016, from http://www.nbcphiladelphia.com/news/local/Youll-No-Longer-Be-Breaking-the-Law-by-Renting-on-Airbnb-308272641.html

Law, S. (2014a, July 30). City legalizes Airbnb, other short-term home rental services. *The Portland Tribune*. Accessed January 26, 2016, from http://portlandtribune.com/pt/9-news/228670-92077-city-legalizes-airbnb-other-short-term-home-rental-services

Law, S. (2014b, December 18). Airbnb resists city efforts to regulate it. *The Portland Tribune*. Accessed January 26, 2016, from http://portlandtribune.com/pt/9-news/244479-112102-airbnb-resists-city-efforts-to-regulate-it

Leland, J. (2012, July 21). They can list, but they can't hide. *The New York Times*. Accessed January 26, 2016, from http://www.nytimes.com/2012/07/22/nyregion/stuyvesant-town-sleuths-keep-vigil-against-illegal-hoteliers-in-their-midst.html

Leland, E. (2015, February 9). Best Western lawsuit: Carbon monoxide deaths could have been prevented. *The Charlotte Observer*. Accessed January 26, 2016, from http://www.charlotte observer.com/latest-news/article10425248.html

Lepore, K. (2015, May 18). How Santa Monica will enforce its Airbnb ban. *89.3 KPCC*. Accessed January 26, 2016, from http://www.scpr.org/news/2015/05/18/51728/how-santa-monica-will-enforce-its-airbnb-ban/

Levy, A., & Goldman, H. (2012, September 27). Airbnb: To tax or not tax a rented bed. *BloombergBusinessweek*. Accessed January 26, 2016, from http://www.businessweek.com/articles/2012-09-27/airbnb-to-tax-or-not-tax-a-rented-bed

Lieber, R. (2015a, April 10). Questions about Airbnb's responsibility after attack by dog. *The New York Times*. Accessed January 26, 2016, from http://www.nytimes.com/2015/04/11/your-money/questions-about-airbnbs-responsibility-after-vicious-attack-by-dog.html

Lieber, R. (2015b, August 14). Airbnb horror story points to need for precautions. *The New York Times*. Accessed January 26, 2016, from http://www.nytimes.com/2015/08/15/your-money/airbnb-horror-story-points-to-need-for-precautions.html

Logan, T., & Alpert Reyes, E. (2015, April 3). Airbnb cuts ties with vacation-rental firms in Los Angeles. *The Los Angeles Times*. Accessed January 26, 2016, from http://www.latimes.com/business/la-fi-airbnb-rift-20150404-story.html

Lomas, N. (2014, December 18). Airbnb to start collecting tourist tax in Amsterdam. *TechCrunch*. Accessed January 26, 2016, from http://techcrunch.com/2014/12/18/airbnb-to-start-collecting-tourist-tax-in-amsterdam/

Lopez, A. (2015, March 18). Louisville Council Committee doesn't want citations issued to AirBnB users for now. *WFPL News*. Accessed January 26, 2016, from http://staging.wfpl.org/louisville-council-committee-doesnt-want-citations-issued-to-airbnb-users-for-now/

Lovett, K. (2015, December 21). Exclusive: New York politicians work to ban Airbnb advertising, stamp out illegal hotels. *New York Daily News*. Accessed January 26, 2016, from http://www.nydailynews.com/news/politics/politicians-work-ban-airbnb-ads-stamp-illegal-hotel-article-1.2472396

Lu, V. (2015, March 18). Noisy Airbnb renters raise ire of Willowdale residents. *Toronto Star*. Accessed January 26, 2016, from http://www.thestar.com/business/2015/03/18/noisy-airbnb-renters-raise-ire-of-willowdale-residents.html

MacBride, M., & Flores, J. (2015, September 29). Man waits inside Ontario hotel room and sexually assaults woman, police say. *ABC7 Eyewitness News*. Accessed January 26, 2016, from http://abc7.com/news/police-man-waits-inside-ie-hotel-room-sexually-assaults-woman/1009080/

Marcin, T. (2014, March 12). Airbnb appeals to the young but the traditional hotel empire is striking back. *Medill Reports Chicago*. Accessed January 26, 2016, from http://newsarchive.medill.northwestern.edu/chicago/news.aspx?id=228878

Mason, M. (2015, April 21). Citing privacy concerns, Airbnb slams bill on short-term rentals. *The Los Angeles Times*. Accessed January 26, 2016, from http://www.latimes.com/local/political/la-me-pc-airbnb-legislation-20150421-story.html

Matier, P., & Ross, A. (2015a, February 18). Airbnb pays tax bill of 'tens of millions' to S.F. *The San Francisco Chronicle*. Accessed January 26, 2016, from http://www.sfgate.com/bayarea/matier-ross/article/M-R-Airbnb-pays-tens-of-millions-in-back-6087802.php

Matier, P., & Ross, A. (2015b, March 22). 'No way of enforcing' Airbnb law, S.F. planning memo says. *The San Francisco Chronicle*. Accessed January 26, 2016, from http://www.sfchronicle.com/bayarea/matier-ross/article/No-way-of-enforcing-Airbnb-law-S-F-planning-6151592.php

McKenny, L. (2014, September 26). Councils threaten home owners with $1 million fine for renting rooms. *The Sydney Morning Herald*. Accessed January 26, 2016, from http://www.smh.com.au/nsw/councils-threaten-home-owners-with-1-million-fine-for-renting-rooms-20140926-10mchq.html

McNamara, P. (2015, August 22). Changes put bite on short-term landlords. *Arizona Daily Star*. Accessed January 26, 2016, from http://tucson.com/news/local/govt-and-politics/changes-put-bite-on-short-term-landlords/article_b3efb530-237f-5533-8cce-03a7dec4eb63.html

Mesh, A. (2014, December 22). City Commissioner Nick Fish berates Airbnb lobbyist. *Willamette Week*. Accessed January 26, 2016, from http://www.wweek.com/portland/blog-32614-video_city_commissioner_nick_fish_berates_airbnb_lobbyist.html

Meyer, D. (2015, February 10). Hotel industry fumes as UK prepares to legalize Airbnb in London. *Gigaom*. Accessed January 26, 2016, from https://gigaom.com/2015/02/10/hotel-industry-fumes-as-uk-prepares-to-legalize-airbnb-in-london/

Morris, S. L. (2015, January 22). Airbnb is infuriating the neighbors. Is it time for new rules? *LA Weekly*. Accessed January 26, 2016, from http://www.laweekly.com/news/airbnb-is-infuriating-the-neighbors-is-it-time-for-new-rules-5343663

Mosendz, P., & Smith IV, J. (2014, July 23). Hiding in plain sight: What Airbnb doesn't want you to know about their new lobbyists. *The New York Observer*. Accessed January 26, 2016, from http://observer.com/2014/07/hiding-in-plain-sight-what-airbnb-doesnt-want-you-to-know-about-their-new-lobbying-firm/

Mulshine, M. (2015, June). After a disappointing Airbnb stay, I realized there's a major flaw in the review system. *Business Insider*. Accessed January 26, 2016, from http://www.businessinsider.com/why-airbnb-reviews-are-a-problem-for-the-site-2015-6

Munshaw, J. (2015, October 28). Visit Baltimore wants Airbnb rentals to be subject to the city's hotel tax. *Baltimore Business Journal*. Accessed January 26, 2016, from http://www.bizjournals.com/baltimore/news/2015/10/28/visit-baltimore-wants-airbnb-rentals-to-be-subject.html

Musil, S. (2014, October 7). Controversial 'Airbnb law' approved by SF supervisors. *CNET*. Accessed January 26, 2016. http://www.cnet.com/news/controversial-airbnb-proposal-wins-ok-by-sf-supervisors/

Nashville.gov. (2016). Short term rental property. *Nashville.gov*. Accessed January 26, 2016, from http://www.nashville.gov/Codes-Administration/Construction-and-Permits/Short-Term-Rentals.aspx

Nerman, D. (2015, April 29). Airbnb nightmare renters leave Calgary home trashed. *CBC News*. Accessed January 26, 2016, from http://www.cbc.ca/news/canada/calgary/airbnb-nightmare-renters-leave-calgary-home-trashed-1.3053555

Nevius, C. W. (2015, November 6). Airbnb says it might be willing to share some data. *San Francisco Chronicle*. Accessed January 26, 2016, from http://www.sfchronicle.com/bayarea/nevius/article/Airbnb-says-it-might-be-willing-to-share-some-data-6616169.php

Newcomer, E. (2015, July 20). Airbnb overhauls service for business travelers. *Bloomberg*. Accessed January 26, 2016, from http://www.bloomberg.com/news/articles/2015-07-20/airbnb-overhauls-service-for-business-travelers

Newcomer, E. (2016, February 24). Airbnb says it removed 1500 listings in New York before data release. *Bloomberg*. Accessed January 26, 2016, from http://www.bloomberg.com/news/articles/2016-02-25/airbnb-says-it-removed-1-500-listings-in-new-york-before-data-release

Nezik, A. K. (2015, April 10). Tourism troubles: Berlin cracks down on vacation rentals. *Der Spiegel*. Accessed January 26, 2016, from http://www.spiegel.de/international/business/berlin-cracks-down-on-estimated-18-000-vacation-rentals-a-1026881.html

Njus, E. (2014, September 3). Portlanders aren't rushing to legitimize their Airbnb short-term rentals. *The Oregonian*. Accessed January 26, 2016, from http://www.oregonlive.com/front-porch/index.ssf/2014/09/no_rush_to_legalize_airbnb-sty.html

Nowicki, A. (2014, April 25). Denver homeowner wants city to alter policies on short-term rental, tiny house. *ABC 7 News Denver*. Accessed January 26, 2016, from http://www.thedenverchannel.com/news/local-news/denver-homeowner-wants-city-to-alter-policies-on-short-term-rental-tiny-house

O'Brien, R. (2015, July 15). Hotel industry targets upstart Airbnb in statehouse battles. *The Center for Public Integrity*. Accessed January 26, 2016, from http://www.publicintegrity.org/2015/07/15/17649/hotel-industry-targets-upstart-airbnb-statehouse-battles

O'Neill, S. (2014, April 30). American hotel association to fight Airbnb and short-term rentals. *Tnooz*. Accessed 26 January 2016, from http://www.tnooz.com/article/american-hotel-association-launches-fightback-airbnb-short-term-rentals/

O'Neill, J. W. & Ouyang, Y. (2016). From air mattresses to unregulated business: An analysis of the other side of Airbnb. *Penn State*. http://www.ahla.com/uploadedFiles/_Common/pdf/PennState_AirBnbReport_.pdf

Ortiz, E. (2015, May 23). Sacramento seeks to accommodate, limit Airbnb rentals. *The Sacramento Bee*. Accessed January 26, 2016, from http://www.sacbee.com/news/business/article21511164.html

Paris, N. (2015, July 22). Airbnb reviews are untrustworthy, user claims. *The Telegraph*. Accessed January 26, 2016, from http://www.telegraph.co.uk/travel/travelnews/11756199/Airbnb-reviews-are-untrustworthy-user-claims.html

Parry, B. (2014, September 5). Queens backs Airbnb, independent poll finds. *Times Ledger*. Accessed January 26, 2016, from http://www.timesledger.com/stories/2014/36/airbnbpoll_tl_2014_09_05_q.html

Pasick, A. (2013, August 8). Myanmar's hotels are full, but it's banning homestays because of unmannered foreigners. *Quartz*. Accessed January 26, 2016, from http://qz.com/113211/myanmars-hotels-are-full-but-its-banning-homestays-because-of-unmannered-foreigners/

Pedler, C. (2016, January 15). The rise of Airbnb has motel owners and Bendigo council concerned. *Bendigo Advertiser*. Accessed January 26, 2016, from http://www.bendigoadvertiser.com.au/story/3664583/airbnb-tourism-and-regional-victoria/

Pellicer, L. (2014, July 16). Barcelona's crackdown on Airbnb renters. *El País*. Accessed January 26, 2016, from http://elpais.com/elpais/2014/07/16/inenglish/1405501012_966041.html

Peltier, D. (2015, February 23). Airbnb faces big fines in Portland if hosts don't get city permits. *Skift*. Accessed January 26, 2016, from http://skift.com/2015/02/23/airbnb-faces-big-fines-in-portland-if-hosts-dont-get-city-permits/

Perry, M. (2015, November 18). Airbnb to start collecting Florida tourist taxes beginning Dec. 1. *Florida Politics*. Accessed January 26, 2016, from http://floridapolitics.com/archives/194890-airbnb-to-start-collecting-florida-tourist-taxes-beginning-december-1

Perthen A. (2012, June 30). Britons facing £15,000 fines in Canaries for letting homes and breaking a law that's not been enforced for years. *The Daily Mail*. Accessed January 26, 2016, from http://www.dailymail.co.uk/news/article-2166981/Britons-facing-15-000-fines-Canaries-letting-homes-breaking-law-thats-enforced-years.html

Pieters, J. (2016, January 13). Airbnb drops Amsterdam properties for violating hotel laws. *NL Times*. Accessed January 26, 2016, from http://www.nltimes.nl/2016/01/13/airbnb-drops-amsterdam-properties-for-violating-hotel-laws/

Plautz, J. (2015a, February 20). Judge evicts NYC tenant for listing rent-stabilized apartment on Airbnb. *Mashable*. Accessed January 26, 2016, from http://mashable.com/2015/02/20/airbnb-nyc-eviction

Plautz, J. (2015b, October 1). Airbnb to start collecting taxes in Washington state. *Mashable*. Accessed January 26, 2016, from http://mashable.com/2015/10/01/airbnb-washington-state/#jtMY5gP1Qmqj

Popper, B. (2015, December 4). Airbnb's worst problems are confirmed by its own data. *The Verge*. Accessed January 26, 2016, from http://www.theverge.com/2015/12/4/9849242/airbnb-data-new-york-affordable-housing-illegal-hotels

Porges, S. (2013, January 23). The Airbnb effect: Bringing life to quiet neighborhoods. *Forbes*. Accessed January 26, 2016, from http://www.forbes.com/sites/sethporges/2013/01/23/the-airbnb-effect-bringing-life-to-quiet-neighborhoods/

Presse Canadienne. (2015, August 9). Quebec will be the first province in Canada to legalize and regulate Airbnb. *The Montreal Gazette*. Accessed January 26, 2016, from http://montrealgazette.com/news/local-news/quebec-to-legalize-and-regulate-airbnb

Pressler, J. (2014, September 23). The dumbest person in your building is passing out keys to your front door! *New York Magazine*. Accessed January 26, 2016, from http://nymag.com/news/features/airbnb-in-new-york-debate-2014-9/

Quijones, D. (2015, August 10). Airbnb and its hosts hung out to dry in Barcelona. *Wolf Street*. Accessed January 26, 2016, from http://wolfstreet.com/2015/08/10/barcelonas-new-mayor-declares-war-on-airbnb/

Rocheleau, M. (2015, August 24). City orders owner to stop renting affordable unit via Airbnb. *The Boston Globe*. Accessed January 26, 2016, from https://www.bostonglobe.com/metro/2015/08/24/city-orders-owner-stop-renting-affordable-unit-via-airbnb/5SsUXOJPKvMQLhKkjFk90M/story.html

Roldan, R. (2015a, May 28). Airbnb ordinance heading for council study. *The Courier-Journal*. Accessed January 26, 2016, from http://www.courier-journal.com/story/news/local/2015/05/28/airbnb-ordinance-heading-council-study/28120339/

Roldan, R. (2015b, August 2). Other cities warn of Airbnb regulation pitfalls. *The Courier-Journal*. Accessed January 26, 2016, from http://www.courier-journal.com/story/money/2015/08/03/cities-warn-airbnb-regulation-pitfalls/30896135/

Rosen, K. (2013). *Short-term rentals and impact on the apartment market*. Berkley, CA: Rosen Consulting Group. http://www.rosenconsulting.com/products/rentalreport.html

Rosenberg, M. (2014, December 8). San Jose set to legalize, tax Airbnb stays like hotel rooms. *San Jose Mercury News*. Accessed January 26, 2016, from http://www.mercurynews.com/bay-area-news/ci_27087863/san-jose-set-legalize-tax-airbnb-stays-like

Rosenhall, L. (2015, March 17). California lawmakers want to regulate home-sharing businesses like Airbnb. *The Sacramento Bee*. Accessed January 26, 2016, from http://www.sacbee.com/news/politics-government/capitol-alert/article15202547.html

Rubin, B. F. (2014, July 10). Airbnb to reviewers: Tell us what you really think. *CNET*. Accessed January 26, 2016, from http://www.cnet.com/news/airbnb-wants-you-to-be-honest/

Said, C. (2015a, October 1). Chesky: Airbnb helps urban middle class make ends meet. *SFGate*. Accessed January 26, 2016, from http://www.sfgate.com/business/article/Chesky-Airbnb-helps-urban-middle-class-make-ends-6543832.php

Said, C. (2015b, November 4). Prop. F: S.F. voters reject measure to restrict Airbnb rentals. *SFGate*. Accessed January 26, 2016, from http://www.sfgate.com/bayarea/article/Prop-F-Measure-to-restrict-Airbnb-rentals-6609176.php

Said, C. (2015c, November 10). Airbnb, Uber cast themselves as saviors of the middle class. *San Francisco Chronicle*. Accessed January 26, 2016, from http://www.sfchronicle.com/business/article/Airbnb-Uber-We-are-the-saviors-of-the-middle-6620729.php

Said, C. (2016, January 7). City implores Airbnb, other firms, to deactivate illegal listings. *SFGate*. Accessed January 26, 2016, from http://www.sfgate.com/business/article/City-implores-Airbnb-other-firms-to-deactivate-6744061.php

Samaan, R. (2015). *Airbnb, rising rent, and the housing crisis in Los Angeles*. Los Angeles, CA: Los Angeles Alliance for a New Economy. http://www.laane.org/wp-content/uploads/2015/03/AirBnB-Final.pdf

Sawicki, E. (2015, April 8). Airbnb to begin collecting taxes for city. *The Malibu Times*. Accessed January 26, 2016, from http://www.malibutimes.com/news/article_df7955b0-de31-11e4-be52-8bccab199937.html

Sayre, K. (2014, July 10). New Orleans City Council toughens ban on unlicensed short-term vacation rentals. *The Times-Picayun* Accessed January 26, 2016, from http://www.nola.com/business/index.ssf/2014/07/new_orleans_city_council_tough.html

Schaal, D. (2013, October 9). Airbnb files petition to block NY subpoena, cites burden to compile data. *Skift*. Accessed January 26, 2016, from http://skift.com/2013/10/09/airbnb-files-petition-to-block-ny-subpoena-cites-substantial-burden-to-compile-the-data/
Schechner, S., & Verbergt, M. (2015, June 25). Paris confronts Airbnb's rapid growth. *The Wall Street Journal*. Accessed January 26, 2016, from http://www.wsj.com/articles/SB12147335600370333763904581058032330315292
Schneiderman, E. T. (2014). *Airbnb in the city*. New York: Office of the New York State Attorney General. http://www.ag.ny.gov/pdfs/Airbnb%20report.pdf
Schumpeter, J. A. (2008). *Capitalism, socialism, and democracy*. Toronto: Harper Perennial Modern Thought (Original work published in 1942).
Sciacca, A. (2015, July 23). SFTravel forges first-ever pact with Airbnb amid San Francisco hotel crunch. *San Francisco Business Times*. Accessed January 26, 2016, from http://www.bizjournals.com/sanfrancisco/blog/2015/07/sftravel-san-francisco-airbnb-hotels-shortage-deal.html
Seaside Courier. (2015, April 22). Carlsbad to regulate short-term vacation rentals. *The Seaside Courier*. Accessed January 26, 2016, from http://www.seasidecourier.com/business/carlsbad-to-regulate-short-term-vacation-rentals/article_bc13bd52-e94b-11e4-81b9-7fedc054dea6.html
Sernoffsky, E. (2015, August 3). Suspect pilfers $35K in loot from Airbnb rental. *San Francisco Chronicle*. Accessed January 26, 2016, from http://www.sfgate.com/news/article/Suspect-pilfers-35K-in-loot-from-Airbnb-rental-6421626.php
Shankman, S. (2014, November 18). The startup businesses built around the Airbnb ecosystem. *Skift*. Accessed January 26, 2016, from http://skift.com/2014/11/18/the-startup-businesses-built-around-the-airbnb-ecosystem/
Shankman, S. (2015, March 27). The Queen of England signs Airbnb-friendly law for London rentals. *Skift*. Accessed January 26, 2016, from http://skift.com/2015/03/27/the-queen-of-england-signs-airbnb-friendly-law-for-london-rentals/
Sheehan, L. R., & Ritchie, J. B. (2005). Destination stakeholders: Exploring identity and salience. *Annals of Tourism Research, 32*(3), 711–734.
Sheehan, L., Ritchie, J. B., & Hudson, S. (2007). The destination promotion triad: Understanding asymmetric stakeholder interdependencies among the city, hotels, and DMO. *Journal of Travel Research, 46*(1), 64–74.
Shute, J. (2014, April 9). Sandbanks locals aren't enjoying the loud party houses. *The Telegraph*. Accessed January 26, 2016, from http://www.telegraph.co.uk/finance/property/10755038/Sandbanks-locals-arent-enjoying-the-loud-party-houses.html
Sidorowicz, J. (2014, November 13). Airbnb licensing to pick up speed in GR, city manager promises enforcement. *Fox 17 West Michigan*. Accessed January 26, 2016, from http://fox17online.com/2014/11/13/airbnb-licensing-to-pick-up-speed-in-gr-city-manager-promises-enforcement/
Slee, T. (2014, March 26). The shape of Airbnb's business. *Whimsley*. Accessed January 26, 2016, from http://tomslee.net/2014/05/the-shape-of-airbnbs-business.html
Smerd, J. (2014, September 9). Bed-Stuy's slice of Airbnb. *Crain's New York Business*. Accessed January 26, 2016, from http://www.crainsnewyork.com/article/20140909/OPINION/309079984/bed-stuys-slice-of-airbnb
Snyder, B. (2014, July 31). Exclusive: Airbnb says it's saving our world with each rented room. *Fortune*. Accessed January 26, 2016, from http://fortune.com/2014/07/31/exclusive-airbnb-says-its-saving-our-world-with-each-rented-room/
Solomon, J. (2014, July 14). No vacancy: Hotels are making a killing. *CNN*. Accessed January 26, 2016, from http://money.cnn.com/2014/07/14/investing/hotel-business-boom/
Specht, P. A. (2015, October 27). Raleigh one step closer to legalizing Airbnb. *The News & Observer*. http://www.newsobserver.com/news/local/counties/wake-county/raleigh-report-blog/article41612481.html
Spielman, F. (2016, January 12). Emanuel proposes regulatory crackdown on Airbnb. *The Chicago Sun Times*. Accessed January 26, 2016, from http://chicago.suntimes.com/news/7/71/1247298/hold-late-post-emanuel-proposes-regulatory-crackdown-air-bnb

Sreenivasan, H. (2015, August 1). Why is New York City cracking down on Airbnb? *PBS NewsHour*. Accessed January 26, 2016, from http://www.pbs.org/newshour/bb/will-new-york-city-shut-airbnb-2/

Staley, L. (2007). Why do governments hate bed and breakfasts? *The Institute of Public Affairs Review: A Quarterly Review of Politics and Public Affairs, 59*(1), 33–35.

Stankus, J. (2012). *How to open and operate a Bed & Breakfast business* (9th ed.). Guilford, CT: Globe Pequot Press.

Stevens, M., & Groves, M. (2014, May 27). Malibu to crack down on short-term rentals via Airbnb, other websites. *The Los Angeles Times*. Accessed January 26, 2016, from http://www.latimes.com/local/la-me-malibu-renting-20140528-story.html

Stone, Z. (2015, November 8). Living and dying on Airbnb. *Medium*. Accessed January 26, 2016, from https://medium.com/matter/living-and-dying-on-airbnb-6bff8d600c04#.poc1jxosx

Sundararajan, A. (2012, October 22). Why the government doesn't need to regulate the sharing economy. *Wired*. Accessed January 26, 2016, from http://www.wired.com/2012/10/from-airbnb-to-coursera-why-the-government-shouldnt-regulate-the-sharing-economy/

Sundararajan, A. (2014, March 3). Trusting the 'sharing economy' to regulate itself. *The New York Times*. Accessed January 26, 2016, from http://economix.blogs.nytimes.com/2014/03/03/trusting-the-sharing-economy-to-regulate-itself/

Swan, R. (2014, October 27). Protesters accuse Airbnb of desecrating San Francisco's neighborhoods. *San Francisco Weekly*. Accessed January 26, 2016, from http://www.sfweekly.com/thesnitch/2014/10/27/protesters-accuse-airbnb-of-killing-san-franciscos-neighborhoods

Swig, R. (2014, August 29). Alt-accommodation impact felt in San Francisco. *Hotel News Now*. Accessed January 26, 2016, from www.hotelnewsnow.com/article/Pdf/14341/

Tam, D. (2013, July 31). Airbnb, Lyft partner with new share-economy advocacy group. *CNET*. Accessed January 26, 2016, from http://www.cnet.com/news/airbnb-lyft-partner-with-new-share-economy-advocacy-group/

Thomas, O. (2015, October 15). With its latest hire, Airbnb gives a clue on how it's going to fight rental laws. *Business Insider*. Accessed January 26, 2016, from http://www.businessinsider.com/airbnb-hires-yahoo-david-hantman-2012-10

Titcomb, J. (2014, January 28). Airbnb denies it is at war with hotel groups. *The Telegraph*. Accessed January 26, 2016, from http://www.telegraph.co.uk/finance/newsbysector/retailandconsumer/leisure/10600282/A irbnb-denies-it-is-at-war-with-hotel-groups.html

Trenholm, R. (2015, March 3). Airbnb exec denies competition with hotels, says an Airbnb trip 'changes you.' *CNET*. Accessed January 26, 2016, from http://www.cnet.com/news/airbnb-exec-denies-competition-with-hotels-says-an-airbnb-trip-changes-you-somehow/

Tsotsis, A. (2015, May 27). Airbnb hopes to have almost a million stays a night by summer. *TechCrunch*. Accessed January 26, 2016, from http://techcrunch.com/2015/05/27/airbnb-hopes-to-have-almost-a-million-stays-a-night-by-summer/

Tussyadiah, I. (2015). An exploratory study on drivers and deterrents of collaborative consumption in travel. In I. Tussyadiah & A. Inversini (Eds.), *Information & communication technologies in tourism 2015*. Switzerland: Springer.

Valencia, J. (2014, December 11). Charlotte, Raleigh, Wilmington wrestle with B&B vs. Airbnb. *WUNC*. Accessed January 26, 2016, from http://wunc.org/post/charlotte-raleigh-wilmington-wrestle-bb-vs-airbnb

Vasagar, J. (2014, April 30). Berlin housing law threatens sharing economy by restricting rents. *Financial Times*. Accessed January 26, 2016, from http://www.ft.com/intl/cms/s/0/1e8299a0-d065-11e3-af2b-00144feabdc0.html

Vivion, N. (2015, February 11). Is Airbnb responsible for the softening in New York RevPAR?. *Tnooz*. Accessed January 26, 2016, from http://www.tnooz.com/article/airbnb-responsible-softening-new-york-revpar

Walker, H. (2014, April 21). Airbnb removed thousands of 'illegal' listings after challenge from New York's top lawyer. *Business Insider*. Accessed January 26, 2016, from http://www.businessinsider.com/airbnb-purging-thousands-of-illegal-listings-2014-4

Walters, A. (2015, February 24). Portland's deadline for Airbnb safety permits passes unheeded, but city won't issue fines. *Willamette Week*. Accessed January 26, 2016, from http://www.wweek.com/portland/blog-32871-portlands_deadline_for_airbnb_safety_permits_passes_unheeded_but_city_wont_issue_fnes.html

Weber, H. (2013a, June 7). After a rough few months, Airbnb receives Amsterdam's blessing. Will other cities follow? *The Next Web*. Accessed January 26, 2016, from http://thenextweb.com/eu/2013/06/07/four-months-after-its-hunt-for-illegal-hotels-amsterdam-lightens-restrictions-on-airbnb-rentals/

Weber, H. (2013b, February 2). Airbnb could be banned in Amsterdam: Local authorities are now hunting for illegal hotels. *The Next Web*. Accessed January 26, 2016, from http://thenextweb.com/insider/2013/02/02/airbnb-may-be-banned-from-amsterdam-local-authorities-are-now-hunting-for-illegal-hotels/

Weinberger, M. (2015, March 23). San Francisco complains it can't enforce its own Airbnb law. *Business Insider*. Accessed January 26, 2016, from http://www.businessinsider.com/san-francisco-calls-airbnb-regulations-unenforceable-2015-3

Whitehouse, K. (2015, January 20). Airbnb to face grilling by NYC City Council. *USA Today*. Accessed January 26, 2016, from http://www.usatoday.com/story/tech/2015/01/19/airbnb-illegalhotels-nyc-renters/21999177/

Williams, O. (2015, February 9). Here's why you might want to rent your home to NWT tourists. *My Yellowknife Now*. Accessed January 26, 2016, from http://www.myyellowknifenow.com/2200/heres-might-want-rent-home-nwt-tourists/

Wohlsen, M. (2013, October 3). Airbnb: Our rooms should be taxed like hotels. *Wired*. Accessed January 26, 2016, from http://www.wired.com/2013/10/airbnb-taxes/

Yglesias, M. (2012a, June 5). Legalize Airbnb! *Slate*. Accessed January 26, 2016, from http://www.slate.com/articles/business/moneybox/2012/06/is_airbnb_illegal_why_hotels_are_so_upset_about_you_renting_a_bedroom_to_a_stranger_.html

Yglesias, M. (2012b). *The rent is too damn high: What to do about it, and why it matters more than you think*. New York: Simon & Schuster.

Yglesias, M. (2013, May 1). Stop "disrupting" everything: How a once-useful concept turned into a meaningless buzzword. *Slate*. Accessed January 26, 2016, from http://www.slate.com/articles/business/moneybox/2013/05/disrupting_disruption_a_once_useful_concept_has_become_a_lame_catchphrase.html

Zabludovsky, K. (2014, May 1). NYC is battling Airbnb, but the home-sharing firm got a green light in Amsterdam. *Newsweek*. Accessed January 26, 2016, from http://www.newsweek.com/nyc-battling-airbnb-home-sharing-firm-got-green-light-amsterdam-249256

Zervas, G., Proserpio, D., & Byers, J. (2015a). *A first look at online reputation on Airbnb, where every stay is above average*. http://papers.ssrn.com/sol3/papers.cfm?abstract_id=2554500

Zervas, G., Proserpio, D., & Byers, J. (2015b). *The rise of the sharing economy: Estimating the impact of Airbnb on the hotel industry*. http://people.bu.edu/zg/publications/airbnb.pdf

Zillman, C. (2015, July 16). Spain's Catalonia region the latest to slap a tax on Airbnb rentals. *Fortune*. Accessed January 26, 2016, from http://fortune.com/2015/07/16/airbnb-taxes-spain-catalonia/

Free Walking Tour Enterprises in Europe: An Evolutionary Economic Approach

María del Pilar Leal Londoño and F. Xavier Medina

Abstract The emergence of the collaborative economy has promoted the rise of numerous profit and non-profit businesses that are flourishing. Some of the business features within this alternative tourism industry are devoted to the support of a moral economy based on social responsibility, sustainable trade, fair labour practices, and social and environmental awareness. In this framework, new trends are appearing within the tourism/travel/leisure industries all over the world. This chapter outlines an exploratory approach to how firms within the collaborative economy operate. The empirical focus is on the "free" or "pay-what-you-want" tours in Europe, which appeal to the free exchange of local knowledge among travellers. It analyses business models and behaviours based on the evolutionary economics concepts of knowledge, innovation and path-dependency. Taking as the main case studies Barcelona and Berlin, this approach allows us to understand the collaborative market and how this affects the relationship between business and tourists by examining the moral affordances, controversies and risks in the context of collaborative economy practices.

Keywords Collaborative economy • Free-walking tours • Business behaviour • Business models • Evolutionary economics

1 Introduction

Escaping the mass-produced uniform travel experience, the collaborative economy is becoming an increasingly valuable source of new products and activities in travel and tourism practices, and it has met consumer demand for more authentic and unique tourism experiences. Nowadays, the collaborative economy is already part

M. del Pilar Leal Londoño (✉)
Ostelea School of Tourism & Hospitality, Barcelona & GRIT-EAE, Carrer d'Aragó, 28, 08015 Barcelona, Spain
e-mail: mleal@ostelea.com

F.X. Medina
Universitat Oberta de Catalunya & GRIT-EAE, Carrer d'Aragó, 28, 08015 Barcelona, Spain
e-mail: fxmedina@gmail.com

D. Dredge, S. Gyimóthy (eds.), *Collaborative Economy and Tourism*, Tourism on the Verge, DOI 10.1007/978-3-319-51799-5_8

of our daily lives and is revolutionising the way we travel and live. The collaborative economy is creating more options for people to travel in different ways. Rental platforms like Airbnb or Uber are popularly recognised sharing practices, however, there are other types of collaborative economy practices emerging that have yet to be explored in the literature, such as free or "pay what you want" walking tours.

As Belk (2014) points out, there are two common points in these collaborative practices: (1) their use of temporary access non-ownership models of utilising consumer goods and services; and (2) their reliance on the Internet. Indeed, one of the main drivers for the move towards the collaborative economy is technology, which allows us to have access to a global market at the click of our fingertips. As explored in this chapter, part of the success achieved by free walking tours in European cities is using the Internet as a marketing tool that allows the spread information all over the world.

Technology has a particularly important role to play, not only because the Internet is crucial as an information source to tourists, but also because the Internet has reshaped the tourist experience. As tourists become more mobile, so does the way they travel. However, far from reducing paid walking tours in cities, technology has prompted the rise of free walking tours or "pay what you want" tours, and is producing even more variations on the guided tour business model. Not only are traditional city walking tour companies tapping into this market, but small and medium-sized tourism enterprises (SMEs) and organisations are also on the guided walking tours scene, and new business models and marketing strategies are also being created to feed the "sharing market".

Generally designed in some form of "loop", the walking tour enables participants to gain an appreciation of aspects of a landscape, both past and present, by interpreting it through a system of signs. An interpretive walk provides not only an opportunity to facilitate learning and to enhance appreciation of an urban landscape, but can also enhance visitors' experience of that place (Markwell, Stevenson, & Rowe, 2004). In this open framework, the concept of a free tour where there is no set charge, and tourists show their appreciation by leaving a tip with their tour guide, is becoming increasingly popular across Europe and beyond. An increase in budget-conscious travel and the ease of word-of-mouth internet marketing is helping drive the trend (Baker, 2013), and tourists themselves are contributing to the expansion of free walking tours across the globe, by sharing their experiences on social media.

This chapter is motivated by the desire to understand the behaviour of tourism enterprises in the framework of the collaborative economy by exploring the phenomenon of free walking tours using evolutionary economics (Dosi, 1988; Nelson & Winter, 1982). This is an important issue in tourism because free walking tours play an increasing role in the marketing, image and visibility of destinations, especially in Europe, and in the debate between where sharing ends and commerce begins (Belk, 2014, p. 7). In the context of the global financial crisis, processes of peer-to-peer sharing of goods, services, transportation, among other things are believed to transform and disrupt capitalist structures. This is associated with the idea that society will change where people demand new business models of access over traditional models of ownership (Owyang, Samuel, & Grennville, 2014).

The starting point for this chapter is the question raised by Koopman, Mitchell, and Thierer (2014): To what degree is the sharing economy creating new markets rather than simply supplanting older forms of transactions? In order to answer this question, the chapter seeks to describe and explain the business models characterising free walking tour enterprises and its moral affordances based on evolutionary economic geography and its fundamental concepts of knowledge, innovation and its principle of path dependency. Secondly, the chapter will critically discuss free walking tours and whether this phenomenon might fit into collaborative economy practices, and whether it is or is not disrupting or transforming tourism. Finally, the chapter explores future perspectives on free walking tours in Europe in the context of the collaborative economy, and its opportunities and challenges for future research and practice.

In the following section, we describe the basic principles of evolutionary economics applied to free walking tour business models, paying particular attention to business dynamics and how these dynamics have been developed. We then explore the characteristics of free walking tours linked to collaborative economy by using primary and secondary data to critically discuss the disruption or transformation caused by this phenomenon on tourism practices. The chapter contributes to a wider knowledge of the free walking tours phenomenon, particularly in Europe. Finally, the chapter addresses some key theoretical and practical issues in the understanding of tourism enterprise models in the context of the collaborative economy. It does this by presenting a dual focus, not just on how ideas and concepts from evolutionary economics can be brought to bear on sharing economic issues, but also on the ambivalent attitudes by stakeholders who are living in a hybrid economy where collaborative consumption and capitalist market structures are continually overlapping.

2 Free Walking Tour Firms Within the Collaborative Economy: An Evolutionary Economics Approach

According to the European Business Innovation Observatory Report (2013), in recent years, a transition from ownership towards accessibility might be observed across a wide variety of markets. In traditional markets, consumers buy products and gain ownership. However, through accessibility-based systems, consumers are increasingly paying for temporary access rights to a product or a service. As a result, sharing platforms in the collaborative economy allow consumers to access goods and services that were normally conducted by traditional businesses.

According with the European Business Innovation Observatory (2013), the most widespread business model deployed by sharing economy companies features an online marketplace through which demand for certain assets or services amongst peers is matched with the ownership of those assets and services by other peers. In the tourism sector, innovation in firms has been driven by the Internet. New business models linked to tourism, like Uber or Airbnb, which are well-established manifestations of the collaborative economy, have reached customers in disruptive ways (Stokes, Clarence, Anderson, & Rinne, 2014). Free walking tour firms are commonly not included or analysed as a collaborative economy example, although they might fit into the pillar of collaborative learning established by Stokes et al. (2014) because they refer to learning experiences where people share resources and knowledge.

In this chapter, we use the evolutionary perspective raised by the relational turn in economic geography, which allows us to understand the dynamics, competitive advantages, economic transformations and the growth of firms within the collaborative economy. Evolutionary economics considers the economy as a dynamic, irreversible and self-transformational system, which opens up a new space for theoretical, ontological and epistemological exploration (Boschma & Martin, 2010, p. 5). The evolutionary approach also allows the analysis of the impact of historical structures and processes on today's firms and their decisions. Evolutionary concepts of change assume that economic and social processes are experienced-based, cumulative and reflexive in nature (Bathelt & Glückler, 2003). From the sociological approach applied to the economy, Granovetter (1985) argues that economic activities are deeply embedded in the structures of social relations. Therefore, firms cannot be analysed as independent entities, but must be viewed within their respective socio-economic contexts.

Collaborative consumption is perhaps an evolution of the economy, it may be a new economy, or it might be seen as a novelty within the existing economy. In fact, novelty is one of the three basic requirements of economic evolution and refers to the creative capacity of economic agents (individuals and firms) and the creative functions of markets to drive economic evolution and adaptation (Metcalfe, Foster, & Ramlogan, 2006). The framework of evolutionary economics innovation and knowledge are essential in helping us to understand the creation and evolution of the business models associated with free walking tours as a phenomenon within collaborative consumption.

Firms absorb, explore and exploit local knowledge because they use different routines, beliefs and habits, and their absorptive capacity is grounded on knowledge bases (Denicolai, Zucchella, & Cioccarelli, 2010). Most free walking tour firms claim to be local firms driven by local people. However, the impact of local firms in and on their local environment depends on local agents, who, according to Denicolai et al. (2010), differ in terms of their absorptive capacity and their accumulation of knowledge and social assets.

Free walking tours might have an impact on destination image and attractiveness because, as stated by Ap and Wong (2001), walking tours are very much responsible for the overall impression and satisfaction of the tour services offered by destinations. One of the main marketing channels for this type of firm is the Internet, demonstrated through a common search in Internet browsers. The Internet and this information technology offer consumers more information about products and services, and it empowers consumers to come together and act on that information (Koopman et al., 2014).

It has been observed that the number of walking tours in cities has increased over the last decade. In Barcelona for example, the number of walking tours has grown from 4253 in 2000 to 14,278 in 2014 according to the Barcelona Tourism Bureau (2014). This fact might be explained by an increase in demand for free walking tours as an innovative tourism product and a non-technological innovation. As Souto (2015) argued, a non-technological innovation, such as a business model or concept, is a way to demonstrate the innovation potential for service firms.

According to Stokes et al. (2014), in the collaborative economy there are four business models that shape the way we participate (see Fig. 1). Some of the most exciting and original participants in the collaborative economy according to the authors, have gone beyond prominent delivery models (such as business–to–consumer or B2C) in favour of less conventional or more peer–driven approaches. However, in the case of free walking tours, the B2C model is the most prominent delivery model, as will be discussed later on in this chapter.

Many of the new tours are set up by local tourism entrepreneurs associated through a network, but also by traditional operators who are taking control on the "sharing market". This statement is supported in research by Stokes et al. (2014) who found that not all organisations operating in the collaborative economy are

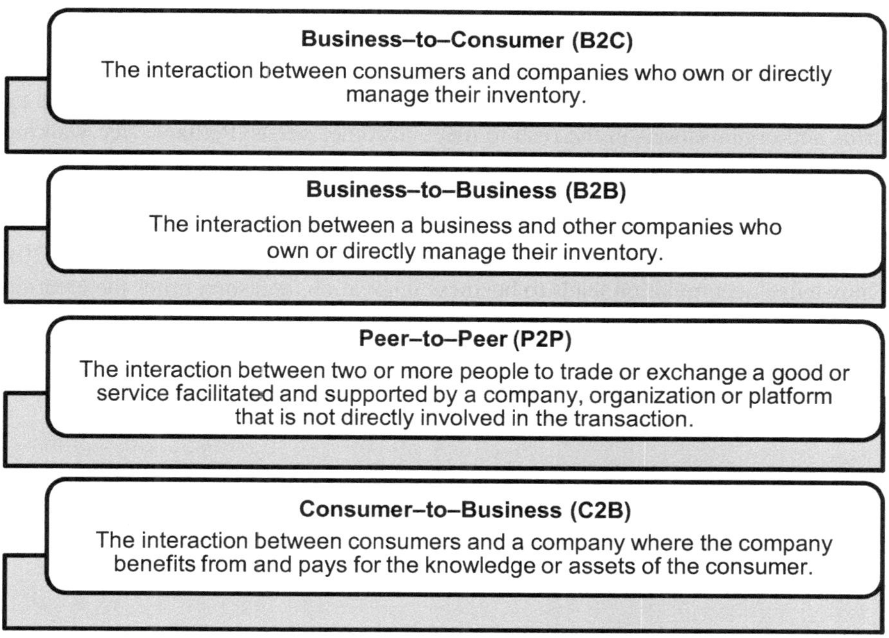

Fig. 1 Business models of the collaborative economy. Source: Author's own based on Stokes et al. (2014)

new. Established corporations are also entering this space, often by aligning themselves with collaborative businesses or adapting their models to incorporate collaborative traits. This fact may reflect a path dependency in the capitalist market economy where firms evolve and adapt to developments in the market place by searching for new ways and mechanisms of distributing their products and services and building market awareness.

As stated by Koopman et al. (2014), the dynamic competition mentioned above encourages firms to discover new ways of doing business and new ways of creating value for their customers. This may also explain the presence of traditional operators offering free walking tours because of heightened business competition. However, in the framework of the collaborative economy, the consumer is empowered via product rating and review systems, thus allowing consumers to influence business behaviour and competition.

The evolutionary economics approach allows us to introduce two questions that will be addressed in this chapter. The first question has to do with how free walking tour firms behave, and how they have developed an innovative business concept known as free walking tours. Based on the previous work developed by Souto (2015), in the tourism industry we distinguish two types of innovation: (a) business concept innovation; and (b) business model innovations that apply knowledge to meet customer needs. Both types of innovation are key for explaining how a business strategy takes form and operates. Taking the case study of the free walking tours, the second question follows the one raised by Dredge and Gyimóthy (2015, p. 9) and asks "Is the collaborative economy just business-as-usual that appropriates an alternative economies logic?"

On this basis, we consider free walking tours as business strategies developed by firms and organisations in the rush to meet customer needs. Perhaps, free walking tours are a B2C business model in which the buying of knowledge takes place. In that sense, and according to the evolutionary economics perspective, firms are agents that compete in a selective environment, and selection is the result of different historical paths of accumulation of knowledge in firms (Giuliani, 2010). Knowledge accumulation leads to business innovation, and sometimes the creation of a knowledge network resulting from business interaction derived from the trade of inputs, services or memberships (Giuliani, 2007). Moreover, firms do not innovate in isolation; collaboration with other companies or institutions increases innovation opportunities especially in the tourism sector (Souto, 2015).

3 Knowledge and Innovation in Walking Tours Firms Within the Collaborative Economy

Knowledge never stands still but is constantly being created. It is this continual process that drives economic evolution and renders capitalism restless and in constant motion (Boschma & Martin, 2010). In the case of firms, and according to Denicolai et al. (2010), in order to manage social assets, firms develop a specific know-how stored in organisational routines, rituals and habits, and it is in the storage and use of this knowledge that innovation can be unlocked. But innovation is also related to the processes of knowledge creation, the development of new technologies and the effects of technological change, especially from a spatial perspective (Bathelt & Glückler, 2003). As argued by Bathelt and Glückler (2003), successful innovations are usually associated with the creation of new knowledge or the modification of existing knowledge. The process of generating new technologies and knowledge is path-dependent in that it depends on the firms' and actors' past experiences and their capacities to modify existing knowledge or create new knowledge.

In this conceptual framework, processes of knowledge creation are based on previous experiences which lead to innovation inside firms. This fact might be translated into innovative business strategies that transform and disrupt the relationship between business and customers. Nonaka (1991) argued that knowledge can be explicit (know-that) which is relatively easily codified and transferred, and tacit knowledge which is more difficult to formalise and, therefore, less easy to interpret and transfer from one organisation to another. Tacit knowledge according to Polanyi (1966) is learned through both individual reflection and collaborative experience. Tacit knowledge might be observed within the United Europe free tours organisation.

In evolutionary economics, firms are not uniform but are characterised by distinctive capabilities. For example, a firm's knowledge can play an important role in innovation and can contribute to the firm's self-constructed competitive advantage (Cooke & Laurentis, 2010). Knowledge is the decisive asset of a firm, and knowledge creation is the key mechanism through which firms produce and sustain competitiveness (Bathelt & Glückler, 2011). In tourism firms, knowledge is a critical determinant in innovative capability (Martínez-Román Tamayo, Gamero, & Romero, 2015).

Previous work by Shaw and Williams (2009) on knowledge transfer and management in tourism confirms knowledge as a competitive advantage for tourism firms. The rise of free walking tours might be seen as an example of businesses building competitive advantage as a response to different drivers of change mentioned by Owyang et al. (2014) such as the financial crisis, new customers and travellers looking for a connection with locals, alternative ways to explore destinations, widespread use of technology, among others. In addition to knowledge as a competitive advantage in firms, Shaw and Williams (2009) stress the importance of knowledge in innovation. However, in order to influence innovation processes, knowledge has to be captured, made explicit and properly understood; it also needs to be interpreted, restored, adapted into specific innovations and recorded (Hjalager, 2010). Based on Hjalager's (2010) categories of innovation, free walking tours show three potential types of innovation:

(1) *Product or service innovations* refer to changes directly observed by the customer and regarded as new approaches to product conceptualisation,

development and delivery. For example, product or service innovation might be seen in traditional paid walking tour companies that incorporate free walking tours into their product range. Alternatively, the reinvented, reshaped and commoditised walking tours may contribute to the launching of new companies and organisations targeting new market segments.

(2) *Management innovations* refer to, for example, new marketing concepts and new relational configurations between providers and customers that enhance, streamline and make more cost-effective market uptake. For example, management innovations inside free walking tour firms can be observed in the way they market their products online. Along with the traditional website, free walking tours base their performance on customer empowerment through reputational feedback mechanisms, such as product rating and review systems, that are posted on the main page of their websites.

(3) *Institutional innovations* refer to new collaborative or organisational structures that enhance accessibility and/or reconfigure traditional supply chains. For example, institutional innovation is reflected on the creation of the United Europe free tours network as independent network that provides quality standards of free walking tours around Europe, although not all free walking tour firms are part of this network.

Innovations in tourism enterprises respond to and are inspired by a range of external and internal factors (Hjalager, 2010). Because firms have histories, path dependencies and evolutionary trajectories, they develop adaptation and survival skills, and in maintaining a relatively unchanging market location they can develop a special capability of transforming themselves to fit new markets (Cooke & Laurentis, 2010). The analysis of the relationship between capacity of innovation, strategies of adaptation and economic performance in tourism firms is a research gap that is yet to be explored (Hjalager, 2010; Martínez-Román et al., 2015).

4 Path Dependency of Walking Tour Firms Within Collaborative Economy

Within evolutionary economics, the notion of path dependency holds that the dynamics of economic development is contained within and explained by specific contexts. For instance, history matters and small chance or random events lead to path dependence and eventually become locked in through a self-reinforcing process (David, 1994). From an evolutionary perspective, yesterday's economic decisions, actions and interactions enable and constrain the context of today's action (Bathelt & Glückler, 2011). In this context, the basic path dependence model proposed by Martin and Sunley (2010) posits four stages of the development of a technological, industrial or institutional trajectory: pre-formation, path creation, path lock-in, and path dissolution. According to these authors, the model has been mainly used to explain the evolution of a particular industry, technology or institution either in a *given* location (region, city), or *across* locations.

In particular, path dependence has helped to explain why regional growth disparities persist; why particular industries and technologies develop in certain locations, but not in others; and to understand why some regional economies are better able to adapt over time than others (Martin & Sunley, 2010). In the case of tourism, path dependence has recently been used to explain the evolution of destinations. In particular, it has been used to understand the emergence, rise and decline of a tourism area and the path dependence and lock-in of dominant tourism products and sectors (Ma & Hassink, 2013) or why destinations change over time (Gill & Williams, 2011; Halkier & Therkelsen, 2013; Sanz-Ibañez & Anton Clavé, 2014).

Ma and Hassink (2013) stress that the path dependence approach can be used to explain the evolution of a particular tourism product, sector or institution either in a given tourism destination or across destinations which can have both positive and negative effects (Martin & Sunley, 2010). As Brouder and Eriksson argue (2013: 379), path dependence studies generally take a reflective, after-the-fact approach to identify the presence of negative externalities that expose regions to some inevitable future shock which in turn leads to a crisis in the regional economy. It can be seen that most tourism studies have been focused on the path dependence of destinations rather than firms. Alternatively, economic geographers have studied firms' and regions' performance over time based on path dependence (Glückler, 2007; Martin & Sunley, 2006, 2010; Stam, 2010).

Within this context, the principle of path dependence applied to collaborative economy might explain why free walking tour enterprises base their performance on traditional business models developed in the capitalist market economy. These free tour enterprises reflect business choices made in the past by emphasising convenience, value and quality or distinctiveness of the services offered. As argued by Owyang et al. (2014), "...for any business that has competed on price, convenience or quality to drive traditional sales, it won't be a huge leap to push those buttons in order to drive sharing".

Following Owyang et al. (2014), the collaborative economy demands nothing short of business model transformation. In that sense, we argue that the collaborative economy is a transformation of the traditional economy shaped by historical structures that configure the current sharing market. Free walking tours exhibit a transformation of traditional walking tour firms that might claim to be innovative. This evolutionary approach suggests that successful routines survive over time, but that the acquisition of successful routines is limited by the bounded rationality of economic actors such as firms and individuals, since firms have a limited capacity to embrace change (Brouder & Eriksson, 2013).

5 Methodology

The current investigation of free walking tours in the collaborative economy is based on a case study analysis of the free walking tours offered by firms in Barcelona and Berlin. Based on the European Cities Benchmarking Report- ECM (2014), these two cities were selected based on two criteria: (a) their tourism performance; and (b) their attractiveness for establishing a business. These criteria are support by the following factors:

(1) Both cities are on the list of the top performing tourism cities. Berlin, Rome, and Barcelona maintained their ranks among the top five tourist cities with decidedly strong year-on-year bed-night growth rates (ECM, 2014).
(2) Both cities are top destinations in Europe and are commonly named as "alternative" due to their culture, art, architecture, and design among other elements. In the case of Berlin, for example, the city is especially attractive to entrepreneurs in the creative sector and the technology industry (Visit Berlin Report, 2015).
(3) Berlin is the ninth best city in the world to open a start-up, according to the 2015 study "Start-up Ecosystem Ranking Report" developed by the firm Compass in 2015.
(4) Arrivals and overnight stays in Berlin and Barcelona have grown significantly, a development unmatched in other European cities (see Table 1).
(5) The economic and social impacts of tourism on the economies of these cities are significant (ECM, 2014).

Primary data were collected through participant observation in Barcelona and Berlin in four different free walking tours. Two tours were conducted with the same firm that operates in Barcelona and Berlin. The other two tours took place with different firms in each case study location. In addition, five informal unstructured discussions were conducted with free tour guides. The information was complemented with three interviews with individuals working in one of the biggest free walking tour firms in Europe. Furthermore, in-field discussions with tourists during the free walking tours in Barcelona and Berlin were carried out. The free walking tour firms were chosen based on two qualifying criteria: (1) one of the biggest firms which offered more free walking tours in different cities in Europe,

Table 1 Tourism data showing increases in tourism in Berlin and Barcelona

	Berlin	Barcelona
Number of visitors (2014)	12.0 million	7.9 million
Number of overnight stays (2014)	28.7 million	17.1 million
Increased of overnight stays (2014)	6.5%	5.6%
% Growth of tourism from 2005 to 2014	83.6%	39.2%

Source: Based on Visit Berlin and Barcelona Tourism websites, 2015

and (2) firms who belong to the United Europe Free Tours and claim to be alternative free walking tour firms.

This primary data collection was complemented with an online survey e-mailed to potential participants in May (2015) and included 28 closed and multi-response questions. The survey was addressed to company managers of free walking tours in Europe and was based on a list available online created by the tour operator 'Free Sofia Tour' and on firms that advertised on the network website "United Europe Free Tours". The consolidated database included 75 operators. The purpose of the survey was to develop a collective description of the free walking tour firms in Europe and their links to collaborative economy.

The online survey was sent to 54 enterprises in the database that had an email address. Two emails were undeliverable so it was assumed that 52 enterprises received the e-mail with the online survey link. At the end of the survey period, 11 usable responses were received giving a 21% response rate. The questionnaire collected information about the characteristics of the business, key characteristics of the free walking tours offered, information about demand for free walking tours, and marketing of tours.

The online survey was analysed using Excel. The country of respondents is presented in Table 2 and shows that responses were concentrated in Eastern Europe, represented by Poland, Romania and Bulgaria. This suggests a positive impact and demonstrates interest in these countries for free walking tours as a way of marketing their destination.

The low responses rate obtained might be explained by the lack of a contact person's name. This impersonal email could provoke mistrust and/or a lack of responsibility for answering by the person who received the email. However, and aware of the small and limited answer response rate, the main purpose of the questionnaire was simply to obtain descriptive data that might complement the information collected through interviews, field notes, photos and participant observation, and was not intended for in-depth statistical analysis.

In addition, the information collected was supported by secondary data including online information available to prospective tourists on their company websites across Europe, academic papers, professional reports, newspapers and internal

Table 2 List of firms' responses to the online survey by country

Country	No. Surveys
Spain	2
Poland	2
Holland	1
Romania	1
Bulgaria	1
Iceland	1
Portugal	1
Italy	1
Germany	1
Total	11

consultant reports. With respect to the interviews and field notes collected from the case study tours in Berlin and Barcelona, due to privacy and confidentiality concerns, we refer to these firms as: firm A, B, C and D. Firms A and B operate to Berlin and C and D to Barcelona.

6 An Analysis of Free Walking Tour Firms: Empirical Findings

The theoretical sections of this chapter explore knowledge, innovation and path dependence as the three main dimensions of analysis. In order to answer the first question raised in this chapter, which relates to understanding the behaviour of walking tour firms and the development of a new concept of walking tours named as free walking tours, the following section will discuss the development of business models around free walking tours in Europe.

6.1 Free Walking Tours Firm Features and Behaviour

One of the main features of walking tours firms that offer free walking tours is that most of them are small enterprises, a fact that may be observed by the number of employees. From the survey responses, 90% of the responding enterprises had less than ten employees. For the European Commission classification, this type of firm would be described as a micro-enterprise. Because the collaborative economy is in its early stages of development, there is no data available about the type of firms involved.

Thus, it might be said that although collaborative economy businesses range in size from start-ups to big companies, free walking tour firms are small companies with 72% describing themselves as independent tour operators and family-owned businesses. Moreover, 27% of survey respondents considered the ownership of their business to be a cooperative and 9% as a non-profit organisation.

Based on field observations and discussions with guides associated with Firms A and C, not all free walking tour firms are small enterprises, family businesses, or a non-profit organisations. Firm A is based in Berlin and England and is present in 15 European cities including Barcelona. According to one tour guide close to the administration in Berlin, the number of fixed employees is approximately about 102 (15 in Berlin and 15 in England and an average of 4 per city) plus more than 250 tour guides. In the case of Berlin, the number of tour guides is around 17 staff: six tour guides for walking tours in Spanish and 11 for tours in English.

Alternatively, firm B and D claim to be "local" in the Barcelona case and "alternative" in the Berlin case. From an evolutionary approach, this might be seen to be an adaptation of firms to a specific environment. In the case of Barcelona, the claim of its products and services being local is due to the current political and social situation regarding the rise of regionalism in Catalonia. On the other hand, the claim of being "alternative" in its product and services in Berlin match with the city's image and the promotion conducted by the local administration (Visit Berlin Website, 2015).

Thus, based on the findings of Benson-Rea, Roderick, and Herbert Sima (2013), we may claim that within the collaborative economy there is a co-existence of multiple business models with pluralistic strategies. One of the dominant business models is the Business-to-Consumer (B2C) model, where there is direct interaction between business and consumers. In this study 60% of respondents surveyed purchased their guided tours without intermediaries illustrating the significance of this B2C model.

A second business model identified was the Business–to-Business (B2B) model, where there is an interaction between free walking tour firms and other businesses in order to market their products or obtain discounts for their clients. In that context, firms establish a win-to-win relationship. This was observed in 40% of firms surveyed who market their guided tours in collaboration with other tourism enterprises or organisations. In addition, it was observed that free walking tour firms usually develop joint ventures with other firms, for example, firm A and C have cooperation agreements with cafes, hotels and other local tourism enterprises, and they claim to have over 750 close partners in a almost 10 countries and over 1000 hostels. This may also be a management innovation (Hjalager, 2010).

A third business model identified was the Peer-to-Peer (P2P) where firms exchange their services facilitated by a third party organisation, such as United Free Tour Europe that is not directly involved in the transaction. However, this platform can also be seen as a network for knowledge exchange and as an institutional innovation (Hjalager, 2010). Although there is variety of business models adopted by free walking tours firms, a commonality is the creation of trust among B2C and B2B, which is also a characteristic of the collaborative economy (Stokes et al., 2014).

Within evolutionary economics, trust is considered as a social asset for firms and is usually an outcome of long path dependent processes, stemming from a series of mutual interactions (Denicolai et al., 2010). As Denicolai et al. (2010) have argued, the development of trust shapes the reputation of firms. This perspective is particularly cogent within the collaborative economy and free walking tours where trust and reputation are created through online reviews made by customers. Reviews and feedback raise a firm's popularity and tour guides also help to improve this reputational capital. This fact was observed after each walking tour when tour guides asked tourists to leave an online comment about their experience.

6.2 Free Tours as a Process of Knowledge and Innovation

Firms are differentiated regarding their capacity to use resources, assets and relationships (Benson-Rea et al., 2013). As knowledge is considered a resource contributing to a firm's competitiveness (Bathelt & Glückler, 2011), firms can understand, absorb and implement external knowledge only when it is close to their own knowledge base (Cohen & Levinthal, 1990). Evolutionary theory predicts that most firms innovate incrementally, exploiting the knowledge they have built up in the past (Boschma & Martin, 2010). In the case of free walking tour firms, innovation is often grounded in knowledge created and managed by traditional paid walking tour firms. Nelson and Winter (1982) have described this as a "local search process". Firm A claims to have been the first firm in Europe to incorporate free walking tours into its offer in 2004. Ten years later, there are over 50 firms offering free walking tours around Europe which is perhaps largely due to a knowledge transfer process.

In this research however, firms' standardisation is hindering rather than enhancing an entrepreneurial and innovative spirit (Hjalager, 2010). In conceptual terms, free walking tour firms have not been innovative, at least visibly, in two main aspects:

(1) Route design: they are following a common geographical pattern as traditional walking tour firms. The tour firms in this study explore just the city centre touristic resources, with the exception of Firm C, which shows an "alternative Berlin" that incorporates famous graffiti sites, local stories, and suburban cultures (see Fig. 2).
(2) Time and schedule: free walking tours follow the normal tour length, which is about two hours. Based on Boschma and Martin (2010), this pattern might be explained by the firms' need to reduce uncertainty and to conform to set routines and market expectations. Because of their tacit and cumulative nature, routines are not easy to change.

Despite the above observations, free walking tour firms might be considered young firms or "newcomers" to the economy, which may indeed have an important role to play in the evolution of economic systems (Stam, 2010). According to Stam (2010), citing Schumpeter (1934), by creating new variations (products, processes, business models) in the economy, such as free walking tours, these innovative new firms compete with incumbent firms, which in turn forces the latter to improve or change their production.

In the emergence of collaborative economy, firms have addressed consumer care by offering innovations, more choices, more service differentiation, better prices, and higher quality services (Koopman et al., 2014). Free walking tours are indeed providing more service differentiation and better prices for tourists, since it was observed that the majority of tourists participating in a free walking tour left a tip for their guide. Tips go from a common €5 tip to €20 or more depending on the

Fig. 2 Tourist observing graffiti during an alternative free walking tour in Berlin. Source: Authors

nationality of tourists. According to tour guides, North Americans and Australians are the most generous tippers. For a tour guide, this might be really lucrative since groups commonly number between 8 and 25 people. Normally in high season a tour guide could have 2 tours per day and work 5 days per week.

The development of free walking tours as a concept created by a traditional walking tour enterprise might be explained using Penrose's (1959) argument that when firms diversify and grow, they tend to expand into related products. In a dynamic economy, fitter routines become more dominant over time through selection, enabling more efficient firms with fitter routines to expand their production capacity and market share (Boschma & Martin, 2010). That is to say, new knowledge combined and applied to the business brings new products to the existing market. In this sense, free walking tours are a business concept innovation (Souto, 2015) or product innovation (Hjalager, 2010). According to Souto (2015), a business concept innovation is a mental model, a notion about the business that has potential to completely change companies.

Business concept innovation positively influences business model innovation and provides new trajectories outside the range of trajectories considered possible in existing business concepts (Souto, 2015). Nevertheless, and following Souto (2015), innovation allows a competitive advantage to be generated, acquired or replicated by other firms until it is replaced by other innovations. This might explain the number of start-ups that are taking part in the free walking tours scene not only in Europe, but also across the globe. However, entrepreneurship might be a crucial factor in the evolutionary redirection of tourism products and increasing competitiveness (Hjalager, 2010).

According to this research, 2010 was an average year for business start-ups. This finding confirmed Stokes et al.'s (2014) findings that 64% of firms operating within the collaborative economy were founded since 2010. Moreover, free walking tour firms based their activity on technology for selling their tours. This is confirmed since 45% of firms surveyed sell tours online. This finding emphasises the young, tech-driven nature of the collaborative economy (Stokes et al., 2014).

6.3 The Path-Dependency of Free Walking Tours

Addressing the second question raised in this chapter, this section focuses on whether free walking tours are an example of the collaborative economy or business-as-usual that appropriates an alternative economies logic. In particular, we will discuss free walking tours as a phenomenon based on the principle of path dependence.

According to Martin and Sunley (2006), all events, circumstances and decisions made in the past, even the most random and unintended, can have long-term consequences. In tourism, path dependence studies have shown how the historical legacy in a given region had an impact (either positively or negatively) on the evolution of the tourism economy over time (Brouder, 2014). Because the dynamics of evolutionary economic change are linked to the way in which political-economic agents operate, the actions of those agents may only be understood through their location in both historical and spatial dimensions.

Value creation in a walking tour is made through the information that is transmitted and interpreted by the tour guides. Therefore, the core of a walking tour is the act of guiding, what appears as "information" may thus be subtly transformed into an interpretation of the visited site intended to influence tourists' impressions and attitudes (Cohen, 1985). Guiding has been extensively discussed by Cohen (1985), and is not a new phenomenon. However, as Cohen (1985) points out, the process of transition from the original to the professional guide's role is closely related to two major sets of variables: the emergence and development of a tourist system, and the often concomitant arrival of institutionalised types of tourists on the tour.

As Cohen (1985) argued, tours have become routinised, advertised in travel brochures and listed in guidebooks, and commercial catering facilities are established or are co-opted at strategic locations along the routes. Furthermore, tourists become more demanding towards the guides, asking for improved service, more information and deeper interpretation of the sights. This leads to an institutionalisation of guiding and the professionalisation of tour guides. In this context, and following Cohen (1985), walking tours have been developed in the context of mass tourism where professional guides have operated mainly in urban areas, and usually working for large bureaucratised travel agencies and tour operators.

Free walking tour firms offer professional tours. On free walking tour firms' websites, for example, statements might read: "We provide travellers with professionally guided tours regardless of budget" (Free walking tour firm in Berlin); or "We offer high quality services" (Free walking tour in Sofia); or "Our guides are local professional guides" (Free walking tour firm in Barcelona). Thus, a professionalisation and institutionalisation of free walking tours is observed that reveals a build-up of the capitalist market structures often associated with mass tourism.

Corroborating this observation, in order to achieve professionalisation of their business activity, free walking tour firms develop a rigorous selection process for their guiding team. This selection process is similar to processes conducted by big enterprises around the world. Our fieldwork revealed that, once the guide has been selected through interviews, they undergo preparation for about 2 months and their performance is filmed so that they may conduct a tour in a language different to their mother tongue. On the first walking tour of a tour guide in Barcelona, for example, owners evaluated the guide's performance in situ by taking notes that helped them to improve their guiding services.

Free walking tours might claim to be the same as traditional tours. There are three steps observed in free walking tours which are similar to purchased tours: (1) introduction, which comprises a set of three sub-stages: (a) the reception of tourists by local guides at a central meeting point. Normally, free walking tours might be booked online, therefore, a confirmation of reservation is made by the guide in charge (see Fig. 3); (b) a general explanation is made by the guide in charge; and (c) the group is split into small groups with assignation to a specific tour guide. The second step is the unfolding of the tour by the guide assigned to each group. The third moment is the end of the tour. At this last moment, the guide asks tourists to make a post about their tour, and the guide mentions the need for good reviews in order to attract further business.

From the perspective of labour conditions, tour guides working with free walking tour firms and organisations are mainly free-lancers. According to our in-field research, guides must give their firms or organisation a minimum amount of money (a kind of a fee per person) which is calculated at between €2 and €5 per tourist. This formula guarantees a fixed income for the firms. However, most of the firms that offer free walking tours see their activity as sharing instead of selling. This statement was reflected at the answers provided by the firms online surveyed. They were asked if they considered free walking tours as "...a socio-economic model based on the shared usage of some kind of commodities", and 70% of respondents agreed with this definition.

Paradoxically, free walking tours are the most successful tours within their tour portfolio according to 70% of respondents. Free walking tours are also a way of connecting with tourists and introducing them to a wider range of payment products. For example, during a free walking tour it is quite normal to promote or sell

Fig. 3 Reception of tourists at the meeting point in Barcelona. Source: Authors

purchased tours. In fact, in a group tour followed in this research, seven people out of 25 purchased paid tours. This fact leads to consumer satisfaction with the service offered by free walking tours. Some of the informal talks with tourists illustrated this observation:

> "...I have done five free walking tours in Europe with the same firm because all the tour guides are quite professional and there is no difference from a payment tour, in fact, free walking tours are much better" (Female tourist from Colombia participating in a free walking tour in Barcelona).

> "... a good walking tour depends much on the guide, and the guides of free walking tours are quite good, I have also done a paid tour with this firm and it was fun" (Male tourist participating in a free walking tour in Berlin).

Although free walking tours may be seen as a collaborative economy phenomenon, there are overlapping processes that mix traditional capitalism with an alternative economy.

7 Discussion and Conclusions

This chapter explores free walking tours within the basic features of the collaborative economy and draws theoretical and practical insights. The findings from the case study provide some answers for the questions raised by Dredge and Gyimóthy (2015) in the sense of an understanding how this new collaborative market and its actors operate, and whether the collaborative economy is just business-as-usual or appropriates an alternative economies logic.

In this chapter, we start from the micro level, focusing on the economic behaviour of free walking tours firms, and how these firms behave within the collaborative economy and how their business strategies and routines are shaped. This leads to firm dynamics in the collaborative economic landscape: some firms are new on the free walking tours market and some are established tourism firms that have increased their market share in the walking tour sector. As we discussed, although firms operating with free walking tours are new business and predominantly small-sized enterprises, traditional and big companies are also looking for a space in this sharing market.

Essletzbichler and Rigby (2010) argued that economic growth and change in the economy might be understood as a simple aggregate of changes in the characteristics of individual business units. Therefore, we might claim that the collaborative economy is a change, but not a disruption within the economy due to aggregate changes inside tourism firms. Tourism firms have adapted to the social and cultural changes produced during the nineties, a turning point in the contemporary history of economic geography (Amin & Thrift, 2000; Bathelt & Glückler, 2003; Yeoung, 2005). These changes have permeated the tourist sphere and been represented in post-industrial practices, and are reflected in the production, distribution and consumption of goods and services in all sectors.

The demand from consumers for an alternative production and supply system to that of industrial production prompts the development of alternative goods and services to those provided by the mass production system. These alternative services are visible on the tourism industry in many ways. Post-industrialism, as a context of action, has brought about a change in the way we perceive and conceive tourism, orienting it towards the flexibility of the product offer and the meeting the personalised needs of tourists who are increasingly seeking to create new experiences. In this context, free walking tours are a manifestation of post-industrial tourism and are creating a new economic relationships based on access to services and products without structured payment, which is a trend driving part of the collaborative economy (Stokes et al., 2014). Customers are able to test product quality and not feel pushed to pay for it. Free walking tours are an affordable product on the tourism market that, in some way, is redistributing the economic value of tourism. However, it can also be claimed that this new product is delivered through a traditional Business to Customer (B2C) model. In this sense, the collaborative economy is more than just disrupting tourism, it is transforming the economic relationships among business and customers within tourism.

From the evolutionary approach, it is important to recognise that the actions of individual agents such as firms occur within contexts that are shaped by broader institutional structures that are themselves created and that evolve over time. Some of these institutions are more durable than others, such as the capitalist modes of production (Essletzbichler & Rigby, 2010). Free walking tours firms reproduce this embedded capitalist mode of production. However, at the same time they are helping customers to save money and this fits into the collaborative economy practices described by Stokes et al. (2014). Free walking tour firms can represent a hybrid relationship, made up of capitalist and collaborative economy practices because, as Brouder and Eriksson (2013) state, the economy is seen as an open system subject to constant dynamic interactions with surrounding agents. Within a post-industrial tourism system, which is more hybridised than the industrial one, there are overlapping processes and practices in traditional supply chains (i.e. structure of the guided tour system) which are breaking down. This case study suggests a path dependence process where tourism firms in traditional capitalist economy are also adopting features of the collaborative economy in terms of firm behaviour and performance. The presence of overlapping processes between the traditional capitalist economy and the collaborative economy performed by the free walking tour firms in this study suggests an evolutionary process resulting from business competition and a specific market environment.

The selection of the environment where firms operate is the result of resources such as knowledge and information. Knowledge creation and accumulation leads to innovation. Therefore, free walking tours might be seen as a business concept innovation that attracts new customers. This new concept and its everyday practices are transforming the tourism scene and have a significant impact on tourist destinations. In this light, free walking tours represent not only concept innovation, based on Hjalager's (2010) classification of innovations, but they were also identified as management and institutional innovations, which positions free walking tours as part of a network that enables and improves firm performance.

On the other hand, free walking tours may be seen as a new marketing strategy—a new business concept developed by firms and embedded in traditional market structures—where one of the main goals is to attract tourists and introduce them to traditional products. Free walking tours show a high level of customer satisfaction and loyalty due to high quality standards of service. In this framework, we may claim that free walking tour firms are path dependent because they are reproducing capitalist market structures visible across five main dimensions: (a) the professionalisation of free walking tours; (b) the staff selection process; (c) labour conditions; (d) marketing strategies; and (e) customer loyalty. In addition, firms operating within the collaborative economy rely on the development of trust, where online reviews shape their reputational capital. Tour guides are the interface between the host destination and visitors and their activity is crucial for shaping the visitor experience.

The Berlin and Barcelona cases illustrate that free walking tours are a localised phenomenon, produced mainly in cities where the impact of tourism is significant. Local and non-local tourism firms identify free walking tours as a lucrative market niche to enter. Therefore, firms that claim to be collaborative are rooted in traditional capitalist market structures, where the creation of economic value constitutes an important driver for its operation, even though firms do not see themselves in this way. In short, this empirical study of free walking tour firms has made many observations and raised a variety of issues and concerns. We have argued for an evolutionary economic lens to understand what is going on, and it has revealed useful insights in the case of free walking tours. This study is, therefore, helpful in understanding tourism firm behaviour in new economic contexts such as the collaborative economy, and it provides a starting point for more in-depth studies in the future.

References

Amin, A., & Thrift, N. (2000). What kind of economic theory for what kind of economic geography. *Antipode, 32*, 4–9.

Ap, J., & Wong, K. (2001). Case study on tour guiding: professionalism, issues and problems. *Tourism Management, 22*(5), 551–563. doi:10.1016/S0261-5177(01)00013-9.

Baker, V. (2013, June 12). *The rise of the 'free' city tour*. The Guardian. Accessed March 22, 2015, from https://www.theguardian.com/travel/2013/jun/12/free-pay-you-want-city-tours

Barcelona Turisme. (2014). *Estadístiques de Turisme a Barcelona*. Barcelona: Turisme de Barcelona.

Bathelt, H., & Glückler, J. (2003). Toward a relational economic geography. *Journal of Economic Geography, 3*(2), 117–144. doi:10.1093/jeg/3.2.117.

Bathelt, H., & Glückler, J. (2011). *The relational economy. Geographies of knowing and learning*. Oxford: Oxford University Press.

Belk, R. (2014). You are what you can access: Sharing and collaborative consumption online. *Journal of Business Research, 67*(8), 1595–1600.

Benson-Rea, M., Roderick, J., & Herbert Sima, S. (2013). The plurality of coexisting business models: Investigating the complexity of value drivers. *Industrial Marketing Management, 42*, 717–729.

Boschma, R., & Martin, R. (Eds.). (2010). *The handbook of evolutionary economic geography*. Cheltenham: Edward Elgar.

Brouder, P. (2014). Evolutionary economic geography: A new path for tourism studies? *Tourism Geographies, 16*(1), 2–7.

Brouder, P., & Eriksson, R. H. (2013). Tourism evolution: On the synergies of tourism studies and evolutionary economic geography. *Annals of Tourism Research, 43*, 370–383. doi:10.1016/j.annals.2013.07.001.

Cohen, E. (1985). The tourist guide: The origins, structure and dynamics of a role. *Annals of Tourism Research, 12*, 5–29.

Cohen, W. M., & Levinthal, D. A. (1990). Absorptive capacity: A new perspective on learning and innovation. *Administrative Science Quarterly, 35*, 128–153.

Compass. (2015). *The global start-up ecosystem ranking report*. San Francisco: Start-up Compass.

Cooke, P., & Laurentis, C. (2010). Evolutionary economic geography: Regional systems of innovation and high-tech clusters. In R. Boschma & R. Martin (Eds.), *Handbook of evolutionary economic geography* (pp. 239–260). Cheltenham: Edward Elgar.

David, P. A. (1994). Why are institutions the 'carriers of history'? Path dependence and the evolution of conventions, organizations and institutions. *Structural Change and Economic Dynamics, 5*(2), 205–220.

Denicolai, S., Zucchella, A., & Cioccarelli, G. (2010). Clusters, networks and economic development: An evolutionary economics perspective. In R. Boschma & R. Martin (Eds.), *Handbook of evolutionary economic geography* (pp. 280–297). Cheltenham: Edward Elgar.

Dosi, G. (1988). Sources, procedures and microeconomic effects of innovation. *Journal of Economic Literature, 26*, 1120–1171.

Dredge, D., & Gyimóthy, S. (2015). Tourism and the collaborative economy: Critical perspectives, questionable claims and silenced voices. *Tourism Recreation Research, 40*(3), 286–302.

Essletzbichler, J., & Rigby, D. L. (2010). Generalized Darwinism and evolutionary economic geography. In R. Boschma & R. Martin (Eds.), *Handbook of evolutionary economic geography* (pp. 43–61). Cheltenham: Edward Elgar.
European Business Innovation Observatory. (2013). *The sharing economy: Accessibility, based business models for peer-to-peer markets*. Brussels: European Commission.
Gill, A. M., & Williams, P. W. (2011). Rethinking resort growth: Understanding evolving governance strategies in Whistler, British Columbia. *Journal of Sustainable Tourism, 19* (4–5), 629–648. doi:10.1080/09669582.2011.558626.
Giuliani, E. (2007). The selective nature of knowledge networks in clusters: Evidence from the wine industry. *Journal of Economic Geography, 7*(2), 139–168.
Giuliani, E. (2010). Clusters, networks and economic development: An evolutionary economics perspective. In R. Boschma & R. Martin (Eds.), *Handbook of evolutionary economic geography* (pp. 261–279). Cheltenham: Edward Elgar.
Glückler, J. (2007). Economic geography and the evolution of networks. *Journal of Economic Geography, 7*, 619–634.
Granovetter, M. (1985). Economic action and social structure: The problem of embeddedness. *American Journal of Sociology, 91*, 481–510.
Halkier, H., & Therkelsen, A. (2013). Exploring tourism destination path plasticity, the case of coastal tourism in North Jutland, Denmark. *ZeitschriftfuerWirtschaftsgeographie, 57*, 39–51.
Hjalager, A. M. (2010). A review of innovation research in tourism. *Tourism Management, 31*, 1–12. doi:10.1016/j.tourman.2009.08.012.
Koopman, C., Mitchell, M., & Thierer, A. (2014). *The sharing economy and customer protection regulation: The case for policy change*. Fairfax: Mercatus Center, George Mason University.
Ma, M., & Hassink, R. (2013). An evolutionary perspective on tourism area development. *Annals of Tourism Research, 41*, 89–109.
Markwell, K., Stevenson, D., & Rowe, D. (2004). Footsteps and memories: Interpreting an Australian urban landscape through thematic walking tours. *International Journal of Heritage Studies, 10*(5), 457–473. doi:10.1080/1352725042000299063.
Martin, R., & Sunley, P. (2006). Path dependence and regional economic evolution. *Journal of Economic Geography, 6*, 395–438.
Martin, R., & Sunley, P. (2010). The place of path dependence in an evolutionary perspective on the economic landscape. In R. Boschma & R. Martin (Eds.), *Handbook of evolutionary economic geography* (pp. 62–92). Cheltenham: Edward Elgar.
Martínez-Román, J., Tamayo, J. A., Gamero, J., & Romero, J. E. (2015). Innovativeness and business performances in tourism SMEs. *Annals of Tourism Research, 54*, 118–135. http://dx.doi.org/10.1016/j.annals.2015.07.004
Metcalfe, J. S., Foster, J., & Ramlogan, R. (2006). Adaptive economic growth. *Cambridge Journal of Economics, 30*, 7–32.
Nelson, R., & Winter, S. (1982). *An evolutionary theory of economic change*. Cambridge: Harvard University Press.
Nonaka, I. (1991). The knowledge creating company. *Harvard Business Review, 69*(6), 96–104.
Owyang, J., Samuel, A., & Grennville, A. (2014). *Sharing is the new buying: How to win in the collaborative economy*. Vision Critical. https://www.visioncritical.com/resources/collaborative-economy-report/
Penrose, E. (1959). *The theory of the growth of the firm*. Oxford: Oxford University Press.
Polanyi, M. (1966). *The tacit dimension*. London: Routledge & Kegan Paul.
Sanz-Ibañez, C., & Anton Clavé, S. (2014). The evolution of destinations: Towards an evolutionary and relational economic geography approach. *Tourism Geographies, 16*(4), 563–579.
Schumpeter, J. A. (1934). *The theory of economic development*. Cambridge, MA: Harvard University Press.
Shaw, G., & Williams, A. (2009). Knowledge transfer and management in tourism organisations: An emerging research agenda. *Tourism Management, 30*(3), 325–335.
Souto, J. E. (2015). Business model innovation and business concept innovation as the context of incremental innovation and radical innovation. *Tourism Management, 51*, 142–155. doi:10.1016/j.tourman.2015.05.017.

Stam, E. (2010). Entrepreneurship, evolution and geography. In R. Boschma & R. Martin (Eds.), *Handbook of evolutionary economic geography* (pp. 139–161). Cheltenham: Edward Elgar.
Stokes, K., Clarence, E., Anderson, L., & Rinne, A. (2014). *Making sense of the UK Collaborative Economy*. London: Nesta and Collaborative Lab.
The European Cities Marketing (ECM). (2014). *Benchmarking report 2013–2014*. Paris: European Cities Marketing.
Visit Berlin. (2015). *Annual Report, everything about Berlin*. Berlin Tourism and Congress GmBH.
Yeoung, H. W. C. (2005). Rethinking relational economic geography. *Transactions of the Institute of British Geographers, 30*(1), 37–51.

Airbnb: Turning the Collaborative Economy into a Collaborative Society

D. Michael O'Regan and Jaeyeon Choe

Abstract New decentralised collaborative platforms are said to be challenging and redesigning traditional business models and reinventing how the tourism business works. Collectively termed the 'collaborative economy', these platforms are increasingly intersecting with the established tourism industry and how a tourist interacts with host communities, destinations and other tourists. By utilising the concept of cultural capitalism to explore the global "disruptive" brand Airbnb, we find that the collaborative economy is not about collaboration at all, and argue that the Airbnb platform is merely reinforcing the values of consumer capitalist society by providing a more efficient means to satisfy tourist wants and desires. While we conclude that collaborative economy in its manifest forms will continue, we believe the tourism industry is well placed to address its impacts, and recommend that authorities should recognise parts of the collaborative economy as predatory laissez-faire platform capitalism in need of regulation.

Keywords Collaborative economy • Sharing economy • Sustainability • Airbnb • Hospitality • Tourism

1 Introduction

We are told we are undergoing a rapid explosion in sharing, bartering, lending, trading, renting and swapping, scaled up in ways never before possible because of new social technologies as well as economic and environmental imperatives. We are told that a new consumptive model is moving tourists and even societies away from hyper-consumption while increasing access to wealth and employment. Its economics of scope is said to offer protection from food, energy and resource scarcity, falling public investment in infrastructure, increasing food prices, unemployment, housing costs and natural disasters. Botsman (2012) believes the collaborative economy is as potentially as important as the industrial revolution as it

D. Michael O'Regan (✉) • J. Choe
Faculty of Management, Bournemouth University, Dorset House D154, Talbot Campus, Fern Barrow, Poole BH12 5BB, UK
e-mail: michael.oregan@gmail.com; jchoe@bournemouth.ac.uk

D. Dredge, S. Gyimóthy (eds.), *Collaborative Economy and Tourism*,
Tourism on the Verge, DOI 10.1007/978-3-319-51799-5_9

reinvents consumer and business models by unlocking assets and driving new sustainable marketplaces as well as productivity, entrepreneurship, intercultural understanding and innovation. This new model is focused on reinventing traditional sharing, re-distributing, bartering, lending, trading, renting, gifting, and swapping through technology and peer communities. It depends on and/or can create new kinds of relationships, changing how we consume, socialise and move. Collectively termed the 'collaborative economy', it presents itself to us in multiple, shifting forms. It has been called the peer-to-peer economy, the access economy, the gig economy, shared capitalism, the on-demand economy, hippienomics, the people economy and the enabling economy. As an encompassing label, Rachel Botsman (2015), a global authority on the collaborative economy, describes it as an "an economic system of decentralized networks and marketplaces that unlocks the value of underused assets by matching needs and haves, in ways that bypass traditional middlemen." The collaborative economy sector has attracted entrepreneurs, the public sector, venture capitalists and start-up corporations to a sector with an estimated a global worth of US$335 billion by 2025 (PwC, 2014). It has also attracted those with consistent and specific motivations to offer, share or lease products, skills and capital deemed valuable to tourist desires and needs. A United States consumer survey conducted by the Travel Technology Association and the Internet Association reported that in 2015 that nearly half of all Americans (46%) participated in one or more aspects of the sharing economy (King, 2015).

Using the concept of cultural capitalism, which refers to the application of capitalist theory to cultural affairs, this paper reveals how critical questions are not being asked about the collaborative economy and explores the unbalanced, short-term and ahistorical rhetoric fostered by collaborative economy evangelists such as Brian Chesky, the co-founder and CEO of Airbnb. We utilise Airbnb as an example of a collaborative economy platform which is said to be disrupting and reshaping the tourism industry and tourist destinations. Through the prism of cultural capitalism, we identify both the impacts of Airbnb on cultural, economic, political, and consumer worlds as well as the opportunities and challenges that Airbnb is bringing the established tourism industry.

2 Theoretical Framework

2.1 Cultural Capitalism

"Cultural capitalism" is a concept developed and/or used by Rifkin (2000), Žižek (2009a) and Holloway (2010) to address a phenomenon that they believe is a new stage of commodification that does not change the basic rules of capitalism. They describe a world where the relationship between an object and its symbol-image is inverted, as an image no longer represents the product, but, rather, the product represents an image (Žižek, 2006). We no longer buy products we want to own, but seek life-experiences to render life meaningful. In a new age of access, where in the "declining relevance of physical capital, the ascendancy of intangible assets, the metamorphosis of goods into pure services" (Rifkin, 2000, p. 114), businesses are increasingly mining assets and resources, and turning them into commodified life experiences and brand communities.

As 'everything is accessed' (Rifkin, 2000, p. 6), experiences are increasingly offered for low transactional cost in order to seduce tourists into buying the true "experiential commodity". Experiential tourism is being immersed as you experience a place, with an increasing popularity of homestays, cooking and craft classes. Access to yachts, private homes and luxury cars serve merely as props, while access to local guides, home cooked meals and paid for romantic dates with locals highlight how the intimate, social and cultural spheres are being pulled into the commercial sphere through vast supplier-user networks controlled primarily by private companies. Žižek (2009a, p. 52) argues that no one any longer sells (and buys), but "in order to render our lives pleasurable and meaningful," one becomes server or client, supplier or user as "social relationality in its very fluidity is directly the object of marketing and exchange" (Žižek, 2009a, p. 139). Holloway (2010) argues that cultural capitalism is the means to expand the capitalist economy by way of capital accumulation in the face of a global, structural crisis. Just as capitalism surged on the dot.com boom as corporations unlocked peoples' homes using sub-prime refinancing (Harvey, 1989), the collaborative economy mines an individual's assets and resources. Collaborative economy platforms have been fully integrated into the market economy by raiding, cracking open, exploiting and releasing surplus value by using resources from private and public sources and repackaging them as cultural commodities and entertainment for the short-term benefit of stockholders, entrepreneurs and venture capitalists, as well as the ultimate tourist consumer.

Collaborative economy platforms have flourished in this context as they seek to persuade people to leverage physical, network, mobility, economic, cultural, human, social assets and other resources so as to capitalise on their liquid and economic value by renting (sharing, leasing) them out to those that demand them. By connecting individuals to information, other people, objects, ideas, lifestyles, capital and physical things such as cars, apartments, tools, relationships, time, bodies and friendship in more efficient ways, rhetoric by collaborative economy evangelists such as Chase (2015), Howard (2015), Kramer (2015) and Krakovsky (2015) claim that the collaborative economy offers health, emotional and spiritual benefits, as well as boosting living standards across the many countries which they span. Blurring the lines between personal-commercial and private-public, anyone can use their assets and resources such as cars (to lease), spaces (parking, a spare room), skills (food preparation, tour guiding, driving) and other goods, products, services and utilities. Tourist focused businesses that seek to unlock 'idling capacity' through platforms that market them as experiences include Dopios (connects travellers with locals who serve as guides and drivers), UrbanBuddy (local concierge), Dufl (someone to pack your suitcase), EatWith (meals cooked by locals), TravellerChic (local dates) and Bellhop (room service provided by locals).

These new businesses are an evolution in the ways they connect tourists with locals, with Botsman and Rogers (2011) describing collaborative economy platforms as a means to disrupt "out-dated" consumption and "anti-innovation" business models propagated by entrenched and monopolistic elements within travel and tourism such as car hire companies, hotel groups and airlines. Largely meeting market-exchangeable needs, with asset owners acting on economic-oriented motivations on the supply side (Hamari & Ukkonen, 2013), these new businesses have recognised the scarcity in tourist infrastructure and experiences, and have sought to trade in these resources using market values. Airbnb has been the leading disruptive innovator in the industry, which Brian Chesky, in his own words, describes as a platform that provides access to social and cultural experiences by helping tourists on a budget visit destinations they might otherwise not go because of cost, as well as unlock latent market demand and thereby offer growth potentials in an otherwise competitive and saturated tourism marketplace (Stephany, 2015).

3 Airbnb

3.1 The Rise and Rise of AIRBNB Inc.

For many, Airbnb is a champion in the libertarian revolt against the oppressive social organisations characterised by entrenched out-dated business models and big government (Lux, 2015). Founded in 2008, Airbnb is part of a new generation of businesses that have, embraced the egalitarian and anti-hierarchical rhetoric of the counterculture to match its many hosts with tourists who rent out their homes and rooms for a fee. It is a strategy that has seen Airbnb increase its value to US$25 billion in 2015 by generating upward of two million listings across more than 34,000 cities across the globe. While striving for an efficient use of existing resources, Airbnb has grown to a global brand by avoiding what they see as outdated regulations, and spending vast sums lobbing lawmakers to deregulate what they see as excessive regulation covering the accommodation sector. Their head of global policy and public affairs, Chris Lehane, who once served as the adviser to former US President Bill Clinton, has lobbied across the globe for a facilitating legal environment. They argue that they should be exempt from existing regulations because their services are ordered over the Web and therefore not subject to 'local' regulation such as existing local housing ordinances or laws pertaining to fire and safety inspections. In practice, this means, for example that in New York, 72%, or more than 25,000 of short-term Airbnb rentals, violate local laws (Schneiderman, 2014).

3.2 Airbnb and Control

Airbnb is a well-funded for-profit business with a vertical, linear structure that uses user interfaces, software and algorithms on its platform to control what is shared, with whom, and for what purposes. It rides on the network effect of the more people who join Airbnb, the more useful it is and the more valuable it becomes as a vehicle to generate revenue. However, the more people join, the more power and control Airbnb have over sellers, who have little to no control over the platforms rules, software, and even their reputation (Gurvich, Lariviere, & Moreno-Garcia, 2015). Žižek (2012, p. 165) argues that contemporary capitalist modernisers like Airbnb seek to "diversify, devolve power, and try to mobilise local creativity and self-organisation", without retaining any of the risks and responsibilities to these independent contractors (Dredge & Gyimóthy, 2015). At the same time that Airbnb promotes itself as a platform for those who have financially over extended themselves in a turbulent world economy, Airbnb exercises control over the conditions and terms by which users secure access to the Airbnb marketplace. At a time of joblessness and high debt levels, as well as poverty in many tourist destinations, Chesky encouraged people to extract value or productivity from their assets to offset rent or mortgages, and make life/austerity/depth bearable. He notes that "I assumed this was a trend that would happen in the aftermath of the recession [in 2008]... I didn't realise this was something that will sustain and become a part of people's lives. It's not too surprising because that's the reason we started this company. We started this because we couldn't afford to pay rent and it allowed me to keep my home in San Francisco. Without being able to rent my rooms, how would I have paid rent?" (Ahmed, 2014).

While lowering start-up friction costs (in the absence of paperwork), there are no protections like health coverage, insurance against injuries, paid vacations, pensions, maximum working hours, a stable income, job security and other safeguards for those hosting via Airbnb and many of those working in the Airbnb ecosystem. From Guesthop (check-in and concierge service) to Proprly (cleaning), Airbnb has facilitated a world without taxes, hourly ceilings, anti-discrimination laws, unions, health and safety regulations and minimum wages. Airbnb does not offer a physical place of work, training, infrastructure or education, and frequently varies the incentives for hosts (i.e. charging hosts an additional 12–15% fee for each booking if their guest found the listing through Google advertising). Data provided by Airbnb rarely reflects host expenses, given sellers must pay third parties (e.g. insurance and self-employment taxes) and other hidden costs of participation, such as the high degree of emotional labour—smiling and conveying friendliness and use of personal time (Hochschild 2003). Through Airbnb videos, guidebooks, and Airbnb Mentors, individuals are trained how to behave and provide hospitality as hosts. As a fragmented, individualistic, temporary, insecure labour force, these "micro-entrepreneurs" have, through little fault of their own, undermined hard-fought protections and regulatory frameworks.

By addressing output over outcome, Airbnb have gained control by way of a superior-subordinate relationship. This is manifested in sellers' fear of algorithms (how they appear in customers' search results) and hidden aspects of algorithms making (or ruining) reputations. While calling its hosts "micro-entrepreneurs", Airbnb controls the keys to the relationship by controlling demand through algorithms, and asking these entrepreneurs to rely on Airbnb to generate leads, market their properties and take payment. The control a seller has (i.e. in setting prices, work hours, income, reputations and refund policies) is exaggerated, as Airbnb terms and conditions supersede their preferences. Given Airbnb is among the top travel booking sites on the planet, its hosts may have few alternatives to source business. Airbnb for example, can delist hosts for no reason (Lynam, 2016), does not allow the host and guest trade email addresses and has very particular demands for hosts to meet the requirements to be a "business ready" host (i.e. no pets, no smoking). For a private corporation, they are also intrusive, by requiring hosts to upload government issued identity documents into third party "secured servers", whilst arguing that the demand by local authorities for the same information about hosting activities is a violation of privacy. In addition, control also includes the fear of leaving a platform because of its "lock-in" nature, high switching costs (inability to move data and reputations to another platform), and the suggestions offered to hosts through the site via their hosting toolkit and hosting tips. The host prices that emerge on Airbnb through its Aerosolve pricing system are created by algorithms that simulate market mechanisms, and are not the result of the free play of supply and demand. The effect ensures prices are set within 5% of Airbnb's algorithmic result, and may lead to surge holiday accommodation pricing. As well as increasing the amount generated from its transactional cut (i.e. Airbnb take approximately 13% off every booking), the Aerosolve pricing system blurs the line between Airbnb as a marketplace and as a more controlling actor.

3.3 Reputation and Capital on Airbnb

Airbnb is dependent on confirming identity, so as to create trust between strangers and enabling trust to be conveyed by way of a bidirectional rating systems, background checks, and frictionless payment systems. Brian Chesky strongly believes that reputation not only serves as a psychological reward or currency, but also as an actual currency, as "[t]he more you broadcast your reputation, the more you'll have access too" (Ferenstein, 2014). By using various verification systems such as giving access to one's social graph on Facebook, creating personal profiles, peer reviews ratings and official verifications (passport, background checks), one is supposed to build reputation capital on Airbnb over time. However, market-based reputation is often about control, manipulation and discipline rather than transparency and accountability. A damaged reputation, even when playing the role of a dutiful and dependent host, may result in the movement of capital away from a host. A tourist's negative review of an Airbnb host because of poor Wi-Fi signal strength can lead to a hosts' account been downgraded in search results. For Debord (1998, p. 18), reputations have become 'malleable and alterable at will by those who control all information.' Debord argues that you cannot believe anything about anyone that you have not directly learned for yourself, with Airbnb customer ratings found to be unreliable and skewed (Zervas, Proserpio, & Byers, 2015b). Airbnb eliminates the possibility that buyers and sellers ever come into contact without some trust mechanism, which in turn makes relationships dispensable. One can leave a reference for the 'Other,' out of lack of pity, empathy or spite, leading to the commodification of culture, and the cultural interaction between hosts and guests.

Airbnb notes in its terms of use, that it merely provides an online platform that connects hosts who have accommodations to rent with guests seeking to rent such accommodations. It notes that Airbnb has "no control over the conduct" of hosts or guests. Airbnb have been accused of facilitating discrimination, with Airbnb hosts in various parts of the world allegedly denying service to consumers with wheelchairs, minorities and guide dog owners. A study by Wang, Xi, and Gilheany (2015) revealed the prevalence of racial discrimination among hosts in California, while another study by Edelman, Luca, and Svirsky (2015) also concluded that Airbnb facilitates discrimination based on a host's race, gender, age, or other characteristics. There is also no reputation mechanism to assist either hosts or tourists denied the use of Airbnb because of discrimination or access to protections that may normally cover accommodation provision and use. A destination fulfilled by only Airbnb may see bodies that are coloured, disabled, queer, sick and obese categorised as 'out of place' by some hosts. There is no backstop to hosts' discriminating, or Airbnb facilitating the threat of violence, racism, sexism and homophobia. Yet Airbnb seeks to control any measures that threaten the extractive nature of their platforms by appealing to their consumers-sellers to push regulators to loosen restrictions and regulatory protections.

3.4 Airbnb's Future Plans

"Dead Capital" is an economic term related to assets which are informally held, but are not legally recognised and not easily bought, sold, valued or used. Airbnb seeks to exploit the precise dead capital of each seller by forcing the value incorporated inside assets, such as socialised spaces like a private home into the open where they can be re-enclosed and commodified. Given that the majority of the world's population are denied access to valuable property or asset ownership, people will increasingly leverage everything they have. The goal of cultural capitalism is to commodify everything, including human relationships, in a process of 'making things exchangeable on markets either actually and/or discursively by framing things as if they were exchangeable' (Sevignani, 2013, p. 733). As the physical economy is shrinking (Rifkin, 2000), the new operative term is "lifetime value" (LTV). This is the theoretical measure of how much a human being is worth if every moment of his or her life were to be commodified in one form or another in the commercial sphere. In 2014, Airbnb began experimenting with a plan to turn their host's homes into restaurants. A San Francisco pilot let diners eat at hosts' homes for US$25 for a three-course meal. In 2015, it launched a pilot option offering "hand-crafted" package holidays and listings especially for business travellers.

Anchored in commerce and enclosure, hosts are not only tourist infrastructure, but also corporate activists. Airbnb has embedded tools and incentives on its site to mobilise hosts in support of less restrictive regulations. Its community organiser program uses hosts to advocate for the company, while also paying its host community directly (e.g. US$10 credit for a 2014 campaign to promote Airbnb thought social media). In fighting Proposition F, a ballot to restrict short-term rentals in San Francisco in 2015, Airbnb asked its hosts to join a local action team to fight the measure by writing to politicians, attend rallies, and become an involved volunteer. Airbnb is also introducing a network of home-sharing guilds in cities across the North America in 2016 to act for the corporation, and become a formidable voting constituency as well offering training, tools and support to these guilds to influence leading elected officials and organisations. This may help to ensure that Airbnb see off future policies or laws that act against its interests.

4 Discussion

Airbnb incorporates the language of the underdog, whilst taking on monopolistic tendencies and accepting existing socio-economic relations built on the conventional economy. Created through venture-capital-backing and a hierarchical structure, it facilitates little more than a transactional form of "collaboration". The utopian spin and frontend of such a service-oriented platform offers the pretence of collaboration, solidarity, community, equality, trust, sustainability, mobility justice, reciprocity and altruism. Airbnb has claimed that they reduce pollution and poverty, and provide more authentic tourist experiences by lowering transaction costs. Botsman and Rogers (2011, p. 216) argue that the collaborative economy is a "systems change", because it converts hyper-consumption into "fewer products, more efficient usage, less material consumed, reduced waste and more social capital" as well as "mopping up the surplus created by overproduction and consumption" (ibid, xvi). Airbnb has been adept at promoting socio-ideological motifs (care for the environment, social responsibility, communal life, social solidarity) and geographical imaginaries (autonomy, intimacy, authenticity) to legitimise their business model. Žižek (2011, p. 236) argues that cultural capitalism promotes solutions as "containing or providing the remedy against the consumerist excess", such as doing one's social and ecological duty. Airbnb evokes the rebellious and anti-establishment spirit of its co-founders, and makes use of its platform for symbolic acts of personal commitment to the causes they invoke (Rifkin, 2000). Paraphrasing Žižek (2009b), tourists are evoked to buy into redemption by being a consumerist. By selling varying slogans and ideas, as helping the environment, or restoring a sense of community, tourist endeavours on Airbnb become capitalism with a human face (Žižek, 2009b). Its 2015 "Never a Stranger" campaign sought to position it itself as sustainable, culturally immersive and a transformative travel experience in cities including Paris, Tokyo, Rio, New York, and Tulum in Mexico. The campaign shows a highly idealised version of the host/guest relationship where a young woman travelling alone buys into a life-style, where consumption and anti-consumerism have been brought together. Latching onto our inherent sentimentality and care for humanity, it promises us we can all feel good (and safe) about using the platform and using the local resources of hosts.

There is nothing wrong with collaboration, sharing, making money or indeed technology. The collaborative economy may be a more efficient means to satisfy every tourist want and desire by expanding lifestyles, niches and brands and may through unintended effects, create some positive social and environmental benefits. Airbnb, however, will not end the financial crisis, climate change, peak oil, inequality, resource scarcity, loss of biodiversity and ecosystem resilience and unemployment. It will not contribute, to any great degree, to a more sustainable world, or more sustainable tourism marketplaces. Airbnb will not create secure and stable jobs and generate greater trust amongst hosts and guests. There is absolutely no evidence to suggest that Airbnb can offset ecological and human damage, make us greener or more ethical tourists and make up for inequality. While Fiske (1992) argues that individuals can live simultaneously in a world where social norms prevail, and where market norms make the rules, Zelizer (2005) argues that trouble ensues when social and market norms collide.

Airbnb ensures that lines between public and private, community and the market, production and consumption, voluntary activity and precarious exploitation, commercial and intimate life, market and non-market, economic value and personal life become more permeable and harder to discern. For governments, these blurred lines mean the illusion of income creation, micro-entrepreneurship, and it makes the degradation of labor, socio-spatial inequalities, intimacy and distributional conflicts associated with Airbnb (somehow) irrelevant. Given that Airbnb is designed to nurture the needs of those who can afford access to paid hosts on the platform, there is a potential breakdown of reciprocity, intimacy, sympathy, understanding and trust between those who perform services and those who pay for them. In a dystopian future, a seller's day might include collecting tourists from the airport, sharing their house, cooking meals, doing their laundry, walking their dog, minding their children and packing their bags. While receiving everything one desires by a commoditised transaction at the touch of an app can be liberating for tourists, it can also be dehumanising, even though Airbnb seeks to conceal any monetising of interaction and intimacy through frictionless payment systems. Our understanding of tourism as a composite commons is being changed by Airbnb in both striking and subtle ways. From demonstrations in Barcelona, where Airbnb is accused of pushing out locals in the old quarter of the city (Arias-Sans & Quaglieri Domínguez, 2016) to the ways we lose something when we forget how to value things without a price tag, a more individualistic, transactional, less creative commons may lead to more manipulation, exploitation, abuse and conflict. The concept of ethical consumption or responsible tourism where autonomy, community or participation is valued now seems quaint as values become guided by the logic of the market.

As the substance and integrity of social life weakens as businesses market interactions, emotions, time and bodies as depreciating assets, the very notion of what can be shared, bought and rented has transformed. As the walls between intimate lives, social relations, community and the market become permeable, what was once thought unthinkable to buy or sell has changed. While one's intimate or private life will never be ruled by the absolute logic of market, the collaborative economy is driving a new kind of flatness or depthlessness (Jameson, 1984, p. 60), leading to the "reductionism of all beings and all cultural differences to a common commodified form" (Harvey, 2000, p. 83). The more you give away via the collaborative economy, the more commercially customised your world becomes. As economic activity degrades intimate relationships (Zelizer, 2005), the very source of culture on which tourism feeds is threatened. As information, knowledge, and culture are produced through market rather than social relations, the lines of difference between culture, entertainment, information and consumption become blurred to such an extent, that almost everything viewed or interacted with becomes an act or object of consumption. Market morality encourages tourists to seek the ease of market exchanges for experiences over serendipity, the uniqueness of the locale, a nuanced appreciation of journey and relationships. The expansion into intimate lives flattens the texture of the social fabric, and the illusion of affluence pushes the poorest, with little to share and little to lose into new terrains of rent extraction (Kaminska, 2015), and a subsequent reduction of the value and meaning of a human life.

4.1 Turning the Collaborative Economy into a Collaborative Society

As an increasing number of politicians and policy makers around the globe adopt the collaborative economy, and destinations such as Amsterdam, Seoul, London and San Francisco describe themselves as "Sharing Cities", Airbnb and similar platforms are here to stay. The collaborative economy can work in many areas of the economy, if sharing businesses work with cities and destinations. However, governments (and unions) must play a pivotal role in ensuring the collaborative economy is more than a modality of economic production (Benkler, 2006), and understand how Airbnb, in particular, violates the spirit and the letter of the law. Its fear of regulation saw it launch an aggressive US$8 million advertising campaign on local TV, billboards and social media in San Francisco in 2015. Using consultants, researchers, canvassers and social media specialists to make the case against regulation, they defeated the measure. Despite this, political debate about the role of the Airbnb, their actual contributions to public good, autonomy and external costs (inequality, discrimination and social exclusion generated by platform use) is slowly emerging. Studies indicate that Airbnb can push up rents (Kusisto, 2015), hit small and medium hotel room revenue (Zervas, Proserpio, & Byers, 2015a) and push rentals off the market. Recent studies have indicated major negative impacts in Barcelona (Arias-Sans & Quaglieri Domínguez, 2016), San Francisco (Budget and Legislative Analyst's Office, 2015) and New York (Schneiderman, 2014). As Airbnb seeks enclosure over the resources once nurtured and protected within communities, the very source of culture on which non-profits and non-governmental organisations such as charities emerge, is threatened. Airbnb has proven to indirectly work against loosely affiliated groups and non-profit entities, who may seek to deliver actual or desired outcomes in a given locality, such as social inclusion, greater equality, cultural understanding and poverty reduction. SERVAS, for example, is an offline, and paper based hospitality exchange system affiliated with the United Nations. As Airbnb refuses to be regulated as it scales up, regulated non-profits are vulnerable to losing their place in tourism. Destinations must invest in the protection of non-profits that could distribute value amongst the value creators, and provide resources for such creators to interconnect technologically (e.g. Platform Cooperativism) to facilitate federations of locally-owned cooperatives.

Adept at paying lip service to poverty, inequality, social and economic exclusion, and beholden to owners, stockholders and investors, there will be market created problems that will soon need innovative solutions. Many solutions from market facing businesses in the tourism industry were structured in forms amenable to non-profit intervention, such as ratings and quality control systems for sustainable businesses and responsible tourism (e.g. Green Globe). However, the more fragmented and decentralised collaborative economy becomes, altruistic interventions may no longer be applicable. While many argue that tourism marketplaces are already exploitive, cultural capitalism has the power to add to its destructive elements. While many collaborative economy platforms package their market communication along the rhetoric of morality and eco-ethics, they do not address or promote moral or ethical decision-making. Airbnb properties, for example, by and large, do not coordinate with the UNWTO Task Force to Protect Children in Tourism, or promote "The Code of Conduct for the Protection of Children from Sexual Exploitation in Travel and Tourism" (ECPAT), or train hosts to spot the signs of child sexual abuse. However, a private trade body called SEUK representing the collaborative economy in the United Kingdom has joined the Skoll Centre for Social Entrepreneurship at Oxford University and Rachel Botsman in 2015 to develop a "trustmark". The idea that Airbnb can regulate and police itself, with the invisible hand of the market protecting the environment, hosts and the public is questionable. Airbnb also throws into question whether a future self-interested consumer, many of whom do not currently pay any taxes on Airbnb, will pay into any future tourism system (i.e. the Balearic Islands accommodation eco-tax, the Dubai tourist tax, the Hamburg culture and tourism tax) and whether policy makers will engage in partnerships with intermediaries such as Airbnb to regulate the accommodation sector (Dredge & Gyimóthy, 2015).

Regulators must decide whether Airbnb's "micro-entrepreneurs" are employees or independent/dependent contractors. Entrepreneurs, for example, should be able to set their own prices and find their own customers. Regulators should also ensure that Airbnb cannot pass the burdens of service, liability, legal, fiscal and social responsibilities onto hosts and consumers in the name of public good and the "big society". Neither should authorities spend resources to enforce existing regulations. Regulators must demand the Airbnb data that they need to enforce regulations and taxation, require hosts to register with local agencies and create new mechanisms to collect taxes, restrict the density of short-term rentals in certain areas, and deal with absentee owners whose guests may become nuisances. In the longer term, margins may not be worth the burden of participation once a "level playing field" between incumbents and Airbnb is introduced and the costs of regulatory, tax and general compliance costs are added. Host "churn" will also impact on host availability. Airbnb also risks becoming a victim of its own success, as it becomes forced to introduce more efficient oversight, host and customer tools, and managerial practices. As it grows, it risks being obscured by new and hungrier platforms. In addition, "micro-entrepreneurs" who begin to invest capital (cleaning staff, redecorating rooms) may end up replicating the existing professional system (Kaminska, 2014) just as the "entrenched" accommodation providers become revitalised as they adapt to the new access-oriented, on-demand environment. Paradoxically, because Airbnb works because of the pretense that it is not a commodity, but an experience, any replication of the existing system and its fixed costs may lead to consumers looking elsewhere for experiences. The venture capitalists who have invested up to US$2.39 billion up to 2015 may also seek to recoup their investments by asking Airbnb management to squeeze even more cash from hosts and raise prices through algorithmic manipulation.

There is no data to indicate the Airbnb threatens entrenched business models, given Airbnb acts to free spare capacity if and when professional capacity falls short. By unlocking spaces at favourable prices, Airbnb actually expands the size of the market. However, spare capacity during peak periods when hotels normally increase prices could affect low and high end independent properties if quality processes and efficiency innovations are not implemented by those independent or chain properties. In addition, Christensen, Raynor, and McDonald (2015) argue that as Airbnb uses nicer host homes in wealthier areas, their disruption to entrenched hotel business models will become more pronounced. However, modest innovation by accommodation providers, either individually or part of a global chain, can be very successful. In 2015, the Hyatt Hotel group become an investor in onefinestay, which rents owners' upscale vacation homes, and allows the platform users an opportunity to freshen up at a Hyatt Hotel, whilst Expedia purchased Homeaway to add vacation rentals to its online travel booking options. Hotel groups, like Ovotel, Citizen M and Marriott International's "Edition" have also sought to incorporate and sell real life "experiences", make better use of customer data and utilise techniques prevalent in Airbnb such as user feedback, flexibility (e.g. self-laundry, flexible check out, co-working spaces), authentic local interactions (i.e. linking guests to local guides), easier transactions and a "lifestyle ethos". Hotels and other accommodation providers increasingly use events, shareable moments and content that speak to customer values, and address the desire for authenticity, flexibility, accessibility, efficiency and adventure. Unlike Airbnb, many hotels (groups) have also made great strides in working with authorities and tourists to protect labor and the environment, and work with cities and those in governance and locally owned platform coops to deliver a real-world service to create sharing destinations where benefits trickle down. In contrast, Airbnb are in conflict with authorities across the globe. They were, for example, fined €30,000 in 2014 for breaching local tourism laws in Barcelona. In Australia and Europe, Airbnb has not fully incorporated any method to show local laws during the listing process, or adequately disclose mandatory fees, such as for service and cleaning in advance, despite regulatory demands.

4.2 *Future Research*

Further research may explore whether the shared resources on Airbnb are really excess capacity from the perspective of hosts, or whether, when fulfilling tourist needs, they create shortages within their immediate social circles (i.e. hosting intermediately rather than seeking higher income, full-time employment). In addition, while Airbnb is delivering progressively more market-sourced income to asset owners, more research is needed to explore whether such income is recycled back locally through taxes, wages and payment for consumer goods and services. Research should explore the emotional impacts of collaboration and sharing on hosts, and whether those who participate freely do so, or are induced to monetise their assets and sociality. It may also be relevant to research the diverse forms, impacts and regulatory responses in different geographical contexts (urban-suburban-peri-urban-rural), including welfare societies and societies in economic crisis. Finally, the impacts of 'short-term strangers' on civic life and the authenticity of neighbourhoods in heavily visited destinations would be useful, as well an examination of the disruption to public policy making in tourist destinations.

5 Conclusions

In its full scope, the collaborative economy encompasses gift transactions and nonprofit collectives and cooperatives. However, despite claims from many advocates, the collaborative economy is, by and large, administered by for-profit companies anchored in commerce and enclosure. As people, their skills, assets and belongings are monetised in a new age of access, Airbnb brings the efficiency and capabilities of the internet to exploit network organisation for the purpose of extraction by connecting tourists with service providers. While boosting economic output without requiring destinations to increase public spending, we argue that parties are as much influenced by economic incentives as by trust underpinned by shared norms, values or protections. While technological infrastructure and entrepreneurial dynamism coupled with regulatory and tax evasion and without proper oversight and proper accountability, Airbnb will continue to grow the demand for experiential travel and make money. However, the organisational ethos of the platform will be increasingly recognised as a symptom of predatory laissez-faire platform capitalism and, therefore, be in need of greater regulation across the globe. While disruption to aspects of the tourism industry as well as destinations themselves are needed to achieve a more sustainable future (e.g. to reduce greenhouse gas emissions from the transportation sector), Airbnb is not a disruptive movement, its venture capital backed business model merely an extractive online tourism marketplace.

References

Ahmed, M. (2014, January 28). Brits turn to Airbnb to make ends meet. *The Times*. Accessed July 22, 2015, from http://www.thetimes.co.uk/tto/business/industries/technology/article3988333.ece

Arias-Sans, A., & Quaglieri Domínguez, A. (2016). Unravelling Airbnb. The case of Barcelona. In G. Richards & A. P. Russo (Eds.), *Reinventing the local in tourism. Travel communities and peer-produced place experiences* (pp. 209–228). London: Channelview.

Benkler, Y. (2006). *The wealth of networks: How social production transforms markets and freedom*. New Haven, CT: Yale University Press.

Botsman, R. (2012, August 20). Welcome to the new reputation economy. *Wired Magazine*. Accessed July 22, 2015, from http://www.wired.co.uk/magazine/archive/2012/09/features/welcome-to-the-new-reputation-economy

Botsman, R. (2015, May 27). Defining the sharing economy: What is collaborative consumption—and what isn't? *Fast Company*. Accessed July 9, 2015 from http://www.fastcoexist.com/3046119/defining-the-sharing-economy-what-is-collaborative-consumption-and-what-isnt

Botsman, R., & Rogers, R. (2011). *What's mine is yours: How collaborative consumption is changing the way we live*. London: Collins.

Budget and Legislative Analyst's Office. (2015). Analysis of the impact of short-term rentals on housing. *City and County of San Francisco Board of Supervisors*. Accessed July 9, 2015, from http://www.sfbos.org/Modules/ShowDocument.aspx?documentid=52601

Chase, R. (2015). *Peers Inc: How people and platforms are inventing the collaborative economy and reinventing capitalism*. New York: Public Affairs.

Christensen, M., Raynor, M. E., & McDonald, R. (2015). What is disruptive innovation? *Harvard Business Review*, 44–53.

Debord, G. (1998). *Comments on the society of the spectacle*. London: Verso.

Dredge, D., & Gyimóthy, S. (2015). The collaborative economy and tourism: Critical perspectives, questionable claims and silenced voices. *Tourism Recreation Research, 40*(3), 286–302. doi:10.1080/02508281.2015.1086076.

Edelman, B., Luca, M., & Svirsky, D. (2015). Racial discrimination in the sharing economy: Evidence from a field experiment. Accessed December 20, 2015, from http://www.benedelman.org/publications/airbnb-guest-discrimination-2015-12-09.pdf

Ferenstein, G. (2014). Airbnb CEO spells out the end game for the sharing economy, in 7 quotes. *Venture Beat*. Accessed November 5, 2015, from http://venturebeat.com/2014/07/02/airbnb-ceo-spells-out-the-end-game-for-the-sharing-economy-in-7-quotes/

Fiske, A. P. (1992). The four elementary forms of sociality: Framework for a unified theory of social relations. *Psychological Review, 99*, 689–723.

Gurvich, I., Lariviere, M., & Moreno-Garcia, A. (2015). *Operations in the on-demand economy: Staffing services with self-scheduling capacity*. Working Paper. Accessed July 25, 2015, from http://www.kellogg.northwestern.edu/faculty/lariviere/research/GLM_Revised_WithNames.pdf

Hamari, J., & Ukkonen, A. (2013). *The sharing economy: Why people participate in collaborative consumption*. Helsinki: Helsinki Institute for Information Technology.

Harvey, D. (1989). *The condition of postmodernity*. Oxford: Basic Blackwell.

Harvey, D. (2000). *Spaces of hope*. Berkeley, CA: University of California Press.

Hochschild, A. R. (2003). *The commercialization of intimate life: Notes from home and work*. Berkeley, CA: University of California Press.

Holloway, J. (2010). *Crack capitalism*. London: Pluto.

Howard, B. (2015). *We-Commerce: How to create, collaborate, and succeed in the sharing economy*. New York: Perigee Books & Penguin Random House.

Jameson, F. (1984, July–August). Postmodernism, or the cultural logic of late capitalism. *New Left Review, 146*, 59–92.

Kaminska, I. (2014, March 27). The unscaling myth. *Financial Times*. Accessed June 5, 2015, from http://ftalphaville.ft.com/2014/03/27/1812572/the-unscaling-myth/

Kaminska, I. (2015, May 21). The sharing economy will go medieval on you. *Financial Times*. Accessed June 5, 2015, from http://ftalphaville.ft.com/2015/05/21/2130111/the-sharing-economy-will-go-medieval-on-you/

King, D. (2015). Survey finds surge in peer-to-peer home rentals, ride-hailing. *Travel Weekly*. Accessed December 13, 2015, from http://www.travelweekly.com/Travel-News/Travel-Technology/Survey-finds-surge-in-peer-to-peer-home-rentals-ride-hailing

Krakovsky, M. (2015). *The middleman economy: How brokers, agents, dealers, and everyday matchmakers create value and profit*. New York: Palgrave MacMillan.

Kramer, B. (2015). *Shareology: How sharing is powering the human economy*. New York: Morgan James Publishing.

Kusisto, L. (2015). Airbnb pushes up apartment rents slightly, Study says. *Wall Street Journal*. Accessed July 19, 2015, from http://blogs.wsj.com/developments/2015/03/30/airbnb-pushes-up-apartment-rents-slightly-study-says/?mod=WSJBlog

Lux, M. (2015). A Libertarian dream: The 'Sharing Economy'. *The Huffington Post*. Accessed October 19, 2015, from http://www.huffingtonpost.com/mike-lux/a-libertarian-dream-the-sharing-economy_b_7313014.html

Lynam, J. (2016, February 15). Airbnb 'delisting hosts for no reason.' *BBC*. Accessed March 2, 2016, from http://www.bbc.co.uk/news/business-35574971

PwC. (2014). The sharing economy. *PriceWaterhouseCoopers*. Accessed July 19, 2015, from http://download.pwc.com/ie/pubs/2015-pwc-cis-sharing-economy.pdf

Rifkin, J. (2000). *The age of access: The new culture of hypercapitalism, where all of life is a paid-for experience*. New York: J.P. Tarcher/Putnam.

Schneiderman, E. T. (2014). Airbnb in the city. New York State Attorney General. Accessed November 15, 2015, from http://www.ag.ny.gov/pdfs/Airbnb%20report.pdf

Sevignani, S. (2013). The commodification of privacy on the Internet. *Science and Public Policy, 40*, 733–739.

Stephany, A. (2015). *The business of sharing: Making it in the new sharing economy*. London: Palgrave MacMillan.

Wang, D, Xi, S., & Gilheany, J. (2015). The model minority? Not on Airbnb.com: A hedonic pricing model to quantify racial bias against Asian Americans. *Technology Science*. Accessed October 1, 2015, from http://techscience.org/downloadpdf.php?paper=2015090104

Zelizer, V. A. (2005). *The Purchase of Intimacy*. Princeton, NJ: Princeton University.

Zervas, G., Proserpio, D., & Byers, J. W. (2015a). *The rise of the sharing economy: Estimating the impact of Airbnb on the hotel industry*. Working paper. Accessed July 10, 2015, from http://papers.ssrn.com/sol3/papers.cfm?abstract_id=2366898

Zervas, G., Proserpio, D., & Byers, J. W. (2015b). *A first look at online reputation on Airbnb: Where every stay is above average*. Working paper. Accessed July 10, 2015, from http://collaborativeeconomy.com/wp/wp-content/uploads/2015/04/Byers-D.-Proserpio-D.-Zervas-G.2015.A-First-Look-at-Online-Reputation-on-Airbnb-Where-Every-Stay-is-Above-Average.Boston-University.pdf

Žižek, S. (2006). *The universal exception*. London: Continuum.

Žižek, S. (2009a). *First as tragedy, then as farce*. London: Verso.

Žižek, S. (2009b, November 24). RSA animate: First as tragedy, then as farce. RSA. Accessed July 10, 2015, from https://www.thersa.org/globalassets/pdfs/blogs/rsa-lecture-slovoj-zizek-transcript.pdf

Žižek, S. (2011). *Living in the end times*. London: Verso.

Žižek, S. (2012). *Organs without bodies: On Deleuze and consequences*. London: Routledge.

Sharing the New Localities of Tourism

Greg Richards

Abstract Geographers have long pondered the role of tourism in producing and shaping space. The description of resort geographies popular in the 1980s and 1990s has gradually given way to the current vogue for place-making and place marketing, re-centering geography in the tourism field. More recently, however, the rise of the sharing economy and "relational tourism" has caused researchers to look beyond the construction and consumption of place and to delve into the co-creation of localities between tourists and residents. These shorter and longer-term "locals" increasingly find each other without the intervention of the traditional tourism industry, giving rise to whole new fields of economic, cultural and social exchange. The growth of companies such as Couchsurfing, Airbnb and Uber not only represents a challenge to traditional views of tourism, but is also reshaping the localities inhabited by tourists. This analysis examines the consequences of the new localities of tourism and they ways in which this might affect the future of tourism itself.

Keywords Sharing economy • Airbnb • Localities • Relational tourism • Place

1 Introduction

From a geographical point of view, tourism can be seen as an activity that produces and consumes space. In the past, there used to be a fairly close relationship between the spaces in which tourism produced tourism experiences, and the spaces in which tourists consumed them. The spatial diffusion of tourism was controlled by a dedicated, narrow value chain that had changed little since the days of Thomas Cook. Tourists went to hotels run by tourism companies, transported there by trains or planes run by transport companies and consumed animation provided by dedicated tourism staff. In the contemporary network society, however, consumers are increasingly able to circumvent the tourism supply chain and become actively

---

G. Richards (✉)
Department of Leisure Studies, Tilburg University, PO Box 90153, 5000LE Tilburg, The Netherlands
e-mail: G.W.Richards@uvt.nl

D. Dredge, S. Gyimóthy (eds.), *Collaborative Economy and Tourism*,
Tourism on the Verge, DOI 10.1007/978-3-319-51799-5_10

involved in the production of their own tourism experiences. The new 'mobile consumer' (Ochoa, 2015) is more directly in contact with a raft of new 'tourism' producers that have little or no contact with the traditional tourism industry.

In this shifting tourism landscape the conventional tourism industry seems to be particularly concerned about the rise of the 'collaborative economy', which arguably facilitates the direct sharing of resources between consumers, without the intervention of commercial intermediaries. The tourism industry itself is beginning to see this as a threat to its business, labelling it a 'shadow industry' (HOTREC, 2014).

This chapter considers the consequences of the shift towards collaborative and co-created forms of supply for the tourism industry and for the production of tourism spaces. We will attempt to assess the ways in which these new 'shared' localities of tourism are re-ordering the relationships between tourism space, place and location, and shifting the distribution of power within the tourism industry.

2 The Rise of the Local

Early analyses of tourism development mirrored the relatively homogeneous and linear processes of mass tourism development in their analysis of tourist space. The models of Barrett (1958), Miossec (1977), Butler (1980) and Smith (1991) all depicted the growth of coastal resorts as stemming from a central zone close to the beach and fanning out in successive temporal waves into the periphery. The market-based nature of such development processes produced a landscape dominated by large-scale tourism consumption. This is one of the central arguments of such seminal works as Sharon Zukin's (1991) *Landscapes of Power,* John Hannigan's (1998) *Fantasy City* and Judd and Fainstein's (1999) *Tourist City.*

However, the development of the collaborative economy is now contributing to a hollowing out of such traditional models of "industrial tourism", because low entry costs mean that local communities are now able to act as micro-producers of tourism. So we are seeing a divergent movement of power in the tourism system, upwards towards global distribution systems and downwards to micro-producers and small local enterprises.

Recently, therefore, the study of tourism geographies more attention has been focussed on the micro level of urban neighbourhoods (Zukin, 2010) or small rural communities (Brouder, 2012) where micro-entrepreneurship is emerging. Sharon Zukin's (2010) *Naked City* explores the development of different neighbourhoods in New York, which in her view are being transformed into consumption zones. She explored the processes by which former working class areas have been gentrified, with the generation of symbolic value in these areas largely being attached to the concept of "authenticity". Essentially, she argues that the "authentic" is now symbolically linked with the local. The question then becomes not "what is authentic?" but "what is local?"

However, the new localism seems to complicate rather than resolve the issue of authenticity. The "global" and "local" are not spatial structures (levels, scales, places, distances, etc.), but different representations of space competing against each other to determine social reality (Guy, 2009). The point is that distances and other spatial measurements simply cannot tell us where to draw the boundary separating what is local and what is global or where the local ends and where the global begins. The adoption of particular temporal or spatial practices can make one a "local", even when s/he has travelled far or stayed a relatively short length of time.

Essentially, in an era of global mobility, it is easy to become a (para)local somewhere else. A range of "soft infrastructure" facilitates this shift, with facilities such as hostels, coffee bars and Internet cafes and local intermediaries offering a 'plug and play' destination (Richards, 2010). Boutique hotels and Airbnb are simply the latest plug-ins for the local experience:

> I think what's similar between a boutique hotel and Airbnb are three key things. Boutique hotels were really all about living like a local. How do you have an experience that feels like a local experience? That was really all around the food experience. Secondly, it was about having a design point of view so the design didn't feel generic. Thirdly, it was about turning strangers into friends. That's why we called staff "host" at our hotels. All of these things apply to Airbnb too. (Chip Conley, Airbnb)

The interesting point about the collaborative economy is that the economic structure itself builds in the "local" dimension, by offering the sharing of goods, services and knowledge between visitors and hosts.

3 The Spatial Effects of Collaborative Tourism Practices

The growth of the collaborative economy points to a new set of practices operating in the field of tourism production and consumption. If we view the situation from a social practice perspective, then we can borrow from Shove, Pantzar, and Watson's (2012) analysis of practices as comprising objects and materials (technologies, things, tools, infrastructure, etc.), skills and competence (know-how, background knowledge) and images and meanings (emotions, motivations, ideas, etc.). A change in any one of the elements of the practice is likely to have recursive effect on the others. For example, the rise of budget airlines (technological change) has stimulated a change in the image of previously peripheral tourism locations (image change) and increased the know-how of local actors about tourist needs and how to meet them (increased skills). Changes in the practice also affect the consumers, who are afforded a range of new destinations, becoming more skilled in researching the possibilities of the destination via the Internet and fuelling the image of new destinations as the 'place to be'.

The usefulness of the practice approach lies in emphasising how the different elements of the tourism system, including the 'locals' and the 'tourists' are interlinked and interact. Transitions in practice reflect changes in the composition of the elements of materials, skills and meanings in the practice. Practices emerge, persist and disappear as connections between different elements are made and broken. New practices involve novel combinations of new and existing elements. The ways in which the different elements of the tourism practice are affected by the collaborative economy are considered below.

3.1 Resources

One of the key dimensions of the collaborative economy is that it has opened up a range of new resources to tourism practices. This is evident in the way that the recent rise of Airbnb has transformed the tourism profile of many cities:

> Nearly 55 million guests have booked the online sharing site since 2007, and 30 million of those were in the last year. Looking just at summer 2015, more than 17 million people booked Airbnb. That's 353 times the number of bookings 5 years ago when Airbnb hosted 47,000 guests during the summer of 2010 (Oates, 2015).

Companies such as HomeAway are also making an impact on local tourism markets, with over 10% growth in 2015. The company is now partnering with online distribution companies such as Kayak and Expedia to expand reach and increase bookings (Oates, 2015: 52). Such companies can have a big effect at local level. In Barcelona, for example, by May 2014 Airbnb was offering almost 7000 entire flats, almost 5000 entire rooms and 285 shared rooms (Arias Sans & Quaglieri Domínguez, 2016). This has had a significant impact on the accommodation supply and revenue in the city:

> Jeroen Merchiers, Airbnb's Barcelona-based general manager for Spain and Portugal, said that last year rentals through his firm had a $128 million impact in Barcelona, much of which helped struggling locals: 77% of the hosts rented out one room in their home and earned an average of 220 euros a month, he said, most of which went toward basic needs. "In southern Europe, people are struggling. Fifty three percent of the hosts say the money they make as a host allows them to stay in the room or house where they are. Thousands of families are using this to make ends meet." (Mount, 2014)

Interestingly, many of these new tourism resources in Barcelona are being provided by foreigners. As Arias Sans and Quaglieri Domínguez (2016) note for example: The knowledge of the Italian language is indicated in more than one fifth of Airbnb listings studied in Barcelona, whilst the proportion of Italian citizens in the whole resident population is relatively marginal. Most of the foreign residents active on Airbnb tend to be white, western middle class "ex-pats" rather than being representative of the migrant of population of the city as a whole.

3.2 *Skills and Competence*

In the emerging collaborative economy of tourism, more formal hospitality and intermediation skills are being replaced by informal ones. The Airbnb host also needs to acquire specific skills in the reproduction of the "local" Airbnb experience. These include how to show "empathy" towards the client and recognise their needs. Airbnb gives specific guidance to hosts on how to develop such skills.

The way in which the host engages with guests is defined by Airbnb in terms of Maslow's hierarchy of needs (Pinchera, 2015). At the basic level, what guests want is a clean environment with wi-fi. At higher levels of need, which Airbnb equates to "success", the important thing is for hosts to give attention to the guest, for example by giving them information about things to do and places to go. But the highest level of "transformation" or self-actualisation is seen as the creative part of the process. This is where personalised experiences are generated through empathy between host and guest. This requires creativity and emotional work on the part of the host, and this is where a networked system such as Airbnb has an important competitive edge over traditional tourist providers. Where hotels and other traditional forms of accommodation have to train their (usually poorly paid) staff to empathise and be creative, Airbnb relies on their feedback system to reward and train the host to deliver transformational experiences. Those who are good at this will receive more positive guest feedback, and therefore more business than other hosts.

But also important in the new collaborative hospitality system is the role of "local" hosts in providing local "buzz" or atmosphere (Bathelt, Malmberg, & Maskell, 2004). Maintaining this buzz also depends heavily on face-to-face contact between key actors, a fact that shapes creative spaces and also provides potential entry points into the local creative field for tourists. Examples include the 'ruin bars' in Budapest (Lugosi, Bell, & Lugosi, 2010), emerging creative clusters in Berlin (Lange, 2012), and creative events such as SXSW (OECD, 2014).

Again there seems to be a specific role for ex-pats in the development of conduits and local buzz attached to tourism. In Barcelona, for example, much of the recent innovation around tourist transport has been led by European ex-pats. This includes the creation of a large number of bike hire companies, predominantly founded by Dutch migrants, and the Cooltra scooter hire company, founded by German brothers living in the uber-cool Gràcia neighbourhood (Richards, 2016). These ex-pats bring with them specific technical skills, but they also have the communication channels necessary to reach foreign markets in the countries of origin, which is far more difficult for most spatially embedded locals.

3.3 Meanings

One of the important meanings attached to the new collaborative tourism systems is that they are not part of the traditional tourism system. Airbnb makes much of the fact that it is not a hotel company. Because each of the dwellings offered by Airbnb is unique, it offers a vast diversity of accommodation options, as a recent review points out:

> [...] while Airbnb has come to be known as the low-key, economical way to travel, it also boasts some seriously incredible, one-of-a-kind accommodations. So, yeah, you could stay in hotel. Or, you could stay in a glass tree house in the Tuscan forest, or a real-life Scottish castle, or even a restored windmill in Santorini (Refinery 29, 2015).

Airbnb also emphasises the fact that it promotes relationships. One important part of the Airbnb practice is that the direct financial transaction between host and guest is removed by the Airbnb website, so that the development of a relationship is not made more awkward by the host having to ask for money. So in this sense it also positions itself as being different from other commercial accommodation providers.

Airbnb also likes to stress that it contributes to local communities by giving them opportunities to earn money directly from visitors. The 'community' role has been strengthened by the opening of Airbnb offices in many different cities around the world. These offices provide a physical point of contact for Airbnb hosts in the city, but they also enable the company to lobby directly with municipal authorities when its interests are threatened.

4 Emerging Practices: Co-Creation Between Tourists and Locals

New practices emerge as a result of new combinations of resources, skills and meanings, such as those discussed so far (Shove et al., 2012). The emergence of a new system of the co-creation of space between tourists and locals has been an important result of these changes. The production of tourist space is no longer simply a question of top-down production of standardised experiencescapes by multinational companies or governments. Increasingly, the development of experiences takes place as a co-creative process between 'tourists' and "locals" linked in networks operating largely outside the tourism system. This changing practice also results in very different types of space or ways of using space.

One of the most evident changes in the practice has been the shifting boundaries of the "tourist" and the "host" or "local". The rise of the mobilities paradigm has underlined the shift from highly directed to much more diffuse and widespread forms of tourist movement. Whereas in the past tourists were fairly easy to identify and localise through their relatively limited range of behaviours, today the concept of the tourist is much more difficult to define. Growing numbers of people travel for a wide range of reasons which may have little to do with the idea of a "holiday".

Many people now travel with a mix of leisure and work or study motivations, such as ERASMUS students, lifestyle entrepreneurs or "global nomads" (Kannisto, 2014). Again, these patterns emphasise the important role of expats in providing the conduits to the local buzz.

In particular, major cities have become places where different groups of relatively mobile cosmopolitans meet with the relatively sedentary "locals". As Russo and Quaglieri Domínguez (2012) have pointed out in the case of Barcelona:

> It is up to the cities and regions to accommodate such diversity and nurture the social and cultural connections or 'atmospheric' elements that determine their capacity to offer a distinct and stimulating atmosphere where, according to the logic of experience marketing, ordinary activities are transformed in memorable experiences.

This makes it clear that what is important for places to attract tourists and other mobile populations is no longer just concrete attractions or tourist infrastructure, but "atmosphere". This atmosphere is often seen as something pertaining to the "local", the "everyday", and particularly the "edgy" aspects of these (Hannigan, 2007). At the same time, "locals" make increasing use of the spaces once reserved for tourists. In fact in some places the tourists themselves have become subject to a "local gaze" that places them as objects of curiosity themselves (Richards & Wilson, 2004).

Locals also become the providers of tourist experiences. In many cases locals become the intermediaries who interpret the places they live in for the tourist, a function that in the past was often taken by the guide travelling with the tourists. Locals are also increasingly supplementing the local accommodation supply. Barcelona research (Richards, 2015) shows that 47% of local residents have provided accommodation to friends and relatives in the past year, supplementing the more commercial spaces provided via Airbnb and the hospitality exchange possibilities of Couchsurfing.

The shared or collaborative tourism model is now being extended to whole communities or cities. For example, Seferihisar in Turkey has become the "world's first homestay holiday village", linking together different houses in the village to provide accommodation for tourists. "Fast-food outlets and chain stores are out. Renewable energy, slow travel and long-held local traditions are decidedly in" (Tomasetti, 2014). As one homestay guest notes:

> And [with our guests] we will pick our own vegetables from our garden. If they want to eat fish at dinner, we will go fishing ourselves in the morning. We will give [visitors] a real opportunity to live in a Cittaslow (Tomasetti, 2014).

The emphasis is on local people, local products and local hospitality. These are elements of the tourism experience that have been gaining momentum in recent years. For example, Gilli and Ferrari (2016) describe the development of the *albergo diffuso* or diffuse hotel in Italy as a new form of network hospitality. In a number of small villages different abandoned houses have been converted into tourist accommodation, and have been linked together with services such as restaurants to produce a network accommodation system. This has helped to regenerate a number of villages that otherwise would have suffered from depopulation and economic decline.

The shift of the collaborative economy from individual producers and consumers towards entire communities has not escaped major players such as Airbnb. Brian Chesky, one of the founders of Airbnb recently coined the idea of the "shared city". "We are committed to enriching cities and designing the kind of world we want to live in. Together, let's build that shared world city by city." The Airbnb vision of the shared city has been extended into the Airbnb Community Compact, which contains three commitments:

- We are committed to treating every city personally and helping ensure our community pays its fair share of hotel and tourist taxes.
- We are committed to being transparent with our data and information and we will help cities understand the home sharing activity in their community while simultaneously honoring our commitment to protect our hosts' and guests' privacy.
- In cities where there is a shortage of long-term housing, we are committed to working with our community to prevent short-term rentals from impacting the availability of long term housing by ensuring hosts agree to a policy of listing only permanent homes on a short-term basis (Chesky, 2015).

The difference between these new places and the traditional spaces of tourism is that their function relies on relationality rather than visual consumption or any type of traditional tourist "gaze" (Urry, 1990; Richards, 2013, 2014). We go there because of the local people and the opportunity to live like them, rather than just to look at them. For cities this places an increasing emphasis on what Richards and Delgado (2003) termed "trusting spaces", where the users of specific spaces can come together and develop relationships of greater or lesser duration. This in turn facilitates the sharing of knowledge and skills, strengthening the practice of relationality itself. Trust development in the Airbnb practice is supported by a number of aspects of the process. The properties have reviews from customers, which the company says "cannot be invented". The reviews are supported by photos of the property, and the trust of guests is increased through a verified ID, by links to social media and a "host guarantee" of up to 700,000 euros.

According to Germann Molz (2014), "sharing with strangers" is one of the key aspects of the new "networked hospitality" model. Through such sharing, Airbnb provides relationality benefits for both hosts and guests, as one host explains:

> As a society we have fewer and fewer opportunities to interact with real human beings, strangers, in person. This is due to the explosion in popularity of smartphones and other technological devices that consume attention in public spaces. (These devices were not as ubiquitous in the past 10 years as they are today). If you look around you as you wait at a bus stop or for the train, you'll see everyone looking at their phones or shut off from the world via their headphones. AirBnB offers people a chance to make those serendipitous personal connections that we are missing in society today. It can be absolutely wonderful to meet random people you would never have otherwise met via AirBnB.
>
> Additionally, the experience of being in someone's home is very different from staying in a hotel. You get a real taste of what life is like for the locals. You can get one of a kind

recommendations and tips from your hosts, who are familiar with the area and who can usually give you more insightful recommendations (and more tailored to you!) than what you will find in a guidebook (Airbnb host, Quora.com, June 2014).

These new practices of tourism therefore require new skills (relationality) to open up new resources (private homes) to tourists and to create new meanings (don't be a tourist—live like a local). These new practices have in turn transformed tourism, and the spaces in which tourism is produced, consumed and performed.

5 How Has the Making of Tourism Spaces Changed?

Recent studies of emergent tourism localities have identified many new types of tourism spaces, such as the Airbnb apartment, the local neighbourhood or the *albergo diffuso*. If we compare the contemporary process of developing new spaces for tourism with the "traditional" model of cultural attraction development, some of the key features can be identified. If we look for example at MacCannell's (1976) model of sight sacralisation, then we can identify a process that proceeds through stages of marking, framing, enshrinement, mechanical reproduction, and social reproduction. These are basically processes that work from discrete and embedded space to more abstract and diffuse social contexts. In many cases, these processes are driven by the competition that emerges between places in the local, regional, national and global search for attention in the modern economy. But in the relational context of contemporary tourism, different processes are at work. As the structures of modern society lose their importance and authority, so does the shared need for identity and self-actualisation begin to take on a more important role, as Airbnb has recognised (Pinchera, 2015). Rather than the sights of tourism being marked and framed by a tourism industry intent on concentrating the tourist gaze, the "local" has now taken on the position of a collaborative marker of authenticity that is co-created between residents (including temporary residents, expats or migrants) and visitors. This tends to shift the focus of tourism activity away from the traditional public spaces of the city towards the private and interstitial spaces of the home, the atelier or the hostel.

The re-location of tourism practices has stimulated a lively debate on the ownership of and access to the city by visitors and by residents creating tourism services. The basic question being posed is: who benefits from these new tourism practices? There is a clear shift in economic benefits away from the traditional tourism sector towards new relational forms of tourism, but there are also other issues at stake.

Airbnb is keen to emphasise the benefits that it brings to local communities. For example, it claims that it helps hosts to make ends meet, and that 50% of hosts are on moderate to low incomes. To emphasise the fact that most hosts are private individuals, Airbnb claims that "82% share only the home in which they live." These hosts not only earn money, but also gain other benefits. For example in

Boston, 48% of hosts said that Airbnb hosting had positively affected their interaction with the local community and 62% said it had positively affected the way they view life (Airbnb, 2014). In terms of the benefits for "travellers", Airbnb says that most visitors want to "experience cities not as tourists, but as locals." According to their surveys, 76% want to explore a specific neighbourhood, and 89% want to "live like a local". This seems to suggest a collaborative benefit for hosts and tourists in constructing a local experience that will appeal to visitors and generate income for local people.

In spite of all the hype about the benefits of the collaborative economy, however, it seems that the outcomes are not always positive. In the case of Airbnb, for example, Arias Sans and Quaglieri Domínguez (2016) argue that the company is flouting local regulations on accommodation provision, producing unfair competition for commercial accommodation suppliers and increasing the concentration of tourism in already heavily visited areas. They also see indications that apartment rentals through Airbnb and other platforms has helped to keep property prices high in such areas in spite of the economic downturn in Barcelona.

Similar problems are now being noted in New York, where a report published in 2014 noted that 72% of Airbnb rentals booked in New York appeared to violate the law (New York State Office of the Attorney General, 2014). In addition, three districts of the city—the Lower East Side/Chinatown, Chelsea/Hell's Kitchen, and Greenwich Village/SoHo—accounted for one-third of private short-term rentals. These three, largely central districts, accounted for host revenue of $186.9 million, which represented 55% of host revenue for private stays in Manhattan. As Arias Sans and Quaglieri Domínguez (2016) found in the case of Barcelona, therefore, the pattern of Airbnb provision in New York seems to strengthen rather than dilute the concentration of tourist accommodation in central areas of the city. The locational concentration also tends to channel income towards particular types of hosts. In Boston, for example, Airbnb figures indicate that around 12% of hosts work in the Arts, design and creative services, 13% in Information Technology, 15% in professional and business services and 20% in education and health services. This seems to indicate a large over-representation of the middle class, or Florida's 'creative class'.

Airbnb has tried to deflect criticism of its operations by releasing a large amount of data on its operations in New York City. The Airbnb presentation of the figures seems to support the picture of local homes being rented out by local residents. About 93% of revenue earned by active hosts in New York City comes from those who share their entire home and who only have one or two rental listings on Airbnb. The median annual host income is roughly $5110—a welcome supplement to the average income, but hardly a commercial business.

However, Airbnb also made the data available to journalists under strict conditions. They could only access the data on Airbnb laptops in a private meeting room, and these data had also been edited by the company, arguably to protect confidential information. Subsequent analysis of these data revealed that of the 35,966 listings for New York City, 55% were for an entire apartment. Under state law it is illegal to rent out an entire apartment for less than 30 days, unless it is a family home. In addition, less than 2% of hosts had three or more listings on Airbnb, but this small group accounted for about 24% of total host revenue in 2015. Analysis by the Huffington Post revealed that about 10,000 hosts were making between $10,001 and $50,000 a year, and about 127 hosts were making between $127,000 and $350,000 a year by renting out their entire homes.

The Verge (2015) concluded:

> Overall the data is a big step toward meeting the company's pledge of transparency. But viewed carefully, the numbers tell a different story than the one put forward by Airbnb. Over the last year, hosts renting out multiple units for long periods of time still represent a significant portion of Airbnb's income in New York, potentially taking housing stock off the market.

In spite of these apparent problems, Airbnb remains extremely popular with hosts, visitors and the market at large. This is presumably because it is giving these parties what they want. The hosts derive income and make new contacts through the platform. The visitors are given a taste of the local, even if this is often manufactured by people operating hotel-like businesses. The Airbnb brand is viewed in a more positive light than most traditional hotel brands (Nguyen, 2013). The performance of the Airbnb platform is therefore also linked with a high market valuation, which has risen from $10 billion to $25 billion in recent years (O'Brien, 2015). The different parties therefore share a positive attitude towards Airbnb, even though they may not actively be collaborating with each other in the accommodation setting itself.

One of the explanations for the popularity of Airbnb may lie in Korczynski and Ott's (2006) concept of the "menu" in mediation. They argue that many products and services are now offered in the format of a menu, which places an emphasis on autonomous choice—the consumer is apparently free to choose from a range of options, as on the Airbnb website. However, the menu effectively hides the structure and power of the global platform. The consumers who choose Airbnb accommodation are not aware of the algorithms that control the menu of properties they are offered, which are designed to maximise sales rather than provide the consumer with a full choice (Bialski, 2016). Thus, Airbnb can continue to appear consumer and host friendly, while at the same time pursuing a more nakedly profit-driven path.

> The fantasy that Airbnb sells is that all its "operators" are small mom and pops who rent out a room to make a little pin money but the studies have shown that many of the Airbnb hosts have many many more than one or two units which they share with short term money paying guests. Some have 50 or more. Those units are off the market for regular rentals and are pulling in $100 a night or more in urban areas where housing for regular residents is scarce (Justice Holmes, Charleston 17 June 2015, quoted in Gelinas, 2015).

Although collaborative tourism practices bring micro-producers and consumers closer together, the public sector is one party that is often conspicuously absent from the practice. Companies like Airbnb have grown up outside traditional regulatory frameworks, and in many cases are operating in contravention of local accommodation regulations. The response of lawmakers has been mixed, with some cities seeming to actively embrace Airbnb's vision of the 'shared city' and others being openly hostile. Amsterdam, for example, has created new regulations covering the temporary letting of private homes by residents, stipulating that these cannot be let for more than 60 days a year and that they should also be occupied during this period by the owners. The owners are also responsible for collecting the local accommodation tax on behalf of the city. In New York, however, here has been a much more antagonistic relationship between lawmakers and Airbnb. Pressure has been put on the city not only by large accommodation providers, but also by local residents objecting to the argued negative impacts of Airbnb rentals. As some have commented, local neighbours are being replaced by tourists:

> New Yorkers and residents of other cities have the right to live in buildings with neighbors, not Dutch tourists with wheelie bags. (Gelinas, 2015).
>
> Should you suddenly suffer a hipster "neighbor," from a foreign country who decides that instead of getting a real job, he'll subsidize his existence by renting out an apartment in your non-doorman, non-elevator, tiny rent-stabilized building to anyone flying in at 2 am from anywhere on the globe, you will understand just how awful Airbnb truly is (Charlotte, New York 6 July 2015, quoted in Gelinas, 2015).

Airbnb has engaged in enrolment and mobilisation strategies (Dredge & Gyimóthy, 2015) in order to counter such criticism from public authorities and social groups. This includes opening offices in cities with large concentrations of Airbnb hosts, and undertaking research to support its case.

6 Conclusions

Tourism as practice has changed dramatically in recent decades. From being a largely top-down Fordist production system, tourism has become a much more dispersed nexus of integrated production and consumption. The impact on tourist space has also been significant—there is now an increasingly integrated type of tourism space emerging where the boundaries between tourism and the everyday are becoming much more vague. The desire to live like a local, combined with the desire of locals to become producers of tourism experiences, has stimulated a new "live like a local" trend that has been met by a range of bottom-up products and experiences.

This involves a reordering of resources, skills and meanings. In contrast to the traditional tourism system, which predominantly colonised public space, the collaborative economy has opened up interstitial private resources for tourism. So the previous situation, in which public resources such as transport infrastructure or cultural attractions, subsidised the private provision of tourism experiences, is being supplemented by a new model in which the private sphere provides an additional economic resource.

In terms of skills, consumers are becoming more skilled, and the gap between producer and consumer is narrowing. Because the consumption of tourism increasingly involves the everyday, the types of skills required become more closely aligned to skills gained from other fields, enabling an expansion of the provision of such experiences by those with no experience of tourism. There has also been a vast increase in peer-to-peer provision of information and skill development, so that the professional gatekeeping function has become far less important. The core competence is no longer the understanding of the tourist, but understanding the source communities of tourists. This has positioned ex-pats as particularly useful collaborative tourism intermediaries.

The meanings attached to the practice of tourism have also shifted as we have all become tourists and many of us are engaged in supplying tourism. Tourists used to be welcomed purely on economic grounds, but they now have a wider range of roles (as citizens, as consumers of culture, as members of the creative class). They also help to provide the carrying capacity for many practices that link the local and the global in terms of resources, skills and meanings.

However, when one examines the effects of such 'Airbnbization' of tourism practices, one sees potential dangers as well as benefits. Clearly the cheapness and flexibility of services such as Airbnb or Uber are good for the consumer. But on the other hand the power of the tour operator or hotel group is replaced by a colonisation of the lifeworld (Richards, 2011), which is even more seductive because the locals seem to willingly collaborate in the colonisation process. The economic crisis in many countries has helped to facilitate this process, as people strive to generate additional income from the assets that they own or rent. This is a virtual miracle of global capitalism—thanks to the network society you can now develop the world's largest accommodation chain without investing a penny in bricks and mortar. Airbnb is currently estimated to be worth around $25 billion, which would make Airbnb worth more than Hyatt Hotels Corp, which has a market value of $8.43 billion.

Unlike Hyatt, Airbnb does not develop tourist enclaves. It may strengthen existing ones, as in the case of the centre of Barcelona. But it can also pioneer new tourist nodes, which are more integrated into local communities. This may be good for some local people who may earn extra income directly from the tourists, but it also raises important questions about the power relationships in the system. There are now interesting battles taking place in cities around the world between vested tourism and travel interests, such as hotel groups and taxi companies, and 'sharing economy' disruptors such as Airbnb and Uber. Interestingly, the hotels, who have traditionally resisted regulation, are now very much for it. The cities where these processes are largely unfolding have not yet found effective ways to control or regulate these developments.

What are the likely outcomes of these new practices? One may be the development of new types of intermediation and tourist occupations. Whereas the growth of the symbolic economy was characterised by an increase in basic service occupations to support the consumption of the middle class (Zukin, 1995), it now seems that the middle classes themselves have been co-opted into the labouring class. Airbnb depends on the relational skills of the middle class or Florida's creative class to make the system work (Bialski, 2016). It is no accident that Airbnb itself was founded by a pair of designers from San Francisco. Although the Airbnb rhetoric is that they are helping the poor in cities like Barcelona, the reality seems to be that they are particularly enlisting the mobile cosmopolitan classes, and in doing so, helping to shift underemployment from the fields of the developing periphery to the streets of the metropolitan core.

The extent to which the collaborative economy has changed the geography of tourism is debateable, since much of the provision of new-style accommodation and other services seems to be centred on established tourism areas. However, it is opening up new spaces in the form of private homes, and producing more direct contacts between tourists and locals. What we are actually witnessing is the colonisation of the lifeworld, as commerce reaches into spaces that were previously beyond its reach (Airbnb) or deregulates service provision (Uber) or privatises space (as in the case of Park Güell in Barcelona). The problem is that as the attractions of tourism become increasingly based on the everyday, and the potential transformation of such spaces into tourism places is apparently limitless.

References

Airbnb. (2014, December 19). *Airbnb's positive impact in Boston.* http://blog.airbnb.com/airbnbs-positive-impact-boston/

Arias Sans, A., & Quaglieri Domínguez, A. (2016). Placing network hospitality in urban destinations: The case of Airbnbn Barcelona. In A. P. Russo & G. Richards (Eds.), *New localities in tourism* (pp. 209–228). Bristol: Channel View.

Barrett, J. A. (1958). *The seaside resort towns of England and Wales.* PhD thesis in geography, University of London (unpublished).

Bathelt, H., Malmberg, A., & Maskell, P. (2004). Clusters and knowledge: Local buzz, global pipelines and the process of knowledge creation. *Progress in Human Geography, 28*(1), 31–56.

Bialski, P. (2016). Authority & Authorship: Uncovering the socio-technical regimes of peer-to-peer tourism. In A. P. Russo & G. Richards (Eds.), *New localities in tourism* (pp. 35–49). Bristol: Channel View.

Brouder, P. (2012). Creative outposts: Tourism's place in rural innovation. *Tourism Planning & Development, 9*(4), 383–396.

Butler, R. W. (1980). The concept of a tourist area cycle of evolution: Implications for management of resources. *The Canadian Geographer, 24*, 5–12.

Chesky, B. (2015, November 11). *Our commitment to communities around the world.* Airbnb Blog. http://blog.airbnb.com/our-commitment-to-communities-around-the-world/

Dredge, D., & Gyimóthy, S. (2015). The collaborative economy and tourism: Critical perspectives, questionable claims and silenced voices. *Tourism Recreation Research, 40*(3), 286–302.

Germann Molz, J. G. (2014, March 3). Toward a network hospitality. *First Monday, 19*(3). http://firstmonday.org/ojs/index.php/fm/article/view/4824/3848

Gelinas, N. (2015, June 16). Airbnb is a problem for cities like New York and San Francisco. *New York Times.* http://www.nytimes.com/roomfordebate/2015/06/16/san-francisco-and-new-york-weigh-airbnbs-effect-on-rent/airbnb-is-a-problem-for-cities-like-new-york-and-san-francisco

Gilli, M., & Ferrari, S. (2016). The "albergo diffuso": A new Italian model of network hospitality. In A. P. Russo & G. Richards (Eds.), *New localities in tourism* (pp. 65–83). Bristol: Channel View.

Guy, J.-S. (2009, Spring). What is global and what is local? A theoretical discussion around globalization. *Parsons Journal for Information Mapping, I*(2), 322.

Hannigan, J. (1998). *Fantasy City: Pleasure and profit in the postmodern metropolis.* London: Routledge.

Hannigan, J. (2007). From fantasy city to creative city. In G. Richards & J. Wilson (Eds.), *Tourism, creativity and development* (pp. 48–56). London: Routledge.
HOTREC. (2014). *HOTREC raises strong concerns about the shadow tourist accommodation market and calls for a level playing field*. Accessed January 26, 2016, from http://www.hotrec.eu/newsroom/press-releases-1714/hotrec-raises-strong-concerns-about-the-shadow-tourist-accommodation-market-and-calls-for-a-level-playing-field.aspx
Judd, D. R., & Fainstein, S. S. (1999). *The tourist city*. New Haven, CT: Yale University Press.
Kannisto, P. (2014). *The global Nomad*. Tilburg: Tilburg University.
Korczynski, M., & Ott, U. (2006). The menu in society: Mediating structures of power and enchanting myths of individual Sovereignty. *Sociology, 40*(5), 911–928.
Lange, B. (2012). Field configuring events: How culturepreneurs use space for the purpose of professionalisation in the design segment of Berlin. In G. Hagoort, A. Thomassen, & R. Kooyman (Eds.), *Pioneering minds worldwide* (pp. 117–121). Delft: Eburon.
Lugosi, P., Bell, D., & Lugosi, K. (2010). Hospitality, culture and regeneration: Urban decay, entrepreneurship and the 'ruin' bars of Budapest. *Urban Studies, 47*, 3079–3101.
MacCannell, D. (1976). *The tourist: A new theory of the leisure class*. Berkeley, CA: University of California Press.
Miossec, J. M. (1977). Un modèle de l'espace touristique. *L'Espace Géographique, 1*, 41–48.
Mount, I. (2014, May 28). Airbnb, Uber under attack in Barcelona. *Fortune*. Accessed January 26, 2016, from http://fortune.com/2014/05/28/airbnb-uber-barcelona/
New York State Office of the Attorney General. (2014). *Airbnb in the city*. New York: State Office of the Attorney General.
Nguyen, H. (2013). *Brand passion index: Airbnb and Hipmunk outpace the big guys*. Accessed January 26, 2016, from http://www.netbase.com/all-posts/brand-passion-index-airbnb-and-hipmunk-outpace-the-big-guys/
Oates, G. (2015). Alternative lodging versus traditional hotels. *Skift Magazine, 2*, 52–53.
O'Brien, S. A. (2015). *'Crazy money'—Airbnb valued at over $25 billion*. Accessed January 26, 2016, from http://money.cnn.com/2015/06/27/technology/airbnb-funding-valuation-update/
Ochoa, G. (2015). *Global tourism chains and local development in the Amazon: Implications for community wellbeing*. s-Hertogenbosch: BOXPress.
OECD. (2014). *Tourism and the creative industries*. Paris: Organisation for Economic Cooperation & Development.
Pinchera, M. (2015). *Are you experienced?* Accessed January 26, 2016, from http://www.mpiweb.org/Magazine/MPINews/2015/11/01/are-you-experienced
Refinery 29. (2015). *30 Airbnbs that will blow your mind (Not your budget)*. Accessed January 26, 2016, from http://www.refinery29.com/crazy-airbnb-rentals#slide
Richards, G. (2010). *Leisure in the network society: From pseudo-events to hyperfestivity?* https://www.academia.edu/1271795/Leisure_in_the_Network_Society
Richards, G. (2011). Creativity and tourism: The state of the art. *Annals of Tourism Research, 38* (4), 1225–1253.
Richards, G. (2013). Tourism and creativity in the city. *Current Issues in Tourism, 17*, 119–144.
Richards, G. (2014). Creating relational tourism through exchange: The Maltese experience. *Journal of Hospitality and Tourism, 12*(1), 87–94.
Richards, G. (2015). Barcelona: A victim of its own success? In S. Hodes (Ed.), *Amsterdam: Anticipating the future* (pp. 58–59). Amsterdam: Architectura & Natura Press.
Richards, G. (2016, September). Tourism and the city: Towards new models? Afers Internacionals, N° 113: «Turismo: perspectivas locales y tendencias globales», Ed. Yolanda Onghena, CIDOB.
Richards, G., & Delgado, E. (2003). *Trusting spaces*. Barcelona: Interarts.
Richards, G., & Wilson, J. (2004). *The global Nomad*. Bristol: Channel View.
Russo, A. P., & Quaglieri Domínguez, A. (2012). From the dual tourist city to the creative melting pot: The liquid geographies of global cultural consumerism. In M. Smith & G. Richards (Eds.), *Routledge handbook of cultural tourism* (pp. 324–331). London: Routledge.

Shove, E., Pantzar, M., & Watson, M. (2012). *The dynamics of social practice everyday life and how it changes*. London: Sage.

Smith, R. A. (1991). Beach resorts: A model of development evolution. *Landscape and Urban Planning, 21*(3), 189–210.

The Verge. (2015). *Airbnb's worst problems are confirmed by its own data*. Accessed January 26, 2016, from http://www.theverge.com/2015/12/4/9849242/airbnb-data-new-york-affordable-housing-illegal-hotels

Tomasetti, K. (2014, August). Slowly does it. *Easyjet in-flight magazine*.

Urry, J. (1990). *The tourist gaze*. London: Sage.

Zukin, S. (1991). *Landscapes of power: From Detroit to Disney World*. Berkeley, CA: University of California Press.

Zukin, S. (1995). *The cultures of cities*. Oxford: Blackwell.

Zukin, S. (2010). *Naked City: The death and life of authentic urban places*. Oxford: Oxford University Press.

Collaborative Economy and Destination Marketing Organisations: A Systems Approach

Jonathon Day

Abstract Destination systems, embedded systems in the larger tourism system, evolve as a result of changes in consumer and stakeholder expectations, social trends and new technologies. New system dynamics necessitate change to traditional supply chains, management practices and relations, and allow the entrance of new players. This chapter examines the changing nature of Destination Marketing Organisations (DMOs) and the challenges they face in providing value to consumers and stakeholders. It also examines the rise of collaborative economy companies and their impact on the destination system. Collaborative economy companies in the destination are leading to new legislative frameworks, a changing competitive landscape, a wider range of product and increased innovation. The chapter also examines the new dynamics developing in the destination system as DMOs and collaborative economy companies respond to the changing system and to each other. Changing DMO roles, new areas of conflict and potential opportunities for collaboration in the collaborative economy are explored.

Keywords Collaborative economy • Destination marketing organisations • Tourism systems • Destination systems • Impacts

1 Introduction

The tourism system (Mill & Morrison, 2009) is constantly changing. As a complex adaptive system (Farrell & Twining-Ward, 2005), tourism adapts to changes in technology, consumer tastes, and financial conditions to name a few factors, by reorganizing, embracing new types of organisations and adapting to new conditions. Driven by changing consumer demands and fueled by enabling technology, the collaborative economy is shifting the equilibrium within the tourism system in a variety of ways. In some ways, these changes are most evident in destinations, themselves systems embedded in the larger tourism systems (Day, Cai, & Murphy, 2011). But

J. Day (✉)
School of Hospitality and Tourism Management, Purdue University, 610 Purdue Mall, West Lafayette, IN 47907, USA
e-mail: gjday@purdue.edu

D. Dredge, S. Gyimóthy (eds.), *Collaborative Economy and Tourism*,
Tourism on the Verge, DOI 10.1007/978-3-319-51799-5_11

collaborative consumption related changes are not the only changes currently taking place in destinations. Technology and new expectations of DMOs are leading to changes in the focus and operation of these actors in the destination system. The current chapter explores such evolution due to the entrance of collaborative consumption related organisations, challenges faced by DMOs and the impacts of collaboration consumption of DMOs.

2 Systems and Value: Destinations, DMOs and the Sharing Economy

Destination systems, like tourism systems more generally, are complex adaptive systems (Day et al., 2011; Volgger & Pechlaner, 2015). They are comprised of a broad variety of types of organisations. The destination system includes a mix of attractions, events, hotels and other lodging, food and beverage, other support industries like retail establishments, infrastructure (water, power, communication, sewage/drainage, healthcare, security), transportation, and hospitality services (Mill & Morrison, 2009). Destinations can be considered "amalgams of tourism products and services, offering an integrated experience to consumers" (Buhalis, 2000, p. 98) or packages of tourism facilities and services (Hu & Ritchie, 1993). Within the destination system, networks of organisations come together to create value for consumers and stakeholders. This value is measured in a variety of ways, the most common of which is what network members will pay for the product, service or experience (Porter & Millar, 1985). Using this economic proxy for value, a business is viable when the value it creates exceeds the cost of performing the value activities. Companies that don't create value are not sustainable. The value chain for a company is the set of activities that must take place to create value (Porter, 1985).

Value chains are embedded in a larger "stream" of activities Porter describes as a "value system". For instance, the value system for tourism includes the value chain of travel providers, destination system members and the consumers themselves. The ability of the destination system to deliver consumer experiences is dependent on the value created by each organisation in the system (Song, Liu, & Chen, 2013). Value chain/value system analysis has been applied in a variety of contexts in tourism research (Mojic, 2012; NDivo & Cantoni, 2015). Porter and Millar's value chain concept is useful in at least two ways—it focuses on value and it recognises the linkages between values that are created by different actors in the system. The value chain/value system approach also recognises the inter-dependencies of actors to create value. As Song et al. (2013) note "every node of the chain can affect the value attained by tourists, which in turn affects the profit of individual actors" (p. 17). However, the traditional value chain and value system approach to tourism has significant limitations derived from its narrow definition of value. One notes that the tourism system is often considered as an "industrial system" and, "tourism is primarily valued as a tool for regional economic development, employment and investment" (Dredge, 2016, p. 2). This characterisation of tourism as a purely economic phenomenon ignores the broader nature of tourism. Tourism takes place in destination communities and impacts life in those communities both positively and negatively. A multidimensional approach to tourism, incorporating a broader set of metrics rather than only economic value is increasingly necessary for analysis of the tourism system.

As the system changes, organisations adapt to create value in new ways and new types of value-creating organisations enter the system. For example, the business model of leisure travel agents has adapted to changes due to innovation in technology, resulting in new organisations like online travel agencies (OTAs), which provide new value chains for consumers. For some time there has been a general understanding that consumer demands are changing and travellers are increasingly rejecting the standardisation and commodification of tourism experiences. This has been evident in the growth of new products promising more authentic or unique experiences and can be seen in the rising popularity of products such as boutique hotel chains and farm to table dining. Stimulated by technology that supports peer-to-peer interactions, these trends have contributed to the growth of the collaborative economy. As noted by Dredge and Gyimóthy (2015) "consuming travel is intimately bound to identity construction and narratives of authentic encounters with local culture" (p. 9). The collaborative economy has enabled travellers to enjoy these types of experiences. Other factors contributing to the growth of the collaborative economy in tourism include the consumer's ability to interact directly with tourism providers and the resultant individualized, "user-focused" service provided by the hosts and collaborative economy providers, and the low incremental capital requirements of companies in providing innovative products (Dredge & Gyimóthy, 2015). These trends, combined with underlying principles of collaborative consumption identified by Botsman and Rogers (2010)—critical mass, idling capacity, belief in the commons and trust in strangers—have resulted in changes in the system.

Many of the same factors that have facilitated the rise of the collaborative economy—new technologies, changing consumer wants and needs, and new social norms—are significantly impacting DMOs and their role in the tourism system. Presently, DMOs face an existential challenge to create value in the destination system (Dredge, 2016) at a time when many of their traditional core competencies are no longer valued or becoming too complex and costly to undertake effectively using current funding models.

3 The DMO's Challenge to Create Value

In some countries, DMOs have existed for over a century. These organisations are known by a variety of names, including national tourism offices (NTOs), regional tourism offices (RTOs) and visitors and convention bureaus (CVBs) and are found across the globe. The acronym, DMO, refers to both Destination Marketing

Organisations and Destination Marketing Organisations (Dredge, 2016). Pike (2004) defined the Destination Marketing Organisation as "any organization, at any level, which is responsible for the marketing of an identifiable destination" (p. 14) while Morrison (2013) described destination management as a "broader and more inclusive concept that includes destination marketing and other activities to manage tourism at the destination" (p. 9). As the role of DMOs adjusts to changing conditions, the concept of destination "management", with particular reference to destination development activities, is gaining favour among DMO managers. While appealing, the ability of DMOs to manage the destination system in a traditional "command and control" sense overstates the capabilities of most DMOs. In recent years, a number of researchers (Beaumont & Dredge, 2010; Song et al., 2013; Volgger & Pechlaner, 2015) have recognised the limitations of so-called "destination managers" and proposed the concept of destination network governance, in which DMOs are framed as network coordinators or network managers, and is a more appropriate description of the role of DMOs in the destination system. As "network managers" their ability to interact with stakeholders in the tourism system is critical to their success (Beaumont & Dredge, 2010; Bornhorst, Brent Ritchie, & Sheehan, 2010; Volgger & Pechlaner, 2014). Indeed, the DMO role of network "management" is more dependent on stakeholder oriented and participative governance than the "top down management" approach commonly associated with company management. DMOs have a singular position in the value chains within the destination system and the larger tourism system. While they rarely have a significant direct role in the consumer's destination experience, they are generally perceived to add value through a set of activities that support the effectiveness of the networks to provide value. Nevertheless, in recent years, the assumption that DMOs add value to the system has been challenged by academics (Dredge, 2016) and practitioners (Gonzalo, 2013; Thompson, 2012). The ability of DMOs to show the value they create is an on-going challenge.

Dredge noted that "DMO functions fall into three broad categories designed to enhance tourism industry outcomes: market enhancing policies, product enhancing policies and policies addressing market failures" (Dredge, 2016, p. 3) and Morrison (2013) identified the following six key roles of DMOs:

- Leadership and Coordination: Setting the agenda for tourism and coordinating stakeholders' efforts toward achieving the agenda.
- Planning and Research: Conducting the essential planning and research needed to attain the destination vision and goals.
- Product Development: Planning and ensuring the appropriate development of physical products and services for the destination.
- Marketing and Promotion: Creating destination positioning and branding, selecting the most appropriate markets, and promoting the destination.
- Partnership and Team Building: Fostering cooperation among government agencies and within the private sector and building partnership teams to meet specific goals.
- Community Relations: Involving local community leaders and residents in tourism and monitoring resident attitudes to tourism (pp. 6–7).

While the list is comprehensive, one may note considerable variation in the activities of DMO from this ideal. Not all DMOs undertake all these roles, and those that do undertake all these actions, do not prioritise them equally. Resource limitations within DMOs (Shankman, 2013) tend to confound the ability to fulfill these roles effectively.

Recognising the challenge to remain relevant in the changing tourism system, Destination Marketing Association International (DMAI) initiated research to provide a "strategic road map for the next generation of global destination marketing". That resulted in the *Destination Next* Report (DMAI, 2014) that advocates a rebalancing of DMO priorities to include adjusting marketing techniques to meet the needs of new consumers (dealing with the new marketplace: broadcast to engagement), increasing stakeholder engagement (evolving the DMO business model: collaboration and partnerships) and developing product and destination products, services and experiences (building and protecting the destination brand: destination managers).

Destination Next emphasises stakeholder engagement. As such it recognises the need for DMOs to engage with their network to create value. This approach is consistent with research proposing the necessity of networked governance of destinations (Bornhorst et al., 2010; Volgger & Pechlaner, 2014). *Destination Next* also advocates significant changes from "business as usual" approaches to marketing. Traditionally, DMOs have focused on marketing and promotion although there has been greater emphasis on product/destination development activities as DMO have revisited the term "marketing". While the concept of the marketing mix is comprised of four P's—product, price, promotion and place (distribution)—introduced by McCarthy (1960), many practitioners continue to tend to equate marketing with promotional activities. DMOs have undertaken advertising campaigns, supported destination publicity efforts, undertaken sales activities, and provided comprehensive (often generic) information about the destination. The evaluation of the value created by DMO activity is dominated by analysis of advertising and promotional activities (Bornhorst et al., 2010). However, effectiveness of DMOs to "add value" through promotional activities is questionable. Criticisms of DMO marketing include that it is underfunded and insufficient to meet the demands of the market place (Gonzalo, 2013; Shankman, 2013; Thompson, 2012). More recently, DMOs have become more engaged in destination development, product development and experience management. Rebalancing of these priorities reflects the response of DMOs to changing conditions. For example, the rise of SoMoLo (Social, Mobile and Local) technologies, drivers of the CE, requires greater emphasis than ever before on the delivery of the product experience. A negative video distributed via social media has the potential to overwhelm positive advertising campaigns. Destination Marketing/Management Organisations are working to ensure that experience delivery measure up to the promise of their promotions.

Product and destination development is a multidimensional construct for DMOs that includes not only stimulating the development of physical product but also supporting human capital development and training. As a result, DMOs are engaging in greater levels of "internal" marketing within the destination. Although Kotler, Bowen, and Makens (2015) defined internal marketing as "marketing to its internal customers, its employees" (p. 274) in the case of a destination, internal customers include employees and stakeholders/actors within the destination system. While many DMOs have moved resources to destination development their ability to impact the destination has also been questioned. Based on current evidence, Pike and Page (2014) suggest that DMOs have very little impact on overall visitor experience.

Whether DMOs are redundant or merely in a period of transition will be revealed in the future. Even as DMOs adjust to the new system dynamics, new organisations are playing increasingly important roles in destination marketing. The rise of Business Improvement Districts (BIDs) or the more tourism focused Tourism Improvement Districts (TIDs) as funding mechanisms for existing DMOs, or alternatives to existing DMOs undertaking marketing and product development (Civitas, 2014), reflects the changing dynamics of DMOs. Nevertheless, DMOs and TID tend to be anchored in the economic value of tourism. Dredge (2016) posited that DMOs are policy tools—organisational instruments—designed to support industrial and economic policies. To create value in the destination system, DMOs are seeking closer relationships with economic development organisations. This approach of DMOs to focus on purely industrial and economic factors restrict the ability of DMOs to contribute to other important considerations, such as social and environmental concerns, and limits the value they can create. This raises the important issue that DMOs must consider: Who they are creating value for? Is it the destination community or the industrial tourism system in the destination community? While *Destination Next* advocates greater stakeholder engagement, the stakeholders are often defined as tourism business operators and governments as opposed to consumers and destination residents.

While traditional DMOs and new organisations like TID are place-based, some authors suggest that being constrained by location is one of the factors limiting the effectiveness of DMOs. It has been proposed that destinations should not be bounded by arbitrary demarcations and that "destinations are socially, politically, spatially and economically mobile" (Dredge, 2016, p. 4). Destinations exist at different scales—local, regional and beyond- simultaneously and the interaction between stakeholders at different levels raises the complexity for DMOs substantially (Dredge & Jamal, 2013). Organisations that market places that are not confined by physical destination boundaries are identifiable in the commercial world as tour operators, travel wholesalers and online travel agencies.

4 Destinations and the Rise of the Collaborative Economy

While DMOs adapt to these new challenges in creating value, other elements of the destination system are rapidly changing. The rise of collaborative consumption represents significant change to the dynamics of the destination as new organisations enter the system and new experiences are generated. Such changes within the system create new opportunities and new rivalries. New actors in the system create new "value chain" networks to deliver tourism experiences. The response to the changing system dynamics, and the disruption to the current system, impacts not only DMOs but also the destination system.

4.1 New Companies in the Destination System

The impacts of companies leveraging the collaborative economy have been widespread, but tourism and visitor related industries have been impacted most dramatically. Core elements of the destination mix, including transportation, accommodations, and tours and attractions have seen new entrants based on the basic principles of the sharing economy. Several such organisations have achieved significant market share. Airbnb, the peer-to-peer accommodation facilitator, has over two million rooms available every night, significantly more than the largest hotel chain, Marriott including newly acquired Starwood, with 1.1 million rooms and the impact of Airbnb has been widespread given that it operates in 191 countries (Chafkin, 2016). In the United States it is currently capturing 1.6–1.8% of traditional hotel demand (Lane & Woodworth, 2016). In several destinations, including New York, Los Angles, San Francisco, and Miami, the number of Airbnb rooms available represents more than 10% of the available hotel rooms. One notes that loyalty to Airbnb is high and average revenue per room beats hotel revenue (Lane & Woodworth, 2016), indicating that the organisation is delivering value not satisfied by traditional hotels. Collaborative economy companies like Airbnb, Uber and others are now important components of many destination systems.

4.2 Innovation in the System

Collaborative economy companies have unleashed a wide range of new experiences for consumers. From unique accommodation styles to tours with local experts, from rideshares with locals to sharing meals in people's homes and learning about their lives, such sharing economy companies provide highly differentiated products with a unique personal flavour. One may note that many of these product types have existed for some time in one form or another. Meals with locals have been available in New Zealand for many years; cycle rental is not new, or couch surfing, or personalized specialty tours. So, one may argue that the social and technological advances that have led to collaborative consumption have ushered in a wave of innovation in the destination system and that these trends have enabled existing business concepts to flourish in new forms.

4.3 Changing Dynamics

Some collaborative economy companies in destinations have entered relatively new market spaces with little controversy. For instance, bicycle-share companies and car-sharing companies have been embraced, even encouraged, by many destinations. Nevertheless, the rise of collaborative economy companies in some destination systems is leading to conflict and change; some of which is predictable but some of which is unexpected. Collaborative economy organisations, disruptors of the current equilibrium, operate new business models and challenge existing legislative frameworks. Policy makers and legislators are responding to these new circumstances in a variety of ways, from embracing the new companies to imposing regulations and taxes, to banning collaborative economy activities completely. While early advocates of collaborative economy proposed that the marketplace could be policed by self-regulatory mechanisms such as social media feedback, and this would be sufficient to govern the collaborative economy, recognition is emerging that new regulatory frameworks designed to meet public safety and market needs is required. In some cases, these new legislative frameworks are reducing legal bureaucracy and sidelining existing structures. In some cases new legislation supports "legacy" organisations, like taxi companies, that have longstanding and highly regulated operating agreements with cities. Such approaches are criticised by collaborative economy representatives as stifling business innovation.

An additional element of complexity in this dynamic is that each destination community is responding in their own way and legislation is not uniform across the sharing economy companies. Rideshare companies compete with powerful, revenue generating and highly regulated taxi companies, and these face different legal battles compared to accommodation sharing organisations. For example, in New York where taxi interests are strong, Uber delayed a government imposed cap on its growth. Adding to the complexity of the change is the fact that many destinations are governed by local and regional authorities with differing perspectives about the value of collaborative economy elements. In the greater Los Angeles area, while the city of Los Angeles accepted Airbnb, Santa Monica has legislated against short-term rentals (Sanders, 2015). In addition to the basic questions of operation, legislation is developing to ensure public health and safety in the new regime where providers are not "professionals". It is certain that there may be many legal battles before a new equilibrium is established in the legal frameworks which allow collaborative economy companies to operate in destinations.

There is also conflict in some sectors of the system where competition between the traditional organisations and new challengers is both direct and immediate. Building on Dredge and Gyimóthy's (2015) conceptual work, Table 1 highlights the traditional enterprises the new businesses are challenging. The competition between ride-share companies and traditional taxi companies is insightful. Uber and other ride sharing companies compete directly with taxi companies, many with long histories and substantial legal protection. The conflict between these two groups of suppliers has been among the most confrontational. Hotel companies,

Table 1 Collaborative economy creates new competition

Destination mix	Collaborative economy A sample of new enterprises	Traditional types of enterprise
Where can I stay? Accommodations	AirBnb Couch Surfing VRBO Luxury Retreats Flipkey Onefinestay Homeaway	Hotel companies
How can I get there/Get around? Transportations	Uber Lyft GrabTaxi (Malaysia) Zipcar Bicycle shares (Liquid) Relay Rides Getaround Sidecar	Taxis
Where can I get travel products, tours and experiences? Tours and Guides	Guidehire Localo ADVLO Likealocal Vayable	Local tour companies
Where can I eat? Food	UberEats Bonappatour UberFresh Eatwith VoulezVousDiner	Restaurants and food delivery

while recognizing the changing dynamics of the accommodations market, have not responded as aggressively to the new competitors; there are differing perspectives about the potential impact of the new collaborative economy. Nevertheless, hoteliers are aware of the changing system dynamics. Commentators have noted the potential impact on traditional supply and demand equations, particularly during peak times (Jordan, 2015; O'Neill, 2015). As new forms of accommodations become popular with both leisure and business travellers, they will impact various parts of the industry in different ways. For instance, hotel room contracting associated with conventions, already changing due to the impact of OTAs, will need to adapt to emerging accommodation trends. While there is challenge for traditional accommodation providers, there is also opportunity for innovation and collaboration. Some hotel chains, such as Starwood, Hilton and Hyatt have partnered with rideshare company Uber. Others have partnered with companies offering complementary products. For example, Onefinestay, a company that offers high-end luxury home rentals, and Hyatt have developed a strategic partnership (Staff, 2015). Interestingly, several major hotel brands have adopted sharing elements of collaborative economy principles. Accor has adopted listing policies similar to Airbnb and increased its property offerings from 3700 to over 10,000 by adding independent, non-affiliated properties (Staff, 2015). Marriott, recognising excess capacity with meeting space, has partnered with LiquidSpace, a sharing company that offers workspace for business (Botsman, 2014).

Less predictable are the conflicts created by new relationships within the system. While in the past commercial accommodations were restricted to hotels and tourists often confined to "tourist bubbles" within cities or other destinations, today house, apartment and room sharing sites bring tourists into the community. This has some advantages as it disperses economic benefits from tourism more broadly throughout a destination. Airbnb study of the impact of *Home-sharing in Portland and Its Neighborhoods* (Airbnb, 2014) describe "neighborhood activation" as Airbnb's ability to "stay in traditionally less visited towns and neighborhoods" (p. 11). While neighborhood activation has possible benefits, it also has the potential to increase community tension. For example, in Barcelona, the headline "Airbnb remains a symbol of Barcelona's growing unease with tourism" (Croft, 2015) leads to a discussion of the mayor "picking a fight with home rental websites as she cracks down on uncontrolled tourism that she fears could drive out poor residents and spoil the Catalan capital's charm" (Croft, 2015). Similar tensions are experienced in a variety of locations including Santa Monica and New York.

4.4 New Business Structures and New Participants in Tourism

Many collaborative economy businesses can be characterised by a larger number of relatively independent operators working with a technology-based "umbrella" system. For example, Airbnb provides a system through which people with excess capacity in their homes (i.e. a spare bedroom) can rent the space to travellers. Similarly, Uber allows people with cars and spare time to provide transportation services. These new "hosts" may not identify as being part of the tourism system and their introduction to the system creates a need for capacity building, training and knowledge sharing to ensure quality delivery of tourism experiences.

5 Collaborative Economy and the Role of DMOs

As collaborative economy enterprises establish their place in the new system, the growth of the collaborative economy in many destinations is challenging DMOs to adjust current practices. While the DMO may be considered a "steward" of the destination, destination and DMO are distinct. DMOs must respond to this changing system dynamic in at least two ways:

- Impact on DMO: They must respond to the specific impacts these new players make on the DMOs themselves.
- Impact on the destination: They must adapt and respond to the rise of collaborative economy companies in order to meet their tourism management goals for the destination.

Responding to these changes, DMOs are presented with a series of potential challenges to DMOs. Using the six roles of DMOs (Morrison, 2013) discussed earlier in the chapter as a framework for analysis, new challenges include:

Leadership and Coordination Partnership and Team Building: DMOs must engage with new collaborative economy players as they work to set the agenda for tourism and coordinate stakeholders' efforts toward achieving the agenda. This process is impacted by several factors including role conflict in the system as new competitors establish roles within the destination, and/or larger numbers of stakeholders and actors who are either new to the tourism industry or do not identify as being part of it. DMOs will need to prove to these new participants the value of DMOs in the system in order to successfully establish their role as leaders, coordinators or potential partners.

Planning and Research The changing dynamics of the system will necessitate new research to better understand the impacts of the CE, and also to identify strategies for attaining a destination's vision and goals. The inclusion of new companies will require adaptation and modifications to destination plans and their inclusion in the destination planning process.

Product Development Planning to ensure the appropriate development of physical products and services for the destination is required. DMOs must respond to changing consumer preferences and emerging business models as they undertake destination planning for product development. DMOs active in product development may influence policy that seeks to regulate collaborative economy companies. As noted previously, more emphasis on destination experience is increasingly placing DMOs in the role of promoting standards of service that are destination brand consistent. Training programs designed to create "destination ambassadors" are becoming more common (Shankman, 2014) as a means of ensuring customer service standards throughout the destination systems. As a new extension to this task, DMOs must engage with collaborative economy travel product suppliers like Uber drivers and AirBnb hosts to ensure high levels of service and brand-consistent messaging.

Marketing and Promotion A key function of DMOs is the creation of destination positioning and branding and selection of the most appropriate markets and promotion of the destination. Several DMOs have recognized the value of crowdsourcing elements of their advertising creative in order to leverage the believability of user-generated content. Australia's: Nothing Like Australia" campaign ("There's Nothing Like Australia—Campaign Strategy," 2012) collected

60,000 stories and images from ordinary Australians and shared them with potential travellers from around the world.

As the impact of collaborative economy on destinations becomes clearer, innovative DMOs are joining in marketing campaigns with collaborative economy partners. In July of 2015, San Francisco announced a first-of-its kind "destination promotion partnership" that leverages the sharing economy to spread the economic benefits of travel and tourism throughout the city (Alderton, 2015). In announcing the program, the San Francisco Travel Association, the city's DMO, emphasised that the campaign would "complement—not replace- its relationship with the (traditional) hospitality community". The campaign reflects many product development components including creating neighborhood toolkits for local merchants and supporting local hosts to share their love of San Francisco. More traditional promotion includes sales activities with meeting and event planners responsible for city-wide conferences and the development of content about local neighborhoods, businesses and experiences across the city.

Community Relations As noted previously, the rise of collaborative economy companies, particularly accommodation sharing companies, has placed residents in new proximity to guests. This is touted as a benefit that supports local business and spreads the benefits of tourism throughout the community. However, also as noted previously, these new tourists have increased tensions in some destinations. While DMOs rarely have direct control over legislation regarding collaborative economy companies or their activities, this is a new challenge that DMOs face in addressing community understanding and appreciation of tourism within the community. Advocacy for the tourism industry is a key role of the DMOs, and this role is expected to become increasingly important in the years ahead according to the *Destination Next* strategic analysis (DMAI, 2014). DMOs will need to reconcile the benefits and the costs of tourism and tourists in new ways and to new stakeholder groups.

6 Responding to the New Destination System Dynamics

The changing dynamics of the destination have practical implications for DMOs beyond the issues associated with the six core roles already identified in the chapter. DMOs governance models are based on the previous system equilibrium and will need to adapt to the changing market place. Perhaps the clearest example is in the funding models of CVBs in the United States. Over 88% of CVBs are funded by room tax from hotels (DMAI, 2015). To some degree, this approach makes policy sense as commercial accommodations were direct beneficiaries of marketing activities undertaken by DMOs. To date, only a handful of destinations require collaborative economy companies to collect occupancy tax (Airbnb, 2016). In the new collaborative economy, where both commercial accommodation and "shared accommodations" benefit from the destination marketing undertaken by the

DMO, at least two issues associated with room tax, or its equivalent, can be identified:

- Shared accommodation not paying room tax or its equivalent is clearly a "free-rider" on the DMO's marketing efforts. While many tourism organisations "ride-free" (i.e. attractions and tour operations) they are rarely direct competitors and the fairness of two competitive accommodation providers (Airbnb and a hotel company for example) operating under different tax rules is problematic; and
- In destinations where room tax funds DMOs and shared accommodation is not room-taxed, the DMO lacks direct financial incentive to encourage visitors to use the shared accommodation.

The issue is significant for both collaborative economy companies and DMOs. San Francisco Travel, recognised as one of the first DMOs to partner in marketing activities with Airbnb, ensured the organisation was collecting occupancy tax, requiring insurance providing the guarantees for business in a similar way to hotels. As Joe D'Alessandro, President and CEO of San Francisco Travel noted "It's about levelling the playing field. It would not have been fair for Airbnb to operate and not collect the hotel tax and not play by the same rules that hotels do (Oates, 2016)." Interestingly, Airbnb has taken the position that it would like to collect the tax, but it is stopped in some cities including New York City, where hotels oppose such legislation since they fear it will legitimise Airbnb's activity (Griswold, 2015).

Despite such issues, collaborative economy companies are appealing to DMOs for a variety of reasons. Collaborative economy companies provide additional capacity at times of high demand. Airbnb is acknowledged as providing important additional rooms for not only major conferences but mega-events like the Superbowl (Oates, 2016), the Olympics, and Papal visits. Additionally, collaborative economy companies are useful to destination markets who typically pursue differentiation strategies (Porter, 1980) as they tend to provide special experiences useful in demonstrating the uniqueness of the destination experience.

Although many of the issues associated with the rise of collaborative economy impact DMOs indirectly, the new sharing economy does present some direct and immediate challenges to DMOs. For instance, DMOs also face challenges as they deal with the democratizing of destination knowledge. They often position themselves as the "authoritative" source of information about the destination. In this new market, where experts can provide customized tours on specific topics, the DMO may have the most general information but there will also be specific experts with greater knowledge in specific fields. How DMOs respond to this changing dynamic will be important in establishing the new equilibrium within the destination. There is clearly potential for other disruption of traditional roles. For instance, collaborative forces could challenge the assumption that DMOs are the "legitimate" destination branders. An early example of this is the "Up Greek Tourism" campaign. Up Greek Tourism was established during the Greek financial crisis by expatriates concerned about the lack of government funding for tourism, an important component of the struggling Greek economy. Funded by crowdsourcing, the marketing campaign ran in 2012 in London, New York, and Washington, DC and featured advertising creative from award winning Greece-based designer ("Up with Greek Tourism").

It should be expected that other challenges will emerge and, while the collaborative economy offers a broad range of product, some organisations have greater likelihood to disrupt traditional DMO roles. As an example, Airbnb is a shared accommodation sales facilitator, connecting homeowners with an extra room to the marketplace. As such, it works with a complex network of "non-professional" product providers to deliver tourism product. The similarity to the role of a DMO is striking; Airbnb provides leadership and coordination to its network, undertakes planning and research to facilitate more efficient sales, supports product development with its host network, markets and promotes the network, fosters cooperation between government entities and within the private sector to meet goals, and engages in community relations. Such similarities represent opportunities for both collaboration and synergy or competition.

6.1 In the Balance

DMOs must assess the value of the collaborative economy to their destinations. With the introduction of new members in the tourism system, DMOs are faced with the challenge of determining which organisations will be most helpful to achieve overall destination goals. Clearly, the costs and benefits of collaborative consumption are different from traditional tourism; some destinations are exploring the value of these new relationships. For instance, Airbnb, with assistance from Visit Portland, examined the value of Airbnb to the Portland community (Airbnb, 2014) and found the company supported household incomes, promoted enterprise and innovation, grew the tourism market by attracting "new" travelers, and "activated" neighborhoods for tourism. As DMOs assess the value of developing relationships with collaborative economy they must consider a variety of factors; the market demand for the products, the positive and negative impacts on the destination, the economic contribution of the CE, the quality of the tourism experience, and others.

While some progressive DMOs, like the San Francisco Travel Association, have engaged with collaborative economy partners, many DMOs are taking a "wait and see" approach to the largest and most impactful collaborative economy companies. As one DMO CEO in a major destination noted, "we don't formally promote it. Airbnb and the Ubers have not approached us. It's an evolving model" (Shankman, 2015). Awareness of collaborative economy and the issues associated with it is growing. Rachel Botsman, co-author of "*What's mine is yours: The Rise of the Collaborative Consumption*" (Botsman & Rogers, 2010) was the keynote speaker at DMAI's, 2014 annual convention. Nevertheless, concern for the impacts of these new approaches is low. DMAI's strategic planning report, *Destination Next* (2014), ranks "the market moving toward a shared economy with assets being rented or bartered outside traditional commercial arrangements (i.e., Airbnb, home exchange)", 45 of 64 important trends impacting destination marketing.

At the same time, collaborative economy companies are assessing the value provided by engaging with DMOs. As new players in the destination system they have a fresh perspective on the relevance of DMOs to tourism system. As noted previously, DMOs are currently addressing a number of challenges associated with changing roles and stakeholder engagement. DMOs recognise a lack of understanding of their work and have embarked on advocacy programs designed to raise awareness of the value created through their actions. Within this broader context, the importance of establishing the relevance of DMOs in the "new" tourism system should not be underestimated. Interestingly, Airbnb's head of global hospitality and strategy, Chip Conley, is reported to have had "immersive sessions" with Hilton, Hyatt and Marriott about "how to be collaborative and how we can work together to promote travel and tourism globally" (Staff, 2015). New players in the destination system must see the value created by DMOs in order to engage.

7 Conclusions

The tourism system and the destination system, in particular, are changing as the result of evolving technology and demand for more authentic experiences. As the system adjusts to the entry of new organisations using innovative business models and distributed workforces, new opportunities for both conflict and collaboration are emerging. Stakeholders within the destination are responding in a variety of ways: new policies and legislation are developing, new sources of competition are emerging, and new opportunities for collaboration to meet the needs of consumers are presenting themselves.

Within this system, DMOs face new challenges to achieve their tourism goals in the changing destination system. DMOs are increasingly balancing traditional promotional priorities with product development responsibilities that range from customer service training to grant programs for attracting new tourism investments. At the same time, DMOs face existential threats to which they are responding with advocacy and stakeholder awareness campaigns highlighting the value they provide to the destination system. At this highly dynamic time in DMO evolution, the disruptive impacts of the collaborative economy are becoming increasingly apparent. Collaborative economy has the potential to impact each of the core roles of the DMO, challenging DMOs to engage with a wide range of new actors and responding to new business models and innovative products. While collaborative economy companies are not currently directly competing with DMOs, they are a disruptive force that impacts DMO operations. As DMOs adjust their approach to achieving their goals in light of the new destination dynamics, they must adjust to systematics inequities as the new equilibrium emerges. DMOs are directly impacted by the conflict concerning collaborative economy lodging companies and lodging taxes, the primary funding mechanisms for DMOs. While there is already concern over the funding model for DMOs, this issue creates urgency for many DMOs to find alternative approaches to funding their operations. The growth of collaborative economy companies in the tourism represents an exciting time of innovation and change in the tourism system. Consumers are embracing new ways of enjoying travel, empowered by new technologies and attitudes toward consumption and social interaction.

References

Airbnb. (2014). *Airbnb: Impacts of home-sharing in Portland and its neighborhoods*. Accessed May 5, 2016, from https://1zxiw0vqx0oryvpz3ikczauf-wpengine.netdna-ssl.com/wp-content/uploads/2016/09/PortlandEconomicImpactReport.pdf

Airbnb. (2016). In what areas is Occupancy Tax Collection and Remittance by Airbnb available? Accessed May 5, 2016, from https://www.airbnb.com/help/article/653/in-what-areas-is-occupancy-tax-collection-and-remittance-by-airbnb-available

Alderton, M. (2015). Airbnb, San Francisco form innovative "Destination Promotion Partnerships". *Successful Meetings*. Accessed May 5, 2016, from http://www.successfulmeetings.com/News/Destinations/West/Airbnb,-San-Francisco-Form-Innovative--Destination-Promotion-Partnership-/

Beaumont, N., & Dredge, D. (2010). Local tourism governance: A comparison of three network approaches. *Journal of Sustainable Tourism, 18*(1), 7–28. doi:10.1080/09669580903215139.

Bornhorst, T., Brent Ritchie, J. R., & Sheehan, L. (2010). Determinants of tourism success for DMOs and destinations: An empirical examination of stakeholders' perspectives. *Tourism Management, 31*(5), 572–589. doi:10.1016/j.tourman.2009.06.008.

Botsman, R. (2014). Sharing's not just for start-ups. *Harvard Business Review*. Accessed May 5, 2016, from https://hbr.org/2014/09/sharings-not-just-for-start-ups

Botsman, R., & Rogers, R. (2010). *What's mine is yours: The rise of collaborative consumption*. New York: Harper Business.

Buhalis, D. (2000). Marketing the competitive destination of the future. *Tourism Management, 21*, 97–116.

Chafkin, M. (2016). Airbnb opens up the world. *Fast Company*, (202), 76–95.

Civitas. (2014). *U.S. tourism district law study*. https://esto.ustravel.org/sites/default/files/ESTO14_Destination_Marketing_Funding_TUESDAY_8.26.pdf

Croft, A. (2015). Airbnb remains a symbol of Barcelona's growing unease with tourism. http://skift.com/2015/08/26/airbnb-remains-symbol-of-barcelonas-growing-unease-with-tourism/

Day, J., Cai, L., & Murphy, L. (2011). Increasing destination competitiveness: Destination brands and their benefits for destination team members. *Asian Journal of Tourism and Hospitality Research, 4*(2), 1–13.

DMAI. (2014). *Destination Next: A strategic road map for the next generation of global destination marketing*. http://www.destinationmarketing.org/sites/destinationmarketing.org/files/DestinationNEXT%20Report%20Phase%201%20July%2022%202014%5B2%5D.pdf

DMAI. (2015). *DMO organizational and financial profile*. http://www.destinationmarketing.org/2015-dmo-organizational-financial-profile-study

Dredge, D. (2016). Are DMOs on the path to redundancy? *Tourism Recreation Research*. doi:10.1080/02508281.2016.1195959.

Dredge, D., & Gyimóthy, S. (2015). The collaborative economy and tourism: Critical perspectives, questionable claims and silenced voices. *Tourism Recreation Research, 40*(3), 286–302. doi:10.1080/02508281.2015.1086076.

Dredge, D., & Jamal, T. (2013). Mobilities on the Gold Coast, Australia: Implications for destination governance and sustainable tourism. *Journal of Sustainable Tourism, 21*(4), 557–579. doi:10.1080/09669582.2013.776064.

Farrell, B., & Twining-Ward, L. (2005). Seven steps towards sustainability: Tourism in the context of new knowledge. *Journal of Sustainable Tourism, 13*(2), 109–122.

Gonzalo, F. (2013). *The destination marketing organization model in tourism is broken*. https://skift.com/2013/07/24/the-destination-marketing-organization-model-in-tourism-is-broken/

Griswold, A. (2015). *Why Airbnb desperately wants to pay hotel taxes*. http://www.slate.com/articles/business/moneybox/2015/02/airbnb_hotel_taxes_why_does_the_sharing_economy_startup_want_to_pay_them.2.html

Hu, Y., & Ritchie, J. (1993). Measuring destination attractiveness: A contextual approach. *Journal of Travel Research, 32*, 25–34.

Jordan, G. (2015). Airbnb not just a worry, but "tectonic shift". http://www.hotelnewsnow.com/mobile/articles.aspx?articleid=16545

Kotler, P., Bowen, J., & Makens, J. (2015). *Marketing for hospitality and tourism* (6th ed.). Boston: Pearson.

Lane, J., & Woodworth, R. (2016). *The sharing economy checks in: An analysis of Airbnb in the United States: Implications on traditional hotel development and market performance going forward*. http://cbrepkfcprod.blob.core.windows.net/downloads/store/12Samples/An_Analysis_of_Airbnb_in_the_United_States.pdf

McCarthy, E. J. (1960). *Basic marketing: A managerial approach*. Homewood Illinois: Richard D. Irwin.

Mill, R., & Morrison, A. (2009). *The tourism system* (6th ed.). Dubuque, IA: Kendall Hunt.

Mojic, J. (2012). Creating value chain model and shaping authentic tourism product: The case of South Serbia. *Tourism and Hospitality Management, 18*(2), 195–211.

Morrison, A. (2013). *Marketing and managing tourism destinations*. New York: Routledge.

NDivo, R., & Cantoni, L. (2015). Economic empowerment of communities through tourism: A pro-poor tourism value chain approach. *Advances in Hospitality and Tourism Research: An International Journal of Akdeniz Tourism Faculty, 3*(3), 116–134.

O'Neill, S. (2015). Airbnb's threat to hotels may be structural, going beyond tax fight. *Tnooz*. Retrieved from Tnooz website: http://www.tnooz.com/article/airbnbs-threat-to-hotels-may-be-structural-going-beyond-tax-fight/

Oates, G. (2016). Interview: San Francisco tourism CEO on getting in bed with Airbnb. https://skift.com/2016/02/09/interview-san-francisco-tourism-ceo-on-getting-in-bed-with-airbnb/

Pike, S. (2004). *Destination marketing organizations*. Oxford: Elsevier.

Pike, S., & Page, S. J. (2014). Destination marketing organizations and destination marketing: A narrative analysis of the literature. *Tourism Management, 41*, 202–227. doi:10.1016/j.tourman.2013.09.009.

Porter, M. E. (1980). *Competitive strategy: Techniques for analyzing industries and companies*. New York: Free Press.

Porter, M. E. (1985). *Competitive advantage: Creating and sustaining superior performance*. New York: Free Press.

Porter, M. E., & Millar, V. E. (1985). How information gives you competitive advantage. *Harvard Business Review, 63*(4), 149–160.

Sanders, S. (2015). *Santa Monica cracks down on Airbnb, bans "vacation rentals" under a month*. http://www.npr.org/sections/thetwo-way/2015/05/13/406587575/santa-monica-cracks-down-on-airbnb-bans-vacation-rentals-under-a-month

Shankman, S. (2013). *The haves and have nots of U.S. State tourism budgets*. https://skift.com/2013/07/17/most-state-tourism-boards-get-peanut-budgets-in-comparison-to-the-top-ten/

Shankman, S. (2014). *How destinations turn locals into their best brand ambassadors*. http://skift.com/2014/08/29/how-destinations-turn-locals-into-their-best-brand-ambassadors/

Shankman, S. (2015). *Interview: Miami Tourism CEO on the significance of partnerships*. http://skift.com/2015/03/31/interview-miami-tourism-ceo-on-the-significance-of-partnerships/#1

Song, H., Liu, J., & Chen, G. (2013). Tourism value chain governance: Review and prospects. *Journal of Travel Research, 52*(1), 15–28. doi:10.1177/0047287512457264.

Staff. (2015). Traditional suppliers and upstarts enter frenemy territory. *Travel Weekly*. http://www.travelweekly.com/Travel-News/Hotel-News/Traditional-suppliers-and-upstarts-enter-frenemy-territory/?cid=eltrdb

There's Nothing Like Australia—Campaign Strategy. (2012, June 5). http://www.tourism.australia.com/media/8242-3284.aspx

Thompson, T. (2012). *3 reasons why the DMO will not survive*. http://travel2dot0.com/ideas/3-reasons-why-the-dmo-will-not-survive/

Up with Greek Tourism. Retrieved Date 10 Oct 2015 from http://www.upgreektourism.gr/

Volgger, M., & Pechlaner, H. (2014). Requirements for destination management organizations in destination governance: Understanding DMO success. *Tourism Management, 41*, 64–75. doi:10.1016/j.tourman.2013.09.001.

Volgger, M., & Pechlaner, H. (2015). Governing networks in tourism: What have we achieved, what is still to be done and learned? *Tourism Review, 70*(4), 298–312. doi:10.1108/tr-04-2015-0013.

Working Within the Collaborative Tourist Economy: The Complex Crafting of Work and Meaning

Jane Widtfeldt Meged and Mathilde Dissing Christensen

Abstract This chapter explores from a critical perspective how workers in the collaborative tourism economy craft meaning and identity in work and discusses transformations on the established labour market induced by the collaborative economy. It does so through the perspectives of guides working with Copenhagen Free Walking Tours, a platform offering guided tours and hosts offering short-term rentals on the platform Airbnb. Both guides and hosts practice job crafting. However, guides and hosts navigate the collaborative economy in different ways. Both markets require hosting qualities drawing on personal competencies when delivering hosting–on-demand. Guides can be characterised as social lifestyle entrepreneurs as they experience guiding as a lifestyle with high social and cultural returns. To the contrary, the Airbnb hosts interviewed can be perceived as micro-entrepreneurs practising pseudo-sharing, and manoeuvring in micro-competitive platform capitalism.

Keywords Airbnb • Copenhagen Free Walking Tours • Informal economy • Job-crafting • Collaborative economies

1 Introduction

The collaborative economy may be examined from a range of interrelated perspectives such as (1) an ideological perspective tapping into sustainability, shared communities and non-profit (e.g. Botsman & Rogers, 2010; Gansky, 2012); (2) an economic perspective presenting new hyper flexible business models eliciting

J.W. Meged (✉)
Department of People and Technology, Roskilde University, Roskilde, Denmark
e-mail: janewm@ruc.dk

M.D. Christensen
Department of People and Technology, Roskilde University, Roskilde, Denmark
Drexel University, Philadelphia, PA, USA
e-mail: mdc@ruc.dk

D. Dredge, S. Gyimóthy (eds.), *Collaborative Economy and Tourism*,
Tourism on the Verge, DOI 10.1007/978-3-319-51799-5_12

hidden resources at extremely low cost facilitated by technological development (Botsman & Rogers, 2010; Gansky, 2012; World Economic Report, 2014); or (3) a critical perspective—albeit a hitherto less widely applied perspective—addressing the impact of the collaborative economy on, for example, working life and on the welfare system, particularly in developed countries (Nielsen, 2015; Skytte, 2014a, 2014b; We-Economy, 2015).

Taking the third perspective above as a point of departure, this chapter explores how the meaning of work and identity are crafted by workers in the collaborative tourism economy. The chapter discusses the transformations on the labour market induced by the collaborative economy, and how workers in the collaborative tourism economy position themselves vis-à-vis the established labour market in a welfare state like Denmark. The collaborative economy envisions a new economic model based on sustainability and sharing, where the glue and tradable value are trust and social capital (Botsman & Rogers, 2010; Germann Molz, 2014a, 2014b; Rifkin, 2014). Rifkin (2014) argues that, in the wake of a third industrial revolution, the economy will be based on abundance instead of scarcity as the Internet of Things (IoT) will lead to extreme productivity at 'near zero' marginal cost, thus producing the next item for 'almost free'. To some extent one can argue that this is already happening in education with MOOCs (Massive Open Online Courses), publishing, communication, entertainment and in areas of tourism. The proponents of the collaborative economy see former workers as prosumers and micro-entrepreneurs engaging in "a distributed, collaborative, open, transparent, peer-to-peer economy as an expression of lateral power" (Rifkin, 2014, p. 241), carried forward by visions of empathy and the common good.

These visions of the benefits of the collaborative economy are already being put to the test as the emergence of the collaborative economy is sending shockwaves through the established economy and labour market. Collaborative enterprises are beginning to overtake old markets, e.g. in hospitality (Airbnb), transport (Uber) and many other services in the tourism economy, disrupting the markets and turning the tables on the "old workers" and professionals in the tourism labour market.

In the Danish labour market, "pay and working conditions are typically laid down by collective agreements concluded between trade unions and employers' organisations. This system of labour market regulation is referred to as 'the Danish Model'" (Ministry of Employment, 2015). This labour model was constructed during the twentieth century, and is based on strong labour market organisations with a high membership rate, which currently is around 70% of workers (Ministry of Employment, 2015; Ministry of Foreign Affairs, 2015). The third party in the employment equation is the state, which by and large leaves the social partners alone to agree on conditions through collective bargaining, but it also ensures universal welfare for all citizens by applying substantial redistribution through healthcare, a free education system and social security. Furthermore, the state supports an active labour market policy by offering guidance, a job or education to all unemployed persons (Ministry of Foreign Affairs, 2015). The result is a generous welfare model, where organised workers are guaranteed a minimum wage well above that of many other countries, which, as of November 2015, amounted to 14.82 euros per hour for an unskilled worker (HK, 2015). Unemployment benefits are also provided at a relatively high level—up to 90% for the lowest paid workers. Furthermore, workers receive other important rights and benefits such as sick pay, six weeks annual holiday and more than a year parental leave.

The model is also referred to as 'flexicurity', as it ensures extensive worker protection while also taking changing production and market conditions into account (Madsen, 2002; Ministry of Foreign Affairs, 2015). This flexibility manifests itself in a high level of job mobility, as employers can easily hire and fire workers to adjust to the market—indeed, about 25% of Danish private sector workers change jobs each year (Ministry of Foreign Affairs, 2015)—but security for the workers when needed. The system builds on mutual trust and responsibility, where public expenditure constitutes as much as 58.2% (2010) of GDP, and simultaneously ranks Denmark amongst the countries with lowest inequality in the world (OECD, 2015).

However, critical voices claim that collaborative economies present a threat to the current organisation of labour within the Danish society. The Danish think tank We-Economy hosted the *Fair Share—dilemmas in a digital job market* seminar in March 2015, which was well attended by the industry, unions, the press and other interested parties. At the seminar, critics draw attention to the notion of 'Platform Capitalism' (Olma, 2014), which views many collaborative enterprises as a 'gig economy' of subcontracting. Along these lines, the leftist newspaper *Information* reported after the seminar:

> ... the [collaborative] services are accused of undermining hard-fought for working rights and further spur a new class of casual labourers, roustabouts or 'self-employed' free-lancers without rights—the so-called precariat. Instead of being micro-entrepreneurs a new group of micro-earners has been created (Kjærgaard, 2015, own translation).

While terms like sharing or collaborative economy may denote acts of friendship and participation, a kind of supplementary part-time job that is half-work, half-social, it is already a global billion dollar business, and many people have made it a way of living, executing small jobs in a gig economy. This has given rise to critical voices in Denmark as well as internationally, reflecting a growing ambivalence against the unintended impact of collaborative economies (Allen, 2015; Mosendz, 2015; Nezik, 2015; Olma, 2014; Quijones & Street, 2015; We-Economy, 2015). Another observation from the seminar was the traditional workers unions' unpreparedness to handle this type of work and workers, which they might consider constitute a fundamental threat to the old structures and ideas of job markets, but that also pose opportunities of new ways of organising old as well as new members. While working in the collaborative economy may be a detriment for workers who crave stability, it may offer flexibility and opportunities for others (The Economist, 2015). We will therefore examine how workers within the collaborative tourist economies negotiate stability, flexibility and opportunity. Which tasks are being crafted working within the collaborative tourist economies? How is meaning created within their working life, and do workers share concerns for the precarious nature of their work, and if so, how are these concerns navigated?

2 New Workers and Lifestyle Entrepreneurs in Tourism

Tourism is an important generator of jobs (Ladkin, 2011), but as part of an economy that is heavily involved in globalisation and restructuration, employment in tourism tends to adjust through flexibilisation strategies, such as numerical flexibility, externalisation, wage flexibility, temporal flexibility and functional flexibility (Buchholz et al., 2009). Many types of tourism workers have always been flexible labourers, such as guides (Meged, 2017), workers in the cruise-ship industry (Weaver, 2005) and hotel employees (Adler & Adler, 2004), with heavy stratification running along the lines of ethnicity, gender and class. However, more than just turning into a flexible labour market, tourism is also a hub for new workers or lifestyle entrepreneurs (Meged, 2017; Veijola, 2009a). This development is characterised by the notion that in tourism "a new emphasis on human and physical capital in the forms of communication and affective labour is prominent: a bodily mode of work that produces social networks, forms of community, biopower" (Veijola, 2009a, p. 114).

To understand how these new tourism workers actually shape their work, we turn to the theory of job crafting, which captures "the active changes employees make to their own job designs, in ways that can bring about numerous positive outcomes, including engagement, job satisfaction, resilience and thriving" (Berg, Dutton, & Wrzesniewski, 2007, front page). Job crafting practices fall into three categories: the first involves changing the job's task boundaries in number or form, the second involves changing cognitive task boundaries, which is how workers alter their view of their work, and the third involves changing the relational boundaries to other actors. Workers job crafting depends on the objective features of their job design, as well as on their motivational orientation; whether they perceive their work as a job where their focus is on financial rewards; as a career, (where focus is on advancement); or as a calling (where focus is on the enjoyment of carrying out socially useful work). Motivation may also be either intrinsic, i.e. doing the work for its own sake, or extrinsic, i.e. doing the work for a reason apart from the work itself, where the former enhances job crafting more than the latter (Berg et al., 2007).

In a recent study, Meged (2017) shows how certified guides are ardent job crafters, who typically act as guides to pursue their passion for people, arts and history. They perceive themselves as natural born guides and by engaging in lifelong learning, networking and creativity, they craft new job opportunities and thereby see themselves as self-employed lifestyle entrepreneurs rather than as causal labourers, although they are effectively hired as such by employers. Guides often take on large amounts of unpaid work, sometimes below market rates, as they may be in fierce competition with colleagues, who are also competitors, and can suffer a great sense of isolation. Garsten (2008) argues from a critical perspective that what is labelled as "freedom of choice", and the use of positive buzzwords like "flexibility", 'lifelong learning and "entrepreneurship", may in fact just be a spin to cover a not-all-that-voluntary adaptation to strong market forces. In reality, adaptation is individualised and internalised, leaving the workers in an isolated, fragmented and highly competitive state in their working life.

In this chapter, we explore how workers or lifestyle entrepreneurs in the collaborative tourism economy perceive their role and how they craft their work, but also, critically, we look at the implicit and explicit cost-benefits of working in an economy operating in the informal sector (Guttentag, 2015, p. 9). We consider two case studies of two different business models in the collaborative tourism economy, namely the global company Airbnb and the small locally run Copenhagen Free Walking Tours, in order to observe the differences and similarities of working within the two businesses. The first company in our case study, Airbnb, is truly global and market-mediatized, while the other, Copenhagen Free Walking Tours, is small, local and self-governed, although it is also market-mediatized. Our analysis utilizes a number of research tools, including netnography, a literature survey, participant observations and interviews with agents working with the respective companies, namely four guides (Guide X, Y, Z and V) from Copenhagen Free Walking Tours and two hosts (Host K and M) from Airbnb.

3 Working with Copenhagen Free Walking Tours

Copenhagen Free Walking Tours (CFWT) was started in 2012 in the city of Copenhagen, Denmark, by a couple of guides. The previous year they had worked with the 'worldwide' company of free guided tours Sandemans New Europe, which had started to offer tours Copenhagen in 2011. Much of the early CFWT model is derived from the co-founders experience with Sandemans, so it is worthwhile to first give some background information on Sandemans. Sandemans was originally set up in Germany in 2004 and offered free guided tours of Berlin, which quickly became popular and helped them expand to other regions and cities. It now operates in 18 cities in Europe, the Middle East and US, and operates an ethos of peer-to-peer guiding, mainly attracting young tourists (Sandemans New Europe, 2010). The concept is a tips-alone based income for the guides who, in return, have to pay 1–2 euros per tourist to the company (guide Z and V). Sandemans works as a franchise, with local offices and management personnel. In its first year of operating in Denmark, the Danish branch did not pay off well enough, and the company suddenly decided to close down activities in Copenhagen in November 2012 (Guide Z). However, as the tourists continued arriving for daily tours, a couple of the guides decided to continue to offer tours but through their own company, and hence, Copenhagen Free Walking Tours (CFWT) was born. In its first year of operation, CFWT offered one daily tour, which attracted around 50–70 tourists in the high season, and the tours proved so successful that within 3 years CFWT had grown exponentially. By August 2015 CFWT were offering four daily tours with three different itineraries, guiding an average of 400–500 tourists daily, and even more on special occasions. However, demand is seasonal, and in low season, they offer only one daily tour; indeed typically in February they may have as few as 20–25 tourists on weekdays, and around 50–60 on weekends. In addition, they have started to offer organised pub crawls. Initially CFWT engaged eight guides, five of whom worked for CFWT as their primary occupation and only source of income; now, just 3 years later, the company engage 15 guides, of which ten of them earn their living entirely by guiding for CFWT. The takings from conducting a tour involving an average of 30 tourists is, according to the interviewees, around 120–200 euros. The tacit norm amongst the guides is that 6.5 euros per tourist is a fair and just tip, although tourists can give any amount they feel is justified.

CFWT is run collectively by all the guides, and an early collective decision was taken to lower the return fee to the company to 65 cents per tourist, to fund the company spending money on marketing, such as brochures, umbrellas, etc. As everybody pool their competences and labour, this permits the company running costs to be close to zero. Guide X explicates the working ethos of CWFT in the frame of collective ownership:

> It is the mindset of Christiania [a small self-governed free town in the centre of Copenhagen], that people create the society, that people themselves create community, like you do on Facebook, If you are not there, Facebook doesn't exist. Nobody from outside is doing it for you, it is the members who create it (Guide X).

During the interviews with the guides, it became clear that all of them put substantial work into the company without additional economic reward, other than the tips they got from the tours. The guides hold monthly meetings, where decisions regarding CFWT are taken in plenary. All the company marketing is planned and carried out by themselves, and each guide has responsibility for a district, in which they regularly distribute flyers. The partner of one guide has cleverly set up their homepage to operate in connection with Facebook and TripAdvisor, where they advertise themselves as the highest rated walking tour in Copenhagen, with a rating of five out of five. Email details are collected from all the tour participants prior to departure with the promise that they will receive only one mail from CFWT. In turn, the guides then take the lead and the same day send a personal email to all the tour participants containing a link to the CFWT Facebook profile, where the photos from the tour groups are posted each day. Additionally, the tour participants are asked to leave a rating on TripAdvisor. This work can be rather cumbersome for the lead guide, as the number of tourists on one tour may be as high as 150–200. One of the co-founders of CFWT explained how they thought of it as a hobby, even the ones who earned their living from being a guide. The co-founder herself had permanent employment elsewhere but had initially continued to work with CFWT, mostly as a key administrative person, responsible for statistics and forecasts and for working out duty rosters etc., besides also guiding some tours.

Clearly the guides subscribe to a collaborative entrepreneurial ethos, where everybody contributes with time and skills without calculating the exact time or cost, and this ethos is also adopted and managed by the constant influx of newcomers. The co-founder interviewed had just left CFWT to focus on a regular job, and explained that since its start in 2012, there was only one of the original guides now left in CFWT, rationalising "Guides are drifters, here today gone tomorrow!" Guide Y described how she had worked as volunteer in a non-profit Copenhagen café, when she first joined CFWT to do tours in German, and she essentially saw CFWT as part and parcel of the environment of volunteers. This points to a generation of super flexible collaborative lifestyle entrepreneurs, who are highly prone to job craft in almost-zero-cost platform enterprises. They cognitively identify themselves with the company, which may be why they are willing to assume a number of unpaid tasks, even if they are only briefly associated with the company.

To explain this commitment, we also have to look at the social fabric of CFWT:

> This group (CFWT) also works as a group of friends, who has a lot of fun together. And there have been the pub crawls in the evenings, so in that way it was a fun crowd to be part of. The tourists also sense that, and they get dragged into it, and it is a kind of an everyday party (Guide Y).

Crafting meaningful connections to colleagues and tourists are important (Meged, 2017), and in CFWT the boundaries between work and privacy have seemingly been erased, as guides are happy to spend their free time with colleagues and even with tourists after a tour, e.g. going to new places or for drinks. Furthermore, CFWT is an integral part of a wider young international community of unskilled tourism workers in Copenhagen, who regularly socialise at a central Kayak bar (Guide Y). The CFWT homepage reveals that only three out of twelve guides are Danish born, indicating a global, flexible workforce working on platform enterprises, which to a large degree eludes national regulations and functions as an informal economy. This is exemplified by the mixed attitudes of the guides in regard to taxation and the formal Danish welfare system. The co-founder clarified that all the guides received an explanation about how to fill out their tax forms, i.e. for when income consists of tips. "It is box 12 in the tax form" (Guide Z); however, it is left to the discretion of the individual guide on how much to fill in. Another guide had discussed the issue with colleagues, and was left with the impression that some would not pay tax at all, while others would, but only to the extent they felt they could afford it, hence considering it as a kind of a private moral issue (guide Y). This demonstrates that CFWT is part of an informal economy. Guide Y explained that she knew that some of her foreign colleagues, who worried about their residence permit, but even though she had permanent residency, she also worried about working in the informal economy:

> As I do not save for my pension, I do not earn paid holiday, I do not build up hours to my unemployment insurance fund, which is important should I need unemployment benefit one day, because the hours I work are not registered anywhere, and I toiled. You are a kind of out of society, you don't exist actually, you are out of the system. What if I can't work anymore, then I have no safety net, because I did not exist in the labour market. But also in the future, if I have to look for other jobs, then I am not present anywhere. It is a little scary. It could have some immeasurable consequences later, which I am not even able to predict

now. A couple of months are ok, but to continue year in and year out would make me feel insecure in all senses (Guide X).

CFWT offers a full lifestyle package for its' guides/workers, but it appears to be connected to a fleeting lifestyle, where people operate in fluid networks loosely attached from the formal structures of society. For some people, this temporary lifestyle may be attractive, as they constantly add to their cultural and social networks and economic capital, but for other people looking for stability it may provoke anxiety. The isolation from society, which Garsten (2008) claims this competitive system fosters, is not between people, as seen with the certified guides (Meged, 2017), but rather an isolation from the formal structures in society. However, in both instances problems are individualised and internalised, as the guides rarely discuss these issues amongst themselves (Guide Y).

4 Working with Airbnb

One of the most successful and well-known collaborative platforms is the accommodation platform Airbnb. Airbnb is, unlike the non-monetised alternative Couchsurfing (Bialski, 2013; Germann Molz, 2007, 2013, 2014a, 2014b) still relatively unexplored, albeit there are a few studies in the literature (Guttentag, 2015; Ikkala & Lampinen, 2015). In Airbnb's business model, users create a profile and either search for a place to rent (acting as a guest) or offer a place for others to rent (acting as a host). Hosts may offer single or multiple rooms, sometimes with the host present in the residence, as well as entire apartments. Accommodation is offered at various standards, accommodating both the budget conscious backpacker as well as the more comfortable traveller. The host determines the price of their accommodation and chooses to accept or reject requests by potential guests.

Airbnb was launched in 2008 and has since grown at an astonishing pace to now operate in more than 190 countries and over 34,000 cities (Guttentag, 2015; New York State Attorney General, 2014). The platform offers more than 1.4 million listings and is valued at US$25.5 billion, with expected revenue of US$900 million in 2015 (Demos, 2015). Airbnb provides the platform that facilitates contact between hosts and guests and offers a safe marketplace through providing three key elements: secure payments, a US$1 million host guarantee and by creating trust through verified profiles, message functions and a review system. Furthermore, support is offered through professional photographs and descriptions of the accommodation, an algorithm guides the host towards prices in comparable accommodation and a 24/7 customer service is offered. Airbnb charges a 3% service fee from the host and a service fee ranging from 6 to 12% from the guest.

Whereas peer-to-peer platforms are creating new structures in the working life of guides, Airbnb also allows users who rarely perceive themselves to be professional hosts to play a role in the tourism industry. Although a user's motivation to host through Airbnb may not necessarily solely be economic (Ikkala & Lampinen, 2015), at times of recession and economic distress income through hospitality exchanges may represent a quite significant income (Primack, 2012). Host M, whose main work is as a waiter, explains how, at times, Airbnb has formed the main, or large part, of her income:

> At that point I was only working part time and sort of needed the money. And it was a really good way to earn some money, rather than risk eviction. It [the apartment] is a Co-op. So I have bills to pay. It was an extra income, a quite important income! Later on, I was out of a job, and I wouldn't go on welfare. At that time it was more or less my (only) income (Host M)

To Host M, the profit from Airbnb presents a significant income, and an essential back-up income in case of economic misfortune, in which case she vacates her apartment and stays with relatives to rent her residence out, which prevents her from having to vacate the residence permanently. Another host (K) channels her income from Airbnb towards an indirect retirement fund, and sees it as an important economic supplement, as she tries to pay off her mortgage before pension, and to help her "butter the bread".

Both interviewees had economic reward as their sole motivation, why they primarily adjust their engagement and availability as hosts on an economic cost/benefit rational basis. Nevertheless, these forms of economic transactions exist, to a large extent, within the informal economy, and even though Airbnb is not illegal in Denmark, various regulations have caused many rentals to be classed as not fully legal, as seen in multiple settings (Guttentag, 2015; New York Attorney General, 2014). Furthermore, much of the resulting income is not taxed, either because it is not reported or because the hosts make sure not to make more profit than allowed within the local tax frames.[1] One host we interviewed was aware that Airbnb rental is not permitted in her housing cooperative, and also admitted that she doesn't keep a keen eye on whether the income exceeds the permitted tax frame. The other host, though, was very aware and careful to stay within the tax-free frame. However, both starkly refused to pay taxes from their income, as they agreed that if you pay taxes, it is simply not worth it. Like the guides in CFWT, the Airbnb hosts perceive themselves as micro-entrepreneurs; however, with a clearly pronounced economic scope. An interesting discussion between the interviewees revealed what they called a "generational" issue. One host, who was nearing her pension refused to depend on such an unstable income, which could be prohibited or made less lucrative in the future, as is happening now in several cities (Quijones & Street, 2015). The other host, who is young and unattached and was neither a member of a union nor an unemployment fund, had no problem of thinking of Airbnb as her safety net in times of trouble, thus indicating her greater reliance on the informal sector than on the welfare state.

[1] In Denmark, a certain amount of income from rent is exempt from tax. The precise amount is determined in accordance with the real estate value.

Although Airbnb is clearly a company of significant scale and value, their commitment to their hosts, who hold the assets that produce the value, is quite detached. As a collaborative platform, it does not act as an employer, and has none of the responsibilities and obligations that employers in hospitality firms normally have, particularly if the parties have signed a collective agreement. On the contrary, as micro-entrepreneurs, hosts are more likely to compete against fellow hosts rather that to unite efforts towards the "employer". Our hosts explained how they consider competition from other local Airbnb hosts when adjusting prices, in order to make sure their price is low enough to attract requests. When Host M had Airbnb as her only income, she lowered her prices further to attract guests. During this period, she let her apartment roughly 15 days a month in order to make ends meet. Conversely, our interviewed hosts raise prices or demand longer stays, when they are in less need of money.

Hosting on Airbnb does not simply mean offering a place to stay. Rather, a long list of tasks is tied into the (unofficial) job of being an Airbnb host. Most obvious perhaps is preparing the home for the guest, e.g. by cleaning and laundering, as well as cleaning and washing after the guest's departure. Hosts often spend time making sure that breakfast is available (if offered). They also organise how to welcome the guest and hand over the key. Both hosts M and K valued meeting their guests personally upon arrival, mainly in order to instruct them about the particularities. This could sometimes involve hours of waiting. However, before an appointment is even made, hosts spend considerable time communicating with potential guests. They try to determine which guests to accept and they answer questions about the destination, often making use of their social capital, when their personal knowledge doesn't suffice. Furthermore, hosts usually remain within reach of current guests during the stay, often through text messages. As such, hosting requires cleaning and accommodation-related tasks, but also other skills, such as the capability to function as a local informant.

Such demands add to the workload and, in particular, one host felt the tasks surrounding hosting, and particularly demands for availability, quite stressful at times:

> Finally it was just like it took over, and I do think you use an incredible amount of time to write and . . .. I have gotten a boyfriend lately, and I felt like I was on the phone all the time. He asked: What are you doing? Oh—it is Airbnb I replied almost every time (Host K).

Both hosts agreed that these pressures are further amplified, if one has limited digital and/or cultural capital. Familiarity with technologies, languages and the cultural aspects of one's town makes the tasks of Airbnb less troublesome. Airbnb's review system was seen as particularly important by the hosts, which is not surprising as a review system translates helpful and fast responses into reputation capital (Botsman & Rogers, 2010; Germann Molz, 2014a). Well aware that the social capital displayed through the review has a very real economic value, hosts feel a pressure to be available all the time.

> You can see it on your rating system, on your profile, how often you answer. Whether you have a 100% answering score, and how fast you answer. So it means something. So usually

> I answer as fast as possible and always within 24 hours, because otherwise it is taken as a no. That adds to your profile (Host M).

These shared practices of monitoring and reporting are an essential part of creating trust between guests and hosts and is considered a basic condition of hosting, "Everybody reviews everybody. They review you and you review them" (Host M). Even though it can been argued that trust and reputation systems are a vital part of the collaborative economy, the disciplining effect of collaborative surveillance practised in the echo chamber of mutual reviews (Germann Molz, 2014a) adds strongly to the complexity of crafting work with Airbnb. In fact, while most of the work undertaken in connection with hosting through Airbnb is done out of necessity, and with the scope of economic reward, it may also be done to secure the hosts' homes, as is the case with our interviewed hosts. Other job crafting practices enhancing personal satisfaction were ranked at a minimum.

5 Discussion and Conclusion

As a common feature between working with CFWT and Airbnb, both guides and hosts practice job crafting. While Aibnb hosts first and foremost mobilise physical idling assets, namely their homes, the guides only mobilise intangible idling assets, namely their personal services, and we see that guides and hosts approach and navigate the collaborative economy in different ways. Both markets require hosting qualities, overlapping private and work spheres and drawing on personal competencies, as well as flexibility and preparedness, when delivering hosting–on-demand. The scope to which this is felt as a burden or a reward appears closely connected to motivational factors, and to the assets being offered. The guides working with CFWT convey strong intrinsic motivation, doing the work for its own sake. Their approach can be characterised as a social lifestyle entrepreneurship. Although they experience quite significant economic rewards, they also consider guiding a lifestyle that offers them social and cultural returns, which is a general trait found in the guide profession (Carnicelli-Filho, 2013; Guerrier & Adib, 2003, 2004; Meged, 2017; Veijola, 2009a). Veijola (2009a) and Valkonen (2010) argue that the job of the guide is a source of happiness and passion, to the point where guides sacrifice their private lives and stay fit to "turn themselves into fountains of hospitality and affective connectivity and their lives into incessant vital labour" (Veijola, 2009a, p. 120).

The CFWT guides practise extensive job crafting, incorporating numerous tasks into their working life. They develop a perspective towards their professional life that appeals to them; they integrate sociality with colleagues and tourists, as well as participating in a collaborative management of the company. For them, the collaborative approach allows them to live a flexible lifestyle, with the opportunity to travel for large parts of the year as well as "being their own boss", also utilizing social, cultural and digital competencies through the collective management structure.

Although other motivational factors exist (Ikkala & Lampinen, 2015), the Airbnb hosts interviewed demonstrated a solely economic and thus extrinsic motivation, which made them less prone to job craft, perhaps as it is a tangible resource that is the key asset offered. However, even though they clearly execute numerous tasks to deliver hospitality-on-demand, they do not perceive themselves as working in hosting, but rather as performing necessary and time consuming supplementary tasks in order to rent their homes to tourists in short-term rentals. They consider hosting "a lot of work", sometimes to such an extent that it even triggers stress. Although often meeting their guests, they have no desire for sociality and perceive them solely as customers. This hospitality-on-demand is guided by the Airbnb review function serving as a surveillance system, as well as their wishes to keep an eye on their property. Such hosts can fruitfully be understood as micro-entrepreneurs practising pseudo-sharing (Belk, 2014). As such, it can be argued that they appropriate a traditional neoliberal approach, and rather than participating in collaborative exchanges with peers, they manoeuvre in micro-competitive platform capitalism (Dredge & Gyimóthy, 2015).

Collaborative platform enterprises in tourism demonstrate remarkable strengths in mobilizing seemingly limitless labour and competences from new workers in high yielding businesses at close to zero costs. The organisational boundaries of collaborative enterprises are porous and ever changing with low entry and exit barriers for individuals. The benefit for workers appears to be precisely this flexibility, as well as the accumulation of economic, digital and network capital, and for lifestyle entrepreneurs, like guides, also cultural and social capital. All these forms of capitals are increasingly vital, and partaking in platform economies may well equip and harness workers for the future of a global labour market with a rapidly decreasing number of fixed positions (Buchholz et al., 2009; Rifkin, 2014).

It could be argued that a precarious, footloose workforce is no stranger to the tourism industry. "Tourism-related jobs, occupations and employment are often precarious, low-paid and labour-intensive; they appropriate embodied presences and personalities and especially feminine skills and female bodies" (Veijola, 2009b, p. 84), and combined with a strong seasonality, the industry has long attracted and absorbed a large uneducated workforce and groups with limited attachment to the organized labour market, such as women, youngsters and immigrants. Furthermore families with limited funds have often been known to rent part of their accommodation to visiting tourists. In recent times, the precarious working conditions in various transnational tourist livelihoods have been addressed e.g. by Meged (2017) covering licenced guides, Weaver's (2005) research on cruise ships workers and Adler and Adler's (2004) work on hotel workers. As such, there are many parallels between the working conditions within the collaborative economies and the traditional tourism industry. However, it can also be argued, that tourism industries have started the process of professionalizing only relatively recently, and there has been an upsurge in tourism educations on all levels (Airey, Dredge, & Gross, 2015). Professionals, like the certified local guides, in Copenhagen have been organised in a union since 1978 and have long participated in collective bargaining with central employers with regard to minimum wages and basic working conditions, even though they still work as casual labourers (Meged, 2017). The collaborative economy puts this development under pressure, causing increased economic competition, and in fact the employers of the Copenhagen certified guides are beginning to opt out of the collective agreements as this chapter is being written, as they want to be able to hire unskilled low cost guides. As such, differences between the established but sometimes precarious industry and the collaborative part of tourism appear to be anchored between the notions of professionalism, formal organisation and also authenticity, which we address below.

Tourism has previously been perceived as an extraordinary practice, but traditionally restricted to tourist enclaves separated from the world of the everyday. However tourist landscapes are created within and coexist with existing landscapes of the everyday (Edensor, 2001, 2007; Larsen, 2008) Accommodation in private homes, and other collaborative practices, can be seen as a counterpart to mainstream tourism, either as a more sustainable mode of travel or symbolically an anti-hotel, representing local identity and connection to the surrounding community. It can be seen as an attempt to enter what Goffman calls the "authentic" back-stage rather than settle with the front-stage performed for the tourist gaze (Bruner, 2005; MacCannell, 1973; Urry & Larsen, 2011).

Collaborative tourist economies seem to attach themselves to strong notions of 'authenticity' and both older and current trends with tourists increasingly demanding 'authentic and special' experiences (Bruner, 2005; MacCannell, 1973). Following such trends, Airbnb promotes itself with strong notions of authenticity and belonging through their slogan 'belong anywhere' (Airbnb, 2015). Furthermore, at a seminar at the Danish Architecture Centre in November 2015, an Airbnb representative argued that not only did the use of Airbnb help disperse tourists throughout the city, it had a strong effect on the types of experiences encountered. Hosts play a vital role conveying, facilitating or maybe even co-creating local authentic experiences. This adds to the expectations and tasks of hosts, and support-services, such as meals (Ferenstein, 2014), transfers and so on are being encouraged by Airbnb (Quora, 2016).

As such, the new actors within the collaborative tourism industries are pressuring established business models by offering service and products tapping into such trends. However, little is known about how such processes affect local urban areas, where the tourism is increasingly dispersed and where tourism overlaps with the spaces and everyday activities of the people there. How authenticity is staged and perceived by guests as well as new collaborative actors and existing businesses should be ground for further research, as this could very likely have strong implications for service and professionalism in the industry, where a professional approach might be perceived as being opposed to the notions of authenticity.

Several of the guides from CFWT and one of the Airbnb hosts appear to subscribe to the values of a global informal economy detached from the welfare state, regardless of whether they had grown up within a welfare system. Short-term rentals or free guided tours offer them the opportunity for income, and in the case of Host M security and flexibility in an unpredictable job market. However, as both guides and hosts navigate the informal economies, they have little of the security and rights that are part of being employed within the formal labour market. This raises concern for some of our interviewees with regard to the fleeting and vulnerable character of their livelihood, which instils a sense of being isolated and left outside the formal structures of the society. They themselves stress that their participation in the collaborative economies must be either limited in time span or they must remain non-dependent on the income generated here, or even must utilize both strategies as a detachment.

Collaborative platform enterprises have grown so rapidly that legislation and labour organisations are lagging behind, leaving a void for the isnformal part of the collaborative economies to flourish (Klarskov, 2015a, 2015b; Thorup, 2015). At a national level, this is acknowledged by the Danish Minister for Business and Growth, Troels Lund Poulsen, who demonstrates a positive attitude towards utilising the collaborative economy as a lever for future growth (see also Dalberg Research, 2014). However, he also states, "We must not make a parallel society, where the sharing economy is exempted from tax and consumer protection does not apply" (Klarskov, 2015b, own translation), and it is his ambition for "Denmark to be one of the best countries in the EU to integrate sharing economies within the ordinary economy" (Klarskov, 2015a, own translation). How and in what way this integration into the ordinary economy should be applied to the rights of workers in the collaborative economy seems less clear, and political attention is mainly focussed on business and particularly taxation issues. However, in the US, where the sharing economy first took off, there are now signs of workers in the collaborative economy taking collective action. The Seattle based Uber drivers have organized the App-based Drivers Association to gain bargaining power and establish some basic rights (Rogers, 2016). This movement may diffuse to other sectors and countries.

The present study questions to what extent this situation is perceived as a problem by workers within the collaborative economy. Although some interviewees voiced concern about working outside formal structures, others did not seem to perceive their working and living conditions as problematic. At the same time, these workers demonstrated a viewpoint that tax should be paid at a minimum or outright avoided. Platform economies, whether "pseudo-collaborative" like Airbnb or fully collaborative like CFWT, create contrasts between flexibility, opportunities and security, which are balanced by the individual. However, such platforms thrive in informal global IT-based structures with subversive traits, which also challenge formal national and regional power regimes, which is why the drive for legislative and organisational changes might just emanate from the latter.

Even though some established actors note that the collaborative platforms are competing in a lower price range of the market, and therefore do not affect competition equally, the collaborative economy disrupts and challenges established ways of working and doing business (Guttentag, 2015). However, there is a further need to understand how the growing number of new workers and micro/lifestyle entrepreneurs in the collaborative tourism economies understand and craft their work, as they shape and change the industry at a micro level. It is also important to further understand the role the collaborative economy plays within the lives and economies of individual workers, not least in times of economic recession (Botsman, 2012; Primack, 2012), and their consequent protests if or when local governments take legal actions against these new structures, such as in New York (Mosendz, 2015), Barcelona (Quijones & Street, 2015) and Berlin (Nezik, 2015).

Clearly, the collaborative economy affects different contexts differently. In the United States, Airbnb hosts defend the platform in public media, arguing that it functions as a social security safety net (Allen, 2015; Primack, 2012). They argue that in times of unemployment or during health issues, Airbnb has kept them from eviction and economic disaster. In contrast, the Danish welfare state offers a (relatively) fine-masked security net; however, the findings of this study indicates that in particular the younger generation are subscribing to the collaborative safety net rather than registering in the systems of the traditional welfare state. The question is how and to what degree this will circumvent the future order of the economy and ways of organising labour, as it potentially may level out national differences, both between individual welfare programs and between welfare states and the rest of world.

References

Adler, P., & Adler, P. (2004). *Paradise laborers: Hotel work in the global economy*. Ithaca: Cornell University Press.

Airbnb. (2015). *Belong anywhere—Airbnb's new mark and identity*. http://blog.airbnb.com/belong-anywhere/

Airey, D., Dredge, D., & Gross, M. J. (2015). Tourism, hospitality and events education in an age of change. In D. Dredge, D. Airey, & M. J. Gross (Eds.), *The Routledge handbook of tourism and hospitality education*. London: Routledge. Accessed May 12, 2016.

Allen, J. (2015). Activists gather at NYC's City Hall to protest Airbnb. *USA Today*. Accessed January 20, 2016, from http://www.usatoday.com/videos/news/2015/01/20/22062641/

Belk, R. (2014). Sharing versus pseudo-sharing in Web 2.0. *Anthropologist, 18*(1), 7–23.

Berg, J. M., Dutton, J. E., & Wrzesniewski, A. (2007) *What is job crafting and why does it matter?* Center for Positive Organizational Scholarship, Michigan Ross School of Business. Accessed April 15, 2011, from http://positiveorgs.bus.umich.edu/wp-content/uploads

Bialski, P. (2013, August). *Not on my couch. The limitations of sharing in the age of collaborative travel and hospitality networks*. Paper presented at the RC21 conference, Berlin, Germany.

Botsman, R. (2012). The currency of the new economy is trust. *Tedtalk*. Accessed September 9, 2015, from http://www.ted.com/talks/rachel_botsman_the_currency_of_the_new_economy_is_trust?language=en

Botsman, R., & Rogers, R. (2010). *What's mine is yours; The rise of collaborative consumption*. New York: Harper Collins.

Bruner, E. M. (2005). *Culture on tour: Ethnographies of travel*. Chicago: The University of Chicago Press.

Buchholz, S., Jabsen, A., Kurz, K., Marold, J., Schmelzer, P., & Blossfeld, H. P. (2009). *Globalization, economic restructuring and increasing uncertainty in old age. A theoretical framework*. Walqing. Work and Life Quality in New and Growing Jobs. EU- Framework 7.

Carnicelli-Filho, S. (2013). The emotional life of adventure guides. *Annals of Tourism Research, 43*, 192–209. doi:10.1016/j.annals.2013.05.003.

Copenhagen Free Walking Tours. (2015). Accessed September 1, 2015, from http://www.copenhagenfreewalkingtours.dk

Dalberg Research. (2014, September). *Analyse af barrierer og udviklingsmuligheder for peer-to-peer virksomheder i Danmark*. Erhvervsstyrelsen.

Demos, T. (2015, June 26). Airbnb raises $1.5 Billion in one of the largest private placements. *The Wall Street Journal*. Accessed January 20, 2016.

Dredge, D., & Gyimóthy, S. (2015). Collaborative economy and tourism: Critical perspectives, questionable claims and silenced voices. *Tourism Recreation Research, 40*(3), 286–302.

Edensor, T. (2001). Performing tourism, staging tourism (Re)producing tourist space and practice. *Tourist studies, 1*(1), 59–81.

Edensor, T. (2007). Mundane mobilities, performances and spaces of tourism. *Social and Cultural Geography, 8*(2), 199–215.

Ferenstein, G. (2014). Airbnbs stealth home dining experiment is going to be awesome. *Venturebeat*. Accessed April 21, 2016, from http://venturebeat.com/2014/06/10/airbnbs-stealth-home-dining-experiment-is-going-to-be-awesome/

Gansky, L. (2012). *The Mesh. Why the future of business is sharing*. New York: Penguin.

Garsten, C. (2008). *Workplace vagabonds: Career and community in changing worlds go work*. Basingstoke: Palgrave MacMillan.

Germann Molz, J. (2007). Cosmopolitans on the couch: Mobilising hospitality and the Internet. In J. Germann Molz & S. Gibson (Eds.), *Mobilising hospitality: The ethics of social relations in a mobile world*. Aldershot: Ashgate.

Germann Molz, J. (2013). Social networking technologies and the moral economy of alternative tourism: The case of couchsurfing.org. *Annals of Tourism Research, 43*, 210–230. doi:10.1016/j.annals.2013.08.001.

Germann Molz, J. (2014a). Collaborative surveillance and technologies of trust: Online reputation systems in the 'new' sharing economy. In A. Jansson & M. Christensen (Eds.), *Media, surveillance and identity: A social perspective* (pp. 127–144). New York: Peter Lang.

Germann Molz, J. (2014b). Toward a network hospitality. *First Monday, 19*(3). doi:10.5210/fm.v19i3.4824.

Guerrier, Y., & Adib, A. (2003). Work at leisure and leisure at work: A study of the emotional labour of tour reps. *Human Relations, 56*(11), 1399–1417. doi:10.1177/00187267035611006.

Guerrier, Y., & Adib, A. (2004). Gendered identities in the work of overseas tour reps. *Gender, Work and Organization, 11*(3), 334–350. doi:10.1111/j.1468-0432.2004.00234.x.

Guttentag, D. (2015). Airbnb: Disruptive innovation and the rise of an informal tourism accommodation sector. *Current Issues in Tourism, 18*(12), 1192–1217. doi:10.1080/13683500.2013.827159.

HK. (2015, December 2). Alt du skal vide om løn, hvis du arbejder i butik. http://www.hk.dk/raadogstoette/emner/loen/handel/loen-butik

Ikkala, T., & Lampinen, A. (2015). *Monetizing network hospitality: Hospitality and sociability in the context of Airbnb*. Paper presented at the Proceedings of the 18th ACM Conference on computer supported cooperative work and social computing.

Kjærgaard, K. B. (2015). Deleøkonomi eller Platformskapitalisme? Dansk Design Center. Accessed May 18, 2016, from http://ddc.dk/2015/03/deleokonomi-eller-platformskapitalisme/

Klarskov, K. (2015a, August 14). Minister vil skabe bedre vilkår for deleøkonomi. *Politiken, Økonomi*. Accessed May 12, 2016, from http://politiken.dk/oekonomi/virksomheder/ECE2795839/minister-vil-skabe-bedre-vilkaar-for-deleoekonomi/

Klarskov, K. (2015b, August 15). Troels Lund vil gøre mere for deleøkonomi—selv om han ikke selv bruger det. *Politiken, Økonomi*. Accessed May 18, 2016, from http://politiken.dk/oekonomi/dkoekonomi/ECE2796089/troels-lund-vil-goere-mere-for-deleoekonomi-selv-om-han-ikke-selv-bruger-det/

Ladkin, A. (2011). Exploring tourism labor. *Annals of Tourism Research, 38*(3), 1135–1155. doi:10.1016/j.annals.2011.03.010.

Larsen, J. (2008). De-exoticizing tourist travel: Everyday life and sociality on the move. *Leisure Studies, 27*(1), 21–34. doi:10.1080/02614360701198030.

MacCannell, D. (1973). Staged authenticity: Arrangements of social space in tourist settings. *American Journal of Sociology, 79*(3), 589–603. http://www.jstor.org/stable/2776259.

Madsen, P. K (2002, May 16). *The Danish model of flexicurity–A paradise with some snakes*. European Foundation for the Improvement of Living and Working Condition. Interaction between labour Market and Social Protection. http://citeseerx.ist.psu.edu/viewdoc/download?doi=10.1.1.199.4437&rep=rep1&type=pdf

Meged, J. W. (2017). Guides crafting meaning in a flexible working life. *Scandinavian Journal of Hospitality and Tourism, Special Issue*.

Ministry of Employment. (2015). *The Danish labour market*. Accessed December 2, 2015, from http://uk.bm.dk/en/Themes/The%20Danish%20Labour%20Market.aspx

Ministry of Foreign Affairs. (2015). The Official website of Denmark. Accessed December 2, 2015, from http://denmark.dk/en/society/welfare/flexicurity/

Mosendz, P. (2015, January 21). Face-Off: NYC Lawmakers Grill Airbnb on Illegal Hotels. *Newsweek*. Accessed September 9, 2015, from http://www.newsweek.com/face-nyc-lawmakers-grill-airbnb-illegal-hotels-301060

New York Attorney General. (2014). *Airbnb in the city*. Accessed May 12, 2016, from http://www.ag.ny.gov/pdfs/Airbnb%20report.pdf

Nezik, A. K. (2015, April 10). Tourism troubles: Berlin cracks down on vacation rentals. *Spiegel Online International*. Accessed September 9, 2015, from http://www.spiegel.de/international/business/berlin-cracks-down-on-estimated-18-000-vacation-rentals-a-1026881.html

Nielsen, J. S. (2015, January 28). Nu raser kampen om deleøkonomien. *Information*. Accessed May 18, 2016, from https://www.information.dk/udland/2015/01/raser-kampen-deleoekonomien

OECD. (2015). *Inequality*. Accessed September 9, 2015, from http://www.oecd.org/social/inequality.htm

Olma, S. (2014). *Never mind the sharing economy: Here's platform capitalism*. Accessed September 9, 2015, from http://networkcultures.org/mycreativity/2014/10/16/never-mind-the-sharing-economy-heres-platform-capitalism/

Primack, D (2012, August 16). How AirBNB helps users save their homes. *Fortune*. Accessed May 12, 2016, from http://fortune.com/2015/08/30/disney-infinity-critics/

Quijones, D., & Street, W. (2015, August 11). Barcelona just declared War on Airbnb. *Business Insider*. Accessed September 7, 2015, from http://www.businessinsider.com/barcelona-just-declared-war-on-airbnb-2015-8?IR=T

Quora. (2016). *Do Airbnb hosts ever provide transportation to their guests*. Accessed April 21, 2016, from https://www.quora.com/Do-Airbnb-hosts-ever-provide-transportation-to-their-guests

Rifkin, J. (2014). *The zero marginal cost society: The internet of things, the collaborative commons and the eclipse of capitalism*. New York: Palgrave MacMillan.

Rogers, W. (2016). Sharing economy workers seek their fair share. *Left Labor Reporter*. Retrieved from https://leftlaborreporter.wordpress.com/2016/01/28/sharing-economy-workers-seek-their-fair-share/. Accessed April 21, 2016.

Sandemans New Europe. (2010). Accessed September 2, 2015, from https://www.youtube.com/watch?v=WHfbYDUxnG4

Sandemans New Europe. (2015). Accessed May 18, 2015, from http://www.neweuropetours.eu/

Skytte, C. (2014a, May 30). Fra forbruger til medbruger. *Information*. Accessed May 12, 2016, from https://www.information.dk/debat/2014/05/forbruger-medbruger

Skytte, C. (2014b). *Skal vi dele? Er deleøkonomien en del af løsningen eller en del af problemet?* Danmark: Skytsengel.

The Economist. (2015, January 3). The future of work. There's an app for that. *The Economist*. Accessed May 12, 2016, from http://www.economist.com/news/briefing/21637355-freelance-workers-available-moments-notice-will-reshape-nature-companies-and

Thorup, M. (2015). Freelance- og deleøkonomi udfordrer solidariteten. *Information*. Accessed March 18, 2015.

Urry, J., & Larsen, J. (2011). *The tourist gaze 3.0*. London: Sage.

Valkonen, J. (2010). Acting in nature: Service events and agency in wilderness guiding. *Tourist Studies, 9*(2), 164–180. doi:10.1177/1468797609360595.

Veijola, S. (2009a). Gender as work in the tourism industry. *Tourist Studies, 9*(2), 109–126. doi:10.1177/1468797609360601.

Veijola, S. (2009b). Introduction: Tourism as work. *Tourist Studies, 9*(2), 83–87. doi:10.1177/1468797609360748.

Weaver, A. (2005). Interactive service work and performative metaphors: The case of the cruise industry. *Tourist Studies, 5*(1), 5–27. doi:10.1177/1468797605062713.

We-Economy. (2015). Er der solidaritet i deleøkonomien? Accessed May 12, 2015, from http://we-economy.net/?p=852

World Economic Report. (2014). Towards the circular economy: Accelerating the scale-up across global supply chains Ellen MacArthur Foundation and McKinsey and Company. World Economic Forum, Geneva, Switzerland. Accessed May 18, 2015, from http://www3.weforum.org/docs/WEF_ENV_TowardsCircularEconomy_Report_2014.pdf

Wrzesniewski, A., & Dutton, J. E. (2001). Crafting a job: Revisioning employees as active crafters of their work. *Academy of Management Review, 26*(2), 179–201.

Part III
Encounters and Communities

Embedding Social Values in Tourism Management: Community Currencies as Laboratories of Social Entrepreneurship?

Rita Cannas

Abstract This chapter explores the Sardex mutual credit system, a social enterprise operating in Sardinia (Italy) as part of the collaborative economy. Sardex is a Local Exchange Trading System (LETS) that was used by local small businesses in response to the economic crisis. The chapter discusses the strategic relevance and contribution of the Sardex network. Based on a qualitative approach, including observation and in-depth interviews with Sardex entrepreneurs, the chapter investigates how exchange mechanisms work among the 195 firms making up the hospitality sector within the network. Beyond tangible and quantitative outcomes, this study shows the intangible role of social values such as trust, reciprocity and mutual support as a means to foster collaborative practices within Sardex firms. The study enriches the debate about the disruptive and/or constructive impacts of the collaborative economy by highlighting the collective social and economic role played by the Sardex network as an innovative driver for local development and community empowerment.

Keywords Social entrepreneurship • Collaborative economy • Tourism consumption • Social values • Community currency • Sardex

1 Introduction: Theoretical Framework and Research Design

The global financial and economic crises from 2008 onwards have generated new business models based on sharing practices that have been presented as alternatives to unsustainable consumption and industrial forms of capitalism (Heinrichs, 2013; Ranchordás, 2015). These new business models within the collaborative economy are capable of reshaping and disrupting existing tourism businesses in, for example, the transport and accommodation sectors (e.g. Uber and Airbnb). Botsman and Rogers (2010, 2011) elaborate the idea of collaborative consumption as a new

R. Cannas (✉)
Dipartimento di Scienze economiche e aziendali, Università degli Studi di Cagliari, Baffi Building, Viale Sant'Ignazio 74, 09123 Cagliari, Sardegna, Italy
e-mail: rita.cannas@unica.it

D. Dredge, S. Gyimóthy (eds.), *Collaborative Economy and Tourism*, Tourism on the Verge, DOI 10.1007/978-3-319-51799-5_13

form of peer-to-peer sharing. The concept involves individuals exchanging, redistributing, renting, sharing, and donating information, goods, and talent, either by organizing themselves or via commercial organization on social media platforms.

The analysis presented in this chapter is inspired by the collaborative economy description presented by Dredge and Gyimóthy (2015). In this description, the exchange of gifts, goods, skills or time among people takes place in different forms across the world. For instance, the mechanism of barter has existed for millennia (Mauss, 1922/1990; Humphrey, 1985; Derrida, 1992), but the global development and widespread uptake of Internet technologies has increased the range of sharing activities, and has permeated the lives of people even though they are not necessarily in geographical proximity. As a result, a broad meaning of the collaborative economy has been adopted in this chapter. According to Dredge and Gyimóthy (2015), the collaborative economy is not only a matter of consumption and production, but it also allows connections between people facilitating better use of skills and goods through Internet technologies (Stokes, Clarence, & Rinne, 2014).

The intention of this chapter is to move beyond the "good" collaborative economy [e.g., altruistic visions of the sharing economy expressed by Botsman and Rogers (2010, 2011)] and the "bad" collaborative economy (critiqued by some community activists and critical scholars as leading to inequality, marginalisation and unfair labour practices). In particular, the chapter asks whether social technologies can unlock hidden wealth by using a community (collaborative) currency. What is the social role of collaborative currencies in reshaping asymmetric market relations towards more symmetric ones? Are there any social, economic and environmental impacts of the sharing economy that emerge from a network of small enterprises cooperating together?

The empirical case for exploring such questions is Sardex, a community currency system which involves 2900 small firms located in Sardinia (Italy), and which is rapidly growing in terms of both members and revenue. The study investigates the role of social values embedded in the Sardex system as a means of fostering collaborative economy and innovative processes, and it pays particular attention to Sardex tourism firms.

The theoretical framework for this study is located in the nexus between the collaborative economy and social entrepreneurship. Particular attention is given to the conceptualisation of social entrepreneurship and how the collaborative economy intersects with this growing sector. Three main research questions form the focus of this study: (1) Is Sardex a social enterprise within the collaborative economy? (2) To what extent are the mechanisms of the Sardex network modifying firms' missions and strategies to incorporate collaborative economy practices while also bringing in and shaping entrepreneurs' social values? (3) In which ways is the Sardex network a sharing community based on collective and individual interests aimed at achieving sustainable goals? By examining these questions, the chapter adds theoretical and practical insights into the collaborative economy in general, and community currencies as a form of collaborative economy, in particular.

The research design is based on a literature review of both collaborative economy and social entrepreneurship in order to better contextualise the topic under investigation. It adopts a qualitative exploratory approach to uncover the overlap between the collaborative economy and social entrepreneurship. The field research involved observations and in-depth interviews with representatives of the Sardex company and tourism entrepreneurs who are members of the community currency circuit. The field research was conducted in Sardinia, Italy, during the period March–October 2015.

The chapter is broken into the following sections: First, a conceptual framework of social entrepreneurship is developed. Second, the case study of Sardex is introduced (the story; the creation of its social value; social innovation in entrepreneurship; creation of new markets/consumers; management implications; etc.) and a focus on Sardex' tourism entrepreneurs is adopted. In the conclusions, some key observations about the contribution of Sardex within the collaborative economy are highlighted.

2 The Multifaceted Meanings of Social Entrepreneurship

The topic of social entrepreneurship is becoming increasingly popular among researchers, as Granados, Hlupic, Coakes, and Mohamed (2011) show in their bibliometric analysis. Although literature on social entrepreneurship reveals several attempts at definition (Dacin et al., 2010), there is wide acknowledgement that it is a contested concept and no unifying theoretical framework has yet emerged (Choi & Majumdar, 2014). In fact, as Dees (1998) points out, the concept of social entrepreneurship means different things to different people, but the same claim can be applied to the concept of entrepreneurship, which also lacks a unifying paradigm (Shane & Venkataraman, 2000).

Within their attempt to conceptualise social entrepreneurship, Mair and Martí (2006) observe that one view is that social entrepreneurship involves not-for profit initiatives in search of alternative funding strategies or management schemes, such as those described by Austin, Stevenson, and Wei-Skillern (2003) and Boschee (1998). A second perspective links social entrepreneurship to socially responsible practices in commercial businesses engaged in cross-sector partnerships (e.g., Sagawa & Segal, 2000; Waddock, 1988). A third perspective, which is adopted in this chapter, considers social entrepreneurship as a tool to alleviate social problems and catalyse social transformation (Alvord, Brown, & Letts, 2004).

Mair and Martí define social entrepreneurship as:

> ...a process of creating value by combining resources in new ways (...) these resource combination are intended primarily to explore and exploit opportunities to create social values by stimulating social change or meeting social needs (...) and when viewed as a process, social entrepreneurship involves the offering of the services and products but can also refer to the creation of new organizations (Mair & Martí, 2006: 37).

While Mair and Martí (2006) stress the creation of social value and action for social change/or addressing social needs, Peredo and McLean (2006: 64) state that:

> . . .social entrepreneurship is exercised where some person or group: (1) aim(s) at creating social value, either exclusively or at least in some prominent way; (2) show(s) a capacity to recognize and take advantage of opportunities to create that value ("envision"); (3) employ (s) innovation, ranging from outright invention to adapting someone else's novelty, in creating and/or distributing social value; (4) is/are willing to accept an above-average degree of risk in creating and disseminating social value; and (5) is/are unusually resourceful in being relatively undaunted by scarce assets in pursuing their social venture.

Important in Peredo and McLean's (2006) definition, is that it incorporates both individual entrepreneurs/groups and teams of entrepreneurs, while earlier definitions framed the social entrepreneur as an individual (e.g. Waddock & Post, 1995).

Social entrepreneurs are innovators just as other entrepreneurs. According to the studies of their personality traits summarized in Peredo and McLean (2006), they are also characterized by special traits (Drayton, 2002) including special leadership skills (Thompson, Alvy, & Lees, 2000); a passion to realise their vision (Bornstein, 1998); and a "strong ethical fiber" (Drayton, 2002: 124). Social entrepreneurs place attention upon the creation/sharing of social value that contributes to the welfare or well-being of a given community (Peredo & Mclean, 2006), and they seek to achieve this using either profit or not-for-profit goals.

Short, Moss, and Lumpkin (2009) move from the process of value creation in entrepreneurship to extend the concept into the realm of social entrepreneurship. They emphasize cross-disciplinary scholarly collaboration and underline the need to establish clear boundaries in the social entrepreneurship framework through a variety of established theoretical lenses. For instance, a conceptual improvement in social entrepreneurship "may provide a context for integrating strategy and entrepreneurship research by enhancing understanding of how organizations simultaneously create social value and achieve competitive advantages" (Short et al., 2009: 173).

Dacin et al. (2010) suggest the adaptation of theories from existing entrepreneurship literature. In their view, efforts to delineate social entrepreneurship as a separate theoretical domain can downplay the potential benefits of drawing from a wider entrepreneurship context. By gathering 37 definitions of social entrepreneurship, Dacin et al. (2010) identify four key factors related to social entrepreneurship: the characteristics of individual social entrepreneurs, their operating sector, the process and resources used by social entrepreneurs, and the primary mission and outcomes associated with the social entrepreneur. Regarding the characteristics of the social entrepreneurs, in the view of these authors, there are many commonalities with entrepreneurship, including types of actors, e.g. conventional agents [who act under new ideas in order to create successful innovation (Schumpeter, 1934)]; institutional agents [who mobilise resources to influence or change institutional rules, to support or destroy an existing institution or establish a new one (DiMaggio and Powell, cited in Dacin et al., 2010)]; and cultural agents [who identify opportunities or act in order to create social, cultural or economic value (DiMaggio, 1982; Wilson & Stokes, 2004)].

In Dacin et al.'s (2010) perspective, significant traits that can help to understand the distinctive nature of social entrepreneurs are *mission*, and *processes and resources*. Briefly, the mission is based on the generation of social values in which the primary goal consists of social change/well-being of shareholders or stakeholders; processes and resources are seen in terms of relational, cultural and institutional resources and associated tension, such as resistance to change. Relational resources, such as social capital and social skills, are the key elements of an actor's social network and these include abilities in social interactions, established networks of formal and informal societal ties, and access to communication channels and networks (Robinson, 2006). An interesting specification that can provide useful insights for the Sardex analysis is observation by Dacin et al. (2010) that:

> ...(t)he existence of a social network in and of itself might be considered valuable, but the real value is created by the unique relationship formed between the social entrepreneur and the network members. It is the interaction between internal organizational human resources and culture and the elements of the social network that generates an advantageous resource (p. 49).

Short et al. (2009) point out that in Peredo and Chrisman's (2006) work there is an interesting attempt to bring new meanings into the social entrepreneurship domain by extending research to develop the concept of community-based enterprise (CBE). In fact, Peredo and Chrisman (2006) combine traits from commercial entrepreneurship, anthropology and social network theory to explain how community-based enterprises may differ from the standard definition of entrepreneurship. They define community-based enterprise as "a community acting corporately as both entrepreneur and enterprise in pursuit of the common good. CBE is therefore a result of a process in which the community acts entrepreneurially to create and operate a new enterprise embedded in its existing social structure" (Peredo and Chrisman, 2006: 310). These authors focus on local communities that create collective business ventures in which their own members act together corporately and collaboratively to achieve social, economic, environmental and cultural goals simultaneously. They see CBE as an unconventional form of entrepreneurship based on collective and individual interests where considerable social capital exists as a result of community culture and a process of social collective learning. This community concept refers to an aggregation of people that share a geographical location, common culture, and relational characteristics. Although Peredo and Chrisman's (2006) work is mainly focussed on the benefits of CBE in less developed countries, the concept of community as enterprise may be implemented in developed economies. It is here that the concept of CBE and collaborative economy come together.

In addition to this brief overview on social entrepreneurship, there is a meaningful point to take into consideration. Social entrepreneurship is more likely to occur where there are significant socioeconomic, cultural or environmental problems that traditional markets have not been interested in addressing because there is a lack of institutional support and/or individual interest in facilitating the development of social ventures (Dacin et al., 2010; Peredo & Chrisman, 2006).

In this chapter, social entrepreneurship is mainly inspired by the views of Dacin et al. (2010). The case of the Sardex network (the company in itself, and the network's membership) is analyzed through the *characteristics* of individual entrepreneurs; the *process and resources* used by them with particular emphasis on relational resources; and their *mission* and *outcomes*. Drawing from from Mair and Martí's (2006) conceptualization, it suggests the need to explore the *social value creation process* within the Sardex network, and its contribution in terms of *social change*. Although many authors stress the need for attention to the role of innovation as a distinctive factor in entrepreneurship as well as in social entrepreneurship, this research echoes Peredo and McLean's (2006) suggestion to show the ways by which innovation is employed in the case of Sardex.

3 The Case of Sardex.Net

Sardex is a system of mutual credit that mainly supports B2B interactions between firms on the island of Sardinia (Dini & Kioupkiolis, 2014; Littera, Sartori, Dini, & Antoniadis, 2014; Melis, Giudici, & Dettori, 2013). The system, is based on the LETS model (see Table 1), and uses a complementary electronic currency named sardex, where each sardex corresponds to one euro. Sardex is also the name of the community currency company that was established in 2009 by a group of young friends who grew up in a small village of Sardinia, Serramanna, where the company set up its headquarters. In 2007, and while living and working in Germany, two of the five core team of members of Sardex were favourably intrigued by the precursor of LETS, the WIR model, an independent complementary currency managed by the WIR Bank in Switzerland (see Table 1). They were attracted by the larger geographical reach and turnover of the WIR relative to other community currencies examples that they had examined (Dini & Kioupkiolis, 2014). Their idea was to implement a similar system in Sardinia as a tool to alleviate the impacts of the financial crises that, in a few years, had deeply affected the Sardinian economy.

Before the case is outlined, it is essential to mention the main socio-economic features of Sardinia. Sardinia has a land area of 24,000 km^2, and a coastline of almost 1900 km. It has a resident population of 1.6 million, resulting a low population density of 68 inhabitants per km^2. Politically and administratively, Sardinia is one of the 20 regions of Italy, but it has its own culture, identity, traditions and language that are substantially different from other regions (Cannas & Giudici, 2015). Sardinia's GDP (€17,700 per capita) is 30% less than the Italian GDP (€26,500 per capita); the unemployment rate increased from 9.8% in 2008 to 18.6% in 2014 (CRENOS, 2015), and the youth unemployment rate is 54% whereas the Italian rate is 40.5% (ISTAT, 2015) and the European Union rate is 20.4% (Eurostat, 2015a). More critically perhaps, the issues threatening Sardinian social capital and social sustainability include emigration of young people (11,000 left Sardinia between 2009 and 2013 (CNA, 2015)), among them early leavers from education and training: Sardinian indicator is 24.7% (CRENOS, 2015) while the

Table 1 Distinctions among types of community currencies

	Origins	Characteristics	Source
WIR	WIR was founded in 1934 by a small group of Swiss entrepreneurs as a means to counteract the financial crisis of the interwar period. WIR was initially named the "Wirtschaftsring-Genossenschaft" (free economic circle cooperative) until it changed its name to the WIR Bank in 1998. WIR aimed at reducing underutilised capacity through a cashless barter system	WIR operates like a bank. The unit of account of the WIR-franc is the Swiss franc: one WIR-franc equals the value of one Swiss-franc WIR charges a 1% fee for each transactions In WIR a member's negative balance is a debt towards the central credit clearing house (WIR Bank)	Studer (1998) and Stodder (2009)
Local Exchange Training System (LETS)	LETS are community-orientated trading networks which aim to develop and extend the exchange of goods and services within a group, re-localising the provision of goods and services LETS was promoted by Michael Linton in the early 1980s in Vancouver (Canada) as a response to the local economic depression Hundreds of LETS are spread around the world	LETS currencies have three distinctive features: (1) their use is normally restricted to members of the local scheme; (2) no interest is charged on debits, nor paid on credit; and (3) the currency is created only through the exchange of goods or services, not issued by a central authority In LETS a member's negative balance is a debt towards the community	Lee (1996), Pacione (1997), Schraven (2000), Schroeder, Miyazaki, and Fare (2011) and Aldridge and Patterson (2002)
Sardex.net	Since 2009 Sardex is a LETS model located in Sardinia (Italy) aimed at pursuing economic and social goals. The members are around 2900 Sardinian SMEs. Sardex is promoting new affiliated circuits in other eight regions of Italy	Sardex is modelled on the WIR but uses only an electronic LETS-like system of credit and debt accounting for any size transaction. Instead of charging a fee for transactions such as WIR, Sardex charges a yearly membership fee that depends on the firm's size Sardex offers not only an internet platform for transaction, but also a team of brokers available by phone, and arrange periodic meetings with members. Frequent face-to-face relationships is its own distinctive and successful *modus operandi*	Dini and Kioupkiolis (2014), Melis et al. (2013), Littera et al. (2014), and Dini, van der Graaf, and Passani (2015)

Italian percentage is 15% and 11.2% is the share in the European Union (Eurostat, 2015b). Although Sardinia is the second largest island in the Mediterranean, the tourism industry lacks competitive products and effective branding strategies. Tourism represents less than 9% of the Sardinian GDP, and the domestic seaside market is still predominantly concentrated in coastal areas and in summertime.

Sardex is defined by Dini and Kioupkiolis (2014) as a company for-social-benefit. As these authors explain, the model of a for-profit company was chosen over a non-profit cooperative because the latter is perceived as "left-wing" in Sardinia, and therefore risky in a region where politics is even more polarised than in the rest of Italy. The founders felt that this could have hampered average businesses in joining Sardex. The Sardex Ltd. bylaws dictate that all profit is to be reinvested in the company.

3.1 Characteristics of Entrepreneurs

The Sardex founders thought that a complementary currency network could positively impact on the Sardinian economy. Their business idea was not only new in Sardinia but also in the rest of Italy. The founders believed that something meaningful, possibly in terms of a collective or community-like effort, had to be done. The Sardex network is based on the social relations of the founders and their shared vision; it is based in both kinship and childhood friendship, and they have worked together on the business and in their political efforts. In this same spirit they involved Sardex members. Among the founders, none had a background in economics or computer science, nor did they have any training in finance: "the group of arts students planned a new currency for their island. It seemed absurd: they had little financial or IT experience, no MBAs and no investor, only the outline of an idea", says Posnett (2015) in the *Financial Times*. Looking back, the founders believed that their lack of training helped them to be creative in developing their business and in building their own knowledge. Only one of the four core members had any previous experience in running a business, such as an advertising and market consultancy (Littera et al., 2014). Therefore, the commitment to learning was high and their attitude to learning remains a distinct trait in their *modus operandi*.

3.2 Corporate Mission and Values

At the beginning of their activity, the Sardex' founders had to face cultural barriers to the business models represented by the LETS and WIR models (Blanc, 2011; Collom, 2011; Schroeder et al., 2011; Williams, 1996) which are based on paying for and receiving goods and services through a non-state currency system. It was very difficult to break the wall of scepticism of local entrepreneurs, since trust is the backbone of the Sardex system. This critical issue has been acknowledged: "rather than adopting the perspective of distant activists or outsiders that aim at social change while never leaving their comfort zones, the whole team wanted to provide a service through creating an employment opportunity for themselves and others" (Littera et al., 2014: 4). Indeed they were determined to subvert the ancient spell inherited from the time of Spanish rule that Sardinians are "few, crazy and disunited" into a new motto: "many, smart and moving together".

The Sardex corporate philosophy emerged clearly in the beginning of its start-up phase where the social value footprint shaped the business's creation. As the founders point out "we studied so much and we saw that there were possibilities to manage the credit system by the members' behaviour based on values such as reciprocity, mutual support, and human relationship, as the main push to creating economic development". Three years along, the Sardex team faced difficult obstacles including the entrepreneurs' own vision of what a network was: "they perceived networks generally speaking as counterparts instead of part of each other. They believed that the Sardex network should have instantaneously brought clients without any effort, by just being in it", said one founder.

Another critical issue they tackled regarded cooperative attitudes and the strength/presence/absence of ties among entrepreneurs: "Sardinian people do not adopt collaborative working models, but we know that sharing attitudes pertain to small circles, such as families, so that we decided to shape the Sardex network on a family based model. Sardex is like a family that helps you [entrepreneurs] when you need help, and we operate like parents who seek to bring their own kids together". The founders underline their attitude of being stubborn and resilient. They understood they have to conquer entrepreneurs' trust day-by-day, by spending time within the entrepreneurs' working place at any time of the day. The topics of their conversations focused not only on the mechanisms of the community currency and how the entrepreneurs might interact with it, but also on entrepreneurs' market strategies related to their own business. The Sardex founders recognised that they needed time to identify the right strategies to involve local entrepreneurs and build strong relationships with them, which were, and still are, based on trust and human ties that often overcome the boundaries of simple working connections. The model of Sardex as a cohesive family network of small and medium enterprises confronted the credit crisis and the difficulty of being insular entrepreneurs, transcended these issues, and became successful.

Sardex is also seen as a laboratory for innovation, a network that promotes continuous improvements following the ability of social entrepreneurs to be engaged in a process of continuous innovation, adaptation, and learning (Dees, 1998). The Sardex team organises an annual event named, Sardinian, "Mitzas" (Springs for the change) which is much more than a simple 3-day workshop. By adopting a talk- show formula, the Sardex team develops open dialogue among academics, entrepreneurs, business consultants, and policy makers, aimed at engaging discussions with different stakeholders and merging innovative ideas. Mitzas is a well-known event that also represents a sort of network celebration for Sardex members for sharing their pride and awareness about their achievements and future activities.

3.3 Resources and Process

As discussed above, Sardex is inspired by the WIR model, but uses only an electronic (digital) LETS system of credit and debt for any transaction size. The credit unit is not convertible into any other currency and it can only be spent and acquired through economic participation in the network. Instead of charging a fee for transactions, Sardex charges a yearly membership fee that depends on the firm's size (between €200 for small enterprises and €3000 for large companies). Operatively speaking, the Sardex network is based on a digital platform. Since its inception, the Internet has played a crucial role both in facilitating the exchange of information and in providing the backbone of the circuit's infrastructure. Sardex. net is the online platform that mediates economic interactions and complements the social face-to-face interactions, and enables the network to scale up to the whole island. The network is also the means to support interactions between members who do not know each other through other channels. By the network service provider, Sardex delivers a wide range of services such as brokering, business networking events, community management, online services, and helpdesk. As one founder observed in the interview "Sardex offers for free the extension of its sales and purchases unit to its members and this opportunity can change their entrepreneurial organisational models... The small entrepreneur cannot bear the cost of any marketing operator within its business, but thanks to Sardex this can be possible".

The circuit works along this simple mechanism: each firm has an account which begins at zero, earning digital currency as it offers goods or services to others in the network. Companies may go into debt but only up to a certain limit, determined by what they can offer other participating firms. By using a centralised system the Sardex administrators track member firms' transactions, occasionally nudging the network to ensure its stability: "we operate to rebalance the members' accounts in order to keep the circuit healthy and alive, as the stationary credits affect not only the single entrepreneur, but also the whole community" says one founder. Often the members are the main ambassadors of the circuit by bringing their own suppliers into it and promoting the network's development, because they really believe the claim "you are the circuit". The sentiment to which any individual feels part of the whole community is quite diverse: "While buying in a shop, any customer who shows their Sardex card to pay, immediately creates a bond with the seller, and then they share information, and stories (. . .) Sardex is like a sharing world. The entrepreneurs are now aware that only by practicing collaborative strategies can they survive" say the founders.

The firm's recruitment process for Sardex membership is mainly fostered by two factors: (1) the marketing strategy of the Sardex team and (2) word-of-mouth among entrepreneurs. The former adopt tools such as periodic meetings to gather potential and actual members at the local level: "we understood we cannot only be a virtual community provider based on Internet, but we needed face-to-face relations by meeting with people in their own places" say the Sardex founders. The direct relations between the Sardex team and Sardex members is the backbone of the Sardex.net's success. The motto "in Sardex we trust" (Littera et al., 2014: 12) illustrates members' attitudes towards being the principle promoters of the circuit to potential members through word of mouth.

3.4 *From Goals to Outcomes*

The founders set up the Sardex service provider, which is also a company and a network of SMEs, to reach the following goals: to enable proximity-based and trust-based relationship building; to foster economic empowerment in and of Sardinia; to create a resilient community; and to define a more equitable environment for trading (Littera et al., 2014). As Posnett (2015: 1) points out, "their hope was that the project would give them a job in the place where they had grown up. But six years later it has turned into a symbol of local action, spreading to create a new network of thousands of businesses". Until in 2010, hundreds of Sardinian firms rejected the idea of joining the circuit, however, currently Sardex.net includes around 2900 SMEs, which generated over €38 million in business transactions in 2014. Sardex.net is also replicating similar systems in seven regions of Italy, using local networks following the Sardex.net principles and sharing the same software infrastructure and governance.

Sardex is not only a local/Italian phenomenon, but also a business model present within other localities. Digipay4growth is a European project co-funded by the European Commission (2014) that brings together Sardex and the Sardinian Governmental Authority and other private and public bodies including Bristol in United Kingdom and Catalan authorities in Spain. The project involves governments, SMEs and consumers and expenditures are made through a digital payment system that stimulates economic growth and job creation by increasing sales and access to credits for SMEs.

4 Building Collaborative Entrepreneurship Within the Sardex's Tourism Firms

Currently there are 195 tourism firms listed in Sardex.net that generate around 15% of Sardex's transactions. Sardex's tourism entrepreneurs are spread all over Sardinia, with the highest concentration in the main Sardinian city, Cagliari. A panel of ten tourism entrepreneurs who operate accommodation facilities (e.g., hotels and bed and breakfast establishments), food and beverage outlets, cultural events, and tour operator services were interviewed for this research (See Table 2). These interviews explored the entrepreneurs' characteristics, their values shared through

Table 2 Sardex tourism firms per type of activity

Entrepreneurial activity	N°
Agritourism	13
B&B	12
Bar, gelateria, paninoteca	20
Restaurant	82
Hotel	51
Pizzeria	7
Residence	5
Pub	5
Total	195

Source: Sardex.net, Marketing & Communication Office, November 2015

the circuit, the internal/external changes in businesses' resources and processes that occurred through their Sardex membership and their business outcomes.

4.1 Entrepreneurs' Characteristics

The tourism entrepreneurs of see themselves as innovators, dreamers, and human relations-oriented entrepreneurs. In fact, one of them said: "I am a dreamer, I like realizing dreams. My business philosophy is to create development (. . .) What I really like is creating innovative projects. I define myself as a man of relations". Another entrepreneur underlined his inclination to walk the unbeaten path: "I approach any business in terms of continuous innovation, I seek to undertake paths that are unusual. This is my philosophy". Entrepreneurs enthusiastically joined Sardex because they perceived the community network as an extension of their own business, as well as of their relational sphere: "I have the sensation of belonging to an amplified sharing network: if the circuits goes well and feels good, then all of us feel well", said one entrepreneur.

While interviewing Sardex entrepreneurs, an exploration was made of the individual's profile "before" and "after" joining the circuit. In other words, the interview investigated the change occurring in entrepreneurs' attitudes as a result of their Sardex's membership. Their answers were quite homogenous: they mirror themselves in Sardex.net. In some cases, relationships that arose through the circuit have directly impacted on their mindset by fostering new stimuli: "My business group has grown up considerably. I graduated while working, and recently I became student in business economics at the University of Cagliari. As I run many companies, and work with managers who are studying postgraduate courses, I need to study too", says one entrepreneur who runs accommodation facilities and restaurants employing 45 people in his group.

Another interesting point regards the entrepreneurs' attitudes to joining other collaborative networks, such as World Wide Opportunities on Organic Farms (WWOOF) and Bartercard: one hotelier manager stated, "I cannot say that Sardex changed my mind, but I found it absolutely coherent with my own philosophy".

4.2 Sharing Values

Tourism entrepreneurs fully recognize the social value of Sardex.net. The community currency was considered a community based on reciprocal help and characterized by friendly relationships: "When I have to go to bank I feel frustrated because for bankers I am just a number not a person, and most of the time (I am) a nuisance; on the contrary when I meet the Sardex team I feel comfortable as I meet friendly people" observed one entrepreneur. The network is also seen as a co-working space based on trust, honesty and loyalty values, and it is here that Sardex grounds its high reputation.

There is a general agreement among the interviewees that Sardex membership is driven to a large degree by economic and social reasons: "Sardex worked like an oxygen tank amidst the asphyxiating financial crisis," says a tourism entrepreneur. Sardex membership was also a question of being dead or alive for such firms, but thanks to Sardex they are still on the market. As one interviewee says, "I know entrepreneurs who kept running restaurants just because they have been fished out through Sardex". As explained in the previous section, the Sardex philosophy is based on supporting firms, and particularly those that experience difficulties (e.g., in cash shortage, decreases in sales, etc.).

Likewise, Sardex.net entrepreneurs adopt a philosophy of mutual help by transacting within the firms' circuit: every day, entrepreneurs organise meetings, eat in restaurants, or they need accommodation for business reasons. Due to their membership, they choose to purchase services in sardex within the Sardex network. The lower costs rule is not the main reason which supports the Sardex' transactions. Sardex is not a "discount community currency". Through the circuit, entrepreneurs sell by the full price of goods/services they trade, as any other Sardex client/supplier, but thanks to Sardex membership they gain extra money by increasing clients, partners and turnover. More than this, Sardex membership incorporates both economic and social benefits: "I choose Sardex restaurants, because I both share relations and I help people like me to keep running their own businesses" says one interviewee.

Participating in the Sardex network means to belong to a social community of entrepreneurs who not only share similar problems, such as the banks' refusal to finance their efforts to improve or save their businesses, but also a communal sense of pride. When Sardex gets visibility in national and international arenas, e.g., in articles in the *Financial Times* (Posnett, 2015) or academic papers by the London School of Economics (Dini & Kioupkiolis, 2014; Littera et al., 2014) and Yale

University (Iosifidis, Charette, Littera, Tassiulas, & Christakis, 2015), each member feels like they are taking part in a play on that same stage.

4.3 The Change in Resources, Processes and Outcomes

The Sardex community currency also activates an important process: each of the 2900 entrepreneurs exchange Sardinian products and services within the network. In doing so, Sardinian entrepreneurs foster local businesses and reinforce the regional economy. Within the Sardinian tourism sector one of the most critical points is with regards to the lack of local/regional supply chains, for instance between hoteliers and the food industry. Due to their Sardex membership, 195 tourism firms embrace the same philosophy by establishing ties with other Sardinian suppliers and customers, and partially reshaping their stakeholders' portfolio: part of their businesses is based on Sardex currency which implies that suppliers' and consumers' choices are driven by community-based values.

The tourism entrepreneurs highlight that their business turnover has increased thanks to Sardex, a fact also pointed out by Dini and Kioupkiolis (2014) who estimated an average of +10%. The reason suggested is because they acquired new clients and new opportunities. One interviewee says "Thanks to Sardex I increased customers, I get new distribution channels, and I pay workers in Sardex"; another one says "Sardex gave me an extra arm, I carried out projects that I could never accomplished such as the development of my product". Due to the network's membership, tourism entrepreneurs who manage accommodation facilities increased their domestic customers also during the low season. Although the number of tourism firms is not so high (when this study started in March, there were 150 firms in Sardex and seven months later there were 195), opportunities to increase tourists may be derived through the other Italian networks. Put simply, new, similar networks mean new potential markets, facilitated by the fact that Sardinia is a well-known and desired destination particularly among Italian tourists.

Another point that has been highlighted during the interviews is with regards to the crucial role of intangible elements, such as the relations generated by Sardex.net. Tourism entrepreneurs are fully conscious of the opportunities that have arisen as a result of the network in which people, and social capital more accurately, are the main wealth. Explicitly or implicitly, Sardex.net activates relationships among entrepreneurs. It goes beyond monetary transactions by developing and sharing new concepts not only for business purposes but also by social value creation. For example, an entrepreneur who manages restaurants and accommodation facilities is developing alternative forms of payments for his restaurant, and in the near future his customers will pay by barter. He says "If you eat in my restaurant you might pay me in goods instead of money. The most beautiful thing in doing business, is to develop relationships (...) What I really like in Sardex is the fact that the circuit commits you to care for your suppliers and customers, because if you do poor work, the circuit works badly as a consequence. You do not think in the same way if you transact by euro". Being an innovation that mixes sharing economy and a community-based value system, Sardex stimulates a non-monetized form of exchange that brings together economic and social needs. In other words, as explained by interviewees, Sardex combines "sharing and caring" (Ranchordás, 2015).

5 Conclusions

The Sardex community currency is a collaborative economy innovation built on a foundation of social entrepreneurship. It is based on social values such as trust, reciprocity, mutual support and human relationships wherein the culture of collaboration among members plays a crucial role. The Sardex entrepreneurs trade in products and services among themselves through a virtual coin which is more than a simple monetary tool. In certain ways, Sardex exemplifies community-based entrepreneurship in which members share similar visions and aims that go beyond pure commercial purposes. They cooperate together against the effects of financial crises, such as the lack of money for lending; they aim to create new jobs and preserve employment; and they ensure that local people can live and grow up with their children in the small towns of Sardinia, which, until this point, have been seriously affected by out-migration. As a result, the Sardex community can also be considered as an agent of social action and change.

The Sardex community currency also operates and affects tourism activity. By adopting collaborative strategies among the tourism entrepreneurs local ties are created and consolidated. Not only is extra revenue generated but this exchange system also has positive socio-economic effects on the Sardinian community. In fact, the Sardex network promotes local supply chains between hoteliers, restaurateurs and other tourism operators, and it creates virtuous circles of trust among entrepreneurs. As a tangible effect, Sardex generates a significant volume of transactions within Sardinian businesses, with regards to both supply and demand. In relation to the former, Sardex promotes local consumption by promoting local Sardinian supply chain relationships, such as in the agribusiness, and it implements shorter supply chain practices. With regards to consumption, Sardex also contributes to capturing new opportunities derived by growth in domestic tourism. Considering its more intangible effects, Sardex promotes connections among dispersed entrepreneurs who enhance their own businesses and create new ones through non-hierarchical relationships. Generating relationships and stimulating social cohesion are precious values on an island like Sardinia, characterized by unsustainable socioeconomic conditions including the loss of social capital due to the emigration of young and skilled people.

Although a collaborative community currency like the Sardex is not a panacea against international financial crises or Sardinia's socio-economic problems, it offers clear support to small businesses that fight every day to survive. By adopting social technologies, asymmetric market relations are being reshaped including, for example, bank-customer relations, as well as tourism relationships between Sardinia and the rest of Italy. Moreover, Sardex is expanding its business model to the Italian peninsula, so that new affiliate community currencies will be opening soon, and it is collaborating with other European organisations to develop broader economic perspectives.

Contrary to potential criticisms that sharing economy practices fall into the 'invisible' economy, Sardex is monitored by the Bank of Italy and the Inland Revenue Authority. No critical issues have emerged regarding tax evasion because Sardex' transactions are trackable, and the circuit fully respects the law. Although the Sardex community currency presents features that demonstrate many positive effects of a collaborative tourism economy based on social entrepreneurship, further investigation is required to extend understandings of the benefits of sharing. For example, more research is needed on the co-marketing strategies, or new business creation processes that have arisen within the tourism enterprises of Sardex and those of similar circuits in the rest of Italy.

Furthermore, considering that face-to-face relationships are one of the key success factors of the Sardinian circuit, this may be altered by the growth of the business and its extension to the rest of Italy. For example, while the leadership team is still made up of the five founders, the growth of Sardex could potentially affect the 'sharing and caring' ethos that is the cornerstone of the initiative. Another challenging point regarding the expansion and upscaling of a very local business model into a national one is that the Sardex founders are local—they are fully integrated within their socio-economic context in which they work and they share common values. Through Sardex they have shaped a distinctive business model in which knowledge and social capital are essential. They have created the new circuits of commerce for Sardinia, by tightly interlinking local communities and their own social values. Maintaining this could be a future challenge.

References

Aldridge, T. J., & Patterson, A. (2002). LETS get real: Constraints on the development of local exchange trading schemes. *Area, 34*(4), 370–381.

Alvord, S. H., Brown, L. D., & Letts, C. W. (2004). Social entrepreneurship and societal transformation. *Journal of Applied Behavioral Science, 40*(3), 260–282.

Austin, J., Stevenson, H., & Wei-Skillern, J. (2003). *Social entrepreneurship and commercial entrepreneurship: Same, different, or both?* Working paper series no. 04–029, Harvard Business School.

Blanc, J. (2011). *Classifying CCs: Community, complementary and local currencies, types and generations*. LEFI (Laboratoire d'économie de la firme et des institutions), Lyon University.

Bornstein, D. (1998). Changing the world on a shoestring. *Atlantic Monthly, 281*(1), 34–39.

Boschee, J. (1998). *Merging mission and money: A board member's guide to social entrepreneurship*. Retrieved from http://www.socialent.org/pdfs/MergingMission.pdf

Botsman, R., & Rogers, R. (2010). Beyond Zipcar: Collaborative consumption. *Harvard Business Review*. Retrieved from https://hbr.org/2010/10/beyond-zipcar-collaborative-consumption/

Botsman, R., & Rogers, R. (2011). *What's mine is yours: How collaborative consumption is changing the way we live*. New York: Harper Collins.

Cannas, R., & Giudici, E. (2015). Tourism relationships between Sardinia and its islands: Collaborative or conflicting? In G. Baldacchino (Ed.), *Archipelago tourism: Policies and practices* (pp. 67–81). Farnham: Ashgate.

Choi, N., & Majumdar, S. (2014). Social entrepreneurship as an essentially contested concept: Opening a new avenue for systematic future research. *Journal of Business Venturing, 29*, 363–376.

CNA (Confederazione Nazionale Artigiani) (2015). *Sesto rapporto sulle imprese artigiane della Sardegna*. Cagliari, Italy: CNA.

Collom, E. (2011). Motivations and differential participation in a community currency system: The dynamics within a local social movement organization. *Sociological Forum, 26*(1), 144–168.

CRENOS (Centre for North South Economic Research). (2015). *Economia della Sardegna. 22° Rapporto 2015*. Cagliari, Italy: CUEC.

Dacin, P., Dacin, M. T., & Matear, M. (2010). Social entrepreneurship: Why we don't need a new theory and how we move forward from here. *Academy of Management Perspectives, 24*(3), 37–57.

Dees, J. G. (1998). *The meanings of "social entrepreneurship"*. Stanford University, Draft Report for the Kauffman Center for Entrepreneurial Leadership, 6 pp.

Derrida, J. (1992). *Given time I. Counterfeit money*. Chicago: University of Chicago Press.

DiMaggio, P. J. (1982). Cultural entrepreneurship in nineteenth-century Boston. *Media, Culture and Society, 4*, 33–50.

Dini, P., & Kioupkiolis, A. (2014). *Community currencies as laboratories of institutional learning: Emergence of governance through the mediation of social value*. Conference Item, LSE (London School of Economics and Political Science). Retrieved from http://eprints.lse.ac.uk/59307/

Dini, P., van der Graaf, S., & Passani, A. (2015). Socio-economic framework for BOLD stakeholders. OpenLaws.eu Deliverable D2.3.d1, European Commission. Retrieved from http://eprints.lse.ac.uk/62819/

Drayton, W. (2002). The citizen sector: Becoming as entrepreneurial and competitive as business. *California Management Review, 44*(3), 120–132.

Dredge, D., & Gyimóthy, S. (2015). The collaborative economy and tourism: Critical perspectives, questionable claims and silenced voices. *Tourism Recreation Research, 40*(3), 286–302.

European Commission. (2014). Digipay4Growth. Project funded by CIP Competitiveness and innovation framework programme (CIP) (2007–2013). Retrieved from http://cordis.europa.eu/project/rcn/191828_en.html

Eurostat. (2015a). News release euro indicators, 174/2015. Retrieved from http://ec.europa.eu/eurostat/documents/2995521/6976371/3-01092015-AP-EN.pdf/

Eurostat. (2015b). Early leavers from education and training by sex. Retrieved from http://ec.europa.eu/eurostat/tgm/table.do?tab=table&init=1&language=en&pcode=t2020_40&plugin=1

Granados, M. L., Hlupic, V., Coakes, E., & Mohamed, S. (2011). Social enterprise and social entrepreneurship research and theory A bibliometric analysis from 1991 to 2010. *Social Enterprise Journal, 7*(3), 198–218.

Heinrichs, H. (2013). Sharing economy: A potential new pathway to sustainability. *GAIA, 22*(4), 228–231.

Humphrey, C. (1985). Barter and economic disintegration. *Man, 20*, 48–72.

Iosifidis, G., Charette, Y., Littera, G., Tassiulas, L., & Christakis, N. (2015, September 23). *Network analysis of the Sardex Community currency*. Yale University, Day of Data, Paper 4. Retrieved from http://elischolar.library.yale.edu/cgi/viewcontent.cgi?article=1066&context=dayofdata

ISTAT (Italian Institute of Statistics). (2015). Noi Italia. Youth unemployment rate. Retrieved from http://noi-italia2015.istat.it/index.php?id=7&user_100ind_pi1%5Bid_pagina%5D=192&P=1&L=0

Lee, R. (1996). Moral money? LETS and the social construction of local economic geographies in Southeast England. *Environment and Planning A, 28*, 1377–1394.

Littera, G., Sartori, L., Dini, P., & Antoniadis, P. (2014). *From an idea to a scalable working model: Merging economic benefit with social values in Sardex*. Conference paper, LSE (London School of Economics and Political Science). Retrieved from http://eprints.lse.ac.uk/59406/

Mair, J., & Martí, I. (2006). Social entrepreneur research: A source of explanation, prediction and delight. *Journal of World Business, 41*, 36–44.

Mauss, M. (1922/1990). *The gift: Forms and functions of exchange in archaic societies*. London: Routledge.

Melis, C., Giudici, E., & Dettori, A. (2013). Revitalizing the Barter: The case of Sardex.Net. In P. Spagnoletti (Ed.), *Organizational change and information system* (pp. 129–136). Berlin: Springer.

Pacione, M. (1997). Local exchange trading systems as a response to the globalisation of capitalism. *Urban Studies, 34*(8), 1179–1199.

Peredo, A. M., & Chrisman, J. J. (2006). Toward a theory of community-based enterprise. *Academy of Management Review, 31*(2), 309–328.

Peredo, A. M., & Mclean, M. (2006). Social entrepreneurship. A critical review of the concept. *Journal of World Business, 41*, 56–65.

Posnett, E. (2015, September 18). The Sardex factor. *Financial Time Magazine*, Retrieved from http://www.ft.com/intl/cms/s/2/cf875d9a-5be6-11e5-a28b-50226830d644.html#axzz3rI6oZeym

Ranchordás, S. (2015). Does sharing mean caring? Regulating innovation in the sharing economy. *Minnesota Journal of Law, Science & Technology*. Retrieved from http://ssrn.com/abstract=2492798

Robinson, J. (2006). Navigating social and institutional barriers to markets: How social entrepreneurs identify and evaluate opportunities. In J. Mair, J. Robinson, & K. Hockerts (Eds.), *Social entrepreneurship*. Basingstoke, UK: Palgrave Macmillan.

Sagawa, S., & Segal, E. (2000). Common interest, common good: Creating value through business and social sector partnership. *California Management Review, 42*(2), 105–122.

Schraven, J. (2000). The economics of local exchange and trading systems: A theoretical perspective. *International Journal of Community Currency Research, 4*, 1–8.

Schroeder, R. F. H., Miyazaki, Y., & Fare, M. (2011). Community currency research. An analysis of the literature. *International Journal of Community Currency Research, 15A*, 31–41.

Schumpeter, J. A. (1934). *The theory of economic development*. London: Oxford University Press.

Shane, S., & Venkataraman, S. (2000). The promise of entrepreneurship as a field of research. *Academy of Management Review, 25*(1), 217–226.

Short, J. C., Moss, T. W., & Lumpkin, G. T. (2009). Research in social entrepreneurship: Past contributions and future opportunities. *Strategic Entrepreneurship Journal, 3*, 161–194.

Stodder, J. (2009). Complementary credit networks and macroeconomic stability: Switzerland's Wirtschaftsring. *Journal of Economic Behavior & Organization, 72*, 79–95.

Stokes, K., Clarence, E., & Rinne, A. (2014). *Making sense of the UK collaborative economy*. Nesta Report. London: Nesta. Retrieved from http://www.nesta.org.uk/sites/default/files/making_sense_of_the_uk_collaborative_economy_14.pdf

Studer, T. (1998). *WIR in Unserer volkwirtschaft*. Basel: WIR. Translation: Beard, P.H. (trans.), 2006.WIR and the Swiss National Economy. Rohnert Park, CA: Sonoma State University. Available as e-book at http://www.lulu.com/content/301348

Thompson, J., Alvy, G., & Lees, A. (2000). Social entrepreneurship—a new look at the people and the potential. *Management Decision, 38*, 328–338.

Waddock, S. A. (1988). Building successful partnerships. *Sloan Management Review, 29*(4), 17–23.

Waddock, S. A., & Post, J. E. (1995). Catalytic alliances for social problem solving. *Human Relations, 48*(8), 951–972.

Williams, C. C. (1996). The New Barter economy: An appraisal of Local Exchange and Trading Systems (LETS). *Journal of Public Policy, 16*(1), 85–101.

Wilson, N. C., & Stokes, D. (2004). Laments and serenades: Relationship marketing and legitimation strategies for the cultural entrepreneur. *Qualitative Market Research: An International Journal, 7*(3), 218–227.

Improvising Economy: Everyday Encounters and Tourism Consumption

Gunnar Thór Jóhannesson and Katrín Anna Lund

Abstract As a part of the rising collaborative economy tourism entrepreneurs are faced with increasing demand of providing opportunities of authentic experiences. Tourist experience has always rested on co-creation and everyday encounters and we argue that the collaborative economy can be seen to include multiple rationalities, manifested in improvised tourism encounters. We contend that by following some of the often mundane encounters between visiting guests and the attraction they visit, it is possible to shed light on how interfering rationalities and multiple levels of collaboration affect the growth of tourism economies. The chapter focuses on improvised encounters between a particular entrepreneur, Siggi, who is the director of the Icelandic Museum of Sorcery and Witchcraft and his guests. It is argued that the value of collaboration and sharing in present day tourism economies is about more than economic transaction and needs to be critically examined as such.

Keywords Collaborative consumption • Co-creation • Tourism encounters • Entrepreneurship • Iceland

1 Introduction

It had been quite a busy day at the Museum of Icelandic Sorcery and Witchcraft, which is located in Hólmavík, a small town in the Strandir region, Iceland. The director, Siggi, and his assistant that day, who happened to be one of the authors of this article, Katrín, had just finished cleaning after closing time and were sitting by one of the tables outside waiting for a phone call from the restaurant in the next street to inform them that their well-deserved pizza was ready for collection. The phone rang, but at the very moment Katrín stood up to run for the pizza, a car stopped outside the Museum and a young woman with a large rucksack, tent and dreadlocks climbed out of the back. "Is the Museum closed?" she called out

G.T. Jóhannesson (✉) • K.A. Lund
Department of Geography and Tourism, Faculty of Life and Environmental Science, University of Iceland, Askja v/Sturlugötu, 101 Reykjavík, Iceland
e-mail: gtj@hi.is; kl@hi.is

D. Dredge, S. Gyimóthy (eds.), *Collaborative Economy and Tourism*, Tourism on the Verge, DOI 10.1007/978-3-319-51799-5_14

anxiously and when Siggi answered that it was, she replied, "No, it is the second time I have tried to visit and then it was also closed, I have always wanted to see this Museum!" Katrín rushed for the pizza and did not hear any more of the conversation or how it continued but a minute or two later she saw the car that the young woman had arrived in drive away. When she came back with the pizza, Siggi was standing outside and said, "I allowed her to go into the Museum". He explained that she had been hitch-hiking around Iceland and a dream of visiting the Museum was the only reason she had stopped in the village; this was her only chance to see the Museum as she had to continue her travels, leaving on the early morning bus the following day.

The woman gave herself plenty of time to explore the exhibits and the pizza had been finished when she came out. She was fascinated by the Museum and had many questions to ask Siggi about the history of witchcraft in Iceland. When he had answered her, it was his turn to ask where she came from and where she had been travelling. She said that she was from Poland and this was her second time in Iceland. She had originally intended to stay for the whole summer undertaking voluntary work for farmers in exchange for food and accommodation in different parts of the country. Unexpectedly, however, just before she left for her visit to Iceland, she met a new partner, which resulted in her reducing her visit to only one month. This meant that she was trying to see as much of Iceland as she could but in a much shorter time.

As the conversations continued, it started raining and suddenly, what seemed to be a light shower, turned into a downpour. All three went inside and Siggi told the young woman that as the forecast was for continual rain throughout the night, she could sleep on the Museum floor rather than going to the campsite. She said she would be fine with putting her tent up but Siggi would not take no for an answer. In the end she stayed the night on the floor of the Museum and when Siggi and Katrín came to work early next morning she had a cup of coffee with them before leaving on the bus.

Although this may count as an exceptional offer to a visitor at the Museum it was certainly not the first time that overnight shelter had been offered due to circumstances affecting travel plans. Indeed this is just a one example of how an exhibition dedicated to witchcraft and sorcery has expanded its function since 2000, both temporarily as well as on a long term basis (Lund, 2015a). In the long term because, although generally called the Witchcraft Museum by locals, it has since 2009 added and developed its services as a restaurant and since 2010 as a tourism information centre for the whole Strandir region (Fig. 1).

Strandir is a peripheral region in Iceland, sparsely populated and like most places in the country, the economy has been based on agriculture and fisheries. During the last 15 years the Museum of Icelandic Sorcery and Witchcraft has slowly become the main tourist attraction in the area and as such, a clear marker of a general societal change in rural areas in the Nordic countries manifested by a burgeoning service economy. The story of the Museum and how it has cemented its place as the centre of tourism activities in the area can be interpreted in multiple ways. One version points to a group of three clever entrepreneurs from the area that effectively

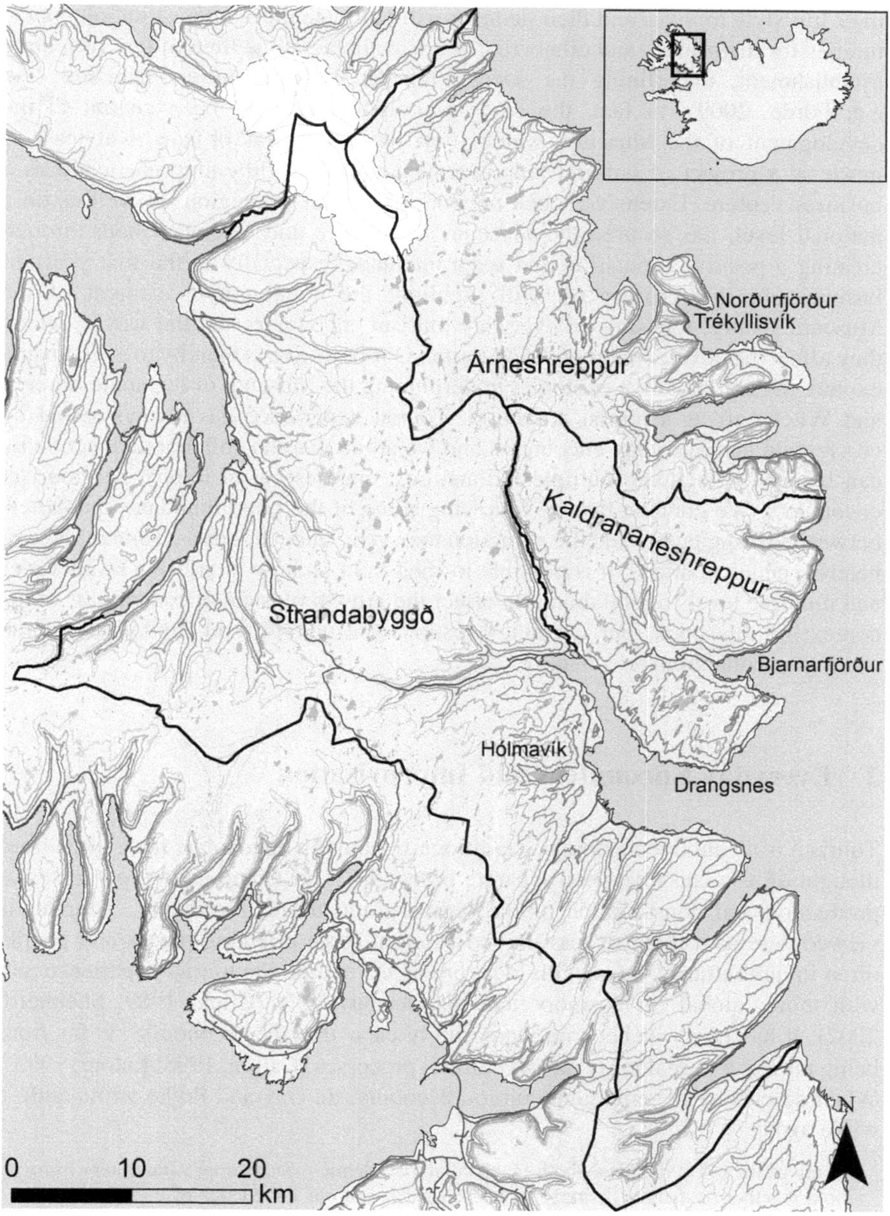

Fig. 1 Map of the Strandir region

made use of a sudden interest by the Icelandic authorities in cultural tourism to muster support to develop their vision of the first (and only) museum of witchcraft in the country (Gunnarsdóttir & Jóhannesson, 2014). Another storyline emphasises their life-style motives and their genuine will to create more interesting job opportunities for themselves and others than were available at the time of the Museum's establishment, underlining the social embeddedness of entrepreneurship (see e.g. Førde, 2009). In fact, the ethos of collaboration has been central in the development of the Museum, which from the outset was organised at least as much as a project of cultural empowerment and lifestyle entrepreneurship as a business venture. Extensive social networking within the region, as well as on a national level, has secured the Museum's existence and extension both through creating a positive reputation and securing funds, especially in the first years of business. In this chapter we will highlight the collaborative element of the Museum's story, focusing on everyday tourism encounters and the way in which they affect the development of the Museum. Our objective is thereby to open up and explore the collaborative ecologies underpinning the Museum of Icelandic Sorcery and Witchcraft as a tourist attraction. Tourist experience has always rested on co-creation and everyday encounters and we argue that the collaborative economy can be seen to include multiple rationalities, manifesting in improvised tourism encounters. We contend that by following some of the often mundane encounters between visiting guests and the attraction they visit, understood as an assemblage of heterogeneous relations, it is possible to shed light on how interfering rationalities and multiple levels of collaboration affect the growth of tourism economies. In the context of this book, our account questions the novelty and limitations of the sharing or collaborative economy.

2 Everyday Encounters and Improvisation

Tourism is all about encounters. Traditionally, tourism encounters have often been thought of as a clash between separate orders, be it hosts and guests, processes of production and consumption or the ordinary and the extraordinary. Tourism is viewed here as a more or less unified external force affecting places and people often in quite drastic ways, with local producers selling the tourist experience and with more 'global' or cosmopolitan tourists buying it (Crick, 1989; Shepherd, 2002). It has however become increasingly clear that the 'economic' is far from being pure or external to social and cultural processes (Callon, 1998; Latour, 1993). When describing the emergent cultural economy, du Gay and Pryke wrote quite a while ago:

> Many of the old certainties—both practical and academic—concerning what makes firms hold together or markets work seem less clear-cut and our knowledge of them feels less secure. Yet among these proliferating uncertainties has emerged—or, better, re-emerged—a belief that something called 'culture' is both somehow critical to understanding what is happening to, as well as to practically intervening in, contemporary economic and organizational life (du Gay & Pryke, 2002, p. 1).

Studies in tourism related to 'the performance turn' (Bærenholdt, Haldrup, Larsen, & Urry, 2004; Edensor, 2000, 2001; Larsen, 2005) and the 'mobility paradigm' (Haldrup, 2004; Hannam, Sheller, & Urry, 2006; Sheller, 2006; Sheller & Urry, 2004) have further illustrated the blurring of conceptual boundaries that have guided much of tourism research (Minca & Oakes, 2014).

The concept of collaborative consumption seeks to grasp the interplay between different kinds of rationalities involved in economic transaction. As such it is open to the idea that the encounter between "producer" and "consumer" or "host" and "guest" involves more than economic motives and a simple exchange of services for money. Belk has suggested that it is useful to think of a continuum of transactions where market exchange of commodities lies at one end "and sharing at the other, with gift giving somewhere in the middle" (Belk, 2007, p. 127). It is possible to think of instances where these forms come about in pure ways. Most of us share things and space with our close family; we take part in ritualised gift giving a number of times over the year, both as givers and receivers and we hardly escape being involved in impersonal market exchanges during the course of the day. The literature on collaborative consumption often highlights how it is different from more "traditional" modes of business transactions and even marks a new and more just or sustainable rationality of production and consumption (Dredge & Gyimóthy, 2015). Collaborative consumption is thus aligned to the sharing-end of the continuum rather than the business-as-usual end with its explicit focus on consumption. In practice, different "shades of sharing" interfere and Belk has argued that many of the activities dubbed as sharing are in fact pseudo-sharing, that is "practices masquerading as sharing" but which are commodity exchange (Belk, 2014, p. 10).

Belk's description of a continuum ranging from a pure sphere of cultural transactions to a pure sphere of economic transactions is useful in that it assists in defining particular types or constellations of collaborative economic activities, not only related to consumption that can be identified in tourism and other spheres of the economy (Dredge & Gyimóthy, 2015). We argue that it is equally important to follow the ways in which the collaborative economy is organised and enacted and how more generally collaborative ecologies emerge through relational practices and co-creation. Instead of taking either sharing or market exchange as a starting point, we begin from tourism encounters and seek to follow the processes, connections and entanglements through which moments of collaborative economy are created (Ren, van der Duim, & Jóhannesson, 2015).

Thereby we approach tourism encounters in relational terms with a focus on how tourist practices entangle with other activities and co-constitute the social (Van der Duim, Ren, & Jóhannesson, 2012). This view dissolves tourism into a multitude of relational practices and orderings (Franklin, 2012). Instead of thinking of tourism as a sector with relatively clear boundaries, as a "matter of fact", tourism becomes multiple and appears always a "matter of concern" (Latour, 2004; Ren et al., 2015). The focus then moves away from definitions of separate variables or classifications towards following the enactment and shaping of what we are used to identifying as distinct categories. In the present context, this involves for instance tracing how guests relate to attractions and take part in weaving together their experience in space and time along with other actors, human and more-than human.

Stating that tourism experiences are accomplished through a process of co-creation, underlines that tourism economies are done and enacted. It may be questionable however how much room there is for creativity when it comes to tourism performances. Tourism is indeed often a carefully staged and choreographed activity (Edensor, 2000, 2001; Larsen, 2005; Urry, 1990). Attractions and destinations are scripted (Gregory, 1999) to a different degree in order to organise the 'tourist gaze' (Urry, 1990) and control the movements and interactions of tourists and hosts, thus creating a stable environment for running and managing business. As managers of every destination management organisation are probably well aware, tourism destinations are never ordered once and for all but are continuously created through practices of multitude of actors (Van der Duim et al., 2012). Any destination is as such constantly in the making; it is an event of 'throwntogetherness' (Massey, 2005) of heterogeneous parts and multiple trajectories.

By focusing on the encounters through which tourist experience is created, the work needed to create and sustain tourism destination is highlighted (Jóhannesson, Ren, & van der Duim, 2015). Tourists and hosts are key actors in the assemblage through which tourism experiences are created but all sorts of materials, emotions and natural forces can also interfere in the process, 'through which the place in question is created both in the mind of the tourist as well as in its matter'(Grit, 2014; Lund & Jóhannesson, 2016). This relational heterogeneity of tourism makes it extremely volatile. Every order is constantly in danger of breaking down; failure in communication leads to misunderstandings: the weather suddenly changes and becomes hostile and demands a change of travel plans; a credit card is cancelled and creates moments of anxiety and even suspicion; or the car breaks down.

If we accept that tourism is constantly in the state of becoming, we might usefully refer to it as a meshwork of interwoven lines of becoming, rather than a network of interconnected points (Ingold, 2011). The tourism encounter is thereby not a clash between two separate entities or orders but the coming together of multiple lines that entangle. One of the implications of this understanding of tourism is that together with ordering and organisation, "doing" tourism in the widest sense of the word, is also very much about improvisation, uncertainties, surprises and disorientation. Ingold and Hallam describe improvisation as relational, as it 'goes on along "ways of life"' that are entangled and mutually responsive (Ingold & Hallam, 2007, p. 7). To improvise is to recognize that there is no script; 'no system of codes, rules and norms that can anticipate every possible circumstance' (Ingold & Hallam, 2007, p. 2) but it is important to note that it is not without rules or limits. Indeed there is a plan or future vision of the Museum's development and past decisions and actions affect possible practices today. Plans however, only go so far. At the end of the day, efforts to improve the tourist experience at the Museum of Icelandic Sorcery and Witchcraft have often been improvised and triggered by everyday encounters and conversations with guests that by themselves demand flexibility and improvisation.

We will begin the next section with a brief description of the Museum and its history. In the narrative we will stay close to Siggi, the Museum's Director, as he is usually in the midst of the 'action' at the Museum and we will follow improvised encounters between him and his guests.

3 Consuming Witchcraft

It can truly be stated that the Museum of Icelandic Sorcery and Witchcraft has from its inception been ordered in a process of improvisation and co-creation. To cut a long story short, during the late 1990s ethnology student, Jón Jónsson, born and bred in the region, was finishing a report for his Master studies exploring the possibilities of initiating cultural tourism in the region. He did this by collecting ideas from local people and listening to what they thought might be interesting topics to pursue. Almost at the end of the report a vague idea appeared about the possibility of using the region's history of witchcraft and sorcery as an instrument for crafting out cultural element for the region, as the region was notorious for these matters in the seventeenth century (Gunnarsdóttir & Jóhannesson, 2014; Lund, 2015a, 2015b; Lund & Jóhannesson, 2016). At this time the Icelandic authorities were encouraging economically weak regions to strengthen their economic sustainability, not least by developing new directions for the local economy to explore, including tourism. Jón, now equipped with ideas, conversed with a local historian, Magnús, and also Siggi, who had purely out of interest and passion, been studying witchcraft and magic; together they received funding to open the Museum. They engaged a professional stage designer to install the Museum, which is located in a low rising building that previously served as a warehouse for fishermen and Siggi was hired as its Director. Jón and Magnús are still at least partially involved with the Museum, Jón as the cultural administrator for the constituency and Magnús as a researcher specialising in the history of the region, with an emphasis on the seventeenth century. His publications are sold at the Museum shop and sometimes he also installs special side exhibitions at the Museum (in co-operation from Siggi), resulting from his research. Daily operation of the Museum is undertaken by Siggi and it can be argued that he has, for many, become an inseparable part of the Museum and even part of its attraction.

Siggi's responsibility as the Museum's Director has been influenced by his passion for the period of sorcery and witchcraft in the region and also his ambitions for sharing his passion with the community as well as making guests feel welcome. Hence, the Directorship is about much more than simply running a museum or a business. On occasions it is about putting on the Sorcerer's garment and acting out magical spells for groups of visitors, or to be photographed or filmed for advertising and introductory material in brochures and on the internet. It is also about storytelling, which is one of Siggi's talents, and if required he takes people on tours during which he narrates the history and folklore in the surrounding landscape (Lund, 2015a, 2015b). Furthermore, he often sets up events such as concerts and poetry reading in the Museum. Much of the work takes place on the internet via the homepage of the Museum and increasingly social media outlets such as Facebook and Twitter, where he promotes the Museum often in person (http://www.galdrasyning.is/). It is also possible to pursue material from the Museum's shop through the internet which is one way to keep in touch with visitors (which he sometimes does), but which has also proved to be a source of income. We could continue listing all the different activities involving the Directorship, but what is more important is to illustrate how these undertakings, in combination with everyday encounters with visitors, have expanded the operation of the Museum to additionally serve as the regional information office for tourists as well as a restaurant, called 'Café Magic'.

It was in 2009 that the tourist information office opened in an unused extended part of the building which also houses the Museum. The opening was a decision negotiated between the local authorities and Siggi. The office had previously been located at the top of the village, by the main road, which meant that tourists did not need to go into the village in search of information. The Museum, on the other hand, is located near the harbour, in the heart of the old village, so re-locating the information centre meant that tourists would actually go into Hólmavík, not just pass by, possibly visiting the Museum at the same time.

Siggi began developing the restaurant in 2009, simply as an experiment. He had for some time been aware that after mid-August, or at the end of the high-season, tourists continued to arrive, many of whom were looking for something to eat, but the only restaurant in the town had closed down. Siggi, as a caring host, started to serve these visitors by making fish soup, which was a great success. He also discovered a new personal passion: food and the preparation of it. He soon decided to try serving food the whole year around, beginning by serving fish soup, from which a menu based mainly on seafood has developed with a mussel platter as the central course (Lund, 2015b).

Although Siggi plays a central role in these two events of the Museum's expansion he is clearly not acting alone. From a relational approach, both instances can be read as effects of improvised encounters where different entities and energies combine. These include local politics, municipal leaders and the perceived need to service tourists when it comes to finding a convenient place for the tourist information centre in the village and also the presence of an unused extension of the Museum building. The launching of the restaurant is a continuation of Siggi's improvisation that is on-going as it requires regular menu changes, sourcing the best ingredients and discovering new recipes, partly to keep up with visitors' wishes and responses but also to continue to carve out the special trade of the Museum as an attraction.

The expansion of the Museum also further extends the space of improvisation through collaborative consumption, or shall we say co-creation. The inventiveness is not merely directed towards expanding business but is rather consequential as ideas and thoughts emerge from interactions taking place amongst the multiplicity of actors; complex and messy entanglements. It is in these entanglements that diverse rationalities become manifested in practice. In this case, aspects of care and caring relations emerge as the essential elements in the encounters and the associated improvisations. As Heuts and Mol (2013, p. 141) write, 'the term "care" suggests enduring work that seeks improvement but does not necessarily succeed. [...] it is a matter of calling on strengths and tinkering with weaknesses'. In the present case we find the notion of care helps us, together with improvisation, in by-passing dualistic notions of altruistic sharing and pure economic rationality and guides us along the collaborative ecologies of tourism encounters at the Museum.

An example of this is how Siggi decided to open a restaurant at the Museum since nobody else was catering for tourists in the village during the low season. He wanted to do this because in his opinion tourists matter. However, another motive was clearly to encourage guests to stay a bit longer in the village and spend more money during their stay. The restaurant was thereby also a potential business opportunity for the Museum and one means for enhancing its reputation and securing its economic survival.

Visitor accounts from Trip Advisor provide another example of how caring is manifested in tourism encounters:

> I was led to the Museum by accident, literally—my vehicle had blown a tire in the mountains the previous evening and Hólmavík was the closest settlement I could limp to on a dicey spare. By the time I would leave I felt I'd been guided there by the spirit of Strandabyggð, the area which claims Hólmavík, and that there may have been good cause for the earlier settlers of Strandabyggð to have been moved to sorcery, witchcraft and divination. In its harsh beauty the region itself inspires reverence and awe (indeed, it's the Helm of Awe painted on the newer exterior of the Museum that alerted me to its existence).
>
> Early on a Saturday morning the only sign of life in Hólmavík was a light in the Museum's door, which when opened yielded the scent of seafood cooking and an elven-looking man patting his pockets. Sigurður looked up and bid me welcome in Icelandic, then, realizing I didn't speak it, switched to excellent English and asked if I had a match. I felt immediately like family.
>
> At first I thought I'd stumbled into just a cafe (through which, it turns out, one passes to get to the Museum), but Siggi asked first if I'd come to see the Museum. I said "not exactly" and told him of my misfortune, which he took immediately in hand, examining my little Renault and running through the small list of possible solutions available in rural Iceland on a Saturday. There were few. Undeterred, Siggi bade me spend my morning in the Museum and he would conjure something to get me on my way again.

In this example, care is strongly linked to the help that Siggi provides in his efforts to sort out the visitor's misfortune. He leaves his task at the restaurant to examine the car before setting out to search for a repair for the tyre, acting now in the role of assistant at the information office and going far beyond what might be expected of him. At the same time he sells the visitor an entrance to the Museum so that he can kill time whilst his car is being sorted out. The boundaries between encounters of care and doing business blur. Siggi's responses to the visitor's problem hints at hospitality that is both spontaneous and genuine and which is consistent with what Lugosi refers to as meta-hospitality, 'existential in nature and emotional in essence' (Lugosi, 2008, p. 19). However, it is seemingly the most mundane incident that cements the positive interaction when Siggi asks for a match, making the visitor feel like part of a family. This is experienced as a moment suffused with a hint of magic which is in line with how the attraction, the Museum of Sorcery and Witchcraft, is scripted, having the helm of awe painted on its exterior and inside it an 'elven-looking man' who appears to be an inseparable part of the interior, as well as exterior, decoration. A snippet from a newspaper interview with Siggi plays on this image of him as well and states:

> The Museum's manager . . . prefers to go by the title 'sorcerer'. This seems fitting with his glinting eyes and unruly hair—often constrained by a peculiar woollen cap—one wouldn't be surprised if he suddenly started chanting and waving around pieces of wood with magical stave carving (Guðmundsdóttir, 2015).

No matter if Siggi is described as an elf or a sorcerer, what matters is that his appearance is in line with visitors' expectations regarding a museum of witchcraft and sorcery. His identity emerges in relation to how the visitor improvises his or her own steps as they explore the settings in their different ways and, for at least some of them, Siggi is indivisible from the attraction, increasing its perceived authenticity. This encounter becomes an event of co-creation or a moment of collaborative consumption. As Tanggaard points out creativity is a collective act and can even be 'conceptualized as dialectical opposites in tension' (Tanggard, 2012, p. 28 and see McLean, 2009). This act is partly improvised, simply because tourism encounters cannot be planned or managed to include every detail. Siggi's bodily appearance has an important agency in creating not only himself as a sorcerer or an elven-like man, but also the sense for the space of the Museum (e.g. Lugosi, 2014). This is not merely an unconscious creation which is revealed in the newspaper interview when he answers the question if he has adopted his appearance to fit the Museum, '. . .with this job, being odd certainly helps'.

Other examples of creative and improvised tourism encounters at the Museum give further insight into the emergent collaborative ecologies underpinning the museum:

> We visited the museum and Hólmavik in March 2013. There is very little else to see in the town itself, which was fine by us because it is truly an oasis of calm. The museum itself was atmospheric and very informative. It gives one a fantastic glimpse into Iceland's dark past. The owner of the museum was incredibly welcoming. You must try the mussels provided. They were excellent. Thank you Siggy and I hope you enjoyed sharing our Baileys! This was certainly one of our best experiences in the whole country. You really mustn't miss it (Visited March 2013).

Another says:

> Many many thanks to the staff who listened to my daughter's stories about every cat she has ever known while we continued to soak in the exhibits. I repeat. . ..the staff at the museum are truly magical (Visited June 2013).

An important part of the short examples mentioned above is that there seems to be time available for Siggi to invest in the emotional labour necessary to realise such moments of collaborative consumption. To improvise through tourism encounters indeed takes more time than to follow a script of 'functional hospitality' (Lugosi, 2008). To hold the balance between connecting to people visiting the Museum and simply providing efficient service to all visitors is a huge challenge for Siggi. While the genuine hospitality seems to play an important part in the image of the Museum being a special, friendly and even mythical place to visit one may ask how far this process of commodification of improvised encounters can go until it begins to deteriorate both Siggi's personal health and well-being. Siggi admits that during periods of heavy traffic to the Museum things are difficult. He says: 'When you don't have the time to talk to people, then I get tired and wasted'. These periods are common during the high season, in fact, the Museum's staff often look up at the end of the day and all they can say to reflect on it is, 'this was a strange day'. A strange day is a day that just seems to disappear as Katrín, whilst working/doing fieldwork at the Museum, often experienced. Once, after a four hour period of Siggi preparing and serving food and Katrín waitressing, as well as selling entry to the Museum and providing information to tourists, they sat down and after staring at each other for a while Siggi said, 'what happened?' and then they burst into laughter. Both felt their communication with tourists had been somewhat superficial and in some cases a hint of irritation had influenced their exchanges due to the differing needs of the tourists. However, by doing their best to service an excellent product, the Museum and what it offers, all grievances were put aside and all visitors left happy; they all had, in one way or another, encountered some kind of magic. Nevertheless, this describes a situation that with the popularity and increasing promotion of the Museum, has become the reality during the high season and for Siggi, as he says, 'this is no fun anymore'.

On the other hand being able to talk to the visitors, connect to their life-trajectories even only for a little while, "re-charges his batteries". He also notes: "You also feel when it is enough, when you cannot give more".

4 Improvising Economy

To draw the discussion to an end we will return to the beginning of the chapter, with the arrival of the Polish woman just after the Museum had closed for the day. She expresses her frustration because she had always wanted to visit it and this was her only chance to do so. Siggi appreciates her interests. The Museum is his creation and he is proud of it so he lets her in. When she has finished her tour, they engage in mutual conversations of cultural exchange; the young woman wants to know more about the history of sorcery in the region and Siggi is eager to listen to her talking about her travels. The exchange brings forth an element of care when he allows her to make a bed in the Museum to shelter from the rain. However, her visit could have been very different. Imagine if she had arrived in the middle of the day during the high season described above. She would probably been sold entrance to the Museum by Katrín and possibly never even seen Siggi since her style of travel was such that she would rather not eat at restaurants so he would not have served her food. Katrín might then have directed her to the bus, and even if she had wanted to find out more about the Museum, there would have been insufficient time for this kind of discussion. A completely different experience; however there is no need to assume that she would not have left happy, as she did actually manage to visit the Museum. Her visit was only improvised due to a particular set of events.

Depending on circumstances, not least the time available to Siggi to spend with visitors, the tourist encounter is improvised in different ways. Sometimes it takes the form of an almost automatic commodity exchange, while at other times it becomes a moment of personal contact and engagement based on the mutual interest of guests and Siggi. Other instances are mediated via the Museum's homepage or its presence on social media and sites such as Trip Advisor. It is however extremely difficult to categorise every encounter. It is not as if encounters are either closed relations of commodity exchanges or open events of altruistic hospitality. Each tourist encounter is a moment of collaboration, a becoming space of co-creation that can turn out in different ways (Lugosi, 2014). Siggi's challenge as a host is to manage the constant fluidity of tourism encounters. When should he open up and engage with visitors and when to draw the line and play the role of the disengaged but professional service worker? There is no straight forward answer to that—it has to be improvised.

Where does this leave us? In this chapter we have moved through the collaborative ecologies underpinning the Icelandic Museum of Sorcery and Witchcraft. Approaching tourism encounters in relational terms allows us to open up the process of transaction, allowing space for the uncertain and unpredictable as well as more nuanced valuations of the collaborative economy. The account above underlines that collaborative economy involves multiple rationalities that cannot be easily boiled down into a single or one dimensional strategy for economic success. The value of collaboration and sharing in present day tourism economies is not only about platform capitalism or monetised digitised market exchange (dubbed as sharing). In Siggi's case, responsibility and care are in constant play in every tourism encounter. In order to critically grasp the potentialities and limitations of the collaborative economy, researchers have to be conscious about their position and agency in the midst of the complex entanglements that tourism encounters manifest. It is important to slow down and attend to the everyday happenings of tourism. Such positionality allows for a glimpse into the network of collaborative ecologies that are always improvised and never completely ordered.

References

Bærenholdt, J. O., Haldrup, M., Larsen, J., & Urry, J. (2004). *Performing tourist places*. Aldershot: Ashgate.

Belk, R. (2007). Why not share rather than own? *The Annals of the American Academy of Political and Social Science, 611*, 126–140. doi:10.1177/0002716206298483.

Belk, R. (2014). Sharing versus pseudo-sharing in web 2.0. *Anthropologist, 18*(1), 7–23.

Callon, M. (Ed.). (1998). *The laws of the markets*. Oxford: Blackwell.

Crick, M. (1989). Representations of international tourism in the social sciences: Sun, sex, sights, savings, and servility. *Annual Review of Anthropology, 18*, 307–344.
Dredge, D., & Gyimóthy, S. (2015). The collaborative economy and tourism: Critical perspectives, questionable claims and silenced voices. *Tourism Recreation Research.* doi:10.1080/02508281.2015.1086076.
du Gay, P., & Pryke, M. (Eds.). (2002). *Cultural economy: Cultural analysis and commercial life*. London: Sage.
Edensor, T. (2000). Staging tourism: Tourists as performers. *Annals of Tourism Research, 27*(2), 322–344.
Edensor, T. (2001). Performing tourism, staging tourism: (Re)producing tourist space and practice. *Tourist Studies, 1*(1), 59–81.
Førde, A. (2009). Creating 'The Land of the Big Fish': A study of rural tourism innovation. In T. Nyseth & A. Viken (Eds.), *Place reinvention: Northern perspectives* (pp. 93–109). Farnham: Ashgate.
Franklin, A. (2012). The choreography of a mobile world: Tourism orderings. In R. Van der Duim, C. Ren, & G. T. Jóhannesson (Eds.), *Actor-network theory and tourism: Ordering, materiality and multiplicity* (pp. 43–58). London: Routledge.
Gregory, D. (1999). Scripting Egypt: Orientalism and the cultures of travel. In J. Duncan & D. Gregory (Eds.), *Writes of passage: Reading travel writing*. London: Routledge.
Grit, A. (2014). Messing around with serendipities. In S. Veijola, J. Germann Molz, O. Pyyhtinen, E. Höckert, & A. Grit (Eds.), *Disruptive tourism and its untidy guests: Alternative ontologies for future hospitalities* (pp. 122–141). London: Palgrave MacMillan.
Guðmundsdóttir, R. (2015). *In Strandir: Sorcery and tourism* [Webpage]. Retrieved from http://grapevine.is/travel/2015/07/30/in-strandir-sorcery-and-tourism/
Gunnarsdóttir, G. Þ., & Jóhannesson, G. T. (2014). Weaving with witchcraft: Tourism and entrepreneurship in Strandir, Iceland. In A. Viken & B. Granås (Eds.), *Destination development in tourism: Turns and tactics* (pp. 95–112). Farnham: Ashgate.
Haldrup, M. (2004). Laid-back mobilities: Second-home holidays in time and space. *Tourism Geographies, 6*(4), 434–454. doi:10.1080/1461668042000280228.
Hannam, K., Sheller, M., & Urry, J. (2006). Editorial: Mobilities, immobilites and moorings. *Mobilities, 1*(1), 1–22. doi:10.1080/17450100500489189.
Heuts, F., & Mol, A. (2013). What is a good tomato? A case of valuing in practice. *Valuation Studies, 1*(2), 125–146. doi:10.3384/vs.2001-5992.1312125.
Ingold, T. (2011). *Being alive: Essays on movment, knowledge and description.* London: Routledge.
Ingold, T., & Hallam, E. (2007). Creativity and cultural improvisation: An introduction. In T. Ingold & E. Hallam (Eds.), *Creativity and cultural improvisation* (pp. 1–24). Oxford: Berg.
Jóhannesson, G. T., Ren, C., & van der Duim, R. (2015). Tourism encounters, controversies and ontologies. In G. T. Jóhannesson, C. Ren, & R. van der Duim (Eds.), *Tourism encounters and controversies: Ontological politics of tourism development* (pp. 1–19). Farnham: Ashgate.
Larsen, J. (2005). Families seen sightseeing: Performativity of tourist photography. *Space and Culture, 8*(4), 416–434. doi:10.1177/1206331205279354.
Latour, B. (1993). *We have never been modern* (C. Porter, Trans.). Cambridge: Harvard University Press.
Latour, B. (2004). Why has critique run out of steam? From matters of fact to matters of concern. *Critical Inquiry, 30*, 225–248.
Lugosi, P. (2008). Hospitality spaces, hospitable moments: Consumer encounters and affective experiences in commercial settings. *Journal of Foodservice, 19*, 139–149. doi:10.1111/j.1745-4506.2008.00092.x.
Lugosi, P. (2014). Mobilising identity and culture in experience co-creation and venue operation. *Tourism Management, 40*, 165–179. doi:10.1016/j.tourman.2013.06.005.

Lund, K. A. (2015a). Just like magic: Activating landscape of witchcraft and sorcery in rural tourism, Iceland. In S. Brunn (Ed.), *Changing world religion map: Sacred places, identities, practices and politics* (pp. 767–782). New York: Springer.

Lund, K. A. (2015b). Magic mussels: Ingredients for improvising a tourism destination. *Journal of Gastronomy and Tourism, 1*(1), 19–31. doi:10.3727/216929715X14298190828831.

Lund, K. A., & Jóhannesson, G. T. (2016). Earthly substances and narrative encounters: Poetics of making a tourism destination. *Cultural Geographies, 23*(4), 653–669. doi:10.1177/1474474016638041.

Massey, D. (2005). *For Space*. London: Sage.

McLean, S. (2009). Stories and cosmogonies: Imagining Creativity Beyond "Nature" and "Culture". *Cultural Anthropology, 24*(2), 213–245. doi:10.1111/j.1548-1360.2009.01130.x.

Minca, C., & Oakes, T. (2014). Tourism after the postmodern turn. In A. Lew, C. M. Hall, & A. Williams (Eds.), *The wiley blackwell companion to tourism* (pp. 294–303). Malden, MA: Wiley Blackwell.

Ren, C., van der Duim, R., & Jóhannesson, G. T. (2015). Postscript: Making headways, expanding the field and slowing down. In G. T. Jóhannesson, C. Ren, & R. van der Duim (Eds.), *Tourism encounters and controversies: Ontological politics of tourism development* (pp. 239–244). Farnham: Ashgate.

Sheller, M. (2006). The new mobilities paradigm. *Environment and Planning A, 38*(2), 207–226. doi:10.1068/a37268.

Sheller, M., & Urry, J. (Eds.). (2004). *Tourism mobilities: Places to play, places in play*. London: Routledge.

Shepherd, R. (2002). Commodification, culture and tourism. *Tourist Studies, 2*(2), 183–201. doi:10.1177/146879702761936653.

Tanggard, L. (2012). The sociomateriality of creativity in everyday life. *Culture and Psychology, 19*(1), 20–32. doi:10.1177/1354067X12464987.

Urry, J. (1990). *The tourist gaze: Leisure and travel in contemporary societies*. London: Sage.

Van der Duim, R., Ren, C., & Jóhannesson, G. T. (Eds.). (2012). *Actor-network theory and tourism: Ordering, materiality and multiplicity*. London: Routledge.

Community and Connection: Exploring Non-monetary Aspects of the Collaborative Economy Through Recreation Vehicle Use

Anne Hardy

Abstract This chapter explores recreational vehicle users' (RVers) non-monetary transactions and tribal behaviour to broaden our understanding of collaborative consumption. The chapter uses a neo-tribal lens to study RVers and their alignment with the collaborative economy. Using an ethno-methodological approach, it argues that there are functional and affective dimensions that underpin non-monetary transactions. Functional dimensions relate to a desire to ensure that RV travellers are able to achieve their travel goals. The affectual dimensions give RVers a sense of belonging, fellowship within a group, and ultimately an opportunity to realise the freedom they seek to experience through RVing. The chapter suggests that the heavy emphasis given to the Internet as the conduit for the collaborative economy to occur may not always be relevant for all styles of travellers. Moreover, it adds depth to previous research into the collaborative economy by demonstrating that non-monetary collaborative transactions can build a sense of belonging, fellowship and shared sentiment.

Keywords Non-monetary Transactions • Recreational Vehicle Users • Neo-Tribes • Collaboration • Tourism • Sharing Economy

1 Introduction

This chapter contextualizes the collaborative and tribal nature of non-monetary transactions within the collaborative economy. It begins with a literature review of the collaborative economy, focussing on the historical and current role of non-monetary transactions. Following this, the chapter argues that recreational vehicle users (RVers) provide a context through which non-monetary transactions and tribal behaviours that occur within the collaborative economy may be explored. Using an ethno-methodological approach the chapter then analyses the non-monetary transactions of RVers and their alignment with the collaborative

A. Hardy (✉)
Tasmanian School of Business and Economics (TSBE), University of Tasmania, Private Bag 84, Hobart, TAS 7001, Australia
e-mail: anne.hardy@utas.edu.au

D. Dredge, S. Gyimóthy (eds.), *Collaborative Economy and Tourism*,
Tourism on the Verge, DOI 10.1007/978-3-319-51799-5_15

economy. In doing so, it contextualises the collaborative nature of travelling within a cultural-historical lens. A significant contribution of this chapter is that it builds upon the positive outcomes of collaborative economy and in doing so, presents an alternative valuing of the non-monetary transactions that take place within the collaborative economy.

In the first chapter of this book it was established that the term collaborative consumption was first coined by Felson and Spaeth (1978, p. 614) as:

> ...those events in which one or more persons consume economic goods or services in the process of engaging in joint activities with one or more others.

Since then, there has been a small yet highly influential body of work that has emerged in this space, much of which putting heavy emphasis on monetary transactions (e.g. Belk, 2007, 2014) as well as on transactional definitions of the collaborative economy involving sharing, bartering, trading and swapping. This chapter argues that an over-emphasis on the monetary aspects of the collaborative economy runs the risk of omitting the broader "sharing turn" characterised by collaborative communities and tribal behaviour.

The case of recreational vehicles users (RVers) will be used to demonstrate this issue. For the purposes of this chapter, RV use has been defined as:

> ...a form of tourism where travellers take a camper trailer, van conversion, fifth wheel, slide-on camper, caravan or motorhome on holiday with them, and use the vehicle as their primary form of accommodation (Hardy & Gretzel, 2011, p. 194).

RVers have long been described as highly social, collaborative community builders (Counts & Counts, 2004; Mattingly, 2005). Their highly mobile, yet tribal behaviour is built upon notions of altruistic sharing and trust (Hardy & Robards, 2015) and has been conceptualized using neo-tribal theory. Neo-tribes were first defined by Maffesoli (1996: 98), then more recently conceptualised as:

> ...networks of heterogeneous persons....who are linked by a shared passion or emotion; a tribe is capable of collective action, its members are not simple consumers, they are also advocates (Cova and Cova, 2002, p. 602).

The characteristics of a neo-tribe have been defined as a grouping that is fluid and ephemeral and based on a state of mind and a lifestyle rather than long-standing involvement (Maffesoli, 1996). Muniz and O'Guinn (2001, p. 414) argued that:

> ...they form, they disperse, they re-from as something else, reflecting the constant shifting identities of postmodern consumers.

Hardy, Wickham, and Gretzel (2013b) propose that neo-tribes can be identified as possessing two characteristics: symbolic and behavioural elements. Symbolic elements include a sense of sharing a lifestyle and being part of community of emotionally connected people. A communal ethic dominates along with a sense of fellowship. The behavioural aspects that define neo-tribes include a physical sharing of space, meeting and performative spaces (Hughson, 2007) and scenes (Bennett, 2011) where individuals group together because of a shared taste. Behavioural characteristics of neo-tribes also include rituals (Hardy et al., 2013b) and signifiers such as goods which may be consumed (Cova and Cova, 2002).

Arguably, RVers' highly mobile lifestyle and social practices represent a neo-tribe. They have been documented as having a strong sense of belonging, fellowship and sense of worth (Counts & Counts, 2004; Hardy, Hanson, & Gretzel, 2013a; Hardy et al., 2013b; Hardy & Robards, 2015). Moreover, and significantly for this study, the social practices of sharing suggest that RVers are a neo-tribe with non-monetary collaborative consumption at its core. Counts and Counts (2004) argued that RVers' sharing habits are often a necessity, as they allow them to maintain their independence, particularly when on the road for extended periods of time, or in remote regions with few services or facilities. Resources which are shared include information on campsites and sharing of information or physical tools in order to perform repairs while on the road. This non-monetary form of sharing differs from economic activities as it also includes sharing that has emotional outcomes; studies have illustrated that the social glue of this highly mobile neo-tribe give RVers a sense of belonging as well as safety (Hardy & Robards, 2015). Despite the location and nature of RVers' non-monetary sharing practices having undergone changes since the development of Web 2.0, there are still significant performative spaces where sharing has occurred for many years and continues to do so.

2 Exploring the Historical Drivers for the Collaborative Economy

There is a persuasive argument for the collaborative economy being a new and technologically facilitated consumption phenomenon. Its rapid and recent growth, particularly in an online context, has been articulated by Owyang (2013) as being the result of three contemporary drivers: (1) societal changes, such as increasing population density and a subsequent desire for sustainability; (2) economic drivers, such as a desire to make money from excess infrastructure or unused/idling assets that one may own, such as property; and (3) technology, such as the development of social media and networking which have largely been a result of the development of mobile Internet devices including tablets and smart phones. Importantly however, there are also other drivers, which include a desire to travel more sustainably and to reduce negative impacts on the environment (Tussyadiah, 2015), and a desire to feel a sense of belonging to a community of like-minded people (Albinsson & Perera, 2012; Botsman & Rogers, 2010; Galbreth, Ghosh, & Shor, 2012; McArthur, 2015; Närvänen, Kartastenpää, & Kuusela, 2013; Tussyadiah, 2015). Dredge and Gyimóthy (2015) add that the rapid uptake of the collaborative economy is a consequence of the recognition of problems inherent in the traditional tourism industrial system. These include unused assets; barriers to investment; large amounts of regulation; high transaction costs; and the use of social media combined with a desire for personalised and alternative forms of tourism and authentic experiences (Botsman & Rogers, 2010). The use of social media has recently received so much attention that the collaborative economy has been defined as denoting the:

> . . .use of Internet technologies in an effort to connect distributed groups of people to make better use of skills, goods and other useful things (Stokes, Clarence, & Rinne, 2014, p. 10).

Similarly, Belk (2014) also emphasised the importance of technology and argued that sharing and collaborative consumption have two aspects in common: (1) their use of temporary access non-ownership models of utilizing consumer goods and services and (2) their reliance on the Internet, particularly websites that allow users to communicate and share content with each other (Carroll & Romano, 2011). This heavy reliance on the Internet as a conduit through which the collaborative economy occurs has also been advocated by Hamari et al. (2015, p. 3), who defined collaborative economy as:

> . . .peer-to-peer activity of obtaining, giving, sharing or gaining access to goods and services, coordinated through community-based online services.

Indeed, Grassmuck (2012) argues that the Web 2.0 era has facilitated what may be defined as the 'sharing turn.'

However, while there is no doubt that the Internet has resulted in the formation of a variety of new ways of monetary based sharing, the Internet has also facilitated older forms of non-monetary sharing on a larger scale (Belk, 2014) such as bartering and the trading of information. These forms of sharing are evident in ancient guidebooks that make suggestions of the best places to visit and the practices of hosting guests in one's home. They do not involve the Internet or an exchange of money and as such may be considered significant antecedents to the modern collaborative economy. Importantly, these historical antecedents suggest that engagement is not just about money. More recently the sharing of photographs and experiences upon one's return from their vacation, serve not only as a tool for recounting adventures and activities, but also allow travellers to share their new-found knowledge of regions and traveller resources.

Non-monetary exchanges have also allowed travellers to actively avoid capitalist systems. The counter-cultural hippies in Amsterdam in 1970s have been documented as gathering in groups, so as to escape the norms of society, institutions and rules. These young travellers from different walks of life coalesced for short periods of time in Amsterdam to share their desire to escape from their routine life at home. Their exchanges of goods, where money was tight and drugs were highly valued, were recorded as being non-monetary and akin to being 'hunter-gatherer-like' (ten Have, 1974). Bartering and exchanges were recorded as well as social engagement (ten Have, 1974). Significantly, this early research concurs with research that reveals similar motivational factors for engaging in the collaborative economy, including economic motivations such as a desire to save money (Bardhi & Eckhardt, 2012; Möhlmann, 2015; Tussyadiah, 2015) or to 'buck the capitalist system' (McArthur, 2015). Moreover, it appears that at the core of these collaborative interactions was a desire to socialise, identify with like-minded travellers and experience a sense of belonging—all akin to the concept of the neo-tribe.

Recently, non-monetary exchanges within the collaborative economy have been explored by McArthur (2015) who argued that economic explanations for the growth of sharing behaviour are inadequate for explaining the success of platforms where no money changes hands. Similarly, Tussyadiah (2015) suggested that the collaborative economy is not just about money but rather people desiring a new mode of travel. However, what both authors demonstrate is an ahistoric view of collaborative consumption. The historical existence of non-monetary transactions within the tourism industry suggests that travellers have engaged in sharing and altruistic behaviour for many years. The neo-tribal lens, which suggests that neo-tribes have affective outcomes (Hardy & Robards, 2015) such as sense of fellowship, belonging and being part of a community of like-minded individuals, provides a cogent lens through which the reasons for engagement in the collaborative economy may be explored. The provision of a contextualised understanding of the collaborative economy will arguably provide rich socio-historical insights into its recent surge in popularity.

2.1 Conceptualising the Recreational Vehicle Market

Recreational vehicle users (RVers) have been defined as highly mobile travellers who are motivated by the desire to experience freedom from the routine of their home life (Counts & Counts, 2004; Fjelstul & Fyall, 2015; Hardy & Gretzel, 2011; Mings & McHugh, 1995; Onyx & Leonard, 2005). In Europe, Australia and the United States, RVers are stereotypically regarded as retirees, called Grey Nomads in Australia or Snowbirds in North America, who travel for extended periods of time (Counts & Counts, 2004; Onyx & Leonard, 2005). However, other groups also exist, including the family market, and those who travel in Caravan or RV club groups and stay only in free or low cost destinations (known as Boondockers in North America and Freedom Campers in Australia). What differentiates this form of travel from others is that the accommodation remains the same for the duration of the vacation and is pre-purchased when the RV is bought. This in itself differentiates the economic structure of this market from others. Consequently, once on the road the expenditure of RVers on 'accommodation' such as campsite fees, appears minimal in contrast to other tourism sectors. This is accentuated by the fact that RVs are now commonly equipped with toilets, showers, grey and black water storage. This facilitates traveller's ability to free camp in locations that have no campsite fee, such as roadside pullovers, national parks and public reserves. Consequently, the RV market is often mistakenly regarded as low income and given a low priority by many local, regional, state and even national tourist organisations. Perhaps for this reason information for these travellers is sparse, particularly considering the size of the RV market. In the United States, it is estimated that 8.9 million households now own an RV and the industry is worth $37 billion (Recreational Vehicle Industry Association, 2014). Similarly in Australia, whose entire population is 23 million, there were 528,869 caravan and campervan registrations at January 2013 (BDO, 2014).

Fellowship that transcends societal status, along with an aspiration for a transformative journey, has been documented as being an essential affective outcome of RVing by researchers (Gretzel, Formica, & Fesenmaier, 2005; Hardy & Robards, 2015; Holloway, 2007; Onyx & Leonard, 2005; White & White, 2004; Hardy & Gretzel, 2011; Viallon, 2012). RVers as a collaborative neo-tribe has been examined in both North America and Australia, both in the pre- and post- Internet era (Counts & Counts, 2004; Guinn, 1980; Mattingly, 2005; Mings & McHugh, 1995; Onyx & Leonard, 2005; Wu & Pearce, 2014). RVers have been noted for their highly collaborative nature such as their daily practices of 'Happy Hour' around the campsite at approximately 5 p.m. and their attendance at rallies and social functions. Their desire to socialise and share experiences, their willingness to help those in need of assistance with their vehicle, and their reliance on sharing information regarding campsites has also been noted (Counts & Counts, 2004; Guinn, 1980; Mings & McHugh, 1995). Prior to the Internet and even at the time of writing, this was done through various channels such as word-of-mouth, different forms of radio including citizens band (CB), club magazines and publications. Word-of-mouth in this community is also paramount; the swapping of information is a social transaction that results in friendships and a spectrum of relational bonds being established but also has a practical role in terms of enhancing RVers safety while on the road (Counts & Counts, 2004; Hardy & Robards, 2015). To date however, it appears that RVing has not been explored as a form of collaborative consumption.

Arguably, the introduction of the Internet has resulted in the highly collaborative nature of RVing becoming far more visible to the outsider. The extent of Internet use by RVers is often misunderstood due to assumptions that Grey Nomads and Snowbirders are older, non-technologically savvy travellers (Hardy & Gretzel, 2011). The reality, however, is that Grey Nomads, Snowbirders and RV club members in particular, are highly connected via web based medium such as GeoWikis, Chat Forums and most recently, sharing platforms such as Park-Sleep, Camplify and My Caravan. Explorations of this market and its reliance on non-monetary transactions provide an opportunity to explore the value of non-monetary transactions that occur within this collaborative economy.

3 Methods

The empirical research that will be presented in this study is the result of four studies derived from ethno-methodological fieldwork that was carried out over the past 9 years (2007–2014) in Canada and Australia on the RV market. Consisting of four major studies (two in Canada in 2006 and 2007 and two in Australia in 2012, 2013 and 2014), the data presented in this research was collated following 50 - in-depth interviews of RVers in Canada in 2007, 22 in 2006, 22 in Australia in 2011 and 50 in 2013. The Canadian data collection methods included 50 interviews of RVers at Dawson Creek in Northern British Columbia. This township marks the start of the famous Alaska Highway, which is a famous landmark for North American RVers. The interviews were semi-structured in nature and were carried out at three RV overnight stops, including two commercial RV parks and one free camping site.

The Australian data set included semi structured interviews that were conducted at three RVing destinations on the East Coast of Tasmania, Australia. Like the Canadian research, differing campgrounds were selected as study sites to reflect the variety of overnight RV sites and styles. Thus, interviews were conducted at one of the Tasmanian Parks and Wildlife Service camping grounds, located within Freycinet National Park, a free camping site maintained by the Tasmanian Parks and Wildlife Service, and a low cost overnight camping area comprising one sports field in a small town.

In addition to interviews, netnographic research (Kozinets, 2010) was conducted to gain further insights into the culture of RVing with pets. Using the principles outlined by Kozinets, two popular RVing forums used by RVers were selected for Canada and Australia: Good Sam's (http://www.goodsamclub.com/forums/) for Canada and the Caravaners Forum (http://caravanersforum.com/) for Australia. In Australia, the Caravan and Motorhome on Tour forum (http://www.candm.com.au/forum/) was used and explored RVers' discussions regarding the iconic outback road, called the Oodnadatta Track, in South Australia.

In all stages of research, the essence of collaborative consumption in the context of RVing was explored. In particular, the elements of sharing and distribution were given focus. While the notion of collaborative economy did not form the original reason for the data collection, the themes that emerged from the transcriptions and subsequent analysis through NVivo clearly demonstrated that RVing is a highly mobile form of tourism that has had a significant and long standing practice of non-monetary collaboration. It was this observation that formed the basis for the current chapter.

4 Findings

In order to explore the value of non-monetary transactions, the data analysis first explores the collaborative spaces and platforms (physical and virtual) where transactions occur and then discusses their value to RVers.

4.1 Performative Spaces for Collaboration

At the campgrounds in North America and Australia where the research was conducted, collaboration was clearly evident at certain times of the day. Most evident was around 5 p.m., when Happy Hour would begin. Happy Hour is a tradition amongst RVers that has been documented by numerous authors (Counts & Counts, 2004; Hardy & Robards, 2015). Around 5 p.m. RVers would assemble outside their RV and have a pre-dinner drink or snack. It is during this time that high levels of socialisation would occur within and between groups of travellers. RV specific language was evident during this time; terms such as *rigs* (the RV), *boondocking* (the name for free camping in North America), *sani dumps* (waste disposal stations) and *hook ups* (where RVs can source electrical power) could be heard. During this time, it was commonplace to hear RVers comparing and evaluating campsites, sharing their stories of different destinations, and recommending attractions to visit which have easy access for their RVs. Rituals of introduction were also evident; some participants in our research explained they used number plates as a point from which to start an introductory conversation.

Outside of Happy Hour, the sharing inherent within RVing was also evident at other locations throughout the campground. As RVers passed each other when walking to the amenities block, when cooking their barbecue on the common barbecues, or when meeting each other while filling their water or disposing of their waste, it was commonplace to witness socialising. These encounters provided the opportunity for collaborative exchanges to occur and acted as opportunities to consolidate relational ties.

> Motorhome User (Canada): I meet a lot of people at RV parks . . . Everywhere we go, I find somebody to talk to. Most of them are the same kind of people I am. We mostly chat—see where they are from, what occupation they have done in the past. We try to find some stuff in common—road, weather or fishing trip.

In addition to face-to-face collaboration, our research established the online environment as an additional site of collaborative performance. There are now countless websites, discussion boards, blogs and books that are dedicated to this activity (Caldicott, Scherrer, & Jenkins, 2014; Counts & Counts, 2004; Hardy et al., 2013a). In Australia this information was evident on the Oodanadatta Track Forum. This virtual space was a location where RVers could gather and share information that would assist in their planning. RVers would post to reflect back on their journey, or ask specific questions to assist in their planning.

In addition to face-to-face and online sharing, collaboration within the RVing community also takes place via radio. In Australia and North America, it was not unusual to find RVs that have CB radios. These radios were installed near the dashboard of the RV and could be operated at any time. CB radio utilises channels and RVers would commonly display the channel that they used on the back of their rig.

4.2 *Why Non-monetary Collaboration Occurs*

When exploring the different performative spaces of collaboration, it became evident that there were different reasons why non-monetary transactions occurred. One set of reasons was related to the function and the practicalities of RVing such as information exchange. The other reasons were related to affective needs, such as a desire to experience a sense of belonging. Thus, the results suggested that the collaborative RVing economy was driven by more than just utilitarian exchange. Moreover, it appeared that different platforms were used to satisfy the differing reasons for collaboration. These will now be explored.

Functional Reasons for Collaboration: Safety The desire of RVers to feel safe and care for their fellow RVers, was determined as an important reason for their collaborative behaviour and was evident at all three performative spaces. Prior to leaving on a new journey RVers relied heavily on the Internet. The Oodanadatta Track Forum (the Oodanadatta Track is an iconic RV route that follows unsealed roads) had many examples of RVers seeking information from fellow travellers in order to assist with their planning. The motivation for these discussions was often expressed as a desire to feel safe and secure in Outback Australia, and a desire to access basic facilities such as food and water.

> Caravanner (Internet Forum): We stayed at Leigh Creek (filled the water tanks there from their excellent dam water) and then overnighted at William Creek and then onto Kulgara (on the Sturt north of Marla). Had one of the best Porterhouse steaks ever at William Creek.

In addition to heat, a great concern to RVers was the possibility of rain, which can result in slippery treacherous, driving conditions. As a consequence, the Oodanadatta Track forum users were regularly seen to be giving advice such as this:

> Tent Trailer User (Australia): Avoid it if wet or chance of rain as sections of it can become very slippery. Recently graded corrugations are not too bad and many sections are quite good gravel road. Just before you travel give a few of the local spots a call to check latest conditions e.g. Maree, William Creek pubs.

During their travels, RVers used CB Radio channels to share information that would enhance safety. In some instances collaboration would extend beyond RVers, to drivers of other types of large vehicles such as trucks:

> Caravanner (Australia): We have a CB radio to communicate with trucks and other travellers as a safety feature.

The function of these radios was to share information about road conditions, weather and other aspects that may affect the RVing experience.

The campground also acted as a performance space where the sharing of important information related to safety, such as weather, road conditions or other aspects affected by seasonality would occur. This performative space allowed RVers to share tips on places they had recently travelled to and those that they considered should be avoided if they recently had become unsafe.

Functional Reasons for Collaboration: Equipment Maintenance and Repair Like safety, collaboration was evident amongst RVers through their sharing of information regarding RV equipment, ongoing maintenance, and on the road-repairs. These functional interactions appeared to be driven by a deeper need to consolidate and build their sense of being a part of the neo-tribe. RVers would discuss how to plan for on the road repairs which may be necessary during travel and what equipment to take on particular journeys. Discussions would regularly centre on the necessary equipment that was required to undertake demanding routes, such as tyres, suspension and even appropriate RV types for differing routes:

> Caravaner (Australia): I am wanting your thoughts. We are thinking of towing our 20 ft Heritage Jayco van with our 100 series 1999 Landcruiser down the Oodnadatta Track next year, and would like to hear from anyone who might have done it and survived, or not survived. Also open to your thoughts. I drive for pleasure no rip doodoo and bust driving, as we enjoy travelling this great country. Awaiting your replies.
>
> And a reply from a fellow Caravaner, Australia: I noted that you had a Jayco Heritage and would suggest that you invert the axles (put the axles under the springs) if you have not already done so to give you better ground clearance, have good quality A/T light truck tyres and have a dust vent in your roof of the van to stop the dust getting in.
>
> And a further reply from a Caravaner (Australia): We recently fitted Kumho AT tyres and have just done the Strzeleki, Birdsville and Oodnadatta tracks—all road conditions plus a bit of sand work without the van on. The tyres are great: good grip, quiet, no chipping on rough stone roads. I got them for $300 each in Sydney, fitted and balanced (17 inch rims). This was $100–200 lower cost than MT, BFG etc.

At the campsite, we noted collaboration related to equipment, maintenance and repair. RVers would share information on the different gear they had purchased. Non-monetary transactions and trading was also evident if something went wrong. It was not uncommon to see one RVer assisting another whose vehicle or equipment was faulty. And bartering, trading and the practice of 'paying it forward' were also evident amongst RVers:

> Motorhome User (Canada): Last night we met three couples, two from Canada and one from Florida. We started talking and another couple stopped by. Eight of us pulled out chairs and sat around fire and it got late before we even realized it. I asked a guy what he was doing while he was fixing the RV and we learned something. You can learn a lot of things from people. Sharing on the road is an everyday thing. I learned some time ago how to unhook the car and a few days ago I passed that knowledge on to some other RVer. Last night we were from four different corners of our continent. We keep in touch. We visited a lady we met earlier. There'll be a lot more Christmas cards this year.

This research established that the CB radio was commonly mentioned as a performative space where collaboration regarding equipment maintenance and repair occurred. Again, this fora enhanced a sense of tribal belonging amongst this highly mobile group of travellers.

Functional Reasons for Collaboration: Sharing Travel Information This research established that the three major performative spaces provided opportunities for collaboration, albeit for different reasons. The online forum played a significant role for RVers to share information on their experiences and assist others with their planning in order to ensure they felt safe. RVers would post questions and these would be answered. It was an asymmetric relationship as some RVers appeared to answer many more questions than they asked themselves. However, once on the road, a more reciprocal exchange was evident, where up to date information on roads, campsites and facilities was shared amongst RVers at Happy Hour and around the campsite.

> Caravanner, Canada: You meet a lot of people from all over the place—pleasant friendly people. We chat about road conditions or traffic. You talk about places that they've been and you haven't. They tell you about road conditions and things like that.

Additionally, while on the road, CB radio allowed real time information to be traded on current road conditions and weather events with fellow RVers or truck drivers.

Functional Reasons for Collaboration: To Save Money and Live and Alternative Lifestyle In recent years, motorhomes and caravans have grown in size and are increasingly self-contained, such that they can store their own water and waste. For large motorhomes, flat ground, wide access and room for turning circles, plus the ability for RVs to avoid having to reverse are common requirements. Access to this information is not always readily available, so the 'bush telegraph' or face-to-face sharing of information was found to be functionally important for these travellers. It also allowed them to share information on free or low cost campsites, that were often not promoted by local visitor information centre.

In addition, this research also revealed that a motivator for collaboration may also be a desire to live an alternative lifestyle. With RVers, this manifested as a desire to escape the norms of society and expectations to retire and leave a routine life. Previously recognised by Counts and Counts (2004) and Hardy and Gretzel (2011), this was evident in the interviews:

> Motorhomer (Canada): I mean we work. So, we typically do that for 20–30 years. We don't move much. . . . I want to experience the people and I want to experience the life outside of my comfort zone if you will and everything I have there.

> Motorhome (Australia): I hate regulation, love freedom.

The desire of these RVers to "buck the system" has synergies with the collaborative economy literature that details participants' desire to live alternative lifestyles and experience alternative, less consumerist experiences (McArthur, 2015). The sharing that they engaged in, either online, in person or via CB radio, allowed them to realise their desire.

The research was conducted prior to the introduction in 2014 and 2015 of sharing communities for RVers, such as Camplify.com and MyCaravan.com. However it did identify a small cohort of travellers in campsites who collaborated to co-purchase a RV in order to be able to afford to purchase an RV and make it more economically feasible and to avoid the idling of assets.

> Caravaner (Australia): We own this [van] in partnership with some friends.

The rationale for these families engagement into an informal collaborative economy was clearly to save money. This has synergies with motivations for engaging in the collaborative economy, as articulated by Bardhi and Eckhardt (2012), Möhlmann (2015) and Tussyadiah (2015).

Affective Reasons for Collaboration: To Experience a Sense of Freedom and Self Actualisation Non-monetary collaboration was found to not only assist in achieving functional outcomes, but it also assisted RVers in achieving affective outcomes. Through all forms of our research, a reoccurring theme was RVers' motivation to experience a sense of freedom through RVing. Sharing and collaboration was seen by them as necessary as it helped RVers to be as independent as possible and escape what many regarded as the shackles of everyday life and routine, and to realise their goals to travel and leave their daily lives behind.

> Caravanner (Australia): Free and easy is me.

> Motorhome (Canada): Freedom, it is my turf. I want to go where I want and when I want.

For RVers, socialisation and the sharing that came with this interaction provided them with the opportunity to meet likeminded people from different walks of life and affirmed their sense of belonging.

Affective Outcomes from Non-Monetary Collaboration: A Sense of Belonging and Being Amongst like Minded People This research concurred with that of others, that RVers derive a great sense of belonging to a large group of like-minded people when on the road (Hardy & Robards, 2015). A reoccurring theme was that RVing was perceived as an activity that resulted in travellers feeling a sense of freedom.

> Caravan owner (Canada): When I travel in my RV I feel free-spirited, alive and excited.

RVers were aware that they shared sentiment and derived a sense of from being with like-minded people. They were both aware and proud of their tribe and its inclusive membership.

> Motorhome (Canada): I think the biggest thing I like is, when you pull into a Walmart, or any campground and you stay, you meet people and you all have the same likes. So, everybody is friends. Automatically you have friends.

The sense of belonging that was so strong amongst many RVers concurs with arguments that the desire to feel a sense of belonging is a central motivator for those who engaging in the collaborative economy (Albinsson & Perera, 2012; Botsman & Rogers, 2010; Galbreth et al., 2012; McArthur, 2015; Närvänen et al., 2013; Tussyadiah, 2015). This aspect is entirely non-monetary and demonstrates the importance of affective outcomes for participants within the broader collaborative economy.

5 Discussion

This chapter has argued that those who engage in the collaborative economy do so in forms that stretch beyond monetary exchanges. Recently, literature on the collaborative economy has focused on the economic and technological aspects of this rapidly growing phenomena (Botsman & Rogers, 2014; Hamari et al., 2015). However, using the example of Recreational Vehicle Users (RVers) this chapter posits that non-monetary collaboration is highly significant and may be categorised as having both functional and affective dimensions. Functionally, RVs are now commonly equipped with toilets, showers and grey and black water storage. Consequently, they demonstrate a high propensity to free camp and as such, often spend relatively little on accommodation. For these travellers, non-monetary collaboration is of significant value because it allows them to share travel tips, source desirable and cost efficient campsites, enhance their sense of safety, and share ideas on equipment, maintenance and repairs, which are necessary when travelling in remote and regional environments. These non-monetary collaborative exchanges present an opportunity to undertake alternative transactions to those that exist in capitalist systems, none of which can be quantitatively measured.

In addition to non-monetary transactions having an important functional value, this research revealed that non-monetary transactions have affective dimensions such as giving participants a sense of belonging, fellowship within a group, and ultimately an opportunity to realise the freedom they seek to experience through RVing. RVers have been documented as neo-tribes (Hardy & Robards, 2015) and this has synergies with Botsman and Rogers' (2010) claim that trust is a key determinant for active participation in the collaborative economy: RVers in this study were found to place great value upon the sense of trust, meaning making, reciprocity and belonging that they gained from being in a large mobile community.

The exploration of the value of non-monetary transactions within the collaborative economy revealed that collaboration occurs in a number of different fora, including RV campgrounds, online sites and also on CB Radio. Interestingly, these transactions take place in the public sphere, away from visitor information centres, or government funded websites. Particularly when planning their trips, this chapter demonstrated that RVers are heavy users of the Internet. In the case of remote and potentially dangerous routes, such as the Oodnadatta Track in Australia, forums and websites devoted to sharing information play a vitally important function, particularly in the planning phases of RVers' travel. This concurred with literature that the Internet plays a highly important role within the collaborative economy (Belk, 2014; Carroll & Romano, 2011; Hamari et al., 2015).

However, the Internet was not the only significant forum for non-monetary collaborative transactions. Face-to-face communication was found to play an equally important role in the collaborative economy of RVers. The use of word-of-mouth communication was evident in campsites, meetings places such as petrol stations and roadside stops. Communication during this time provided RVers with information on campsites, road conditions and destinations, as well as reassured them that they belonged to a neo-tribe of like-minded people.

While driving on the highway, a third mode of non-monetary collaborative transactions were found to be of great importance to RVers. Despite the rise of the Internet, CB radio remains a common method of communication where information on road conditions and campsites is often shared. The reasons for this continued use of this communication method is likely to be related to a lack of Internet access in remote areas and RVers desire to feel safe and reduce their risks where possible.

The findings pertaining to collaboration suggest that the heavy emphasis given to the Internet as the conduit for the collaborative economy to occur (Belk, 2014; Carroll & Romano, 2011; Hamari et al., 2015) may not always be relevant for all styles of travellers. Significantly, the use of CB radio and face-to-face communication at campsites and meeting places challenges Grassmuck's (2012) proposition that the Web 2.0 era has facilitated a 'sharing turn', as it demonstrates that sharing has existed amongst travellers for many years prior to and following the Web 2.0 era.

Moreover, the research adds depth to the work of Dredge and Gyimóthy (2015) by demonstrating that non-monetary collaborative transactions can build a sense of belonging, fellowship and shared sentiment. These are some of the potentially positive aspects of the collaborative economy that previously have been overlooked.

While writing this chapter, several new sharing websites have opened for RVers, using similar models to platforms such as Airbnb. RVers who are not using their rig are encouraged to rent them out. Other sites advertise areas suitable for RVers to camp at with minimal cost and have been developed for owners to utilise their unused assets. The implications of this are that RVers can now converge and collaborate on multiple online platforms, which may affect their social and tribal dynamics in the future. Further research is now needed to decipher whether these sites have reinforced, enhanced or changed the nature of non-monetary collaborations.

To conclude, this chapter has broadened the discussion of collaborative economy by exploring of the character of non-monetary and non-digital collaborative transactions. It argues that non-monetary transactions play important roles within the collaborative economy and may even lie at the very heart of this phenomenon. Moreover, neo-tribal formations may adopt these collaborative platforms, thus reinforcing the already strong bonds that exist their community.

References

Albinsson, P. A., & Perera, B. Y. (2012). Alternative marketplaces in the 21st century: Building community through sharing events. *Journal of Consumer Behaviour, 11*(4), 303–315.

Bardhi, F., & Eckhardt, G. (2012). Access based consumption: The case of car sharing. *Journal of Consumer Research, 39*, 881–898.

BDO. (2014). *Caravan and campervan data report: August 2014*. Unpublished report produced for the Caravan, Industry Association of Australia. Stafford Heights, Queensland: Caravan Industry Association of Australia.

Belk, E. (2007). Sharing. *Journal of Consumer Research, 30*(5), 715–734.

Belk, E. (2014). You are what you can access: Sharing and collaborative consumption line. *Journal of Business Research, 67*, 1595–1600.

Bennett, A. (2011). The post-subcultural turn: Some reflections 10 years on. *Journal of Youth Studies, 14*(5), 493–506.

Botsman, R., & Rogers, R. (2010). *What's mine is yours: How collaborative consumption is changing the way we live*. New York: Collins.

Botsman, R., & Rogers, R. (2014). You are what you can access: Sharing and collaborative consumption online. *Journal of Business Research, 67*, 1595–1600.

Caldicott, R., Scherrer, P., & Jenkins, J. (2014). Freedom camping in Australia: current status, key stakeholders and political debate. *Annals of Leisure Research, 17*(4), 417–442.

Carroll, E., & Romano, J. (2011). *Your digital afterlife: When Facebook, Flickr and Twitter are your estate, what's your legacy?* Berkeley, CA: New Riders.

Counts, D. A., & Counts, D. R. (2004). *Over the next hill: An ethnography of RVing seniors in North America* (2nd ed.). Peterborough: Broadview Press.

Cova, B., & Cova, V. (2002). Tribal marketing: The tribalisation of society and its impact on the conduct of marketing. *European Journal of Marketing, 36*(5/6), 595–620.

Dredge, D., & Gyimóthy, S. (2015). Tourism and the collaborative economy: Critical perspectives, questionable claims and silent voices. *Tourism Recreation Research, 40*(3), 286–302.

Felson, M., & Spaeth, J. (1978). Community structure and collaborative consumption: A routine activity approach. *The American behavioural Scientist, 21*(4), 614–624.

Fjelstyl, J., & Fyall, A. (2015). Sustainable drive tourism: A catalyst for change. *International Journal of Tourism Research, 19*(5), 460–470. doi:10.1002/jtr.2013.

Galbreth, M. R., Ghosh, B., & Shor, M. (2012). Social sharing of information goods: Implications for pricing and profits. *Marketing Science, 31*(4), 603–620.

Grassmuck, V. (2012). The sharing turn: Why we are generally nice and have a good chance to cooperate our way out of the mess we have gotten ourselves into. In W. Sützl, F. Stalder, R. Maier, & T. Hug (Eds.), *Cultures and ethics of sharing*. Inssbruck: Innsbruck University Press.

Gretzel, U., Formica, S., & Fesenmaier, D. R. (2005). Tribal marketing for destination websites: A case study of RV enthusiasts. In *Proceedings of the 36th Annual Travel and Tourism Research Association Conference*. Boise, Idaho: Tourism and Travel Research Association.

Guinn, R. (1980). Elderly recreational vehicle tourists: Motivations for Leisure. *Journal of Travel Research, 19*(9), 9–13.

Hamari, J., Sjoklint, M., & Ukkonen, A. (2015, July). The sharing economy: Why people participate in collaborative consumption. *Journal of the Association for Information Science and Technology*. doi:10.1002/asi.23552.

Hardy, A., & Gretzel, U. (2011). Why we travel this way: An exploration into the motivations of recreational vehicle users. In D. Carson & B. Prideaux (Eds.), *Drive tourism: Trends and emerging markets* (pp. 194–223). London: Routledge.

Hardy, A., & Robards, B. (2015). The ties that bind: Exploring neo-tribal theory's relevance to tourism. *Tourism Analysis, 20*(4), 443–454.

Hardy, A., Hanson, D., & Gretzel, U. (2013a). Travelling neo-tribes: Conceptualising recreational vehicle users. *Journal of Tourism and Cultural Change, 11*(1–2), 48–60.

Hardy, A., Wickham, M., & Gretzel, U. (2013b). Neglected stakeholder groups: The pitfalls of tourism policy development. *Journal of Corporate Ownership and Control, 11*(1), 348–359.

Holloway, D. (2007). See Australia and die: Shifting discourses about gray nomads. *Tourism, Culture and Communication, 7*, 161–168.

Hughson, J. (2007). A tale of two tribes: Expressive fandom in Australian Soccer's A-league. *Culture, Sport, Society, 2*(3), 10–30.
Kozinets, R. V. (2010). *Netnography: Doing ethnographic research online*. London: Sage.
Maffesoli, M. (1996). *The time of the tribes*. London: Sage.
Mattingly, G. A. (2005). *Individualistic roamers or community builders? Differences and boundaries among RVers*. Unpublished Master's Thesis. Mississippi State University.
McArthur, E. (2015). Many-to-many exchange without money: Why people share their resources. *Consumption, Markets & Culture, 18*(3), 239–256.
Mings, R., & McHugh, K. (1995). Wintering in American sunbelt: Linking place and behaviour. *The Journal of Tourism Studies, 6*(2), 56–61.
Möhlmann, M. (2015). Collaborative consumption: Determinants of satisfaction and the likelihood of using a sharing economy option again. *Journal of Consumer Behaviour, 14*(3), 193–207. doi:10.1002/cb.1512.
Muniz, A., & O'Guinn, T. (2001). Brand community. *Journal of Consumer Research, 27*(4), 412–432.
Närvänen, E., Kartastenpää, E., & Kuusela, H. (2013). Online lifestyle consumption community dynamics: A practice-based analysis. *Journal of Consumer Behaviour, 12*(5), 358–369.
Onyx, J., & Leonard, R. (2005). Australian grey nomads and American snowbirds: Similarities and differences. *Journal of Tourism Studies, 16*(1), 61–68.
Owyang, J. (2013). *The collaborative economy: Products, services and market relationships have changed as sharing startups impact business models. A Market Definition Report*. Altimeter. Retrieved August 31, 2016, from http://www.slideshare.net/Altimeter/the-collaborative-economy
Recreational Vehicle Industry Association (RVIA). (2014). *RVIA news release: New RVIA research shows record level of RV ownership*. Retrieved August 31, 2015, from http://www.rvia.org/?esid=trends
Stokes, K., Clarence, E., & Rinne, A. (2014). *Making sense of the UK collaborative economy*. Retrieved August 31, 2016, from http://www.nesta.org.uk/publications/making-sense-uk-col laborative-economy
ten Have, P. (1974). The counter culture on the move: A field study of youth tourists in Amsterdam. *Mensch en Maatschappi, 49*, 297–315 http://rjh.ub.rug.nl/MenM/article/viewFile/13341/10840.
Tussyadiah, I. (2015). An exploratory study on drivers and deterrents of collaborative consumption in travel. In I. Tussyadiah & A. Inversini (Eds.), *Information and communication technologies in tourism, Proceedings of the international conference in lugano, Switzerland* (pp. 817–830). Legano: Springer. doi:10.1007/978-3-319-14343-9_59.
Viallon, P. (2012). Retiree snowbirds. *Annals of Tourism Research, 39*(4), 2073–2091.
White, N. R., & White, P. B. (2004). Travel as transition: Identity and place. *Annals of Tourism Research, 31*, 200–218.
Wu, M., & Pearce, P. (2014). Chinese recreational vehicle users in Australia: A netnographic study of tourist motivation. *Tourism Management, 14*(10), 22–35.

Collaborative Economy in Tourism in Latin America: The Case of Argentina, Colombia, Chile and Mexico

Helene Balslev Clausen and Mario Alberto Velázquez García

Abstract This chapter addresses collaborative economy in four Latin American countries: Argentina, Colombia, Chile and Mexico. It challenges one of the taken for granted assumptions about the collaborative economy that it creates a more equal society with a fairer, more inclusive economic model (Botsman and Rogers, Harvard Business Review, 2010). The chapter argues that the collaborative economy is underpinned by fundamentally different rationales and structures in Latin America compared to Western societies. The chapter's Latin American perspective suggests limitations in existing conceptualizations of the collaborative economy. In Latin American societies, digital collaborative economy is adopted into a sociocultural, political and economic context and has become an extension of well-established and social embedded historical practices of collaborative production and consumption. It has often replicated old patterns of privileged access for some and denial for others. Even though the digital collaborative economy has increased significantly, and Latin America is characterized by a solid information technology, it becomes clear that the informal sector keeps playing a pivotal role in the understanding of practices related to collaborative economy.

Keywords Collaborative economy • Latin America • Sharing economy • Exchange • Informal economy

1 Introduction

The collaborative economy has been characterised as a worldwide phenomenon with distinct features aligned with equality and accessibility. It is also claimed to be a more inclusive economic model assumed to be valid across all cultural and

H.B. Clausen (✉)
Department of Culture and Global Studies, Aalborg University, A.C. Meyers Vænge 15, Copenhagen 2450, DK, Denmark
e-mail: balslev@cgs.aau.dk

M.A. Velázquez García
Colegio de Estado de Hidalgo, Pachuca, Mexico
e-mail: mar_002@hotmail.com

D. Dredge, S. Gyimóthy (eds.), *Collaborative Economy and Tourism*,
Tourism on the Verge, DOI 10.1007/978-3-319-51799-5_16

geographic contexts. This chapter argues that, in Latin American societies, practices of exchange in the collaborative economy are underpinned by fundamentally different rationales and structures than in Western societies. For centuries in Latin America a range of economic, sociopolitical and cultural practices have been intimately linked to what Western societies are now calling the collaborative economy. Acknowledging the importance of Web 2.0, this chapter will discuss how digital technologies have brought about new collaborative consumption patterns and we address the question of whether the technology-induced collaborative economy has created new economic and sociocultural settings or if it reproduces already existing ones.

In this chapter, we conceptualise the collaborative economy in relation to an old economic model of collaboration that has historically existed in Latin America. This framing provides us with an understanding beyond the current collaborative economy in Western post-industrial societies. To define collaborative economy in Latin American societies, we first need to recognise that relations established in the exchange of goods and services are tied in some way to historical, spatial and sociocultural conditions linked to the informal economy, social inequality and exclusion. We assert that the digitalised collaborative economy is reproducing collaborative practices that are intimately linked to marginalisation and social exclusion, which remain societal challenges despite the region's economic growth (World Bank, 2016a, b). For reasons of scope, this chapter focuses on four countries representing the largest economies and most important tourism destinations in the Spanish speaking part of Latin America: Argentina, Chile, Colombia and Mexico. We emphasise how shared societal features and challenges (e.g. inequality, exclusion and informal economy) play out in digitalised collaborative consumption in ways that are substantially different from the Western world.

2 Collaborative Economy

Our interpretation of collaborative economy is inspired by Felson and Spaeth (1978) who define acts of collaborative consumption as "those events in which one or more persons consume economic goods or services in the process of engaging in joint activities with one or more others" (1978, p. 614). Additionally, Belk's definition draws attention to the motivation of compensation: "people coordinating the acquisition and distribution of a resource for a fee or other compensation" (2014, p. 1597). Sharing is also characterised by the collective strength of often very weak ties according to Granovetter (1973), wherein individual collaborative action accumulates in collective results. The distinction between offline and online collaborative exchange also warrants discussion, since inequity and exclusion can be present in both digital and non-digital spheres. In studies of the collaborative economy, Cammaerts (2008, 2011) found that digital technologies cannot be treated as separate to the economic, political and cultural realities of the traditional, offline world but are very much entangled. Instead, digital technologies offer new opportunities for economic participation by providing an extended network and new avenues for exchange. However, digital technologies also go hand-in-hand with exclusion and control, reinforcing power relations and hegemonies.

Collaborative consumption can be understood as a form of economic exchange whereby the use of idle goods and services not only benefits the owner or service provider, but also a wider community. The very existence of the exchange network extends a set of relational ties that makes a collective, and this collective or community has future potentials beyond the simple exchange between giver and receiver. For instance, Botsman and Rogers (2010) identify idle capacity as a key characteristic of the collaborative economy, e.g. a car owner using digital platforms such as "BlaBlaCar" or "Tripda" to connect with and offer seats in a car to persons who want a ride to the same destination. This type of exchange is reinventing not only what is consumed but also how we consume it. It also redefines the practices that are taking place in diverse areas ranging from the financial world to technological and educational worlds. One stated benefit of these practices is to create a fairer, more inclusive and equitable economic model (Botsman and Rogers, 2010).

In industrial and post-industrial societies, technology has contributed to the commodification of culture. For example, the Internet and rapid expansion of digital technologies have fed collaborative consumption. Increasing access to the Internet on mobile devices has scaled up sharing quite radically; it takes place in a context of (very) weak ties, often across international boundaries, and on a global scale. It is not only the scope of sharing that has increased exponentially as a result of digital technologies, but also the breadth of what is available to be shared or traded online.

Increased access to and interconnectedness between different actors enable new exchange opportunities, although emphasise that these technologies are appropriated in different ways. Arguably, the term "network" denotes a new social morphology of informational capitalism in which communication technologies such as the Internet facilitate the decentralisation of transactions. Castells emphasises that digital technologies do not necessarily bring old practices of power to an end but allow for new forms of control to emerge. They also have the potential to generate more democratic and egalitarian practices. This is in line with a World Bank report (2016a, b) that argues that access to information and communication infrastructure is by no means the miracle solution to social inclusion and social cohesion. Digital technologies require knowledge, skills and a commitment from government in terms of education and communication programs.

The concept of "the digital divide", which is a term originally coined to describe the disparities in Internet access in the United States, might be useful to understand the existing inequalities between those with access to digital technologies and those without access. The ability of an actor, be it a company, individual, government or other organization, to form part of, and participate in, the network is determined by the degree to which they can contribute to the goals of the network. Individuals who cannot access and/or use new technologies are those with nothing to offer the network and are therefore excluded (Cammaerts, 2008). For instance, even though the above-mentioned World Bank report (2016a, b) states that Latin America has solid investment in information technology infrastructure, production and knowledge, it flags concerns that governments are not seeking to close the digital gap. For instance, Mexico has 68 million people without access to the Internet, 61.8% of the total population of 110 million (World Bank, 2016a, b).

Digital technologies connect individuals, groups or collaborative economy businesses and create different mechanisms, such as reputational measures, feedback forums and ratings, to increase trust and address informational asymmetries in the exchange process. However, social media trades on cultural homogeneity and established social networks both online and in real life (Munar, Gyimóthy, & Cai, 2013). Whenever new connections are built, it often replicates old patterns of privileged access for some and denial for others. Cultural encounters are likely to occur between like-minded and privileged members of the creative middle class, rather than within low-income communities or across a broader spectrum of consumers (Stokes, Clarence, Anderson, & Rinne, 2014). Further, the benefits of the collaborative economy do not necessarily trickle down to the needy, and there are some who partake in sharing out of necessity (Kassan & Orsi, 2012) as seen during the recent financial crisis in Spain, Portugal and Greece.

3 The Informal Sector in Latin America

This chapter challenges one of the taken for granted assumptions about the collaborative economy that it creates a more equal society with a fairer, more inclusive economic model (Botsman & Rogers, 2010). As already stated, scholars have demonstrated that new digital technologies do not necessarily generate greater equality. In Latin American societies with a significant informal sector, we argue that the inclusion of the informal sector is pivotal in assessing the impacts of the collaborative economy. Often however, the informal economy is disregarded because data on the informal economy are often unreliable by virtue of the fact that it is hidden and operates in a grey zone outside official record keeping. However, as a tentative picture of its relevance, this sector makes up 52% of employment in Latin America. As such, the informal economy constitutes a structural condition of Latin American societies, and it has consequences for accessing goods and services in the regulated economic market.

There are also contradictions in the different forces at work that make it difficult to understand the collaborative economy as a formal-informal phenomenon. Under a modernisation agenda (an agenda historically pursued by global organisations such as the World Bank), the informal sector is depicted in decline everywhere, being replaced by structured, systematic approaches to production and consumption. Digital innovation, as represented by the collaborative economy, is encouraged for its innovation and is perceived as a way of expanding markets and growing the economy. Conversely, under globalization, the economy is depicted as universally growing as a deregulated, frictionless global economy (e.g. Portes & Haller, 2005). Globalisation, as it takes form in collaborative economy peer-to-peer transactions, appears to promote and even accelerate informal transactions occurring outside the formal economy. A significant part of the activities embedded in the concept of the collaborative economy is hitherto part of the informal sector (Hart, 1973).

In a context-bound understanding of collaborative economy, we must acknowledge particular economic, environmental, social and institutional factors influencing exchange in a given society. This suggests that the informal economy is the product and driver of advanced capitalism and the site of the most entrepreneurial aspects of the urban economy in the Global South. For instance, exchanges outside the formal economy can be understood as a response to the regulated, normative market as well as a set of behavioural practices in communities that resist, are opposed to, or excluded from participating in regulated formal markets for a variety of reasons (Portes & Haller, 2005). Ghezzi and Mingione (2003, 2007) argue that the informal sector is not a marginal element of the service economy in Southern economies. On the contrary, new patterns of employment that encourage flexible jobs lead to increasing job opportunities within the informal sector (World Bank, 2016a, b). This change in employment patterns does not occur in isolation but is also part of broader changes taking place that reflect the legal and cultural revalorisation of the informal economy. Flexibility and some of the informal sector's practices, such as certain types of micro-entrepreneurship and individual or group initiatives, are gaining acceptance in this new economic sphere even though they were considered illegal before. These micro-entrepreneurships are set up, for instance, at the *tianguis* or flea markets, and these collaborative practices are mediated by digital technologies that legitimise and reinforce existing social practices.

4 Inequality and Exclusion

For some sectors of the Latin American population, the collaborative economy is a collective strategy to generate jobs and purchase goods, where the latter is particularly related to new technologies. The scope of the collaborative economy is intimately linked to societal conditions such as inequality and to political, economical, cultural and social exclusion, which in turn create the drivers for seeking alternatives outside the regulated market to solve basic needs. In the Global North, the collaborative economy has been mooted as a strategy to address market failures such as overconsumption and overuse of resources, to unlock the economic potential of idle resources, to supplement incomes, and to reduce transaction costs for example, which are all arguments related to formal economic exchange.

However, in Latin American countries the collaborative economy is more appropriately understood as a societal structure and set of practices related to the unregulated or informal economy (Schneider, Buehn, & Montenegro, 2010). In this perspective, the collaborative economy becomes yet another visible manifestation of societal and structural challenges. Due to the lack of opportunities to integrate into the established social and economic systems, or a lack of belief in the institutionalised formal economy, certain social groups adapt to and participate in the collaborative economy. In Latin America in 2012, the total population was 575 million of which 167 million (29%) lived in poverty and 66 million (11.5%) in extreme poverty. In 2013, 68% of the population in the region was identified as 'lower class', with the 'middle class' 30% and 2% classified as 'upper class' (Latinobarómetro, 2013). As Table 1 shows the presence of poverty in the overall population of Argentina, Chile, Columbia and Mexico, illustrating that despite the region's progress in fighting poverty and inequality over the last two decades it still remains a central and urgent problem (World Bank, 2016a, b).

Building upon the above picture of the region, Table 2 illustrates that Latin America is one of the most unequal regions in the world. In 2014 the richest 10% of the people in Latin America has amassed 71% of the region's wealth (World Economic Forum, 2015). In 2009 taxes and transfers reduced the income inequality in 19 Gini points in Europe, whereas in Latin America it was 2 Gini points (OXFAM, 2014a, b).

Despite strong economic performance in Latin America over the last decade, its vibrant economic growth and significant reduction in poverty and inequality, approximately 20 million young people between the ages of 15 and 24 are neither studying nor working. The integration of this group, known as "ninis" (from the Spanish phrase "ni estudia ni trabaja"), is a persistent challenge for governments. One of the main groups of protagonists for the collaborative economy is the youth, which is estimated to be 140 million young people. 39% of this group (more than 54 million individuals) live in poverty and 10% in extreme poverty. Only 35% of working youth have health insurance, 32% are enrolled in a pension system, and of those working only 10% have a regular job. As a group, youth are characterised by increasing education levels and they also have access to social media platforms for exploring alternative ways to gain access i.e. to work or social networks.

In developing societies, digital technologies divide those who have access to a wider range of social and economic opportunities and those who do not. This digital gap tends to open along generational and educational lines: the younger generations generally enjoy greater use of digital technologies, and the higher the educational level, the greater the use of digital technologies (World Bank, 2016a, b). Globally, there is a trend towards an increase in the actual value added by the information technologies in the services sector (World Bank, 2016a, b). However, despite increased access to technologies in developing countries, this has not necessarily led to an increase in uptake of digitalised platforms (World Bank, 2016a, b) such as Uber, Airbnb or Touristlink. As noted above, one of the key points of difference between Western and Latin American societies is the way capitalism operates: in developing countries inequality, exclusion, and the informal sector are contributing to structural problems and alternative economic practices that do

Table 1 Poverty ratio (in %) in the population of Argentina, Chile, Colombia and México

	1990	2000	2010	2013
Argentina	S/D+	S/D	7.6	S/D
Chile	38.59	20.22	14.1	14.4
Colombia	S/D	S/D	44.9	28.5
México	S/D	41.1	49.6	53.2

Source: Cepal (2013)
+S/D, No information available

Table 2 Gini[a] index in Argentina, Chile, Colombia and México

	2000	2005	2010	2013
Argentina	51.1	49.3	44.5	42.3
Chile	55.3	S/D	S/D	50.5
Colombia	58.7	55	55.5	53.5
México	51.7	51.1	48.1	S/D

Source: World Bank http://data.worldbank.org/indicator/SI.POV.GINI/countries/1W-CN BR?display=default
[a]A Gini index of 0 represents perfect equality, while an index of 100 implies perfect inequality

not exist to the same extent in Western economies. This leads to a set of rather different rationales of participation in the digital collaborative economy in developing countries to those operating in Western societies. As discussed below, rather than being a response to a financial crisis and a driver to supplement formal incomes as seen in Greece, Spain and Portugal, the collaborative economy in Latin America reinforces and synthesises the existing power asymmetries, unequal distribution of resources and knowledge gaps.

5 The Historical Context of Collaborative Economy: *Tianguis* and Flea Markets

Understanding Latin America's setting for collaborative consumption activities requires an understanding of the flea markets or *tianguis*. In the *tianguis*, exchanges of goods and services take place in an unregulated, informal market system and provide the local population (lower and middle classes) access to a variety of products and services otherwise outside their reach. In recent studies by Olavarrieta, Manzur, Hidalgo, and Farías (2008), the flea markets in Chile expanded considerably in the 1980s due to the country's severe economic crisis. By 2003 the country had 6000 outlets and attracted over two million visitors a year. In the 1990s Argentina suffered yet another economic crisis, which led to a considerable increase in not only second hand markets but also illegal/copy-merchandise markets. Currently in Buenos Aires more than 100 markets of this type exist. La Salada, a market in the city of Buenos Aires emerged in 1991. It was originally organised by Bolivian immigrants with only a few stalls, but now it has approximately 40,000 small stalls selling different products (El País, 2015a, b).

Another significant redistributive market given its size, history and cultural significance is Tepito in Mexico City. It comprises of an enormous area and is intimately linked to trade in the pre-Hispanic times. At the end of the Mexican Revolution (1910–1920), the area became known for its production of shoes, which in the 1970s transformed into a marketplace for the distribution and exchange of illegally imported goods and services (in Spanish, *fayuca*). The emergence of this type of market provided the local population (middle class and lower middle class) access to products and services that would otherwise be unavailable. In 2001, approximately 12,500 sellers worked in this market and were linked to 64 different trading organisations (Najar, 2001). Several federal and local Mexican governments have tried to regulate and even close this market, however the population has created a whole range of different social practices, internal organisations and strategies of negotiation with external actors (i.e. local and federal authorities), which have paved the way for the market to gain relative independence. Consequently, the failure of several attempts by local and federal authorities to take control of the market cannot be understood simply in terms of the capacity of the market to organise itself and advocate its interests. Rather it is about tolerance from and complicity with authorities (Olavarrieta et al., 2008; Najar, 2001; El País, 2015a, b; La Nación, 2014).

These populations have created an array of social and cultural practices, internal organisations and strategies of negotiation to control and manage the *tianguis* or flea markets. Consequently, these negotiated spaces are seen as the failure of authorities to take control and they also represent opportunities to gain access to new technologies and forms of consumption (e.g. cell phones, computers, software, films, music) which otherwise would have been impossible to access for the marginalised segments of the population due to the existing structural barriers discussed above (Velázquez & Clausen, 2017, forthcoming). For instance, in 2005 the International Intellectual Property Alliance (IIPA) ranked Mexico as the fourth in the world for selling pirated products and goods, surpassed only by Russia, China and Italy (Posada, 2007). These older forms of collaborative economy are historically embedded sociocultural practices in the exchange of goods and services. They are also connected to the digital collaborative economy in unique ways.

6 The Informal Economy in the Digital Era

The informal and non-institutionalized spaces of collaborative economy have not only open new avenues to access goods and services for marginalised and excluded segments of the population, but have also generated unique consumption patterns. Contrary to Western consumer societies wherein digital technology devices (e.g. smartphones, tablets and computers) have a short lifespan, in all four Latin American societies described in this case the flea markets or *tianguis* have developed specialised businesses in which they repair hardware or install copies of software. Computers or cell phones which are discarded in the US or European markets are repaired or re-used as parts to repair other devices. This brings about a kind of sustainable re-use and environmentally beneficial practice and it also represents a novel business sector generating new job opportunities albeit in the informal economy.

These flea markets provide the opportunity to stage collaborative consumption in spatially-fixed, but highly socialised platforms and they are integrated into some of the must-see sites and principal tourist attractions of Buenos Aires, Mexico City, Santiago de Chile and Bogota. Contrary to the Western ideas of collaborative economy these social platforms are face-to-face exchanges of goods and services, which also represent the integration of economic, political and social reality with digital technologies (as opposed to being mediated by digital technologies). These sites play a significant economic role in the informal sector. The Argentine Chamber of Commerce calculated a 55.9% increase in the sale of such products from 2013 to 2014 in Buenos Aires (La Nación, 2014). In March 2015 the Argentina Chamber of Commerce counted a total of 2659 illegal stalls, which represent an increase of 21.4% compared to 2014 (CAC, 2015). Turning to Colombia the sale of illegal products generated in 2013 a surplus of 720 million US, which corresponds to approximately 1.3 trillion Colombian pesos. The lost revenue of illegal products in Mexico is considered to be 200,000 million Mexican pesos. The most affected market sectors are the production of music and software (El País Colombia, 2014). Even though these markets have turned into strategically significant spaces of commerce, these markets also reproduce existing societal structures of exclusion and inequality.

7 Digital Gap in Latin America

As has already been stated, in Latin America there is a deep divide between people with and without access to digital technologies, and this divide is exacerbated by generational differences (World Bank, 2016a, b). In Latin America, only a small proportion of the population has access to or knowledge about new digital technologies. Not one of the countries in the region is listed among the top 30 countries that have managed to reduce the digital divide (World Economic Forum, 2015). The gap persists in spite of economic growth in the region. For instance, Chile leads the region with 61% of its population enjoying access to Internet whereas in Columbia it is 49% and in Argentina it is 56% (Latin American Science, 2016). To participate in and benefit from the digital collaborative economy, access is required to new technologies, particularly in relation to financial systems (e.g. banking and credit card systems). Even though the Latin American market has been one of the fastest-growing regions for card payment volume in recent years, cash payment still remains the most prevalent form of payment accounting for more than half of the region's total consumer payment transactions (Euromonitor, 2015).

Several studies argue that technological progress will increasingly enable the poor to afford and use digital financial services. However, the population's ability to reap the dividends from these investments will be largely determined by the state's capability to provide supporting policies such as educational and technical programs about how to use the Internet. Moreover in Latin America the new technologies automate many tasks but for workers not possessing the skills that technology augments, the outcome will be greater inequality rather than greater efficiency. Poor regulation, little competition and a historically volatile currency has prompted consumers to move to the informal or unregulated economy, making access to established financial systems (e.g. credit cards and loans) difficult. Consequently, access to and use of digital collaborative economy platforms such as Uber and Airbnb are inaccessible to a large proportion of the population both as producers and consumers. It is noteworthy that, for example, in Mexico a sharing service such as Uber is only available in the major cities of Mexico City, Monterrey, Ensenada and Guadalajara. In other words, as revolutionary as these new technologies may be, participation is bound by both the local sociocultural context, political realities and histories of marginalisation and exclusion that characterise these societies.

8 The Collaborative Economy in Tourism in Latin America

Despite the impediments outlined above, Latin America has witnessed the establishment of digital collaborative economy companies such as Uber and AirBnB. Airbnb, for example, has access to 7000 properties in Argentina and 8000 in Mexico (Herrera, 2014). A large number of Latin American platforms have also started up (see Table 3).

In a Latin American context, Uber is a very successful company with an increasing customer base since 2013. The constant growth of this company is explained by the lack or inadequacy of transportation services provided by traditional taxi companies in this region, and issues relating to service quality and safety and security issues including taxis in poor condition, too expensive, the waiting time to get hold of taxis, rude or unlicensed taxi drivers etc. In Colombia, Uber reported that hundreds of thousands of people have benefitted from their service and have further generated jobs for five thousand people according to the acknowledged newspaper El País (2015a, b). The Colombian government hesitated to intervene but has recently announced certain measures to regulate this service which might even be to close it down due to the providers' unwillingness to pay taxes (El País, 2015b). In Mexico, Uber also has exhibited strong growth in the major cities as Mexico City, Monterrey, Guadalajara and Tijuana. The service has enjoyed broad acceptance, however consumers are from the upper and middle classes with access to digital sharing platforms and credit cards (El Universal, 2015a, b).

Table 3 Collaborative economy businesses in Argentina, Chile, Colombia and Mexico

Service areas	Foreign entrepreneurs	International businesses
Accommodation		Airbnb Zukbox Segundohogar Homeaway
Mobility	Autocompartido (Ecuador, Perú y Colombia) CompartoCoche (Argentina) Coviajero (Argentina) ADedo (Chile) Aventones SincroPool (Argentina) DameUnAventon (México) Rutear Ecobicy (Argentina and Mexico) Bikla (México) EnCicla (Colombia) CiciLasCondes (Chile)	Uber BlaBlaCar Carpling
Tasks/Services	Zolvers (Argentina and Mexico)	Nubelo
Others	MercadoLibre Alamaula Gratiferia (Argentina, Chile y Mexico) BioEcon (Argentina) TuOla (México) HackerGarage (México) MandarinaHub (México) Centraal (México) NoblezaObliga (Argentina) Eventdoo (Argentina) La Fulana (Argentina) QuieroAyudar (Argentina)	UrbanStation TicketBis Entrusters (Argentina) TrocaFone (Argentina)

9 Concluding Considerations and Reflections

In this chapter we have discussed how the collaborative economy in Latin America responds very differently to the needs and interests of two segments of the population: (1) the marginalized and excluded groups; and (2) the middle and upper classes. In the four countries examined, the collaborative economy represents an alternative model for the production of goods and services, and for employment of marginalised and excluded segments of the population. This especially counts for the youth who do not have access to the educational system or job opportunities within the formal economic system. However, the collaborative economy is not only about job opportunities or acquiring products. It also provides a lens to understand how specific segments of the population are excluded from the regulated economic market.

Even though the expansion of digitalized collaborative initiatives related to tourism consumption has increased significantly, and Latin America is characterized by a solid information technology: infrastructure, production and knowledge according to the World Bank's latest report (2016a, b), it also becomes clear that the informal sector keeps playing a pivotal role in the understanding of practices related to collaborative economy. It might be yet another way for the populations to express their critique in a non-violent way of the existing political and economic model implemented by the governments in this region. Marginalised and poor people depend on the spatial fixed *tianguis* and flea markets in Latin America to access the world of new technologies and products which otherwise would be out of reach. These spaces are turning the sector of collaborative consumption into a more sustainable alternative by re-using and repairing goods and products e.g. computers and cell phones. However, for the middle and upper classes, these new digital technologies are an additional tool providing access to an international arena representing and constituting new forms and practices of economic, socio-cultural and political integration with their national as well as international peers.

The above-discussed Latin American perspective suggests limitations in existing conceptualizations of the collaborative economy offered by Botsman and Rogers (2010). In Latin American societies, digital collaborative economy is adopted into a sociocultural, political and economic network. As such, it becomes an extension of well-established and social embedded historical practices of collaborative production and consumption, that replicates old patterns of privileged access for some, and denial for others.

In this chapter we have aimed to advance conceptualisations of the collaborative economy by reflecting on structures, rationales and practices in countries characterised by high levels of equality, exclusion and large sectors of informal economic activity. In this way, we have demonstrated that there is a deeply historical collaborative economy that operates outside the formal sphere and that bears little resemblance to the new digital collaborative economy described by contemporary Western protagonists. That said, the contemporary digital economy manifested by global platforms such as Airbnb and Uber is growing rapidly in Latin America, propelled by the middle and upper classes. However, as is the case in countries where this digital collaborative economy is driven out of necessity (such as Italy, Greece and Spain), in Latin America it is not necessarily taking place on digitalized platforms (World Bank, 2016a, b). In Latin America it would appear that the marginalized and informal workers remain unable to access this form of economic exchange because they lack both skills and access to digital capabilities as well as access to creditworthiness to become either producers or consumers. It seems reasonable to conclude that the new digital technologies might provide new avenues of change however we do not think we are witnessing a dramatic shift to more equality, to a fairer and more equal economic model based on the collaborative economy's principles rather these collaborative practices are to be understood and bound up on the sociocultural and political realities in a Latin American context.

References

Belk, R. (2014). You are what you can access: Sharing and collaborative consumption online. *Journal of Business Research, 67*(8), 1595–1600.

Botsman, R., & Rogers, R. (2010). Beyond Zipcar: Collaborative consumption. *Harvard Business Review*. Accessed May 1, 2016, from https://hbr.org/2010/10/beyond-zipcarcollaborative-consumption/

Cámara Argentina de Comercio (CAC). (2015). Informe de venta ilegal Callejera y Piratería en la Ciudad de Buenos Aíres. Accessed May 1, 2015, from http://www.cac.com.ar/documentos/22_VI_Ab15.pdf

Cammaerts, B. (2008). Critiques on the participatory potentials of web 2.0. *Communication, Culture & Critique, 1*(3), 358–377.

Cammaerts, B. (2011). Disruptive sharing in a digital age: Rejecting neoliberalism? *Continuum: Journal of Media and Cultural Studies, 25*(1), 47–62.

Cepal. (2013). *Panorama social de América Latina*. Naciones Unidas. Version digital. Accessed March 14, 2015, from http://www.asocamerlat.org/CEPAL_PanoramaSocial2013_AmericaLatina_diciembre2013.pdf

El País. (2015a). *La salada, el gran mercado negro de Latinoamérica*. Periódico. Accessed March 14, 2015, from http://internacional.elpais.com/internacional/2015/03/13/actualidad/1426276499_218087.html

El País. (2015b). *El Gobierno de Colombia lanza una ofensiva contra Uber*. Accessed March 14, 2015, from http://internacional.elpais.com/internacional/2015/03/14/actualidad/1426303113_247877.html

El País Colombia. (2014). *Piratería en Colombia dejó pérdidas por $1,3 billones en 2013*. Accessed June 17, 2015, from http://www.elpais.com.co/elpais/economia/noticias/pirateria-colombia-dejo-perdidas-por-13-billones-2013

El Universal. (2015a). *Guadalajara, Tijuana y Monterrey, contra Uber*. Accessed May 30, 2016, from http://www.eluniversal.com.mx/estados/2015/impreso/guadalajara-tijuana-y-monterrey-contra-uber-99149.html

El Universal. (2015b). *Edomex no permitirá operación de Uber*. Accessed May 28, from http://www.eluniversal.com.mx/ciudad-metropoli/2015/edomex-no-permitira-operacion-de-uber-1103345.html

Euromonitor. (2015). *Consumer payments 2015: Trends, developments and prospects* (Euromonitor International Report). London. Accessed January 3, 2016, from http://www.euromonitor.com/

Felson, M., & Spaeth, J. (1978). Community structure and collaborative consumption. A routine activity approach, American. *Behavioral Scientist, 21*(4), 614–624.

Ghezzi, S., & Mingione, E. (2003). Beyond the informal economy. New trends in post-fordist transition. In J. Friedman (Ed.), *Globalization, the state and violence* (pp. 87–106). New York, NY: Altamira.

Ghezzi, S., & Mingione, E. (2007). Embeddedness, path dependency and social institutions an economic sociology approach. *Current Sociology, 55*(1), 11–23.

Granovetter, M. (1973). The strength of weak ties. *American Journal of Sociology, 78*(6), 1360–1380.

Hart, K. (1973). Informal income opportunities and urban employment in Ghana. *Journal of Modern African Studies, 11*(1), 61–89.

Herrera, C. (2014). Airbnb takes a local approach in Latin America. *Pulso Social*. Accessed May 20, 2015, from http://pulsosocial.com/en/2014/05/20/airbnb-takes-local-approach-latin-america/

Kassan, J., & Orsi, J. (2012). Legal landscape of the sharing economy. *The Journal of Environmental Law & Litigation, 27*(1), 1–20.

La Nación. (2014). La venta ilegal callejera y la piratería registraron un récord en. Buenos Aires. Accessed December 8, 2015, from http://www.lanacion.com.ar/1750560-la-venta-ilegal-callejera-y-la-pirateria-registraron-un-record-en-buenos-aires

Latin American Science Organization. (2016). Accessed April 12, 2016, from http://latinamericanscience.org/2014/05/latin-americas-digital-divide/

Latinobarómetro. (2013). *Informe 2013*. Accessed June 2, 2015, from http://www.latinobarometro.org/documentos/LATBD_INFORME_LB_2013.pdf

Munar, A. M., Gyimóthy, S., & Cai, L. (2013). Critical digital tourism studies. In A. M. Munar, S. Gyimóthy, & L. Cai (Eds.), *Tourism social media: Transformations in identity* (pp. 245–262). Emerald: Bingley.

Najar, A. (2001, August 5). Retrato de un barrio agónico. Tepito por dentro. *La Jornada*. Accessed March 12, 2015, from http://www.jornada.unam.mx/2001/08/05/mas-tepito.html

Olavarrieta, S., Manzur, E., Hidalgo, P., & Farías, P. (2008). Un análisis a los atributos relevantes de los mercados de las pulgas para los compradores: Evidencia desde América Latina. *Revista de Ciencias Sociales. Universidad del Zulia, XIV*(3), 468–478.

OXFAM. (2014a). *Gobernar para las elites. Secuestro democrático y desigualdad económica*. Accessed March 12, 2015, from https://www.oxfam.org/sites/www.oxfam.org/files/bp-working-for-few-political-capture-economic-inequality-200114-es.pdf

OXFAM. (2014b). *Justifica fiscal para reducir la desigualdad en Latinoamérica y el Caribe*. Accessed March 12, 2015, from https://www.oxfam.org/sites/www.oxfam.org/files/file_attachments/justicia_fiscal_para_reducir_la_desigualdad_en_latinoamerica_y_el_caribe_.pdf

Portes, A., & Haller, W. (2005). The informal economy. In Smelser and Swedberg (Ed.), *Handbook of economic sociology* (pp. 403–425). London: Russell Sage Foundation.

Posada, M. G. (2007). México, cuarto lugar mundial en la venta de piratería y contrabando. *La Jornada*. Accessed July 4, 2015, from http://www.jornada.unam.mx/2007/07/04/index.php?section=economia&article=027n1eco

Schneider, F., Buehn, A., & Montenegro, C. (2010). New estimates for the shadow economies all over the world. *International Economic Journal, 24*(4), 443–461.

Stokes, K., Clarence, E., Anderson, L., & Rinne, A. (2014). *Making sense of the UK collaborative economy. Collaborative lab*. London: NESTA. www.nesta.org.uk.

Velázquez, M., & Clausen, H. (2017). Tianguis and collaborative consumption in Latin American societies, Pasos, 15 (forthcoming).

World Bank. (2016a). Accessed 20 September 20, 2016, from https://openknowledge.worldbank.org/handle/10986/22349

World Bank. (2016b). *Digital dividends. World Bank group*. Accessed January 15, 2016, from http://www.worldbank.org/en/publication/wdr2016

World Economic Forum. (2015). *Conozca los 10 países latinamericanos major ubicados en el ranking TIC del FEM*. Accessed August 30, 2015, from http://tecno.americaeconomia.com/articulos/conozca-los-10-paises-que-lideran-el-ranking-tic-del-foro-economico-mundial-en-latina

Peer-To-Peer Accommodation: Drivers and User Profiles

Juho Pesonen and Iis Tussyadiah

Abstract The tourism industry is currently dealing with the impacts of collaborative consumption, with tourists increasingly using peer-to-peer (P2P) services such as Airbnb and Uber. This study aims to extend our knowledge of why P2P accommodation services are not just succeeding, but thriving, from the consumer perspective, and it contributes to an understanding of the reasons for the popularity of P2P accommodation services and how consumer heterogeneity affects consumer choices. In this study, the drivers of P2P accommodation services are examined in order to better understand consumer characteristics and behaviour. Based on a survey of Internet users in Finland, the major drivers affecting the use of P2P accommodation services are the age of consumers, active use of the Internet and online technologies, and the frequency of international travel. Cluster analysis identified two user profiles corresponding to consumer motivations for using P2P accommodation services. The first consumer group uses P2P accommodation services to make their trips more convenient, while the second uses them mostly for social reasons.

Keywords Peer-to-peer accommodation • Segmentation • Motivations • Sharing economy • Drivers • Collaborative economy

1 Introduction

Collaborative consumption is becoming more prevalent in many industries and having a profound impact on consumer behaviour. With more and more consumers using peer-to-peer (P2P) services such as Uber and Airbnb, collaborative consumption is becoming increasingly important and is expected to transform the

---

J. Pesonen (✉)
Centre for Tourism Studies, University of Eastern Finland, Joensuu, Finland
e-mail: juho.pesonen@uef.fi

I. Tussyadiah
University of Surrey, Guildford, GU2 7XH, United Kingdom
e-mail: i.tussyadiah@surrey.ac.uk

D. Dredge, S. Gyimóthy (eds.), *Collaborative Economy and Tourism*,
Tourism on the Verge, DOI 10.1007/978-3-319-51799-5_17

tourism industry in the coming years. However, information regarding who the consumers are, why they are attracted to these services and what their scale of use is remains unclear. Indeed, Sigala (2015) has called for more international research on the numerous personal and contextual factors that influence collaborative consumption, highlighting the need for a better understanding of the increasing popularity of this consumption behaviour and the drivers behind it. Additionally, Guttentag (2013) has specified several topics of importance for future research regarding Airbnb, including the demographic and psychographic characteristics associated with its use. P2P accommodation services can be regarded as a type of collaborative consumption in which anyone can rent out their property (e.g., houses, apartments, cabins, rooms) for guests to stay in. With this definition, the focus is on a market-mediated sharing economy, one which involves the monetary element (i.e., renting) in collaborative consumption. This is congruent with Belk's (2014, p. 1597) definition, which states that "collaborative consumption is people coordinating the acquisition and distribution of a resource for a fee or other compensation".

Marketing literature regards segmentation and customer profiles as one of the cornerstones of understanding consumer behaviour (Pesonen, 2013). Consumers are heterogeneous in their behaviour, characteristics, motivations, needs and wants; different people prefer different things for different reasons. In particular, motivations have been regarded as an efficient way to analyse and understand consumer behaviour in travel and tourism (Bieger & Laesser, 2002; Park & Yoon, 2009; Pesonen, 2013). Therefore, researchers assume that those engaged in collaborative consumption are not a homogenous group and that the reasons for using P2P services differ from one person to the next. However, while attempts have been made to better understand consumer motivations for engaging in collaborative consumption (e.g., Hamari, Sjöklint, & Ukkonen, 2016; Tussyadiah, 2015), the users of P2P services are typically regarded as a homogenous group. Several recent studies have sought to explain in more detail consumer heterogeneity within the sharing economy. Ozanne and Ballantine (2010) identified four groups of toy library users who share different characteristics. Stokes, Clarence, Anderson and Rinne (Stokes, Clarence, Anderson, & Rinne, 2014) found regional and socio-demographic differences between users and non-users of sharing services. Finally, Tussyadiah and Pesonen (2015) identified minor differences with respect to the drivers of P2P accommodation use between consumers in Finland and the United States. Due to the limited findings presented in previous research, there still exists a gap in the field with regard to market heterogeneity as well as the factors influencing the use of collaborative consumption services. To that end, this study compares users and non-users of P2P accommodation services and identifies how they differ from each other, especially in terms of the personal and behavioural factors that drive collaborative consumption. Furthermore, this study explores further the profiles of P2P accommodation users to uncover the different reasons for participating in collaborative consumption among different user profiles.

2 Literature Review

2.1 *Drivers of Collaborative Consumption*

Collaborative consumption services are growing fast and becoming more and more popular all over the world. This phenomenon is driven by a large number of different factors: societal, economic and technological factors (Owyang, 2013). The societal drivers of collaborative consumption identified in the literature include consumer concerns about sustainability and social relations. According to Botsman and Rogers (2010), people are becoming more and more aware of the negative impacts of their consumption habits and are starting to shift their preferences towards more eco-friendly consumption patterns. The sharing economy makes efficient use of existing resources and reduces the need to invest in buying new products or building new infrastructure, such as hotels, thus reducing the environmental impact of travel. This, in turn, also allows for cost savings. Indeed, Belk (2014) has identified consumer attitudes towards consumption as one of the major drivers of the sharing economy. Buying and owning are losing importance as technology enables more and more efficient sharing. Consumers are willing to pay for temporal access to goods and services instead of buying and owning them outright (Bardhi & Eckhardt, 2012). The increased financial flexibility that non-ownership provides is the primary economic driver of the sharing economy (Owyang, 2013). Finally, technology is regarded as the third major driver behind the sharing economy. Mobile technologies, online communications, social media and developments in ICT, including payment systems, have all made possible the wider adoption of a sharing economy on a global scale (Belk, 2014).

Some scholars have argued that people do not participate in the sharing economy just for the sake of sharing, but for the benefits it provides. The benefits that consumers receive from consumption have been identified as a major driver of their consumption choices (Haley, 1995). However, in many cases the benefits are inseparable from or else very hard to distinguish from motivations (Pesonen, 2012). The very question that motivations and benefits aim to answer in this case is why consumers are using P2P accommodation services instead of other options. In this study, the benefits that a consumer receives and the motivations that drive a consumer to seek such benefits are treated as one and the same.

While the extant literature on the sharing economy generally suggests these three drivers—economic, societal and technological (Owyang, 2013)—there is limited information on the relative importance of each driver. For example, Hamari et al. (2016) studied the adoption of collaborative consumption services and identified factors such as sustainability, enjoyment of the activity and economic gains as motivations for using collaborative consumption services. Their results also suggest that sustainability is not an important motivation for everyone, but those for whom ecological consumption is important are more likely motivated by the sustainability aspect of collaborative consumption. Tussyadiah and Pesonen (2015) examined how the social and economic appeal of P2P accommodation services contributes to changes in the travel patterns of tourists due to the use of such services. They found that both social and economic factors have a significant influence on increases in the length of stay, participation in various activities, selecting from a wider range of destinations and the frequency with which people travel. Despite becoming a prominent research field, there needs to be more empirical research to confirm and estimate the effects of different drivers of collaborative consumption, including how they affect the use of P2P accommodation services.

2.2 Choice of Accommodation and Reasons for Choosing P2P Accommodation

Contemporary tourists have a wide range of accommodation types available to them, including hotels, hostels, friends and relatives, chalets and cottages, or free accommodation services such as Couchsurfing. With all these different options available, it is important to better understand the reasons for why P2P accommodation services such as Airbnb are thriving in a marketplace with a high level of competition. Tourists are looking for variety when choosing between different types of accommodation and some selection factors are more important than others. In terms of hotel choice, the topic has been relatively well researched, with a number of studies explaining the different factors influencing accommodation selection (see, e.g., Kim & Perdue, 2013; Sohrabi, Vanani, Tahmasebipur, & Fazli, 2012). For example, Wong and Chi-Yung (2002) identified price, quality, location, brand and room type as the most significant factors affecting hotel selection. However, these studies focus on why consumers choose one hotel over another instead of why they prefer hotels over other accommodation options.

Guttentag (2013) states that the demand for P2P accommodation services such as Airbnb is not a given, as Airbnb lacks many benefits that traditional options such as hotels provide, including service quality, brand reputation and security. However, guests in P2P accommodations benefit from better prices, amenities, local experience and the possibility to stay in a 'non-touristy' area. Indeed, one of the growing tourism trends is the search for authenticity (Wang, 1999; Yeoman, Brass, & McMahon-Beattie, 2007). There is less and less space to accommodate mass tourism in the modern world. Tourists are increasingly seeking genuine, authentic, local, unique and, especially, memorable experiences (Cohen, 2010; Sims, 2009; Tung & Ritchie, 2011). Ritzer (2007) argues that commercial hospitality is inhospitable because commercial advantage is driving hospitable behaviour instead of genuine motives such as a desire to please and welcome others. Tourists want human contact that is both local and real (Yeoman et al., 2007). Indeed, Week

(2012) analysed individuals who view themselves more as travellers than (traditionally defined) tourists, individuals who desire more local and authentic travel experiences. P2P accommodation services can provide tourists with authentic experiences by creating opportunities to form meaningful relationships with local hosts. Furthermore, P2P accommodation services enable tourists to tap into destination resources through the local hosts. These meaningful host-guest interactions are what make P2P accommodation services unique compared to other types of accommodation.

The literature also recognises sustainability as an important factor for consumers when making accommodation decisions and that consumer concerns about the environment are become more and more important (Han, Hsu, & Sheu, 2010; Kalafatis, Pollard, East, & Tsogas, 1999). For example, the green marketing of hotels has been a topic of interest in hospitality literature in the last decades (Han & Kim, 2010; Kim & Han, 2010; Lee, Hsu, Han, & Kim, 2010; Manaktola & Jauhari, 2007). Researchers have suggested that consumers are increasingly placing greater levels of importance on sustainability and, consequently, considering the potential environmental impacts of their travels when making accommodation choices. Indeed, sustainability, as one of the drivers of collaborative consumption, manifests itself in the form of reselling, renting, co-owning or gifting practices (Owyang, 2013), all of which reduce the need to invest in new products, facilities and infrastructures.

P2P accommodation services require interaction between hosts and guests, implying that the culture of each plays a central role in the creation of customer experience. Plog (1974) presented a tourist typology based on motivations, demonstrating that some tourists prefer exotic experiences whereas others prefer more familiar destinations. Thus, some tourists might avoid P2P accommodation services when travelling internationally (i.e., to minimise interactions with unfamiliar cultures), but use them when travelling domestically. On the other hand, others might prefer P2P accommodation services in international travel precisely because they want to experience new cultures and local customs. Prior travel experiences influence a person's degree of familiarity with particular tourist destinations. Tourists who often travel internationally, and who are exposed to different cultures, might be more familiar with and interested in local customs in faraway destinations. Therefore, travel frequency might be reflected in the use of P2P accommodation services. This suggests that the novelty of the host culture could be one of the drivers of (or barriers to) P2P accommodation services.

In previous studies, P2P accommodation users are often regarded as a homogenous group of people. For example, Guttentag (2013) has suggested that the users of P2P services are often young, technology savvy, budget conscious consumers because of the unique attributes of P2P accommodation services and reservation process, which involve lots of interaction with the host. Likewise, Stokes et al. (2014) have stated that people who are employed either full-time or part time, managerial, professional and administrative workers, and people with children in the UK are more likely to take part in the online collaborative economy than others.

Tussyadiah and Pesonen (2015) have also identified differences between consumers in Finland and the US in terms of how P2P accommodation services ultimately lead to changes in travellers' behaviour. However, as researchers obtain more information about the users, it is becoming obvious that different motivations and reasons for using P2P accommodation services are important for different people. Specifically, motivations are often used to segment and profile tourists since they provide a stable and actionable base for marketing purposes (Pesonen, 2015). In the context of P2P accommodation services, consumer motivations can provide an excellent base for user profiling (e.g., Tussyadiah, 2015).

3 Aim of the Study

Based on the literature review, we identified two central themes for research. First, the drivers of collaborative consumption need to be examined in order to establish what particular factors drive the use of P2P accommodation services in general. Then, to challenge the assumption that those who use P2P accommodation services comprise a homogenous group, we provide a more detailed examination of the users of P2P accommodation services. Assessing the various groups of people who use P2P accommodation services allows us to understand heterogeneity in the market place and how the drivers of collaborative consumption are manifested in the different market segments. This study analyses at a deeper level the factors that drive user participation in collaborative consumption and, therefore it contributes to our understanding of the adoption and use of P2P accommodation services from a user perspective.

4 Data and Methods

To achieve the goals of this study, an online survey was created to solicit responses from Internet users in Finland. To examine the reasons for using P2P accommodation services, items prepared by Tussyadiah (2015) and Tussyadiah and Pesonen (2015) were used. These survey items were derived from relevant previous studies in the existing literature (see Botsman & Rogers, 2010; Gansky, 2010; Guttentag, 2013; Kohda & Matsuda, 2013; Owyang, 2013) and reflect the motivations and benefits for consumers to use these services (see Fig. 1). The items were measured using a 5-point scale with agree–disagree anchored statements (ranging from −2, "Disagree Completely", to 2, "Agree Completely"). Additionally, nine items were used to measure respondents' opinions of the environment, use of the Internet and travel behaviour. The items were part of a larger study on Finnish lifestyle choices and were based on studies conducted by Mustonen and Lindblom (2013). The measurements were deemed valid for the purpose of this study via principal component analysis (Table 1). The questions were also presented in a similar

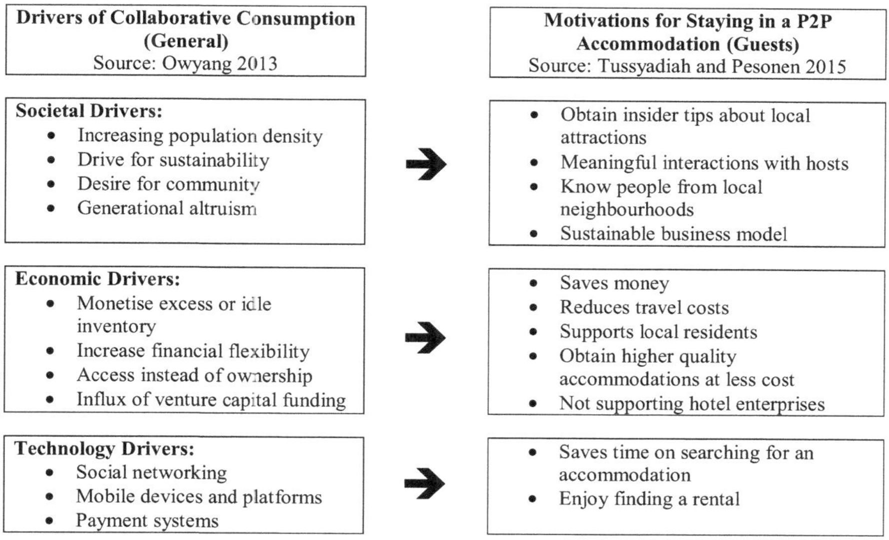

Fig. 1 Reasons for using P2P accommodation based on collaborative consumption drivers

5-point Likert scale. Personal annual income was measured using seven categories, and respondents were also asked to state how often they take domestic and international holidays per year on average.

First, we collected a representative sample of Finnish residents using an online panel survey ($N = 1026$). The sample represents Finnish consumers both in terms of geographic location and gender. Also, different age groups among the population are well represented, but the mean age of the sample was higher than the mean age of the Finnish population (50 years in the sample compared to 41.5 for the general population). This data was used to respond to the first research question about the drivers motivating the use of P2P accommodation services among the general population in Finland. Since only 70 users were captured in the first survey, additional data were collected using the same panel survey and targeting only those who had used P2P accommodation services before. The additional survey was conducted by directing the survey at the national population and asking whether or not people had previously used P2P accommodation services. All of the respondents who agreed with the statement were regarded as P2P accommodation users. This resulted in an additional 220 responses just from the P2P accommodation users.

Data analysis was divided into two parts. To obtain more knowledge about the drivers of P2P accommodation services among the general public, a principal component analysis (PCA) with Varimax rotation was conducted using all of the collected data on the lifestyle items, including travelling, Internet use, and environmental friendliness. PCA identifies the underlying shared dimensions of the

Table 1 Principal component analysis of lifestyle items

Principal component and items	Mean	S.D.	Loading	Eigenvalue	Variance explained	Cronbach α
Environmental friendliness				3.256	36.181	0.882
Environmental reasons have reduced my consumption	2.87	10.78	0.890			
Environmental reasons have affected the choices I make during trips	2.71	10.67	0.875			
I take environmental factors into account when making consumption choices	3.08	1.004	0.829			
Environmental reasons have reduced my travelling	2.45	1.045	0.815			
Active use of the Internet				1.596	17.731	0.642
I do daily grocery shopping online	1.61	1.022	0.808			
I actively follow blogs	2.20	1.227	0.774			
Travelling				1.354	15.048	0.596
Travelling is an important way for me to spend my leisure time	3.42	1.154	0.817			
I am interested in culinary cultures in other countries	3.43	1.131	0.804			

various constructs and group items based on participant responses (Hair, Black, Babin, & Anderson, 2010). Regression scores of each principal component were saved for further analysis, with the aim being to compare the importance of these principal components. Then, we used discriminant analysis to explain the differences between users and non-users of P2P accommodation services in terms of three consumption behaviour factors identified via PCA. During this particular phase of the analysis, only one sample from the first round of data collection was used (n = 1026). Additional responses collected just from P2P accommodation users were thus not included during this phase of the study. The sample was randomly divided into two groups, namely an analysis group and a validation group. Regression scores from the PCA were used for the discriminant analysis to examine the discriminatory power of the factors of P2P accommodation use. The analysis also included additional explanatory factors from the literature, such as number of annual trips abroad, number of annual domestic trips, personal annual income, and age. Age was explained via the logarithmic transformation score.

During the second phase of the analysis, we assessed at a deeper level the users of P2P accommodation services. During this particular phase, we included all respondents who had reported using P2P accommodation services during both data collection rounds, resulting in a total of 290 responses. In order to examine whether the users form a homogenous group or whether different kinds of user segments can be identified, we used hierarchical cluster analysis. This is a very popular approach to addressing market segmentation in tourism literature (Dolnicar, 2002). Hierarchical cluster analysis groups the observations into a treelike structure, with similar observations being grouped together. With Ward's method, the similarity of clusters is measured using the sum of squares within the clusters summed for all of the variables (Hair et al., 2010). Different cluster solutions, ranging from two to five, were compared and, based on the dendrogram and interpretability of the results, two cluster solutions were chosen. The two clusters were then compared with respect to the importance of lifestyle factors.

5 Results

5.1 Drivers of P2P Accommodation

The principal component analysis of lifestyle factors identified three underlying dimensions: "Environmental Friendliness", "Travelling" and "Active Use of the Internet" (see Table 1). The Kaiser-Mayer-Olkin MSA test yielded a score of 0.760, with a significance of $p < 0.001$. The three components explained 68.96% of the total variance. The item "I often shop online" was removed from the analysis because it decreased the reliability of the principal component that it was associated with.

The main results of the discriminant analysis are presented in Tables 2 and 3. Box's M statistics for discriminant analysis proved to be statistically significant ($p < 0.001$). The results show that users and non-users of P2P accommodation services differed the most with respect to their "active use of the Internet", whereas they did not differ much statistically in terms of the sustainability component ("environmental friendliness") of the analysis. In terms of travel frequency, the

Table 2 Discriminant analysis classification function coefficients

	Respondent groups	
	Users	Non-users
Environmental friendliness	−1.166	−1.393
Active use of the Internet	5.237	4.666
Travelling	−0.248	−0.511
Personal annual income before taxes	32.225	34.025
Age	−0.669	−0.776
Frequency of international travel	0.213	−0.419
Frequency of domestic travel	2.712	2.776
(Constant)	−64.484	−69.061

Table 3 Tests of the equality of group means and structure matrix

	Tests of equality of group means			Structure matrix
	Wilks' Lambda	F	Sig.	Function
Environmental friendliness	1.000	0.079	0.779	0.034
Active use of the Internet	0.961	21.771	0.000	0.567
Travelling	0.976	13.057	0.000	0.439
Age	0.964	19.604	0.000	−0.538
Personal annual income before taxes	0.997	1.645	0.200	0.156
Frequency of international travel	0.953	26.112	0.000	0.621
Frequency of domestic travel	0.992	4.063	0.044	0.245

frequency of international leisure travel clearly differentiated P2P accommodation users from non-users more so than did the frequency of domestic travel. Also, age significantly differentiated users from one another, with younger respondents being more prone to use P2P accommodation services. Additionally, those who reported that they regard travelling as important are more likely to be P2P accommodation users.

The coefficients were generally lower for those who reported not having used P2P accommodation services, except with respect to age, travelling and personal income. The variables with the greatest differences in Table 2 explain the differences between users and non-users. Table 3 shows that "environmental friendliness" and personal income do not significantly affect whether or not someone used P2P accommodation services. Tests on the equality of group means (Table 3) measure each independent variable's potential before the model has been created. Additionally, the structure matrix provides information regarding how well each variable correlates within the function. Coefficients with large absolute values correspond to variables with a greater ability to discriminate between users and non-users. This means that age, travelling abroad and "active use of the Internet" discriminate between users and non-users the most, whereas frequency of domestic travel, "environmental friendliness" and personal income are poor indicators of P2P accommodation use. The mean age of P2P accommodation users was 39.7 years, whereas it was 49.5 years for those who reported not using such services.

5.2 *Heterogeneity of P2P Accommodation Users*

We randomly divided the data into two samples to test the discriminant function. The function presented in this study managed to group correctly 71.4% of the unselected original group cases when the prior probabilities were calculated using equal group sizes.

To analyse the heterogeneity among P2P accommodation users, users were profiled based on their reasons for using P2P accommodation services in order to

Table 4 Motivation scores among clusters

I chose to stay at a P2P vacation rental because...	Pragmatists (n = 121)	Idealists (n = 145)
...it saved me time in searching for accommodations	−0.50	0.86
...I wanted to get insider tips on local attractions	−0.41	1.28
...the location was convenient	0.32	0.68
...finding the rental was an enjoyable experience	−0.21	1.32
...it saved me money	0.28	0.69
...I wanted to have more meaningful interactions with the hosts	−0.33	1.19
...it helped lower my travel costs	0.19	0.86
...I wanted to support local residents	−0.43	0.89
...I wanted to get to know people from the local neighbourhoods	−0,26	0.84
...it was a more sustainable business model	−0.29	0.98
...I wanted to have higher quality accommodations while spending less money	0.00	0.34
...I did not want to support hotel enterprises	−0.44	0.86

better understand the structure of the markets. We used hierarchical cluster analysis with Ward's method and squared Euclidean distances. This resulted in a clear two-cluster structure in the data with respect to motivations for using P2P accommodation services, as presented in Table 4. The first cluster rated all motivations as being lower than the second cluster. Only three types of motivation received positive scores for cluster 1: location, saving money, and reducing travel costs. The members of the second cluster rated all reasons as important, especially insider tips, the enjoyment that comes from finding a rental and meaningful interaction with the hosts.

Based on the results, we labelled the first cluster *Pragmatists*. The main reason that they reported using P2P accommodation services is that such services offer a convenient way to travel, providing cheaper and better accommodation at a more suitable location. They are not interested in the social or sustainable aspects of P2P accommodation services. The second cluster consists of *Idealists*. They reportedly embrace all aspects of P2P accommodation, but especially the community aspects of the service, such as interaction with the hosts. They reported that using services such as Airbnb to find the rental is an enjoyable experience. These results suggest that *Idealists* might actually consider what type of people they will meet when they are choosing to use a P2P accommodation service and do not just look at price, location and quality of the accommodation itself, as the *Pragmatists* do.

Regarding lifestyle (Table 5), members of the second cluster reportedly regard "environmental friendliness", "food and travel" and "consumption and shopping" as being more important than do members of the first cluster. We found no

Table 5 Lifestyle differences among clusters

	Pragmatists (n = 121)	Idealists (n = 145)	Sig.
Environmental friendliness*	−0.1853	0.1302	$p = 0.015$
Traveling*	0.4316	0.9580	$p = 0.288$
Active use of the Internet	−0.5733	−0.4056	$p < 0.001$

*$p < 0.05$

Table 6 Differences in socio-demographics and P2P accommodation experiences

	Pragmatists (n = 121)	Idealists (n = 145)	Sig.
Gender			$p < 0.05$
Men	83 (68.6%)	75 (51.7%)	
Women	38 (31.4%)	70 (48.3%)	
Overall, how satisfied are you with your stay at P2P accommodation rentals?			$p < 0.05$
Very dissatisfied	4 (3.3%)	0	
Dissatisfied	4 (3.3%)	0	
Somewhat dissatisfied	11 (9.1%)	4 (2.8%)	
Neutral	52 (43.0%)	9 (6.3%)	
Somewhat satisfied	22 (18.2%)	54 (38.0%)	
Satisfied	21 (17.4%)	57 (40.1%)	
Very satisfied	7 (5.8%)	18 (12.7%)	
How likely are you to use P2P vacation rentals in the future?			$p < 0.05$
Very unlikely	10 (8.3%)	2 (1.4%)	
Unlikely	13 (10.8%)	8 (5.6%)	
Undecided	49 (40.8%)	18 (12.5%)	
Likely	36 (30.0%)	86 (59.7%)	
Very likely	12 (10.0%)	30 (20.8%)	

statistical differences in terms of "active use of the Internet". The only socio-demographic difference between the clusters was gender, with the first cluster having considerably more men than women, whereas in the second cluster the gender balance was equal (see Table 6). It also seems that members of the second cluster have been much more satisfied with their P2P accommodation experience, reporting that they are much more likely to use P2P services in the future and will also use them more often than members of the first cluster when travelling abroad. The clusters were also compared with respect to other profiling items, but we have not found statistically significant differences in terms of the following items: age, frequency of P2P accommodation usage, travel frequency, education, phase of life or personal income. The mean age of the first cluster was 39 years, whereas it was 41 years for the second cluster, with medians of 37 years for both groups.

6 Discussion

The results of this study confirm the assumptions presented in previous studies regarding the drivers of collaborative consumption in the context of peer-to-peer accommodation services. We identified three aspects of Finnish lifestyles (i.e., travelling, environmental friendliness and active use of the Internet) and examined how they affect people's willingness to adopt and use P2P accommodation services. We also included income, age and frequency of international and domestic travel in the analysis. The results show that those who are younger, who actively use the Internet and who travel abroad more often are more likely to be P2P accommodation users. These findings confirm the assumption that the consumers of P2P accommodation services are younger and technology-savvy people who travel more often and earn more than the general population. The most important drivers are "active use of the Internet", age and frequency of travels to abroad. Travelling in general is an important factor in explaining the use of P2P accommodation services, as those people who travel more frequently are also the ones who are more likely to use P2P accommodation services. However, even though P2P accommodation users are younger than non-users, most of them, at least in Finland, are well over 30 years of age, with the median age being 37. However, a standard deviation of 15 years demonstrates the fact that users come from many different age groups and generations. Income proved to be a non-significant factor in accounting for P2P accommodation use, meaning that people from all income categories are likely users of P2P accommodation services. Finally, contrary to suggestions made in previous studies, "environmental friendliness" is not a driving force behind the use of P2P accommodation services.

We identified two different user profiles with respect to P2P accommodation users. We labelled the first group *Pragmatists*. This group of people reported that they use P2P accommodation services only because such services are convenient. They can find accommodations at relatively affordable prices when using P2P services. Still, they reported being generally less satisfied with the P2P accommodations and less likely to use them in the future than the members of the other group. In terms of demographics, the *pragmatist* primarily consisted of men. Regarding lifestyle, they reportedly are not active users of the Internet, as are the members of the other segment, nor are they as environmentally friendly in their opinions. We called the other group *Idealists*. This group had an almost equal number of men and women. They reported appreciating all aspects of P2P accommodation services, but especially the interaction with hosts and the booking process itself, which includes the chance of interacting a great deal with the hosts. For them, the convenience offered by P2P accommodation services was the least important motivation. They reported being quite satisfied with P2P accommodation services and highly likely to use them again in the future. The groups were of almost equal size, thus the P2P accommodation market in this study could be divided quite evenly. However, Wards method tends to form clusters of an equal size (Hair et al., 2010), and segment sizes obtained via cluster analysis do not necessarily represent the actual marketplace; which should be kept in mind when interpreting the results (Pesonen, 2014). There were no differences between the segments regarding the phase of life, income or age.

7 Conclusions

This study identified several drivers of collaborative consumption and their effect on differentiating between users and non-users. The results clearly demonstrate that the sharing economy thrives on the use of the Internet, just as an important prior study suggests (Belk, 2014). Without the Internet and its users, there would be no sharing economy at a global scale. As Sigala (2015) states, collaborative consumption fulfils the requirements for it to be considered a disruptive technology, one which appeals to enthusiastic early adopters. Also, travel behaviour significantly influences this consumption practice, as those who travel abroad more frequently are more likely to embrace P2P accommodation services.

This study in part challenges the assumption that sustainability is a driving force behind collaborative consumption, especially in the case of P2P accommodation services. When comparing the driving forces that account for why some people choose to use P2P accommodation services and others do not, we found that environmental friendliness does not play much of a role. Airbnb (2014), for example, differentiates itself from hotels based on sustainability arguments. However, the results of this study do not confirm the assumption that environmentally friendly consumers choose to use P2P accommodation services in greater numbers. When looking at the two user segments, we found that *Idealists* are more environmentally friendly than *Pragmatists* and also regard P2P accommodation services as a more sustainable business model compared to other accommodation alternatives. However, for *Idealists* sustainability only ranked as the fourth most important reason for choosing to use P2P accommodation services out of the 12 reasons measured in this study. This also confirms the assumption made by Hamari et al. (2016) that sustainability indeed is important only for those whom ecological consumption is likewise important. We can conclude that at least in Finland, the environmental sustainability, or ecological footprint, of the accommodation is not a major concern for consumers when choosing a holiday. However, this study does not tell the whole story regarding the topic, as sustainable consumption can already be an organic part of the Finnish lifestyle and only manifest itself when terrible sustainability practices are witnessed, or else perhaps tourists just want to take a break from sustainable practices during their holidays (Barr, Shaw, Coles, & Prillwitz, 2010).

The division of P2P accommodation users into *Idealists* and *Pragmatists* suggests that collaborative consumption has a different appeal for different people. *Idealists* are looking for social connections. They use P2P accommodation services not only to find a place to stay, but also to connect with local people and engage in positive social interaction. For them, the host can be even more important than the rental accommodation itself. *Pragmatists*, on the other hand, do not seek to interact much with the hosts. For them, a P2P accommodation is just a way to find conveniently located places to stay with a good price-quality ratio. This means that *Pragmatists* probably compare P2P accommodation options with other possibilities, such as hotels, to find the optimal location-price-quality combination with respect to an accommodation. *Idealists*, on the other hand, prefer to say in P2P accommodations because the social aspects of such stays are something that hotels struggle to provide. *Idealists* are much more likely to use P2P accommodation services in the future as well and are considerably more satisfied with their previous P2P accommodation experiences than *Pragmatists*.

Tussyadiah (2015) identified economic drivers as one of the most important reasons for choosing to use P2P accommodation services and argues that users consider such accommodations to be less expensive than other accommodation options. The results of this study also provide insights into the role of economic benefits as a driving force in collaborative consumption. This study found that people who have a higher level of personal income are more likely to use P2P accommodation services. However, collaborative consumption services such as Airbnb are not just for low-income and budget-conscious people (Guttentag, 2013). Many people are willing to pay prices that are equal to hotel prices just for an alternative experience. For *Pragmatists*, the main reason for using P2P accommodation services is that such services help them save money, and so for this segment of the population the findings presented in previous studies are quite relevant.

The distinction between *Idealists* and *Pragmatists* also reflects typologies posited in earlier literature. For example, *Idealists* are similar to Week's (2012) travellers in that they seek authentic experiences, whereas *Pragmatists* are similar to the type of tourists that Week defines in his study (Week, 2012). The results also reflect the tourists' need for authenticity (Yeoman et al., 2007). In searching for authentic experiences, tourists desire human contact that is both local and real (Yeoman et al., 2007). P2P accommodation services are probably for many closer to the genuine hospitality experience (Ritzer, 2007) than are hotels, especially for *Idealists*. The results also show that the more respondents claimed to travel internationally, the more likely they reportedly are to be P2P accommodation users. However, taking more annual domestic trips does not mean that a person is more likely to use P2P accommodation services. It seems that P2P accommodation services are used especially when travelling abroad, which means that especially for *Idealists*, the local culture is a significant factor when choosing an accommodation and when choosing a P2P accommodation over other types of accommodation.

A critical part of collaborative consumption, one that affects the tourism industry quite strongly, is how to generate interest in using a particular product or service. The results of this study show that P2P accommodation services are just beginning to become popular, at least in Finland. Only a small minority, less than 10% of Finnish consumers, have used P2P accommodation services. However, the average age of the users was 40 years, meaning that P2P accommodation services are not just for young people; older age groups have also started using these services. The average age of the respondents who reportedly do not use P2P accommodation services was almost 50 years. The fact that more mature consumers are willing to use P2P accommodation services indicates that collaborative consumption business models will likely be more widely adopted in the future.

The reasons presented and analysed in this study provide an answer to why people use P2P accommodation services. For some consumers, they provide a way to find an accommodation that is better located or of a higher quality than would have otherwise been possible on a more limited budget, especially compared to such options as hotels. For others, a P2P accommodation provides opportunities for social interaction that enable them to feel more like travellers (Week, 2012); they seek the chance to mingle with locals instead of just being stuck in the typical tourist bubble. Guttentag (2013) argues that Airbnb lacks many benefits provided by such traditional options as hotels, including service quality, brand reputation and security. However, Airbnb has managed to create a brand for itself and offer a level of service that earlier homestay services had not managed to provide. The Airbnb brand offers customers the security and brand reputation that they value in major hotel chains.

The results are interesting for traditional accommodation companies such as hotels and hostels as well as P2P accommodation companies. It can be suggested that approximately half of all P2P accommodation users represent a potential market for hotels, as *Pragmatists* are not looking for anything that the hotels could not provide. However, *Idealists* are clearly consumers who prefer P2P accommodations over more traditional accommodation options, mainly due to the unique attributes of P2P accommodations (for example, social interaction between the guest and host), attributes which the various hotel chains may lack entirely. *Idealists* are also more likely to respond to green marketing than *Pragmatists*, as they tend to be more environmentally friendly in their lifestyle choices. The results of this study carry both positive and negative implications for hotels. The good news is that for many P2P accommodation users, hotels are still a viable option when deciding on accommodations for a holiday. *Pragmatists* compare different options and, given more convenient accommodation choices, are less likely to use P2P accommodation services than *Idealists*. *Idealists*, on the other hand, are indeed a difficult market segment for hotels. *Idealists* want genuine hospitality, contacts with local people and also to feel less like tourists and more like travellers. On the one hand, small hotel chains and boutique hotels have the possibility to cater to this segment of the market via more personalised marketing and services; on the other hand, these hotels are also probably the ones that lose the most customers to P2P accommodation services, especially in the *Idealists* segment. According to Tussyadiah and Pesonen (2015), the availability of P2P accommodation services expands tourists' destination choice sets and enables them to travel more. *Idealists* are probably the consumers that especially enjoy additional travel possibilities because of P2P accommodation services.

Theoretically, this study contributes to our understanding of the driving forces behind the P2P accommodation phenomenon by studying the importance of the different forces at play. The study also challenges existing assumptions about sustainability being the determining factor, as P2P accommodation users are homogenous in their motivations and needs. This study also provides insights into collaborative consumption from the customer perspective. People use collaborative consumption services for different reasons. The markets are most likely also heterogeneous regarding forms of collaborative consumption other than just P2P accommodation services; rather than just focusing on customers in general, there are possibilities for providing niche services if such niches and market segments can be better identified.

In conclusion this is the first study to segment P2P accommodation users based on their motivations to use P2P accommodation and also increases our knowledge on what factors drive the use of P2P accommodation. The two segments identified, *Idealists* and *Pragmatists*, provide an interesting viewpoint on the use of P2P accommodation for future research. The segment structure also helps practitioners, both traditional accommodation providers as well as P2P accommodation providers, to understand the users of P2P accommodation better and how customer motivations impact their businesses.

References

Airbnb. (2014). *New study reveals a greener way to travel: Airbnb community shows environmental benefits of home sharing*. Accessed 2016, December 10, from https://www.airbnb.fi/press/news/new-study-reveals-a-greener-way-to-travel-airbnb-community-shows-environmental-benefits-of-home-sharing

Bardhi, F., & Eckhardt, G. M. (2012). Access-based consumption: The case of car-sharing. *Journal of Consumer Research, 39*(4), 881–898.

Barr, S., Shaw, G., Coles, T., & Prillwitz, J. (2010). 'A holiday is a holiday': Practicing sustainability, home and away. *Journal of Transport Geography, 18*(3), 474–481.

Belk, R. (2014). You are what you can access: Sharing and collaborative consumption online. *Journal of Business Research, 67*, 1595–1600.

Bieger, T., & Laesser, C. (2002). Market segmentation by motivation: The case of Switzerland. *Journal of Travel Research, 41*(1), 68–76.

Botsman, R., & Rogers, R. (2010). *"What's mine is yours." The rise of collaborative consumption*. New York: Collins.

Cohen, S. (2010). Searching for escape, authenticity and identity: Experiences of 'lifestyle travellers'. In M. Morgan, P. Lugosi, & J. R. B. Ritchie (Eds.), *The tourism and leisure experience: Consumer and managerial perspectives* (pp. 27–42). Bristol: Channel View Publications.

Dolnicar, S. (2002). A review of data-driven market segmentation in tourism. *Journal of Travel and Tourism Marketing, 12*(1), 1–22.

Gansky, L. (2010). *The mesh: Why the future of business is sharing*. London: Portfolio Trade.

Guttentag, D. (2013). Airbnb: disruptive innovation and the rise of an informal tourism accommodation sector. *Current Issues in Tourism*. doi:10.1080/13683500.2013.827159.

Hair, J., Black, W., Babin, B., & Anderson, R. (2010). *Multivariate data analysis* (7th ed.). Upper Saddle River, NJ: Prentice Hall.

Haley, R. (1995). Benefit segmentation: Decision-oriented research tool. *Marketing Management, 4*(1), 59–62.

Hamari, J., Sjöklint, M., & Ukkonen, A. (2016). The sharing economy: Why people participate in collaborative consumption. *Journal of the Association for Information Science and Technology, 67*(9), 2047–2059.
Han, H., & Kim, Y. (2010). An investigation of green hotel customers' decision formation: Developing an extended model of the theory of planned behavior. *International Journal of Hospitality Management, 29*(4), 659–668.
Han, H., Hsu, L. T. J., & Sheu, C. (2010). Application of the theory of planned behavior to green hotel choice: Testing the effect of environmental friendly activities. *Tourism Management, 31* (3), 325–334.
Kalafatis, S. P., Pollard, M., East, R., & Tsogas, M. H. (1999). Green marketing and Ajzen's theory of planned behavior: A cross-market examination. *Journal of Consumer Marketing, 16*(5), 441–460.
Kim, Y., & Han, H. (2010). Intention to pay conventional-hotel prices at a green hotel—A modification of the theory of planned behavior. *Journal of Sustainable Tourism, 18*(8), 997–1014.
Kim, D., & Perdue, R. R. (2013). The effects of cognitive, affective, and sensory attributes on hotel choice. *International Journal of Hospitality Management, 35*, 246–257.
Kohda, Y., & Matsuda, K. (2013, October 31–November 2). *How do sharing service providers create value? In Proceedings of the Second Asian Conference on Information System (ACIS 2013)*. Thailand: Phuket.
Lee, J. S., Hsu, L. T., Han, H., & Kim, Y. (2010). Understanding how consumers view green hotels: How a hotel's green image can influence behavioural intentions. *Journal of Sustainable Tourism, 18*(7), 901–914.
Manaktola, K., & Jauhari, V. (2007). Exploring consumer attitude and behaviour towards green practices in the lodging industry in India. *International Journal of Contemporary Hospitality Management, 19*(5), 364–377.
Mustonen, P., & Lindblom, T. (2013). Urbaanien nuorten aikuisten monenkirjavat elämäntyylit. *Kvartti, 2*, 69–85.
Owyang, J. (2013). *The collaborative economy: Products, services and market relationships have changed as sharing startups impact business models. To avoid disruption, companies must adopt the collaborative economy value chain* (A market definition report). San Mateo, CA: Altimeter.
Ozanne, L. K., & Ballantine, P. W. (2010). Sharing as a form of anti-consumption? An examination of toy library users. *Journal of Consumer Behaviour, 9*(6), 485–498.
Park, D.-B., & Yoon, Y.-S. (2009). Segmentation by motivation in rural tourism: A Korean case study. *Tourism Management, 30*(1), 99–108.
Pesonen, J. A. (2012). Segmentation of rural tourists: Combining push and pull motivations. *Tourism and Hospitality Management, 18*(1), 69–82.
Pesonen, J. A. (2013). *Developing market segmentation in tourism: Insights from a finnish rural tourism study*. Dissertations in Social Sciences and Business Studies No. 69, University of Eastern, Finland.
Pesonen, J. A. (2014). Testing segment stability: Insights from a rural tourism study. *Journal of Travel and Tourism Marketing, 31*(6), 697–711.
Pesonen, J. A. (2015). Targeting rural tourists in the internet: Comparing travel motivation and activity-based segments. *Journal of Travel and Tourism Marketing, 32*, 211–226.
Plog, S. (1974). Why destination areas rise and fall in popularity. *The Cornell Hotel and Restaurant Administration Quarterly, 14*(4), 55–58.
Ritzer, G. (2007). Inhospitable hospitality. In C. Lashley, P. Lynch, & A. Morrison (Eds.), *Hospitality: A social lens* (pp. 129–139). Oxford: Elsevier.
Sigala, M. (2015). Collaborative commerce in tourism: Implications for research and industry. *Current Issues in Tourism*. doi:10.1080/13683500.2014.982522.
Sims, R. (2009). Food, place and authenticity: Local food and the sustainable tourism experience. *Journal of Sustainable Tourism, 17*(3), 321–336.

Sohrabi, B., Vanani, I. R., Tahmasebipur, K., & Fazli, S. (2012). An exploratory analysis of hotel selection factors: A comprehensive survey of Tehran hotels. *International Journal of Hospitality Management, 31*(1), 96–106.
Stokes, K., Clarence, E., Anderson, L., & Rinne, A. (2014, September). *Making sense of the UK collaborative economy*. Nesta Collaborative Lab.
Tung, V. W. S., & Ritchie, J. B. (2011). Exploring the essence of memorable tourism experiences. *Annals of Tourism Research, 38*(4), 1367–1386.
Tussyadiah, I. (2015). An exploratory study on drivers and deterrents of collaborative consumption in travel. In I. Tussyadiah & A. Inversini (Eds.), *Information and communication technologies in tourism. Proceedings of the international conference in Lugano, Switzerland, February 3–6, 2015 (pp. 817–830)*. Heidelberg: Springer.
Tussyadiah, I. P., & Pesonen, J. (2015). Impacts of peer-to-peer accommodation use on travel patterns. *Journal of Travel Research*. doi:10.1177/0047287515608505.
Wang, N. (1999). Rethinking authenticity in tourism experience. *Annals of Tourism Research, 26* (2), 349–370.
Week, L. (2012). I am not a tourist: Aims and implications of "traveling". *Tourist Studies, 12*(2), 186–203.
Wong, K. K., & Chi-Yung, L. (2002). Predicting hotel choice decisions and segmenting hotel consumers: A comparative assessment of a recent consumer based approach. *Journal of Travel and Tourism Marketing, 11*(1), 17–33.
Yeoman, I., Brass, D., & McMahon-Beattie, U. (2007). Current issue in tourism: The authentic tourist. *Tourism Management, 28*(4), 1128–1138.

Part IV
Futures

New Frontiers in Collaborative Economy Research in Tourism

Dianne Dredge and Szilvia Gyimóthy

Abstract This chapter reflects on the challenges of defining the collaborative economy in a tourism context. We argue that an all-encompassing definition of the collaborative economy is problematic and that efforts might be better spent in understanding the social, cultural and economic pluralism of the collaborative economy rather than locking up its conceptualization in universal assumptions and producing knowledge that is highly contextual to that definition. In an effort to address growing concerns about the hidden values and self-interest underpinning collaborative economy research, this paper sets out a framework that helps researchers articulate their research choices.

Keywords Collaborative economy • Sharing economy • Tourism • Future research • Research framework

1 Introduction: Perspectives on the Collaborative Economy

The aim of this book has been to explore and theorise the nature, character and operation of the collaborative economy and its relationship to tourism. In the unfolding of the preceding chapters we have seen that the collaborative economy is much wider, deeper and more complex that we had initially anticipated, and that in the process of exploration we have come to appreciate that it has wide reaching social, economic, political and environmental consequences. The collaborative economy crosses disciplinary and sectoral boundaries, and it creates tensions and contradictions that take considerable skill, knowledge and patience to unravel and understand, much less construct purposive interventions.

D. Dredge (✉) • S. Gyimóthy
Department of Culture and Global Studies, Aalborg University, A.C. Meyers Vænge 15, Copenhagen 2450, Denmark
e-mail: dredge@cgs.aau.dk; gyimothy@cgs.aau.dk

D. Dredge, S. Gyimóthy (eds.), *Collaborative Economy and Tourism*, Tourism on the Verge, DOI 10.1007/978-3-319-51799-5_18

We deliberately adopted a broad interpretation of the collaborative economy at the outset of this book project. We adopted this approach in order to allow researchers the latitude needed to explore all that it *could* mean without limiting it to current discussions about the digital collaborative economy epitomised by a few well-known digital platforms. Without a doubt, this approach paid off in terms of the rich insights gathered from chapter authors who adopted a range of disciplinary perspectives, research approaches and contexts for their investigations. We overview these below, but we would first like to share some insights about how this collection of chapters has emerged, and the implications this has for knowledge building and a social science agenda for researching the collaborative economy.

In developing this book and in the initial call for papers, our first preconceptions were that we would indeed attract a range of contributions interrogating the digital collaborative economy, its transactions, its impacts and its controversies in tourism. Additionally, we were particularly keen to explore how "the global" plays out in the local, and how "the local" influences what happens globally in the collaborative economy. We wanted to seek out explorations of the de/re/structuring of tourism systems, and the wider economic, social, political and environmental implications of the collaborative economy. Coming from this perspective, it came as quite a surprise to us that, in late 2015, when we first announced the book proposal, few tourism researchers had heard of the collaborative economy. By mid-2016 however, we believe that the situation had changed dramatically and that there is growing awareness. To date however, research has remained quite narrowly focused on understanding markets, quite often using very limited data sets, and on critiquing of particular platforms. Wider interrogations have been limited and there are few explorations of the global-local interactions and processes of de/re structuration being facilitated by the collaborative economy either inside tourism or in the wider research arena. In Dredge and Gyimóthy (2015), we posit the reasons why research has been slow to take off include the absence of clear analytical frameworks and lenses, the difficulty of securing access to data, and the need for an appreciation of wicked complexity of the collaborative economy as a multidisciplinary and multisectoral problem. These issues remain problematic and will need to be addressed in the future.

As a result, and as we pointed out in the first chapter, researching the collaborative economy from a holistic social science perspective is not an easy task. However, our chapter authors rose to the challenge and interpreted "collaborative economy" in a kaleidoscope of ways giving depth, variety, contrast and meaning in ways that we never expected. In the light of their varied and insightful investigations, it therefore makes sense to revisit the meaning of the collaborative economy, and how we might unfold and investigate this term in the future. Put simply, using an inductive approach, we are now able to draw attention to the meanings of the collaborative economy and its intersections with tourism in a manner that we were unable to at the beginning of this project.

2 Definitional Reflections: Towards Social, Cultural and Economic Pluralism

As promised in the introductory chapter, we return to explore the meaning of the collaborative economy in this final chapter. There are many definitions of the collaborative economy, which reflect both the diverse values of authors and the purposes for which they seek to define it. Contradictions abound. It is both old and new; it is global and local; it may be monetized or non-monetized; and it is manifested in both formal and informal economies. It is collective in name and also demonstrates a high level of individualization. It is said to redistribute wealth, democratize economic systems (Gorenflo, 2013; Parsons, 2014a, 2014b) and increase the accessibility of travel (PWC, 2015). Conversely, it is also seen as nothing more than platform capitalism, extracting wealth from precariat workers and the commons, redistributing and concentrating it within the wealthier echelons of capitalist society including venture capitalists, hipsters, property investors and the creative class (Scholz, 2014; Slee, 2016; Thrasyvoulou, 2014). Another unresolved contradiction is whether the collaborative economy represents resistance to traditional forms of capitalism, ownership and over-consumption, or whether it is simply a new form of capitalism. Botsman (cited in Kade, 2015) has suggested that the collaborative economy might be a form of resistance to hyper-consumption, consumerism and resource depletion:

> . . .what originally drew me into the space was how these ideas can empower both providers and customers to exchange in more direct and human ways. At its best, power is taken from the hands of the 'big company' and back into the hands of millions of users.

O'Regan and Choe (chapter "Airbnb: Turning the Collaborative Economy into a Collaborative Society") counter this argument with observations that the collaborative economy incentivizes monopolistic, commercial and profit-seeking behaviours, where the offering of multiple properties by the same owner on collaborative accommodation sites such as Airbnb, or Uber's move into fleet cars demonstrates this point (SMH, 2016). It seems that the more attention the collaborative economy receives, the more new contradictions emerge.

Not surprisingly, definitions of the collaborative economy tend to reflect the particular reality for which the definition is generated; the author's way or understanding or positioning of themselves within the discourse; and the particular value sets held by authors or their clients. For example, consultants and so-called sharing economy experts focus on the disruptive and innovative elements of the collaborative economy, buying into a framing that heightens the value of their expert contribution in helping to navigate the uncertainty of disruption. Economists and business consultants might focus their definitions on elements such supply chain and market dynamics, demand and consumption, while social researchers might concern themselves with the distribution of impacts on different communities, aspects of power, trust, reputation and the accumulation/redistribution of wealth. In other words, definitions are shaped by a range of ontological (i.e. ways of understanding), epistemological (i.e. ways of knowing) and axiological (i.e. ways of valuing) assumptions. Under these circumstances, an all-encompassing definition of the collaborative economy is unlikely to emerge. Efforts might be better spent in understanding the social, cultural and economic pluralism of the collaborative economy rather than locking up its conceptualization and meaning in universal assumptions and producing knowledge that is highly contextual to that definition (e.g. see Howitt & Suchet-Pearson, 2006).

So what reflections can be learned from the deliberations contained within the chapters of this book that might help to direct attention towards developing greater social, cultural and economic pluralism of the collaborative economy? In the chapter "Business models of the collaborative economy", Gyimóthy shows that the collaborative economy is also characterised by diverse business models. Whilst it is easy for our thinking to be dominated by the recent rise of the digital collaborative economy, and for our theoretical endeavours to become narrowly fashioned around the digital focus, the importance of maintaining awareness of wider ontologies of collaborative economy is essential. Drawing upon Kennedy (2015), Gyimóthy ("Networked cultures in the collaborative economy") alerts us to three ontological perspectives on the collaborative economy that have been reflected within the chapters of this book:

- An ***economy*** driven by social capital (i.e. the sharing economy/collaborative economy) demonstrated in, for instance, the chapters by Guttentag ("Regulating innovation in the collaborative economy: an examination of Airbnb's early legal issues") as well as Pesonen and Tussyadiah ("Peer-to-peer accommodation: drivers and user profiles").
- A mode of ***resource distribution*** (i.e. sharing platforms) demonstrated in, for instance, the chapters by Cannas ("Embedding social values in tourism management: community currencies as laboratories of social entrepreneurship?") and Leal Londoño and Medina ("Free walking tour enterprises in Europe: an evolutionary economic approach").
- A site of ***social intensification*** (i.e. symbolic exchanges, tribal belonging and bonding among community members, which has been demonstrated in the chapters by Cannas ("Embedding social values in tourism management: community currencies as laboratories of social entrepreneurship?"), Johannesson and Lund ("Improvising economy: everyday encounters and tourism consumption"), Hardy ("Community and connection: exploring non-monetary aspects of the collaborative economy through recreation vehicle use").

In the chapter "Networked cultures in the collaborative economy", Gyimóthy examines the sociological dimensions of collaboration and sharing to illustrate that the motivations of actors in the collaborative economy also vary as does the way it is valued. She highlights that the historical framing and dominance of communitarian "sharing" discourses have led to romanticized notions of collaboration, solidarity, sustainability and social responsibility that can misrepresent what is really going on. She argues that "sharing is positioned as a 'morally correct act', transporting its rhetoric and positive associations to companies facilitating peer transactions against a fee". Gyimóthy's explanation of the algorithmic manipulations taking place on digital platforms illustrate that we need to remain cautious to the communitarian claims of the digital collaborative economy, and be aware of the ethos, motivations and logics underpinning digital "collaborative economy" models. The chapters of Cannas ("Embedding social values in tourism management: community currencies as laboratories of social entrepreneurship?"), Johannesson and Lund ("Improvising economy: everyday encounters and tourism consumption") and Hardy ("Community and connection: exploring non-monetary aspects of the collaborative economy through recreation vehicle use") provide us with alternative examples of the collaborative economy demonstrating that solidarity, sustainability and social responsibility can indeed be present. Furthermore, if we foreground the social (as opposed to the nature of economic exchange), we reveal other insights about the nature of collaboration, individualization, relational bonds and connections.

In sum, we decline to offer an all-encompassing definition for the above discussed reasons, and instead argue for conceptualizations that allow the social, cultural and economic pluralism of the collaborative economy to flourish. The collaborative economy might be very old, but it is also evolving, hybridizing and morphing at a very rapid rate. Narrowing to a preferred definition runs the risk of closing down yet-to-be-imagined models. Remaining open to alternative ontological, epistemological and axiological perspectives must therefore form part of any future research agenda. However, this position requires that authors take the time to explicate their ontological, epistemological and axiological foundations.

3 Reflections on Complexity: Collaborative Economy as a Perfect Policy Storm

The rise of the collaborative economy has been described as a "perfect storm" (Gansky, 2010). "Perfect storm" is an expression used to describe the confluence of issues where the synergies produced are significantly more complex and difficult to deal with than if individual issues were addressed separately (Dredge, Gyimóthy, Birkbak, Jensen, & Madsen, 2016). The metaphor is particularly apt in policy contexts where a number of policy and regulatory issues coalesce, where there are diverse stakeholder interests at play, and the complexity of taking action involves weighing up a range of interconnected policy options and their known and unknown consequences (e.g. see Head, 2008a, 2008b; Rittel & Weber, 1973 for a discussion of wicked policy problems). The rapid growth of the collaborative economy at a global scale has contributed to this perfect (policy) storm.

Both Richards' chapter ("Sharing the new localities of tourism") and O'Regan and Choe's contribution ("Airbnb: Turning the Collaborative Economy into a Collaborative Society") illustrate this perfect policy storm in their renderings of the global-local complexities of the collaborative economy accommodation sector.

City destinations are raising concerns over the impact of the rapid rise of the collaborative economy accommodation sector that has occurred at a time when many localities in various corners of the globe are feeling the impacts of decades of pro-growth tourism strategies. Strong sustained growth in visitor numbers, fuelled by growth in low cost airline passenger capacity, city branding and promotion efforts, the increased use of events as economic development tools, and increases in hotel investment, have contributed to an intensification of tourism activity. Physical signs of overcrowding and visitor saturation, particularly in inner-city locations close to tourist attractions, are evident. Psychological effects of overcrowding are manifested in increased political conflict (e.g. demonstrations in Barcelona and negative social media in many cities). In some instances, falling rates of residential occupancy in some neighbourhoods have resulted in the closure of community facilities such as schools where there is no longer a population demographic to support the service. These policy issues are broadly the consequence of tourism growth and development policies. The seeds of these current problems existed prior to the rise of collaborative economy tourism accommodation sector and the pace of uptake of the collaborative economy by both producers and consumers has exacerbated these pre-existing policy issues (Dredge et al., 2016).

The rise of the collaborative economy has also coincided with pre-existing housing shortages and affordability issues in many cities. The causes of these housing issues are complex and historically embedded in, for example, the evolution of national and regional housing markets, infrastructure and investment policies. These policies have shaped the supply and demand for housing; they have shaped the behaviours of markets and investment, and in turn contributed to current housing shortages and affordability issues. The collaborative economy tourism accommodation sector has grown, in part, due to the natural tendency for capital to maximise return on investment. In many cities, local economic and investment conditions dictate that short-term tourism accommodation rental is more profitable than renting to permanent residents. As a result, investors seeking to maximise their returns have been drawn to the collaborative economy accommodation sector where small investors with as little as one apartment to rent can access the global marketplace (Dredge et al., 2016).

These conditions create considerable challenges for policy makers and regulators. Diverging national rules and local regulations have created uncertainty and policy and regulatory environments have become highly politicized in some locations. Not only have existing policy and regulatory approaches and frameworks struggled to keep up with the pace of innovation in the collaborative economy, but opportunities to share information, compare and contrast public administration responses and experiences in different contexts have been difficult. Accordingly, the policy environment in all its multi-scalar complexity is both a facilitator and/or an inhibitor to the collaborative economy and understanding of policy complementarities and trade-offs must be part of a future research agenda.

4 Reflections on Knowledge Needs and Information Asymmetries

In our earlier work exploring the landscape of the collaborative economy and tourism, we identified a range of concerns about the lack of reliable data, the dearth of independent research and the information asymmetries that have been emerging as a result of power imbalances in the collaborative economy (Dredge & Gyimóthy, 2015). Governments and industry require good, reliable data in order to devise well-conceived responses to the collaborative economy. Put simply, the fundamentals of robust decision-making about what to do includes using valid and reliable data; analysis, conclusions and potential actions that are derived from independent and systematic inquiry drawn from multiple sources of evidence; and establishing a level of trust among stakeholders that these former conditions have been met (Pawson, 2006).

At present in the collaborative economy, reliable and publically accessible data is limited and the data that is available or made public is often presented through a lens of self-interest (Gordo, de Rivera, & Apestegia, 2016; Slee, 2016). For a variety of commercial and political reasons, collaborative economy platforms are unwilling to share their "raw data" and even when it has been forthcoming it has generally been in the form of high-level trend or descriptive data that supports the overall position or interests of the platform. CleanTech's research report on the environmental sustainability of Airbnb, briefly discussed by Dredge in the chapter on "Responsibility and care in the collaborative economy", illustrates this point. Adding a further level of murkiness, there have been specific incidences where data supplied have been "cleaned" or manipulated prior to its sharing, which has eroded trust between Airbnb and its stakeholders (Cox & Slee, 2016).

The targeting of data collection exercises is also problematic. Existing data collection initiatives such a visitor surveys, census data collection, accommodation data, industry reporting and so on do little to shed light on the collaborative economy in tourism. While additional questions are now starting to be offered within these existing data collection tools, their ability to capture the extent and nature of the collaborative economy is questionable because their application and target audiences may not reach collaborative economy participants. In the tourism sector, the mobility of travellers adds an additional challenge to data collection. For example, collaborative economy visitors often circulate outside traditional tourist zones and/or communication channels making them difficult to identify and survey. Hosts may also not self-identify for fear of the regulatory burden or tax obligations they may be subjected to.

The impacts and consequences of the collaborative economy in tourism also extend well beyond impacts on traditional industry players, hosts and guests. As discussed in the opening chapter "Collaborative economy and tourism", stakeholders may be directly or indirectly affected by the collaborative economy and impacts may emerge over time. As a consequence, a broader set of stakeholders and longitudinal data collection must also be included when considering what information is required, and from whom, in responding to the collaborative economy.

5 Reflections on Myths

Myth-making is prevalent amongst advocates of the collaborative economy. In the opening chapter, "Collaborative economy and tourism" we identified a number of myths that have been reproduced so often that they are fast becoming taken-for-granted "truths" that normalise the way we view the collaborative economy. Following Couldry (2015), the concern we raise is that these myths are framed around certain socio-political values and self-interests and can impede and even distort balanced understanding of the collaborative economy. Myths also tend to be characterised by over-generalisation and high levels of simplicity. The contributors to this book have explored the complexity of the collaborative economy and its relationship to tourism, and while they have not directly sought to dispel the myths identified, their interrogations help to shed light on the relative strengths and weaknesses of such assertions.

The first myth was that the collaborative economy supposedly unlocks hidden wealth by turning idle assets, dead capital and surplus resources into economic opportunity. The chapter authors have, through their diverse explorations, rendered a picture of the collaborative economy as being much more than a system of economic transactions unlocking hidden wealth. For example, Cannas' chapter, "Embedding social values in tourism management: community currencies as laboratories of social entrepreneurship?") highlights the hidden wealth of communities who seek to collaborate, but motivations are not as simple as unlocking hidden wealth. In the Sardex case, economic reasons for collaboration cannot be separated out from social bonds of a community seeking to survive the financial crises that have unfolded in Sardinia. This social dimension of exchange, the diversity of non-monetised transactions, and the social and cultural value of the relational encounter itself tend to be minimised in this myth. These transactions have a personal individual quality (Jóhannesson and Lund), and they also have a collective, bonding value (see also Hardy's and Clausen and Velázquez's chapters). This myth thus oversimplifies social-economic entanglements, and over-focuses on economic value to the detriment of deeper understandings. The complexity of social-economic linkages justifies a broader social science approach as will be detailed in the research agenda later in this chapter.

The second myth was that the collaborative economy embraces openness, inclusivity and the commons, it reallocates wealth across the value chain, and it carries the seeds of a more fair, just and equal society. A range of chapters offers insights into the claims embedded in this myth. There were elements of truth in this myth in Leal Londoño and Medina's chapter ("Free walking tour enterprises in Europe: an evolutionary economic approach") investigation of free-walking tours. They found that easy access to the collaborative economy marketplace had opened up opportunities for local guides and given them choices that they may not have had previously. However, Clausen and Velázquez dispel this myth in their discussion of the collaborative economy in Latin America, finding that it is linked to pre-existing patterns of economic and social organisation. They argue that the collaborative economy is not new, but an extension of existing informal economies that has been propelled by digital technology. Examining the collaborative economy from the perspective of labour, Meged and Christensen ("Working within the collaborative tourist economy: the complex crafting of work and meaning") also note that the collaborative economy does not redistribute wealth nor create a fairer or more just society. They find the reverse—that the collaborative economy undermines existing labour rights and protections and has the potential to make society less fair. Drawing from the insights offered by the collection of chapters, we find that such a myth oversimplifies the nature of transactions and generalises across a wide range of collaborative economy models. It demonstrates Gyimóthy's chapter ("Networked Cultures in the collaborative economy") concern over the romanticisation of the collaborative economy as an altruistic phenomenon, which has been problematized by authors such as Guttentag ("Regulating innovation in the collaborative economy: an examination of Airbnb's early legal issues"), O'Regan and Choe ("Airbnb: Turning the Collaborative Economy into a Collaborative Society") and Richards ("Sharing the new localities of tourism").

The third myth is that the collaborative economy focuses on community lifestyle and living local movements, it is an antidote to the failures of capitalism, and it contributes to a moral turn towards more responsible production and consumption. Some of the chapters in this book render very intimate understandings of collaboration, and leave little doubt that deep relational bonds can emerge from collaborative transactions. Jóhannesson and Lund ("Improvising economy: everyday encounters and tourism consumption") explore the connections between museum staff and a visitor in the Icelandic Museum of Sorcery and Witchcraft. They draw our attention to the encounter and to the meaning and relational attributes of genuine collaboration, which in the case of the museum curator is about responsibility and care. It is neither monetised or digitized. Hardy ("Community and connection: exploring non-monetary aspects of the collaborative economy through recreation vehicle use") follows a similar trajectory, where in her investigation of grey nomads, she arrives at the conclusion that collaboration is about a sense of belonging, fellowship and shared sentiment. Among the grey nomads, transactions take a variety of forms and may or may not have an explicit economic value. Moreover, money is often ancillary to the highly valued collaborations that take place. So while we see partial support for this myth within the chapters, any semblance of truth in this myth depends heavily on the characteristics of the particular collaborative economy model and the actors involved. Gyimóthy ("Networked cultures in the collaborative economy"), O'Regan and Choe ("Airbnb: Turning the Collaborative Economy into a Collaborative Society"), Meged and Christensen ("Working within the collaborative tourist economy: the complex crafting of work and meaning") and Richards ("Sharing the new localities of tourism") all explore the digital collaborative economy, returning an alternative conclusion that it is not a more responsible form of consumption and is often nothing more than business as usual capitalism.

The fourth myth is that the collaborative economy represents a free, unfettered and more efficient market place where producers and consumers exchange goods and services without heavy-handed regulation. Chapter contributors (e.g. Guttentag, O'Regan and Choe) have raised a range of concerns about the capacity of the collaborative economy to deliver more efficient markets. Of particular concern is the way in which digital P2P platforms can bypass regulatory requirements with issues emerging around health and safety, consumer protections, labour rights. Again, this myth does not take into account the diversity of collaborative economy models nor the effects and unintended consequences of these efficiency dividends. Day ("Collaborative economy and destination marketing organisations: a systems approach") draws attention to the way in which the collaborative economy has potential to bypass Destination Management Organisations (DMOs), and in the process a range of core DMO functions (e.g. training, promotion, business support) that contribute to destination image, service quality and so on are placed at risk. Day's findings suggest that a measured response in needed towards the collaborative economy and that the bypassing and/or dismantling of all regulatory mechanisms and government functions in relation to tourism is not necessarily the best outcome for the future of innovative and competitive tourism systems.

The fifth and final myth was that the collaborative economy possesses the capacity to self-regulate and address market failures. Chapter authors contribute a number of observations with regard to this myth but all suggest that there are a range of issues, unintended consequences and impacts that have not yet been fully and concretely identified much less researched. Dredge's exploration of politics, policy and the regulatory challenges ("Responsibility and care in the collaborative economy") draws attention to the need for a more nuanced approach to regulation that responds to the different collaborative economy models and the consequences for diverse stakeholders and communities of interest. Importantly, this myth is perhaps also designed to progress the argument that the collaborative economy needs a "regulation-lite" approach from government. It seeks to confirm a fundamental tenant of neoliberal capitalism: that self-regulation is better and more efficient than government regulation. However, it would seem that it is too early to make such a claim that the collaborative economy has the capacity to self-regulate. The discussions contained in chapters by Guttentag, Richards, Gyimóthy and O'Regan and Choe also appear to support the need for more detailed, critical and independent studies about the relative merits of self—versus government regulation.

6 Researching the Collaborative Economy and Tourism

In this section we seek to lay the foundations for a research agenda on the collaborative economy that enables us to pursue the social, economic, cultural and political pluralism that we believe is necessary. As previously discussed, a commitment to ontological, epistemological and axiological pluralism can help to generate alternative understandings of the collaborative economy and tourism.

The contributions contained within this book demonstrate that the collaborative economy is very complex. It is not just a tourism problem; its tentacles extend into urban planning, economic management, community development, fiscal policy, investment, labour and mobility to name a few sectors and policy spheres. There is no single best approach to its study—it is multi-sectoral and multi-disciplinary, and it also involves a myriad of stakeholders and communities of interest. The contradictions and competing claims that have emerged, which have been discussed herein have arisen in part because of the wide range of values and self-interests lurking beneath both research and advocacy activities in the collaborative economy. In order to explore these contradictions and competing claims there is a need for researchers to be more explicit about the worldview they adopt; to be clear about the knowledge devices, disciplinary influences, frameworks and tools they are using to frame and focus their research; and there is a need to be clear about the values and beliefs that shape their position as a researcher.

Figure 1 captures the elements of this values-based framework for the collaborative economy and tourism. This framework can be used as a guide to assist researchers better articulate the choices and influences upon their research into the collaborative economy by making explicit the ontological, epistemological and axiological decisions that have influenced their research approach. On the left side of the Figure, the researcher is prompted to articulate ontological, epistemological and axiological choices. The shaded boxes in the middle of the Figure contain examples of the choices that were made by the chapter authors within this volume.

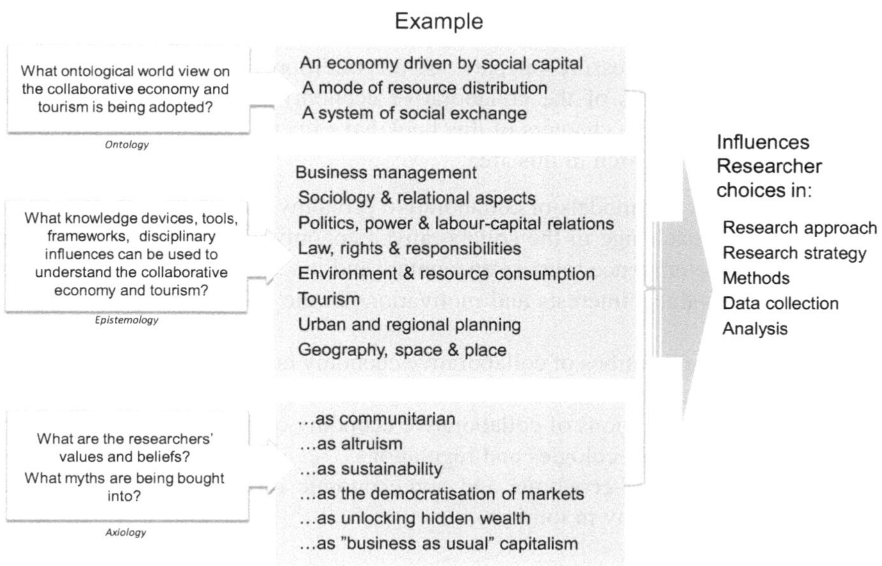

Fig. 1 Social, economic, cultural and political pluralism in the collaborative economy: a research framework

A commitment to social, cultural and political pluralism addresses the choices available in framing or positioning future research in the collaborative economy and tourism. But what might be the substantive directions for a research agenda for the collaborative economy and tourism? In this final section, we can now identify a number of research opportunities that have emerged and which provide important lines of theoretical and practical inquiry into the future. We frame this agenda around the need to engage more thoroughly in three overlapping sets of concerns emerging from this volume: (1) better understandings of the characteristics of the collaborative economy in tourism; (2) improved insights into the societal impacts of the collaborative economy and tourism; and (3) what can be done about it. While the first two enable us to better understand the nature of the collaborative economy and tourism and its impacts, the latter channels the knowledge of the first two and prompts us to ask the hard questions about values, ethics, responsibility and judgement. We deal with each in turn.

6.1 Characteristics of the Collaborative Economy and Its Relationship with Tourism

It is evident from the preceding chapters that some parts of the tourism system are being transformed by the collaborative economy. We have also illustrated that the collaborative economy is not a homogeneous "thing", neither does it "hit equally". Rather, it is a collection of business models, practices, relational networks, technologies, and stakeholders with different interests, resources and power that together are placing pressure on parts of the traditional tourism system. More nuanced understandings of the collaborative economy and its relationship with tourism are needed. The chapters of this book have opened and contributed to the following lines of research in this area:

- Characteristics and models of collaborative economy businesses in tourism
- Sociology of exchange in the collaborative economy and how these relational characteristics influence tourism encounters and practices
- Stakeholder values, interests and motivations in the collaborative economy in tourism
- Impacts and implications of collaborative economy on traditional and/or incumbent industry actors and destination management organizations
- Impacts and implications of collaborative economy on tourism systems, supply chains and business ecologies and regulations
- Alternative forms of economic and non-economic forms of value creation in collaborative economy in tourism.

6.2 Societal Impacts of the Collaborative Economy

The idea that tourism can be a tool for social good—that it can add social and economic value, help to protect natural resources, and contribute to community cohesion and sustainable livelihoods for example—is well established in the literature. Similarly, some models of the collaborative economy are also aligned with the altruistic view that it can help to deliver social, cultural and political value in addition to economic growth and innovation. Together these ideas—that tourism collaborative economy can create a better world—has become a simplistic but potent argument gaining increasing momentum. Critical voices put forward an opposite interpretation, claiming that the collaborative economy is the purest form of capitalism, exploiting individual lives and private resources beyond the safety net of welfare systems. However, both positions remain ideological and provide an overtly crude appraisal of a phenomenon that is not yet consolidated nor well understood. The collaborative economy is seeping in the cracks of dysfunctional capitalist and welfare systems, creating partial solutions but also new ruptures as it infiltrates existing institutional and social structures. Hence, more detailed investigation is needed to better understand the complex societal impact of the collaborative economy in tourism. From these deeper understandings we can better identify strategies and actions to maximise the positive benefits and minimise the negative effects.

Drawing from the preceding chapters a number of lines of further inquiry have been identified, such as:

- Impacts and implications of collaborative economy on destination sustainability
- Economic impacts of tourism collaborative economy sectors (e.g. accommodation, transport, services, etc.)
- Employment consequences of the collaborative economy including full time and part time job creation, estimates of formal and informal labour and multiplier effects on employment in other parts of the economy
- Impacts and implications of the collaborative economy on housing, livelihoods, labour rights and relations
- Characteristics of participation (e.g. demographics, gaps, biases and impediments) leading to insights about social inclusion and exclusion and the democratization of the marketplace
- Evaluations of the direct and indirect social and cultural impacts of the collaborative economy on communities
- The impacts and consequences of the collaborative economy across different policy sectors, the policy complementarities and trade-offs involved in managing the collaborative economy
- New models of public-private governance that invoke new thinking about regulatory roles, responsibilities and structures
- Opportunities and impediments to partnerships and collaboration in the collaborative economy

- Implications and consequences of the collaborative economy on different types of destinations at different scales and geographical locations, e.g. urban, rural and coastal destinations, major tourist hubs and smaller localities.

6.3 What Can Be Done About It?

Taking a social science perspective, many of the chapters within this volume have galvanized around the notion of a more caring and responsible research agenda with respect to the collaborative economy. While the above two areas of future research dwell on understanding the impacts and characteristics of the collaborative economy in tourism, this last set of research ideas focuses on what we ought to do about it.

The collaborative economy is unfolding at lightening pace, and there exist many possible scenarios for its future. At the same time, our slide into a post-fact, post-truth world (Majoo, 2011) is creating significant challenges in understanding what is *really* going on, what "truth" to believe, and what is the entire pool of options available, not just what we are given to select from. In this post-fact world, collaborative economy advocates, consultants, platforms and researchers are contributing insights and knowledge about the collaborative economy by marshalling the best possible evidence drawn from their own cloisters. Knowledge sharing occurs only to the extent it comes from those sharing the same (or similar) ontological stage, and alternative insights are distanced, dismissed and/or not given credence. Each knowledge network has a truth of its own, and the politics of pluralism allows alternative insights to be ignored despite the potential utility, rigor and salience for other groups of actors. This dissent into fragmentation stymies opportunities to develop broad-based, textured and contextualised understandings of the collaborative economy. Non-action is easier than action in such circumstances. This last set of research directions is aimed at addressing this potential inertia.

Earlier we raised an issue with the asymmetries of information that characterize the collaborative economy and tourism and called for greater attention to ontological, epistemological and axiological orientations that underpin research and knowledge generation. Tourism researchers can and should play an important role in shaping this future, and we encourage our colleagues to live up to this responsibility. It requires going beyond the role of documentary chroniclers, industrial consultants driven by a particular agenda or alienated critiques, and repositioning ourselves as responsible scholars. To be clear, we are not proposing an instrumental research agenda that prescribes what ought to be done, nor are we advocating that a consensus can be reached about what is true, valuable or useful knowledge in the collaborative economy and tourism. To the contrary, we argue that diverse types of knowledge are useful in different circumstances and we call for wider engagement in the generating and sharing of knowledge, and for researchers, consultants, advocates and platforms to span knowledge-making boundaries. Within this line of inquiry we also believe it is important to identify opportunities for action by different actors; to examine, compare and contrast the impacts of policies, strategies and initiatives already adopted; and to also consider the ethical dimensions and moral responsibilities upon stakeholders to do something about the issues and implications that are unfolding. In this sense, research that addresses both "big picture questions" and "small contextualised explorations" is needed. In order to produce research that is concrete, salient and useful, researchers must embrace strategies that entail:

- Detailed engagement with practical problems and contradictions
- A level of independence from politics
- Space for political deliberation
- Insights from experiences in different institutional contexts (national and international)
- Acknowledgement of the institutional and organizational realities
- Political robustness—i.e., present knowledge that is politically acceptable and has taken into account various stakeholder perspectives
- Epistemic robustness—i.e., adopt research methods and approaches that are considered appropriate within the disciplinary context and be scientifically sound in terms of knowledge claims (see Budtz Pedersen, 2014; Head, 2008a, 2008b; Lentsch & Weingart, 2011).

Drawing from the preceding chapters and the principles above, a particular approach is emerging, that defines a viable and morally responsible direction for researchers not only studying but actively shaping the future of collaborative economy. This necessitates engaging with collaborative economy problems and challenges as follows:

- Establish dialogue-based approaches and collaborative platforms to identify value creation mechanisms and shared value across diverse stakeholder groups
- Identify and navigate among the moral responsibilities of those involved in the collaborative economy and tourism
- Assess the consequences of current regulatory regimes in regard to fair and equitable competition in the tourism industry
- Assist in the development of balanced regulatory measures, policy strategies, actions and initiatives aiming at maximising value for stakeholders on different levels.

From the above we acknowledge that the collaborative economy is bringing significant transformations to certain parts of the tourism system. Despite our best efforts and those of the chapter authors within, there is limited research to date, and we know little about how it will all play out. However, we are certain that the collaborative economy is deeply entangled in, and has the potential to deliver positive outcomes for, a range of urgent societal challenges (e.g. the need for alternative, less-consumptive economic models, sustainability, social cohesion, local livelihoods, etc.). What is needed though, is to step back from and balance out the simplistic claims of benefit generated by collaborative economy advocates and platforms. Collaborative economy prospects, impacts and implications are also deeply intertwined with a range of policy sectors (e.g. housing, transport, economic development, fiscal policy, community development, etc.). Indeed, we argue that questions about the collaborative economy and consideration of possible actions are intrinsically connected to big picture thinking about the future. In order to navigate this future, we need to be armed with research that rises above the political interests of platform capitalism; that recognises the complex interest structures embedded within the collaborative economy; and that keep a keen eye on the future and rises to the societal challenges we face.

Using different research approaches and in different contexts, the chapter contributors have all directed their attention to the need for a caring research agenda. Drawing from Dredge (chapter "Responsibility and care in the collaborative economy"), this is a social science for the collaborative economy and tourism, wherein:

> *Context matters*. A caring response necessarily requires an appreciation of the experiences, capacities, histories and relationships with others.
>
> *Relationships matter*. A caring response recognises relational entanglements, interdependence and dependence, and the flow of impacts and consequences in different directions.
>
> *Values and emotions matter*. Emotions, such as empathy, injustice and inequity, and values such as respect, reciprocity and mutuality inform and motivate moral commitment and can trigger deeper and more personal actions.
>
> *Individual and collective action matter*. Care ethics involves an action orientation that is both an individual and a collective responsibility to care.

In the spirit of collaboration, this vision for a social science research agenda for the collaborative economy and tourism also embraces an open collaborative researcher network, shared data and knowledge co-creation. Efforts are needed to break down the current researcher-advocacy silos and to create new platforms for researcher-society-industry-community collaboration. Technological advances and societal innovations that have paved the way to new collaborative business models may also inspire the building of disruptive knowledge sharing initiatives (living lab, governance lab) across institutional and geographical boundaries.

References

Budtz Pedersen, D. (2014). The political epistemology of science-based policy-making. *Society, 51*(5), 547–551.

Couldry, N. (2015). The myth of "us": Digital networks, political change and the production of collectivity. *Information, Communication and Society, 18*(6), 608–626.

Cox, M., & Slee, T. (2016). *How Airbnb's data hid the facts in New York City* (pp. 1–16). Retrieved from http://insideairbnb.com/reports/how-airbnbsdata-hid-the-facts-in-new-york-city.pdf

Dredge, D., & Gyimóthy, S. (2015). The collaborative economy and tourism: Critical perspectives, questionable claims and silenced voices. *Tourism Recreation Research, 40*(3), 286–302.

Dredge, D., Gyimóthy, S., Birkbak, A., Jensen, T. E., & Madsen, A. K. (2016). *The impact of regulatory approaches targeting collaborative economy in the tourism accommodation sector: Barcelona, Berlin, Amsterdam and Paris* (Impulse paper no. 9). Brussels: European Commission.
Gansky, L. (2010). *The Mesh: Why the future of business is sharing*. New York: Penguin Books.
Gordo, A., de Rivera, J., & Apestegia, A. (2016). Facing the challenge of collaborative consumption in Europe: The time of independent metrics. In *Second International Workshop on the Sharing Economy (#IWSE)* (pp. 1–28). Paris: Second International Workshop on the Sharing Economy. Retrieved from http://cibersomosaguas.net/files/Facing the challenge of Collabora tive Consumption in Europe.pdf
Gorenflo, N. (2013, March 19). Collaborative consumption is dead, long live the real sharing economy. *PandoDaily*. Retrieved from http://pando.com/2013/03/19/collaborative-consumption-is-dead-long-live-the-real-sharingeconomy/
Head, B. W. (2008a). Three lenses of evidence-based policy. *Australian Journal of Public Administration, 67*(1), 1–11.
Head, B. W. (2008b). Wicked problems in public policy. *Public Policy, 3*(2), 101–118.
Howitt, R., & Suchet-Pearson, S. (2006) Rethinking the building blocks: Ontological pluralism and the idea of "management." Geografiska Annaler, Series B: Human Geography, 88(3), 323–335.
Kade, M. (2015, October/November). The rise of collaborative consumption: A conversation around connecting humanity to themselves. Aspire. Accessed 2016, June 12, from http://rachelbotsman.com/wp/wp-content/uploads/2015/09/Aspire_WFW-Magazine-Sept-2015.pdf
Kennedy, J. (2015). Conceptual boundaries of sharing. *Information Communication and Society, 19*(4), 461–474.
Lentsch, J., & Weingart, P. (2011). *The politics of scientific advice: Institutional design for quality assurance*. Cambridge: Cambridge University Press.
Majoo, F. (2011). *True enough learning to live in a post-fact society*. Hoboken, NJ: Wiley.
Parsons, A. (2014a). *The sharing economy: A short introduction to its political evolution*. Accessed 2016, June 12, from https://www.opendemocracy.net/transformation/adam-par sons/sharing-economy-short-introduction-to-its-political-evolution
Parsons, A. (2014b). *The sharing economy: A short introduction*. Accessed 2016, June 12, from https://www.opendemocracy.net/transformation/adam-parsons/sharing-economy-short-introduc tion-to-its-political-evolution
Pawson, R. (2006). *Evidence based policy: A realist perspective*. Thousand Oaks: Sage.
PWC. (2015). *The sharing economy. Consumer intelligence series*. New York. https://www.pwc.com/us/en/technology/publications/assets/pwc-consumer-intelligence-series-the-sharing-economy.pdf
Rittel, W., & Weber, M. (1973). Dilemmas in a general theory of planning. *Policy Sciences, 4*(2), 155–169.
Scholz, T. (2014). Platform cooperativism vs. the sharing economy. *Medium.com*, 1–9. Accessed 2016, June 12, from https://medium.com/@trebors/platform-cooperativism-vs-the-sharing-economy-2ea737f1b5ad
Slee, T. (2016). *What's yours in mine: Against the sharing economy*. New York: OR Books.
SMH. (2016, April 23). *Uber attracts more car-less drivers as entrepreneurs buy up ride-share fleets*. Accessed 2016, June 12, from http://www.smh.com.au/business/innovation/uber-cars-used-all-day-and-night-as-drivers-take-turns-using-cars-20160419-goa0ip.html
Thrasyvoulou, X. (2014). *What's next for the collaborative economy?* Accessed 2016, June 12, from http://www.forbes.com/sites/theyec/2014/03/20/whats-next-for-the-collaborative-economy/#6fbce44223f5

MIX
Papier aus verantwortungsvollen Quellen
Paper from responsible sources
FSC® C105338

If you have any concerns about our products,
you can contact us on
ProductSafety@springernature.com

In case Publisher is established outside the EU,
the EU authorized representative is:
Springer Nature Customer Service Center GmbH
Europaplatz 3, 69115 Heidelberg, Germany

Printed by Libri Plureos GmbH
in Hamburg, Germany